Controversies in Psychotherapy and Counselling

edited by

Colin Feltham

SAGE Publications
London • Thousand Oaks • New Delhi

First published 1999

SAGE Publications Ltd
6 Bonhill Street
London EC2A 4PU

SAGE Publications Inc.
2455 Teller Road
Thousand Oaks, California 91320

SAGE Publications India Pvt Ltd
32, M-Block Market
Greater Kailash – I
New Delhi 110 048

British Library Cataloguing in Publication data

A catalogue record for this book is available
from the British Library

ISBN 0 7619 5640 9
ISBN 0 7619 5641 7 (pbk)

Library of Congress catalog card number 99–073782

Typeset by Mayhew Typesetting, Rhayader, Powys
Printed in Great Britain by The Cromwell Press Ltd, Trowbridge, Wiltshire

Contents

Part III   Professional Issues

Notes on contributors

John Berridge is Senior Lecturer in Personnel Policy, Manchester School of Management, University of Manchester Institute of Science and Technology (UMIST). He trained as a sociologist at the London School of Economics and has taught and researched widely in Britain, Europe and the USA. He is author of *Employee Assistance Programmes and Workplace Counselling* (Wiley, 1997) with Cary L. Cooper and Carolyn Highley-Marchington and has edited the journal *Employee Relations* since 1990.

Mary Connor is Head of Individual and Organization Development Studies at the University College of Ripon and York St John, in York. Her extensive teaching has included specialist lecture tours in the Far East, and she is currently developing collaborative partnerships in counselling training in Greece and Argentina. Her publications include *Training the Counsellor* (Routledge, 1994).

Jennifer M. Cunningham works as a community paediatrician in the Child Development and Communication Disorder assessment teams within the Balvicar Child Centre, Yorkhill NHS Trust, Glasgow. Most of her work entails the developmental assessment of preschool children who may have special needs or autism.

Albert Ellis is the founder of rational emotive behavior therapy (REBT), the pioneering cognitive-behavioural therapy. He is President of the Albert Ellis Institute for REBT in New York, practises considerable individual and group therapy every week, gives many talks and workshops throughout the world and has published over 65 books on psychotherapy.

W.M. Epstein teaches social policy in the School of Social Work, University of Nevada, Las Vegas. He is the author of *The Dilemma of American Social Welfare* (Transaction, 1993), *The Illusion of Psychotherapy* (Transaction, 1995), *Welfare in America* (University of Wisconsin Press, 1997) and *Children Who Could Have Been: The Legacy of Welfare in Wealthy America* (University of Wisconsin Press, 1999).

Colin Feltham is Head of the Counselling Development Unit, School of Education, Sheffield Hallam University. He is a British Association for Counselling (BAC) Accredited Counsellor and a BAC Fellow. His publications include *Psychotherapy and its Discontents* (with Windy Dryden, Open

University Press, 1992), *What Is Counselling?* (Sage, 1995), *Which Psycho-therapy?* (Sage, 1997), *Time-Limited Counselling* (Sage, 1997) and *Witness and Vision of the Therapists* (Sage, 1998). He also edits the series 'Professional Skills for Counsellors' and 'Perspectives on Psychotherapy' for Sage.

Derek Gale is an author and humanistic psychotherapist in private practice in Essex and London specialising in voice, psychodrama and group work. He is currently developing his work as a consultant to industry. He is the author of *What is Psychotherapy?* (Gale Centre Books, 1989) and *What is Psychodrama?* (Gale Centre Books, 1990).

Jan Harvie-Clark is a psychoanalytic psychotherapist in private practice and supervisor and teacher at the Highgate Counselling Centre, London. She is a member of the British Association of Psychotherapists and is registered by the British Confederation of Psychotherapists.

Jeremy Holmes is Consultant Psychiatrist/Psychotherapist in North Devon. His books include *John Bowlby and Attachment Theory* (Routledge, 1995), *Introduction to Psychoanalysis* (with Anthony Bateman, Routledge, 1995), *Attachment, Intimacy, Autonomy: Using Attachment Theory in Adult Psychotherapy* (Jason Aronson, 1996), and *Healing Stories: Narrative in Psychiatry and Psychotherapy* (with G. Roberts, OUP, 1998).

Alex Howard has for many years been a tutor and manager in adult education. His fourth book, *Challenges to Counselling and Psychotherapy* (Macmillan, 1996), was highly acclaimed. *Philosophy in Counselling and Psychotherapy* (Macmillan, 1999) will relate over 30 philosophers, from ancient Greece to the present, to the contemporary practice of counselling.

David Howe is a Professor in the School of Social Work at the University of East Anglia, Norwich. His research interests include applications of attachment theory, particularly in the fields of child maltreatment, parenting and adoption. He is the author of a number of books, the most recent being *On Being a Client: Understanding the Process of Counselling and Psychotherapy* (Sage, 1993), *Attachment Theory for Social Work Practice* (Macmillan, 1995) and *Patterns of Adoption: Nature, Nurture and Psychosocial Development* (Blackwell Science, 1998).

Tim Kendall was Director of the Centre for Psychotherapeutic Studies, University of Sheffield, and is now a Consultant Psychiatrist in the NHS. He is also Chair of the Universities Psychotherapy Association. He has studied medicine, neurochemistry, psychiatry and psychoanalytic psychotherapy. His research interests include power and subjectivity in psychoanalysis and other therapies, and technique in psychotherapy.

Ann Macaskill is Principal Lecturer in the Psychology of Health and Illness in the School of Health and Community Studies, Sheffield Hallam University. Her research interests and publications are in components of the therapy process, treatment of depression, stress and other aspects of health psychology and health education.

Norman D. Macaskill is Senior Lecturer in Psychotherapy at the University of Leeds. He was previously a consultant psychotherapist in the NHS, with honorary lectureships at the Universities of Sheffield and Nottingham. He has trained as both a psychodynamic and cognitive-behavioural therapist, and has published extensively on many themes, including cognitive-behavioural therapy for depression and personality disorders and integration of pharmacotherapy with psychotherapy to optimise treatment outcomes.

Jim McLennan has been practising, teaching, researching and supervising in counselling and psychotherapy since 1970. He has worked in a range of counselling and psychotherapy settings and is a Member of the College of Counselling Psychologists of the Australian Psychological Society. He is currently an Associate Professor of Psychology at Swinburne University of Technology in Melbourne.

Richard Mowbray has over 20 years' experience as a practitioner of Primal Integration. Together with Juliana Brown he is co-director of the Primal Integration Programme in London and is a member of the Open Centre, one of the UK's longest-established growth centres. Publications include *The Case Against Psychotherapy Registration: A Conservation Issue for the Human Potential Movement* (Trans Marginal Press, 1995).

Tim Newton is a Lecturer in Organizational Studies at the Department of Organizational Psychology, Birkbeck College, London. He is researching subjectivity and the self; management of knowledge; sociology of emotion and the body. His publications include *'Managing' Stress: Emotion and Power at Work* (Sage, 1995).

Marjorie Orr, originally a BBC documentary producer and journalist, is now a Jungian psychotherapist. In 1991 she founded Accuracy About Abuse, an international information service on sexual abuse. She is on the editorial board of *Trauma/Treating Abuse Today*, lectures extensively in the UK and elsewhere and has several publications in this field.

Ian Parker is Professor of Psychology at Bolton Institute and Director of the MSc Critical Psychology programme. His publications include *Psychoanalytic Culture: Psychoanalytic Discourse in Western Society* (Sage, 1997) and *Deconstructing Psychotherapy* (edited, Sage, 1999). He is a member of Psychology Politics Resistance and the North West Right to Refuse Electroshock Campaign.

John Rowan is the author of *The Reality Game* (2nd edn, Routledge, 1998) and many other books on counselling and psychotherapy. He teaches at the Minster Centre in London and has a private practice in therapy and supervision in north-east London. He is also a Fellow of the British Psychological Society. With Mick Cooper he has edited *The Plural Self* (Sage, 1999).

Stephen Saunders received his doctorate from Northwestern University, studying with Kenneth Howard. He is currently Assistant Professor at Marquette University and an executive board member of the Center for Addiction and Behavioral Health Research. He has published extensively in the area of help-seeking and psychotherapy outcomes.

Roger Scotford is Director of the British False Memory Society. Previously an engineer officer in the Royal Navy, and businessman, he broadcasts and writes on false memory and lives with his second wife and eldest daughter and her family in Bradford on Avon.

Valerie Sinason is a poet, writer, adult psychoanalyst and child psycho-therapist. She is Director of the Clinic for Dissociative Studies, and Consultant Research Psychotherapist at St George's Hospital Medical School Psychiatry of Disability Department. She specializes in work with learning disabled and abused/abusing clients. She lectures nationally and internationally and was made a Life Member of Poms, the Swedish psychology organization, and an Honorary Consultant at University of Cape Town Child Guidance Clinic. Her books include *Mental Handicap and the Human Condition* (Free Association Books, 1991), *Memory in Dispute* (Karnac, 1998) and *The Shoemaker and the Elves: Working with Multiplicity* (Routledge, forthcoming).

David Livingstone Smith is the author of numerous publications on psycho-analysis, philosophy and related subjects including *Approaching Psycho-analysis: An Introductory Course* (Karnac, 1999), *Hidden Conservations: An Introduction to Communicative Psychoanalysis* (Rebus, 1999) and *Freud's Philosophy of the Unconscious* (Kluwer, 1999). He is a registered psycho-therapist as well as a trained philosopher, and is clinical supervisor for Kids Company, a charity providing psychotherapy and counselling for inner city children. He is visiting lecturer on psychoanalysis at a number of UK universities.

Peter Speedwell has worked professionally in the arts, writing and directing for Channel 4, and writing for theatre. He completed a PhD on Bakhtin and psychoanalysis, and is now undertaking a research project on scapegoating and sacrifice.

Sheelagh Strawbridge is a Chartered Counselling Psychologist in inde-pendent practice. She has a background in university teaching on degree courses in social science and professional courses in counselling and social work. Her publications include *Exploring Self and Society* (with Rosamund Billington and Jenny Hockey, Macmillan, 1998).

Digby Tantam is Clinical Professor of Psychotherapy at the Centre for Psychotherapeutic Studies, University of Sheffield, Associate Medical Director of the School for Health and Related Research, Director of the Centre for the Study of Violence and Reconciliation, and an Honorary Consultant Psychotherapist for Community Health Sheffield. He has previously been Chair of the Universities Psychotherapy Association, and Chair of the United Kingdom Council for Psychotherapy, and is currently Registrar of the European Association of Psychotherapy. He has been the author of over 90 published scientific articles, and the author or editor of eight books, including *Clinical Topics in Psychotherapy* (Gaskell, 1998).

Brian Thorne is a Professorial Fellow and Director of the Centre for Counselling Studies at the University of East Anglia, Norwich. He is also a Professor of Education in the College of Teachers, London. He has contributed substantially to the professional literature and is an international figure in the world of person-centred therapy. His most recent books are *Person-Centred Counselling and Person-Centred Christian Spirituality* (Whurr, 1998) and *Person-Centred Therapy: A European Perspective* (co-edited with Elke Lambers, Sage, 1998).

E.M. Thornton is a medical historian specializing in the history of psychiatry and neurology, and is a Fellow of the Royal Society of Medicine (History of Medicine Section). Her books include *Hypnotism, Hysteria and Epilepsy: An Historical Synthesis* (Heinemann Medical Books, 1979) and *Freud and Cocaine: The Freudian Fallacy* (Blond & Briggs, 1983). She is currently engaged in a historical study of Darwinism.

Fay Weldon is one of Britain's leading writers. Novelist, screenwriter and critic, her work is translated the world over. Her novels include, most famously, *The Life and Loves of a She-Devil* (Flamingo, 1983), *The Cloning of Joanna May* (Flamingo, 1998) and *Big Women* (Flamingo, 1989), a fictional perspective on 25 years of feminism.

Sue Wheeler is a counsellor and psychotherapist, supervisor and Senior Lecturer in Counselling at the University of Birmingham. She has many years of experience as a counsellor in further and higher education, and as a counsellor trainer and supervisor. She is a course tutor for the MA Counselling and course director of the Certificate in Supervision at the university. She is the author of *A Handbook for Personal Tutors* (with Jan Birtle, Open University Press, 1994) and *Training Counsellors: The Assessment of Competence* (Cassell, 1997), and of many articles and book chapters related to counselling and supervision of counsellors.

1 Controversies in psychotherapy and counselling

Colin Feltham

An honest man speaks the truth, though it may give offence; a vain man, in order that it may.

When a thing ceases to be a subject of controversy, it ceases to be a subject of interest.

(William Hazlitt, 1778–1830)

It is easily forgotten perhaps that psychotherapy has always been (or originally was) a deeply controversial field, many of its early controversies being associated with theories of the unconscious and infantile sexuality which offended ordinary citizens 100 years ago. But it has also been controversial within professional ranks, medical practitioners and lay analysts having had their share of conflict over ownership, effectiveness and theoretical correctness. Therapist has fought with therapist, sometimes quite acrimoniously, and broken away from close colleagues to form new alliances. So in itself the presentation of controversy here is nothing new.

What we see in our own time is a mixture of controversies old and new. There are still debates about what the unconscious is and whether it is a valid concept, for example, and there are still debates about who has the right to own and control the field. Indeed there is very little about which consensus exists. In an emerging profession that is characterized by over 400 different schools of thought and practice, practitioners agree on almost nothing – except perhaps the general worthwhileness and effectiveness of therapy, the sacrosanct nature of confidentiality and the taboo against sexual contact with clients. Disagreement is rife on the best ways to train practitioners, who has the right to oversee the field, which theories and methods are valid and proven. Beneath the public relations front and professional alliances made for economic and survival purposes, controversy rules!

For the sake of making progress with this introduction, I have already had to overlook the problem of terminology: exactly what the differences are between psychotherapy, counselling, counselling psychology, clinical psychology and related activities; whether it is more accurate to speak of clients, patients, analysands, helpees, and so on, are all topics of ongoing debate. One speaks as if this is in some sense a unified field – and no doubt it is if compared with completely different fields of endeavour – but beneath the public image of its professional umbrella bodies it may be said to be at best a lively arena of restless debate on best methods for alleviating human suffering, at worst an utterly dishonest and disorganized mess of warring factions.

So controversy is unavoidable, unless one buries one's head in the sand of one or another of the many orthodoxies available. However, colleagues often point out to me that media and academic critics already do a good hatchet job, therefore why should any of us within the profession add to our problems? I depart company from some colleagues here. For some, counselling and therapy are legitimate acts of faith based on deeply subjective truths, on the personally transformational experience of therapy received as trainees, for example. Criticisms, analyses and research may often be regarded by such defenders of the faith as completely missing the point, as merely betraying their authors' own defensive attitudes. In this scenario, therapy resembles religious experience: those who have been saved *know* the truth of the matter and *know* that the content of most of these controversies is stale and trivial.

Having been a client in a number of therapies, a practitioner, colleague, supervisor, trainer and academic in this field for many years, I cannot *not* know just how divided and controversial it is. I know that what one colleague believes (apparently *knows*) passionately, another considers complete nonsense. Very little has been established beyond dispute except that many (but not all) people report positive experiences of therapy (however so defined) as consumers, and often report therapists' attitudes as the most significantly helpful factors. It is not even established what the contribution of training is to clients' perceived satisfaction, or whether training adds much if anything to ordinary human qualities like warmth, interest, concern, and so on. There is plenty of debate, much research and many assertions in this as in other areas.

In irresistible ways therapy can and perhaps should be compared with religion. People want it and are often very emotional about it, but all its central tenets are highly questionable. Is there a God at all? Should we have priests, and if so, how should they be trained? How can the public be protected from errant priests? How do I know if I am saved? Can I save myself or must I attend church and engage in particular rituals? How can I know which is the most suitable church for me? Whose version of theology of which aspects of my religion is to be believed above others'? How can I know if I am or am not deluding myself? If I am happy with what I get, does all this matter anyway? Psychotherapy and counselling are in a similar position, facing the same kinds of questions and engendering similar passions.

Although I am a practitioner, I have never regarded it as my role to be unquestioningly faithful to any particular position in the field of therapy and counselling. Although a public relations avoidance of controversy may be expedient, there is ultimately no purpose in defending theories and practices that cannot stand up to challenge. Falsification, exaggeration, convenience and lies surely have no place in therapy. Arguably what heals is truth, an old-fashioned and often derided concept. Rightly understood, as a relentless logical *and* emotional erosion of untruths, truth seeking has a perennial function, and controversy tends to be a rich opportunity for truth seeking.

Controversy may be presented as simply unavoidable, then. It may be served up as of historical or academic importance. It is certainly often used as a means of sniping, offloading grievances, seeking sensation, media attention and newspaper and book sales. Soberly, it is often defended as something from which we can and should learn how to improve our practice, clean up our act, and so on. Controversy can and arguably should be utilized as a teaching aid, prompting students to think critically about the subject from the outset. Or it can be regarded simply as one part of the field itself and as part of the larger human search for truth, or passion for eliminating untruths, of which (I believe) psychotherapy and counselling are ultimately dispensable components.

Structure of the book

Taking a number of obvious and not so obvious, but largely current, debates and controversies in the field, I invited known authors to agree to 'take sides' on various issues. This book does not represent every conceivable controversy. Not represented, for example, are arguments as to whether homosexuality is psychopathological (a debate almost too controversial to be included, and considered by most to have been firmly resolved); whether psychotherapy is simply a substitute religion; whether it is a scientific pursuit; whether research in this area is useful and conclusive or trivial and inconclusive; and so on. The final, necessarily non-exhaustive selection of controversies is based on certain expressed interests, current debates and willing authors.

I have ordered the book in more or less opposing pairs. In some cases viewpoints are diametrically opposed, in others different but not necessarily polar opposite viewpoints are presented. The writers were not shown each other's chapters but were asked to present or defend a certain case. Readers may be interested to decide on what basis they themselves take sides, and to judge how and why the present writers have come to the acceptant or sceptical positions they adopt. I have divided the controversies into areas of interest but I make no pretence that these are in any way watertight areas.

The book opens with a number of theoretical issues. In Part I E.M. Thornton questions the very concept of an unconscious mind, something upon which many consider the whole psychoanalytic edifice to stand or fall; and Tim Kendall and Peter Speedwell defend the concept. Jennifer M. Cunningham denies the existence of retrievable accurate memories of birth trauma and casts serious doubt on therapies built on the retrieval of such early memories; John Rowan puts the case for the reality of such trauma and argues that it is of crucial importance in therapeutic work. Roger Scotford presents the case for a critical stance on behalf of false memory syndrome, in particular against the recovered memory movement which claims to have unearthed widespread childhood sexual abuse and concomitant phenomena; Majorie Orr presents the counter-evidence.

Part II, on what I have called 'clinical issues', opens with the ongoing debate on clinical outcomes, which owes much of its initial thrust to Hans Eysenck. W.M. Epstein questions the research methods and evidence of those claiming to have firmly established the effectiveness of psychotherapy, while Stephen Saunders puts the case for the strength of the evidence for proven effectiveness. Albert Ellis challenges the currently fashionable view that the therapeutic relationship is the main change agent in psychotherapy, while David Howe puts forward the argument for its centrality. The traditional diagnosis of psychopathology, its underlying assumptions and consequences, are deconstructed by Ian Parker, while Norman D. Macaskill describes the positive and perhaps indispensable contributions of psychodiagnosis. Boundaries, considered so crucial by many therapists, are stretched and questioned by Derek Gale, and sharply defended by David Livingstone Smith.

Exactly how professional this field is, and what constitutes the parameters and assumptions of this professionalism, are the ingredients of the Part III of the book. Ann Macaskill reviews the evidence, or lack of it, in support of the argument that personal therapy for trainees is necessary and beneficial, a position that is hotly contested by many therapists and psychotherapy organizations, here represented by Valerie Sinason. Going to the very core of professionalism, Jim McLennan presents the evidence against the assumption that training and supervision are necessary and of proven impact; Mary Connor, to the contrary, argues strongly for the need for and the known benefits of rigorous training. A common assumption across most trainings is that a core theoretical model must be identified and should permeate courses; Colin Feltham denies the validity of this assumption whereas Sue Wheeler champions it. On the topical issue of the means of professionalism, that is to say, on the question of accreditation and registration, Richard Mowbray argues that this is not the best or inevitable way forward, and that it does not protect clients; Digby Tantam, however, presents the case for the necessity and benefits of registration. Finally in this part, Brian Thorne refutes the common assertion that counselling and psychotherapy are distinguishable, while Jan Harvie-Clark defends the case for separation.

Part IV opens with an analysis by Tim Newton of popular stress discourse which suggests that all is not at all what it seems in the world of stress management and employee counselling; and John Berridge presents the case for the reality and peculiarity of contemporary stress, its effects, management and treatment. Alex Howard radically questions whether counselling and psychotherapy and their recent rapid growth are desirable and defensible; Jeremy Holmes, to the contrary, argues strongly in favour of therapy as of demonstrated benefit and suggests that it is an important health provision to which people should have the right of access. Finally, Fay Weldon renews her attack on therapy, or Therapism, as something of a substitute religion, something which perhaps offered real hope when it began but is now enfeeblingly pervasive and dubious; Sheelagh Strawbridge argues that, for all its faults, therapy has provided a voice, a narrative channel for many seriously hurt and traumatized people, and is therefore ultimately more empowering than otherwise.

It is my belief that many of these controversies go to the core of what psychotherapy and counselling are all about. In certain instances we do seem faced with either–or dilemmas to be resolved: either there is or there is not an unconscious; birth may or may not be traumatic and therapy capable or not of unearthing and healing such traumas; training is or is not necessary and beneficial, an improvement on good intentions or common wisdom; registration is or is not inevitable and beneficial. In such dilemmas we are faced with questions resembling a crisis in religious faith: either there is or is not a God; either there is one true God or there are many gods; and so on. It may be that therapy, like religion, works by placebo effect, by faith alone. It can certainly be argued that science, scientific method and scientific demands for evidence ultimately have no place in the therapeutic enterprise. Yet, without some scientific anchorage, therapy inevitably becomes a matter of emotional faith alone. The tension within these controversies is perhaps that between what we want to believe and what we are called to question. The survival of psychotherapy and counselling is of course economically and ideologically important to its practitioners but relatively unimportant in the larger historical context of the overriding human quest for an understanding of suffering and its alleviation. Given the quite pervasive human tendency towards self-deceit and delusion, what would surely be the most controversial position of all is to assert that in psychotherapy and counselling we have finally found the solutions to our most profound human dilemmas.

PART I

THEORETICAL ISSUES

---

2 Does the unconscious mind really exist?

E.M. *Thornton*

Can there be such a thing as an *unconscious* mind? And is the concept in itself not a contradiction in terms? After all, what we call the mind is not a substantive entity with volume and dimensions. Thus it cannot have 'hidden depths', 'deeper layers' or repressed material 'brought to the surface' (into *what* has it been repressed?). 'The mind' is a mere descriptive term, a convenient abstract appellation to encompass our *conscious* awareness of ourselves and our surroundings, and the cognitive activities involved in their interaction, perceiving, thinking, remembering, feeling. All these functions are co-existent with consciousness. On purely rational grounds, therefore, the term 'unconscious mind' is a contradiction in terms.

True, there are underlying *brain* processes subserving mental activity of which we are unaware, in the same way as we are normally unaware of the circulation of the blood, but these do not in the aggregate constitute a mind. It is only when the end products emerge into consciousness that mental activity begins to take place. We know, for instance, that there are vast stores of memories present in the temporal lobes of our brains, but we have to recall a memory to consciousness before we can make use of it. Experiments have been performed with brain-damaged patients showing that some elements of perception are still present even when their sight has been irreparably damaged. But isolated instances of perception do not make a mind. Similarly experiments on patients who have undergone cerebral commisurotomy for the treatment of severe epilepsy have been cited to show that neither hemisphere appears to know what the other is doing, and these have been put forward as showing some evidence of unconscious mental activity. However, all these experiments were performed on *fully conscious* subjects and thus can have no valid application to the subject of an *unconscious* mind. Subliminal advertising was once put forward as a feasible option for attracting trade, but was soon discarded by hard-headed businessmen to whom results were more important than theory. Similarly, nothing is now heard of 'sleep learning', once entertained as a workable proposition. The hard fact remains that if a student falls asleep during a dull lecture, or even allows his or her attention momentarily to wander, that part of the lecture is lost to him or her for ever.

The astonishing thing about the concept of the unconscious mind is that its existence has never been experimentally proved, nor even scientifically investigated with any rigour. It has entered common currency by the back door as it were, as a component of the entire Freudian corpus, without any of the controversy and critical appraisal that would be normal in the consideration of such a fundamental issue. When all the historical leads are explored, the concept of the unconscious mind appears to have received its wide acceptance solely on the untested and unopposed word of Sigmund Freud.

What were Freud's grounds for adopting the concept, and, moreover, for making it the central postulate of his psychology?

Freud had become convinced of the existence of an unconscious mind from the phenomena of hypnotism. At the time he was formulating his basic postulates in the 1890s, hypnotism had been undergoing a major revival and was being investigated in many important medical centres in Europe. The phenomena themselves were called 'somnambulism' as the hypnotized subjects were assumed to be walking and talking in their sleep, though still appearing capable of rational thought processes, hence the emergence of the concept of the unconscious mind. It was not a new one and Freud claimed for it no originality. It had, in fact, enjoyed a considerable vogue earlier in the century, again inspired by hypnotism (then called 'animal magnetism'). Eduard von Hartman had written an influential book on it, *The Philosophy of the Unconscious*, in 1870. Ideas of an unconscious mind had indeed persisted since the days of the ancients, who, ignorant of the autonomic nervous system, had explained the continuation of breathing and other vital functions during sleep by claiming for the soul an unconscious faculty.

Freud regarded hypnotism as the decisive evidence for the existence of the unconscious mind. 'The "unconscious"', he wrote, 'had, it is true, long been under discussion among philosophers as a theoretical concept, but now, for the first time, in the phenomena of hypnotism, it became something actual, tangible and subject to experiment' (Freud, 1924). His disciples, in their own writings, echoed him in citing hypnotism as their authority for the existence of the unconscious mind. For Freud, the 'unconscious mind' contained sinister forces, homicidal impulses and incestuous desires repressed only with the greatest difficulty by the conscious mind. It could, however, be explored by psychoanalysis 'for the purpose of making conscious what has so far been unconscious' (Freud, 1914).

Dreams were 'the royal road to the unconscious' and thus dream interpretation became an important part of psychoanalytical practice. The unconscious 'wishful impulses' requiring such treatment were generally of a repellent kind. 'They are an expression of immoral, incestuous and perverse impulses or of murderous and sadistic lusts' (Freud, 1925).

There are two things wrong with this exposition. In the first place its central postulate is untrue. Subjects in the hypnotic trance are *not unconscious*: numerous electroencephalographic (EEG) studies in the decades since its discovery in 1929 have shown no evidence of sleep. Without exception they show only the typical tracing of a waking record.

Second, modern research on dream physiology has overtaken Freud's theory of the dream. It has been revealed by the electroencephalogram that sleep passes through regular cycles, progressing in orderly sequence from Stages I to IV and then back to Stage I every 90 minutes or so, these stages having definite EEG correlates. It has been found that the 'rapid eye movement' (REM) stage in which dreaming takes place occurs in regular cycles throughout the night in orderly sequence and that the proportion of REM sleep to non-dreaming sleep is constant. If the subject is deprived of sleep for a considerable time, the length of the periods of REM sleep in proportion to non-dreaming sleep is extended in compensation, but the pattern remains regular and constant.

It is difficult to conceive of forbidden wishes arising in orderly sequence at regular intervals throughout the night, lasting for a fixed period of time, the length of which is in fixed proportions to non-dreaming sleep and only at these times. It has also been found that infants have a much larger proportion of REM sleep to non-dreaming sleep and it is difficult to believe that newborn infants need to dream to disguise *their* repressed wishes. So once again another of Freud's central postulates falls to the ground.

How, then, did Freud and countless psychoanalysts after him imagine they were penetrating the secrets of the unconscious mind? It is evident that psychoanalysis is ultimately a process of *interpretation* – of the random associations and dreams of the subject under analysis. The question is: is this interpretation derived from the subject's unconscious mind or *from the psychoanalyst's own conscious mind*? This question is aptly illustrated in the first comprehensive psychoanalytical case history Freud published – the 'Dora analysis' of 1900 (Freud, 1905).

Dora, the subject of the analysis, was sent to Freud in 1900 for treatment. An intelligent girl of 18 with 'engaging looks', she suffered from epileptiform attacks and recurrent episodes of an illness accompanied by cough and loss of voice lasting for several months at a time. Dora had been the object of unwelcome attentions from a friend of the family, Herr K. To complicate the situation, Dora's father had shows signs of having an illicit affair with Herr K's wife. The two families lived in close contact and Dora had formerly been on good terms with Frau K, but since her suspicions of her father's attachment, this friendship had ceased. So distressed was she by the whole situation she had threatened suicide. It was in these circumstances that Freud began his analysis.

The analysis revolved around two dreams. In the first, Dora woke to find her father beside her bed telling her the house was on fire. She dressed quickly. Her mother wanted to stop and save her jewel-case, but her father said he refused to let himself and his two children be burned for the sake of the jewel-case. Asked by Freud to make associations from this dream, Dora produced the information that her parents had been arguing about her mother's practice of locking the dining room at night from which her brother's room had its sole exit. This led *Freud* to associate – and with a characteristic flight of ideas. 'The word "Zimmer" ["room"] in dreams', he said, 'stands very frequently for "*Frauenzimmer*" [literally, "women's apartment"].' 'The question whether a women is "open" or "shut" can naturally not be a matter of indifference,' he continued. 'It is well known too, what sort of "key" effects the opening in such a case' (Freud, 1905).

The fact of her mother wanting to save her jewel-case caused Dora to mention that Herr K had made her a present of an expensive jewel-case a little while before. This led to the following exchange:

> 'Then a return present would have been very appropriate. Perhaps you do not know that "jewel-case" is a favourite expression for the same thing that you alluded to not long ago by means of the reticule you were wearing – for the female genitals, I mean.'
>
> 'I knew you would say that.'
>
> 'That is to say, you knew that it *was* so. The meaning of the dream is now becoming even clearer.' (Freud, 1905)

The allusion to the reticule was as follows: having been invited to confess that she had masturbated in childhood, Dora had flatly denied that she had ever done so. But her fidgeting with her purse was interpreted by Freud as 'a fantasy of masturbation', the purse being (to him) a representation of the female genitals.

In the second dream, Dora dreamed she was walking about in a town she did not know, with streets and squares strange to her. Then she came to the house where she lived and went up to her room, where she found a letter from her mother lying there. Her mother had written to her to say that as Dora had left home without her parents' knowledge, she had not wished to tell her that her father was ill. 'Now he is dead, and if you like you can come' (Freud, 1905). Dora went to the railway station, which she had difficulty in finding, going through a thick wood to reach it. Then she arrived home to be told that her mother and others were already at the cemetery. She went upstairs to her room and began reading a big book that lay on her writing table. The patient had seen precisely the same thick wood the day before, in a picture at the Secessionist exhibition. In the background of the picture there were nymphs. This last item played an important part in Freud's interpretation.

> At this point a certain suspicion of mine became a certainty. The use of '*Bahnhof*' ['station', literally 'railway court'] and '*Friedhof*' [literally 'peace court'] to

represent the female genitals was striking enough in itself, but it also served to direct my awakened curiosity to the similarly formed *Vorhof* ['vestibulum', literally 'forecourt'] – an anatomical term for a particular region of the female genitals. (Freud, 1905)

The nymphs in the background of the thick wood were declared to be the nymphae (labia minora) 'which lie in the background of the "thick wood" of the pubic hair'. Freud acknowledged that his patient would have been unlikely to know such anatomical terms. The 'big book' Dora was reading on her return home was therefore arbitarily declared to have been an encyclopaedia – 'the common refuge of youth devoured by sexual curiosity'. Thus the dream represented 'the fantasy of a man seeking to force an entrance into the female genitals' (Freud, 1905).

But the patient had *not used the anatomical terms* – they had been associated not by her but by Freud himself from the ordinary everyday words 'station' and 'cemetery'. And Freud *did* have a medical training and *did* know the anatomical terms. In addition, there was a significant selection in the association to the word 'vestibulum' and hence to the female genitals. In anatomy, the term 'vestibulum' simply means the space at the entrance to a canal. It can be applied to several other organs in the body, but its usual application is to the oval cavity of the internal ear forming the approach to the cochlea. The use of the term without other qualification in describing the female genitals would be unlikely to be found in any encyclopaedia. A recent researcher (Anthony Studland) has in fact examined the extant encyclopaedias which Dora could have consulted in 1899. 'The word "Vorhof" does not appear at all,' he says, 'either in its own right or under an entry on sexuality. Nymphen is mentioned only fleetingly. Thus, Freud's assertion that Dora had read both words in the encyclopaedias is empirically disproved' (Studland, 1989: 199).

Freud's interpretation of this dream is therefore the clearest indication that what purported to be emanations from the patient's 'unconscious' were, in fact, the products of his own *conscious* mind, showing, in its strained strivings after sexual connotations, his own peculiar monomania.

The analysis proceeds along similar lines. Freud's final interpretation of his patient's throat symptoms illustrates his current preoccupation with incest and sexual deviations. Dora had insisted that Frau K only loved her father because he was a 'man of means'. This led Freud to infer that 'behind this phrase its opposite was concealed' and that her father, as a man of means, was, in fact, impotent (this might have been a fact known to Freud as the father had also been his patient, but is hardly likely to have been known by a young daughter in the nineteenth century). From there he deduced that Dora, knowing of her father's impotence, had pictured his affair with Frau K in 'scenes of sexual gratification *per os*'; moreover, she must have, in that fantasy, been putting herself in Frau K's place and 'identifying' with her, thus revealing an unconscious desire to indulge in oral sex with her own father.

The Dora analysis provides irrefutable evidence that what Freud claimed to be material emanating from his patient's 'unconscious' was in reality derived from his own *conscious* mind. He was, at the time of the analysis, currently preoccupied with his Oedipus theory and interpreted her dreams accordingly. Yet only a few years previously he had been interpreting his patients' dreams and associations to fit in with his then current theory of infantile seduction.

Many years ago, Hans Eysenck (1973) pointed out that Freudian analysts interpreted their material according to Freudian symbols while Jungian analysts used totally different ones. Psychoanalysis therefore would seem to be largely a process of *interpretation*, and, moreover, interpretation guided by theories and principles very much in the analysts' *conscious* minds. Since there are now said to be over 400 competing schools of psychotherapy, it is woefully probable that their advocates are all interpreting their clients' material according to the various rules and principles of their different systems.

The dependency on interpretation can be traced further. Up to 1984, Freudian analysts gave the orthodox Oedipal interpretation, or derivatives of it, to the material gleaned from their clients. With the publication of Jeffrey Masson's book that year, *Freud: The Assault on Truth* (Masson, 1984), all this changed almost overnight. In this book, Masson claimed that, in abandoning his infantile seduction theory, Freud had shown a 'failure of courage' and that he should have believed his patients when they told him of their childhood experiences of sexual abuse. In fact, they had *not* told him of any such experiences. *Freud* had told *them* they had been seduced in childhood. They themselves had strenuously denied any memory of such events. This is clear from the original papers Freud published at the time. Additionally the Oedipus theory, which replaced the seduction theory as, for instance, explored in the Dora analysis, was, with its reliance on infantile sexuality, to the nineteenth-century Viennese, potentially far more scandalous than the latter. Nevertheless these deficiencies in Masson's thesis appear to have been overlooked and it was taken up with enthusiasm. No-one evidently took the precaution to check the original contemporary papers. Before long, analysts and psychotherapists all over the United States were interpreting their material in terms of childhood sexual abuse, generally by the father. The trend spread to other countries. Astonishingly this dubious material was accepted by the courts and fathers were sent to prison and families broken up as a consequence. The recent condemnation by the Royal College of Psychiatrists, London, (Brandon et al., 1998) may help to redress these iniquities, but for many it will have come too late.

Even if the concept of the unconscious mind were true, how would it be possible to disentangle the contributions from the conscious mind of the analyst from those of the so-called 'unconscious' of the analysand? Once an unconscious mind to which the analysand does not have access, the contents of which can only be revealed by psychoanalysis, is postulated, anyone can put into it anything they wish without fear of being disproved – even the murderous or incestuous impulses cited by Freud, whose heavy use of cocaine at the time undoubtedly influenced his judgement (Thornton, 1983). Events the analysand denies remembering are accounted for by the premise that they have been 'repressed' into the 'unconscious'.

The dubious concept of 'repression' is also coming under critical scrutiny, many reputable authorities denying its existence altogether. Raymond Tallis, for instance, following Sartre's argument, points out that

> the unconscious has to know what it is that has to be repressed in order (actively) to repress it; it has also to know that it is shameful material appropriate for repression. If, however, it knows both these things, it is difficult to understand how it can avoid being conscious of it. (1996)

There is, to my knowledge, no experimental or empirical evidence that memories *can* be repressed. Repression appears to be another concept that has crept in via the back door as part of the entire Freud package. On the common-sense level, it is completely contrary to everyday experience, which is that unhappy and traumatic events are those that stand out most vividly in the memory. We may try to 'put them out of our head', that is, turn out attention to something else, but they will return unbidden in all their pristine freshness when recalled to memory by some chance association. But the concept of repression was of immense value to Freud in allowing him to postulate in his patients any motive his fertile imagination could conceive, and has continued to be so in succeeding generations of psychoanalysts.

What if the analyst has a somewhat morbid imagination, which *has* happened? Allegations of witchcraft and human sacrifice have been made under these conditions which have proved to be completely without foundation when investigated, but the trauma inflicted on families by the allegations has been immense. Children have been taken from their beds in midnight raids by social workers with police back-up and put into care, with fathers arrested and imprisoned as a result of these dubious allegations.

Psychoanalysis, previously regarded as the harmless preoccupation of the bored, the self-absorbed or the unhappy, has suddenly assumed a more sinister aspect. But it is not only in the psychoanalytical relationship that danger lies. Freudian concepts, including that of the unconscious mind, form the backbone of the theoretical foundation of the training of many social workers, probation officers, educationists and others who not only accept the untested and unproven theories of Sigmund Freud but actually put them into practice in their daily work. As a result of the large input of Freudian theory absorbed in their training, many social workers see their function as that of psychoanalysing their clients rather than giving them the practical help they need. They are conversant with all the jargon of Freudian theory while being woefully ignorant of the rules governing the social security system, for instance. The heavy involvement of social workers in the witchcraft and similar false memory cases testifies to the harm that can result from the application of Freudian theory to social casework.

Up until recent years, psychoanalytical theory did little serious harm. But the potential for harm was always present in the very nature of the concept of an unconscious mind. The events of recent years have shown us the formidable extent of this potential. It has now become urgently necessary that the whole concept of the unconscious mind be brought under rigorous scientific scrutiny before further damage is done and fresh traumas are inflicted on innocent people.

References

Brandon, S., Boakes, J. Glaser, D. and Green, R. (1998) Recovered memories of childhood sexual abuse. *British Journal of Psychiatry*, 172: 296–307.

Eysenck, H. (1973) *Experimental Studies of Freudian Theories*. London: Methuen.

Freud, S. (1905) 'Fragment of an analysis of a case of hysteria', in J. Strachey (ed.), *The Standard Edition of the Complete Psychological Works of Sigmund Freud*, Vol. 7. London: Hogarth Press.

Freud, S. (1914) 'On the history of the psycho-analytic movement', in J. Strachey (ed.), *The Standard Edition of the Complete Psychological Works of Sigmund Freud*, Vol. 14. London: Hogarth Press.

Freud, S. (1924) *The Standard Edition of the Complete Psychological Works of Sigmund Freud*, Vol. 19. London: Hogarth Press.

Freud, S. (1925) 'Some additional notes on dream interpretation as a whole', in J. Strachey (ed.), *The Standard Edition of the Complete Psychological Works of Sigmund Freud*, Vol. 18. London: Hogarth Press.

Masson, J.M. (1984) *Freud: The Assault on Truth*. London: Faber & Faber.

Studland, A. (1989) 'Was Dora ill?', in L. Spurling (ed.), *Sigmund Freud: Critical Assessment*. London: Routledge.

Tallis, R.C. (1996) 'Burying Freud', *The Lancet*, 347: 669–71.

Thornton, E.M. (1983) *Freud and Cocaine: The Freudian Fallacy*. London: Blond & Briggs.

3 On the existence of the unconscious

Tim Kendall and Peter Speedwell

An impractical notion

The idea of the unconscious, as conceived by Freud in the closing years of the nineteenth century, is at best a metaphor. At worst, the unconscious appears to be not much more than a misused and abused caricature of a much richer Nietzschean version of beasts, bodies or 'The Self' (Nietzsche, 1969: 61–3). Its paradoxes produce a kind of dyspepsia, so that whatever you have swallowed keeps returning, as if to tell you that you should be more careful about what you consume. On the one hand, the unconscious simply refers to those ideas and motivations within ourselves of which we are usually unaware, the personal psychological unknown (with no connotations of some sleeping giant lying in wait for us). However, if, by definition, we are not aware of the unconscious, can we be sure it exists? We can't touch it, smell it or see it, and yet Freud assured us that it exists and the reason that we don't know about it is because it's unconscious. It appears that we are being asked to believe in something because we are unable to experience it. This, it seems, is a triumph in double talk.

From our dreams and phantasies, from our jokes and slips of the tongue and from all the odd quirks of human behaviour, *fin-de-siècle* Freud began to elaborate a Gothic edifice and sunk it below ground like an Ethiopian religious temple (Freud, 1900/1953). Now the unconscious was a seething cauldron of violent and amorous desires, of murderous and incestuous wishes, which, if not sublimated or indirectly expressed in socially acceptable ways, would explode into apparently senseless action or mental illness. In any case, and this is true for everyone of us, in investigating the unconscious routes to what we are and what we do, Freud revealed the unstable, lustful and violent core of human subjectivity. (Surely this is a testament to the sort of person Freud was: half-crazed through the use of cocaine and seeking 'unconscious' excuses for his immoral relationships and desires.)

For Freud, the deeper historical core of this human interiority was indeed the unexplored 'dark continent' of our primitive and incestuous desires, those arising within the world of mother and infant. But (and here's the rub) Africa could be proved to exist. The unconscious could not. It seems absurd that Freud wished to be considered seriously as a scientist.

After all, a scientist is most assuredly interested in what can be proved, and what can be proved is surely a matter of empirical inquiry.[1]

Further peculiar practices took place under the aegis of this most questionable non-phenomenon. Psychoanalysts were now given *carte blanche* to ask invasive questions concerning their patients' murderous or sexual desires and, when the reply was a negative, the psychoanalyst could smile smugly with the rejoinder, 'I wonder if you aren't resisting your own impulses and wishes.' Angry at the suggestion, the patient protests. But the analyst insists on the reality of the unconscious, by way of the reality of resistance, to prove that the patient really is dominated by wishes that are beyond his or her ken! 'We are sure it's there, because you are sure it isn't. And when you're really sure it isn't there, we're convinced it is.' From double talk to perfect double bind.

This widely disseminated caricature of Freud, whether taken up by his 'followers' (and few psychoanalysts would class themselves as followers of this interpretation of Freud) or his accusers (Thornton, 1983; Webster, 1995), does not take into account the complexity of Freud's thought. Nor do these very polarized and, we believe, unengaged accounts of psychoanalysis take cognizance of the continual revision to which the dissatisfied Freud subjected his theories.

Justification

In 1915, Freud wrote a paper called 'The Unconscious' which laid out a genuinely radical concept of human subjectivity (Freud, 1915b/1957). In many ways it exploited the radical aspects of some of his earlier works which placed language as central to the psychoanalytic venture, such as *The Interpretation of Dreams* (Freud, 1900/1953) or perhaps *The Psychopathology of Everyday Life* (Freud, 1901/1960). The 1915 paper was an important summary of Freud's view of how conscious human experience was influenced by motivations, intentions, desires, hopes, wishes and fears. Most importantly, this paper was a clear and accessible theory of these influences as they occurred unconsciously, that is, without the person being aware of this happening. Freud went further in his theories and provided a very necessary justification for the use of the concept (Freud, 1915b/1967: 166–71).

First, our consciousness contains so many 'gaps' that we really cannot begin to understand our actions and thoughts in their entirety without some notion of mental processes of which we are not aware. These gaps in conscious experience include psychotic and neurotic symptoms, dreams, slips of action and comprehension, and jokes.[2] Second, as Freud found out through the analysis of his own neurotic symptoms, our conscious experience of these symptoms or gaps can be changed through finding a different meaning for those neurotic symptoms, meanings not derived from consciousness. This is one example of how our conception of the unconscious can be used to design methods (in this case psychoanalysis) that can influence our conscious experience. Alternative methods include hypnosis and post-hypnotic suggestion, in which it is possible to show that people are capable of acting under commands of which they are not consciously aware. Third, the notion of the 'unconscious' leads to a gain in meaning, to an increase in our sum of knowledge about ourselves and our subjective lives (through the conception of internal objects, drives, unconscious processes, and so on).

One of the crucial points concerning our understanding of the unconscious, raised in the 1915 paper, is how useful it is to us. After all, we do not know, at least we cannot directly prove, that atoms exist. We cannot touch them, taste them or see them. And yet by using this concept we make sense of, and we can alter more predictably, the physical world in a way that is now widely regarded to be indispensable. Is the unconscious a practical notion that can be made use of, or is it some kind of poetical notion that has its beauty but which cannot be applied?[3]

Although the notion of the unconscious may appear illogical, in many ways it is a simple idea. Those ideas which are not in consciousness but have an influence upon our behaviour or activity are rightly regarded as unconscious (non-conscious if you prefer, as the cognitive psychologists do). Now it is not difficult to show empirically that someone's consciously executed performance on simple exercises can be influenced by non-conscious factors, and that the impact of these non-conscious factors upon consciousness is directly related to their emotional content. There are some creditable experiments that persuade us that, parallel to our conscious life, unconscious conflicts exert great pressure (Shevrin et al., 1996). Sometimes these experiments can have quite startling or funny results, as in the following example.

Using a tachistoscope you can flash up onto a screen words or images for periods of time that are too short for a person to be able to consciously perceive what he or she has seen. Using such an instrument a woman, an academic, who was in her middle years, and who was deeply sceptical of psychoanalysis and in particular of the concept of the unconscious, was exposed to the word 'Mother' for gradually increasing periods of time starting at one millisecond exposure. Normally, people see nothing up until between 8 and 12 milliseconds and can only see the word clearly at between 12 and 15 milliseconds. This woman saw the word 'Conflict' from 12 to 14 milliseconds and, at 15 milliseconds, blushed with an intense sense of embarrassment when she realized her error.[4]

Freud wrote the paper on the unconscious shortly after the 'technical papers' had been largely completed (Freud, 1911–15/1958). These can be seen as a culmination of a series of very practical papers with very practical instructions and justifications: how to do psychoanalysis and why we do it this way. As such, this period of Freud's writing (1911–15) knits free association, and therefore language, into a meta-psychological and practical framework for the treatment of neuroses.[5] The unconscious becomes

directly understood in terms of the analytic interaction, and in two con-
temporaneous papers Freud outlines how the transference, as an unconscious process, can be utilized to redirect repetitive actions and behaviour
patterns into speech (Freud, 1914/1958, 1915a/1957). In one of these papers
what is forgotten, what becomes unconscious and forces an endless
sequence of seemingly inexplicable repetitions, is early hurts in love. Once
the analysand becomes attached to the physician (therapist or analyst),
these are unconsciously repeated in the relationship with him/her in an
unconscious process central to all of human life, the transference.

For Freud discovered in his clinical work that patients would reveal
extremely strong feelings about the analyst, of intense love or hatred, which
were not necessarily appropriate to the clinical setting. It was Freud's
theory that these feelings belonged to the history of the patient and his/
her relationships and that they were being 'transferred' to the analyst. In
fact, if we consider it, all feelings of intense love (or hate) may be called
transference. For, in love, we are capable of the most extraordinary self-
deceptions and idealizations to keep our beloved on his/her pedestal. But in
psychoanalysis, it is hoped, the pattern might be changed and the sad
repetition of disastrous romantic engagements might be resolved in analysis
rather than replayed, once again.

Thus, Freud in this period was beginning to see the importance of
relationships (especially our very early relationships, given their 'affective
power') in unconsciously dominating the present. He also began to see how
these early relationships might dominate the way we view ourselves. In
'Mourning and melancholia', which was also written during this fertile
reworking of his theories, Freud began to ask the question why some
people, especially those in depression, should be so hostile to themselves
and continually berate themselves (Freud, 1917/1957). Freud related
depression (melancholia) to the natural process of mourning whereby, after
a certain period of grief, the mourner identifies with the lost loved one and
internalizes him/her. This seems to be the ego fooling us into thinking that
we really have not lost the one who has died: he or she lives on in us, and
this offsets the immense and inexplicable pain of loss.[6]

For the depressive, something similar is going on, but the relationship
with the internalized parent (usually) has been much more problematic in
that there has been a deal of uncommunicated, unthinkable and therefore
unconscious hatred between the depressive and the one he/she mourns. By
internalizing the lost and ambivalently loved one, the depressive offsets the
loss only to find him- or herself full of self-hatred. Moreover, the extent of
these self-attacks increases in proportion to the degree that the depressed
person could not communicate his or her hatred to the lost person in
question during life. Incidentally, Freud's 'Mourning and melancholia' is
widely valued, even by his more ferocious critics (Webster, 1995: 166).

That human beings go through serial losses, identifications and ambivalent identifications, led Freud to a more dynamic conception of internal
life, in which we are built up from forces and relationships which do not

always co-exist in harmony. Deduced from the point of view that symptoms and language, indeed conscious life itself, were the product of the interaction of these antagonistic internal forces and relationships, and which (when seriously divided) operate like separate internal psychological agencies, Freud (1923/1961) developed a dynamic and structural model of the human mind made up of 'I', 'It' and 'Over-I'. These 'parts', or 'psychic agencies' (ego, id and superego), are most clearly formed during the period of very intense and mostly ambivalent attachments during early childhood. This is Freud's Oedipal period that ends in the formation of the superego.

Freud believed that the superego was formed from a child's reactions to his or her mixed feelings and ambivalent identifications with parents (against incest, rivalry or murderous rage, for example), combined with his or her internalized commands, prohibitions and ideals. The superego rejected the wishes and impulses of the id, that part of us that is made up of the drives that overtake us without social negotiation (represented by phrases such as 'It gripped me', or 'It affected me'). The third in the triad is the ego, which, having cut its teeth on mediating between a greedy and uncontrolled infantile id, has now developed to become a mediator between the two conflicting forces of id and superego as well.

Communication and the unconscious

One of Freud's crucial insights in his essay on the unconscious is that for an idea to become conscious it needs to be attached to language, in other words it needs to take part in communication. As psychoanalysis in large part takes place through language and communication, and these internal conflicts, forces, relationships and agencies are capable of 'talking' and 'not talking', of being thought and 'unthought', then the picture of our internal and external relationships can be seen either as a result of communication and 'excommunication', or in terms of conscious and unconscious (Speedwell, 1998). In both cases the conception is dynamic in that our experience is the synthesized product of conflicting forces. Moreover, to the degree that our conscious experience of our selves and our world is coherent and well synthesized, we can assume that such experience is also mediated by an ego whose prime functions are compromise and synthesis.

So, the ego (which will therefore be divided between communication and 'excommunication', between conscious and unconscious) synthesizes our experience and maintains the coherence of our perceptions. It gathers together the disparate, fragmented and conflictual elements of our internal and external world and turns it into a coherent whole, a gestalt, upon which we can rely. But part of this synthesis includes how we see ourselves; and we like to see ourselves as rational, consistent beings and not as divided persons, so when we do something strange we need an explanation. Our conscious part excludes contradiction and puts together a rational explanation as far as possible, until things begin to break down.

We might say that the conscious ego constructs little narratives to fool itself, to maintain a coherent narrative. But any coherent narrative excludes the details and contradictions that make up a rich pattern of life. Thus, there will be a part that is 'excommunicated' from the stories that we tell about ourselves and that society tells about us (Speedwell, 1998).

Thus, at one level, the id is comprised of that which has been dialogically excluded from the narrative of how we know ourselves. If we wish to belong to a rational society, we do not want to know that we harbour murderous thoughts against our loved ones, we do not wish to know that we entertain incestuous impulses, and so we excommunicate them. We do not let them see the light of language. However, because these desires are not negotiated through language, they can act upon us in the most forceful way through direct influence upon our behaviour, actions and conduct. Thus psychoanalysis is something very different from some kind of liberation theology based on the de-repression of desires. Rather, it is a technique for self-mastery where excommunicated desires can be communicated, and therefore made conscious, and then can be mastered and controlled.

We would readily recognize that this formulation of the unconscious is a reworking of Freud's theory, and in particular of his drive model of repression. However, we believe that the conception of the unconscious as that which is excommunicated from our self-narratives has many advantages.[7] First, it is a flexible notion and does not have to be filled with preconceived ideas concerning the contents of the excluded narrative. Second, it gives room for historical change and can account to some extent for the fact that symptoms change over historical time and do not always demonstrate the eternal verities of Freud's versions of the unconscious. Third, it embraces some notions of the unconscious which were inimical to Freud's theories, particularly the existential conception of 'bad faith', which is reformulated as 'self-deception' by Mirvish (1990). Finally, it helps us to explain the importance of language and communication as the medium for what takes place in the consulting room.

The unconscious in practice

Let us take a couple of practical examples. A young, intelligent boy suddenly begins to do badly at school. He fails in all his tests. Where has his intelligence (in itself a highly disputed notion) gone? When asked about his difficulties, the child cannot give a proper account in spite of efforts to do so. Such a child may be sent to a child therapist. As he begins to play or talk and as he builds up trust in his therapist, he may begin to communicate his difficulties. However, before this moment, we have to accept that the causes of his difficulties were unknown to him. He was unconscious or unaware of them. This does not mean that the cause is locked away in a vault somewhere. It is rather that their connections with language have been severed or never developed. It is quite possible and quite likely that his difficulties are incommunicable to his parents in the home, that they are excluded from allowed or acceptable family narratives. The failures at school are a communication only that something is going wrong.[8]

Or: A man in his mid-sixties comes to see me (TK) with a full-blown delusion. He believes that something is wrong with his drains at home. He has called plumbers, heating engineers, 'sewerage experts' and used hundreds of cleaning agents in his sinks, bath and toilets. He has had the hot-water tank changed and is considering replacing his central heating and cold-water plumbing systems. He isn't sure if there might not be a nasty and unseemly smell emanating from his drains (although he cannot smell it). He is convinced that the draining of his 'water-works' is the prime problem, although he cannot be sure that someone isn't tampering with them. But something is still wrong. I begin to talk to this man, who is frightened to see me because I am a psychiatrist. He has been rejected by his family; they have insisted that he should seek medical (psychiatric) treatment.

Now it is possible to operate on the preconception that his symptoms are the results of a chemical imbalance in the brain. This would lead to a conclusion that the form of his experience (fixed and false belief held tenaciously against all the evidence) is the result of such imbalance, but the content of his experience (that his 'water works' were seriously faulty) is irrelevant to his 'illness'. In other words he is talking nonsense and will continue to do so until the balance is chemically restored, when he would begin to talk sense again. I could assume, on the other hand, that he is showing evidence of deeply placed and repressed homo-erotic tendencies. Or even that he has become possessed by evil spirits! In any of these interpretations what he says is only for diagnostic purposes, and there would be little concern with why he says it, nor to whom he is saying it, and whom, we could assume, he wants to hear it. This is not to say that in some ways these 'diagnoses' may not contain some truths.

Alternatively, I could maintain a respect for what I am being told, and then all I can presume is that within the metaphor of the rotten drains he is telling his family (and me) there is a story. It is both pointing towards and hiding, at the same time, something that he and his family would collusively prefer not to share or be conscious of.[9]

I continue to talk to this man. I find out that his wife died some four years ago of a sexually transmitted disease and that at this time he had discovered that his wife had a long-term affair with a man in the South of England. After his wife's death the lover from the South of England telephoned my patient and asked what his wife had died from. He could not tell the truth and pretended it was cancer, although he felt a strong desire to reveal the true cause of his wife's death. A couple of years later, the lover's own wife telephoned to tell my patient that her husband (the lover) was dying and asked if her husband had had an affair with my patient's wife. My patient felt again a strong desire to reveal the true cause of his wife's death, but he could not follow this through. His depressive 'symptoms' developed from this time.

I ask the patient how his wife's terminal illness had manifested itself before she died. She had developed urinary tract infections and blockages, and eventually renal failure, a complication associated with her illness. I consider that there may well be some connection between his wife's renal failure and the difficulties he experienced with the drains. I ask him if he might be confusing the two. It was as if her diseased and faulty 'water-works' had become the 'diseased' and faulty water-works in the house. He could not accept her death, nor undertake the work of mourning so long as he could not communicate it (along with how he felt about her and her disease) to himself or others.[10] The effect of my tentative suggestion was palpable and physical. He became shocked. He was stunned by what I had said, reiterating it with a sense of realization. His delusions quickly abated, becoming something more like a neurotic obsession with keeping the drains clean, although he became more miserable and despairing over the coming weeks.

I could not help this man without some conception of the unconscious and of necessary self-deception. Indeed this accepts that there are some facts of life and death that are so powerfully painful that they seem unbearable. This is why we hide the awful truth from ourselves and others and can only hint at it. This is why we hide from ourselves, and our nearest-and-dearest, the forcefulness of our love and hate, and how much we fear our own destructiveness.

As connections are progressively made and the patient begins to make a new pattern or narrative concerning his life, something comes to the fore, sometimes quite slowly, as he pieces together the events and fictions concerning his family life. On the other hand, sometimes (but less often than is popularly believed) a traumatic memory is unearthed which either shakes the conventional family narrative to the roots or confirms the new perspectives that the patient has achieved.

The pursuit of self-knowledge has been, since the ancient Greeks, an honoured practice both necessary and useful to gain a greater degree of mastery over ourselves. This implies that what we don't know about ourselves tends to make us unstable and out of control, and, further, that knowing about these darker sides of ourselves helps to give us a greater degree of stability in our lives. The ideas that seem the most repugnant and destabilizing will also often be the most forceful in determining our behaviour (hence the need to know ourselves better and so gain better control).

It is a great pity that some critics of Freud have reduced his concepts (plural intended) of the unconscious to a narrow dogma as a rhetorical sparring partner against which to promote their own dogmatic theories. Indeed, it seems more than curious that the notion of the unconscious should be rejected. Do we really think that all our motivations are rational and known, or that we hide nothing from ourselves? If we do, we are in danger of sliding into a quite irrational confidence in our conscious rationality, the dangers of which we have already seen in this century.

Notes

1. Science is not a unified way of investigating the world which is reducible to empiricism (for example, compare the different methods used in cosmology, non-observable physics, chemistry and health services research, each of which has very different standards for evidence, verification and the point at which one claims something to be true). Nevertheless, 'scientific' psychology and psychiatry regard nomothetic inquiry to be *the* paradigm for investigating our psychological lives (and the Randomized Control Trial is the gold standard of investigation).

2. From Descartes to the end of the nineteenth century, we assumed an identity between what is conscious and what is mental. This was purely a matter of convention, not one based upon evidence. Moreover, Freud argues, to take such a view dooms us to psychophysical parallelism in which events in our minds are causally connected.

3. These are not mutually exclusive positions for either atoms or the unconscious: both concepts have their beauty and are practically useful.

4. This sort of error can be understood most easily by comparison to errors in typing. For example, when we mix up the letters 'm' and 'n' we are unsure if this is a result of their similarity of appearance or sound. Alternatively, we might mix them up because, for some psychological reason, we were drawn to type 'mumbers' instead of 'numbers' and we never mixed the letters 'm' and 'n' when typing other words. Finally, it might be because 'm' and 'n' are simply next to each other on the keyboard. The error of subliminally confusing 'Mother' and 'Conflict' most likely fits the latter type of error: that is, that the subjects 'Mother' and 'Conflict' are physically close to each other, in the way that her internal life is linguistically structured.

5. The term 'neurosis' is a complicated and rather broadly used concept. It is useful as a term applied to conscious waking experiences (behaviours, thoughts and images) which do not make meaningful sense without reference to (and interpretation of) unconscious processes and 'objects'. This is a psychoanalytic use of the term and can be applied to some aspects of everyone's experience. However, to use the term 'neurosis' as a distinction from the normal and psychotic is, we would suggest, more problematic. This is a psychiatric use of the term (mixing up the two has not worked well).

6. In Freud's words: 'The shadow of the object fell upon the ego . . .' (1917/1957: 249).

7. Although it may be objected that the unconscious is still an unwieldy notion, it is worth maintaining, for the following reasons: as a direct translation of Freud's *Unbewusste* it means simply that which we are not aware of. Thus it need not be visualized as a dustbin for our more bestial desires but, rather, can be understood as dispersed throughout the psyche–soma as long as the link of communication is broken. Thus the unconscious, although socially determined, is a burden borne by the individual as it is unshared knowledge (see note 9, below).

8. It is worth noting that Thomas Szasz elaborated an important distinction in communicative modes between discursive (two-way, more sophisticated and socially accessible) and iconic (one-way, like a picture, idiosyncratic, less sophisticated). The latter is developed and most easily seen in family life and in religious domains, and is typified by 'sulking' and 'mental illness'. When discursive communication fails, we all tend to revert to iconic signs. In other words, psychological symptoms are

metaphorical and idiosyncratic and 'one-way' communications are used when more social forms of communication fail (Szasz, 1972: 111–52).

9. Etymologically, 'conscious' means 'knowing together', and has the same etymological route as 'conscience' (many languages, including French, do not distinguish conscious from conscience).

10. It may be important to know that his own mother died when he was just seven years old, a fact that he could communicate very little about.

References

Freud, S. (1900/1953) *The Interpretation of Dreams*, in J. Strachey (ed.), *The Standard Edition of the Complete Psychological Works of Sigmund Freud*, Vols 4–5. London: Hogarth Press.

Freud, S. (1901/1960) *The Psychopathology of Everyday Life*, in J. Strachey (ed.), *The Standard Edition of the Complete Psychological Works of Sigmund Freud*, Vol. 6. London: Hogarth Press.

Freud, S. (1911–15/1958) 'Technical papers', in J. Strachey (ed.), *The Standard Edition of the Complete Psychological Works of Sigmund Freud*, Vol. 12. London: Hogarth Press.

Freud, S. (1914/1958) 'Remembering, repeating and working through', in J. Strachey (ed.), *The Standard Edition of the Complete Psychological Works of Sigmund Freud*, Vol. 12. London: Hogarth Press.

Freud, S. (1915a/1958) 'Observations on transference love', in J. Strachey (ed.), *The Standard Edition of the Complete Psychological Works of Sigmund Freud*, Vol. 12. London: Hogarth Press.

Freud, S. (1915b/1957) 'The unconscious', in J. Strachey (ed.), *The Standard Edition of the Complete Psychological Works of Sigmund Freud*, Vol. 14. London: Hogarth Press.

Freud, S. (1917/1957) 'Mourning and melancholia', in J. Strachey (ed.), *The Standard Edition of the Complete Psychological Works of Sigmund Freud*, Vol. 14. London: Hogarth Press.

Freud, S. (1923/1961) 'The ego and the id', in J. Strachey (ed.), *The Standard Edition of the Complete Psychological Works of Sigmund Freud*, Vol. 19. London: Hogarth Press.

Mirvish, A. (1990) 'Freud contra Sartre: repression or self-deception?', *Journal of the British Society for Phenomenology*, 21 (3): 216–33.

Nietzsche, F. (1969) *Thus Spoke Zarathustra*. Harmondsworth: Penguin.

Shevrin, H., Bond, J.A., Brakel, L.A.W., Hertel, R.K. and Williams, W.J. (1996) *Conscious and Unconscious Processes*. New York: Guilford.

Speedwell, P. (1998) 'Time and the polyphony of mind'. Unpublished PhD thesis, University of Sheffield.

Szasz, T. (1972) *The Myth of Mental Illness*. London: Grafton.

Thornton, E.M. (1983) *Freud and Cocaine: The Freudian Fallacy*. London: Blond & Briggs.

Webster, R. (1995) *Why Freud Was Wrong*. London: HarperCollins.

4   Primal therapies – stillborn theories

Jennifer M. Cunningham

Her clients included a woman who suffered migraines until therapy revealed that in a past life she was put to death with a metal band around her forehead.

This was the by-line of an interview with psychotherapist Deike Begg, recently arrived in Scotland to bring relief to sufferers of millennium anxiety and other psychosocial morbidities. Having specialized in rebirthing and past-life therapy for 10 years, Begg attributes a wide range of symptoms including ulcers, abdominal problems, headaches and mental problems, to past-life traumas. She admits: 'I would think the medical body would think it is complete lunacy.' Nevertheless, she argues, scientific thought changes constantly, and rebirthing could yet find itself on the orthodox curriculum (Pallister, 1998).

For the foreseeable future, past-life experiences will remain a matter of faith, not susceptible to rational investigation or theorization. However, most primal therapists (despite differing approaches among practitioners[1]) make their starting point the repressed memories of trauma during child-birth and early childhood – memories that are believed to underlie adult neuroses and psychosomatic disorders. This at least can be the subject of scientific inquiry.

Arthur Janov, who popularized primal therapy with the publication of his book *The Primal Scream* in 1970, writes two decades later: 'It is a therapy that has been investigated for over fifteen years by independent scientists, and the findings are consistent. Primal Therapy is able to reduce or eliminate a host of physical and psychic ailments in a relatively short period of time with lasting results' (1993: xvii–xviii). Claiming therapeutic success is not sufficient to establish the scientific basis of any therapy; especially when, as in the case of primal therapy, relatively few have been objectively evaluated – and where they have been, results are less then conclusive.[2] A well-founded explanation of why the therapy should work is also required. Primal therapy has to be able to clarify the nature of infantile memory and the mechanism of repression in terms that are consistent with our current understanding of child development and neuro-science. In this I believe it fails.

Remembering birth trauma

There is nothing unworldly about obstetrician Frederick Leboyer's harrowing descriptions of newborn babies in *Birth Without Violence*:

> The child? Oh, dear God, it can't be true! The mask of agony, of horror; and above all the hands, raised to the head in the classic gesture of despair. This is the gesture of the mortally wounded, the moment before they collapse. Can birth hold so much suffering, so much pain? (1975: 10)

Leboyer was convinced that babies could suffer overwhelming trauma during birth and he advocated gentler obstetric practices, both during and after delivery.

Even primal therapists must recognize that there is a danger here of projecting adult feelings onto neonates; of assuming that superficially similar manifest behaviour signifies an equivalent emotional experience. Suffering, in its human sense, is not a simple biological phenomenon. It is an intellectual and emotional understanding of the consequences of pain, danger, death or a lack of freedom. There is a related difficulty in accepting that what people report about re-experiencing early life traumas, or what therapists observe in 'regression' to neonatal states, are *real* primal experiences and not the vivid imagery of the adult mind.

Theologian and psychiatrist Frank Lake argued that what impressed him and other psychiatrists treating neuroses and personality disorders with lysergic acid (LSD) in the 1960s was the frequency with which patients remembered their first year of life and the accuracy with which neonatal movements were mimicked. He and his colleagues were reporting 'the reliving of birth trauma so frequently that the evidence became overwhelming' (Lake, 1978: 230). Clearly one should exercise some scepticism about ideas and behaviours elicited under the influence of probably the most potent hallucinogenic drug.[3] But we must also be cautious about accepting the veracity of memories of early childhood obtained in the emotionally evocative circumstances of primal therapy, regression and hypnosis.[4] This is particularly so given the accumulated evidence that our memories can be both flawed and subject to suggestion.

Many studies have demonstrated the impact of mood states on the recall of past events. For example, acutely depressed people describe their parents in more negative terms than both non-depressed controls and remitted depressed subjects (with a history of depression but not depressed during the study) – remembering them as having been more emotionally rejecting (Lewinsohn and Rosenbaum, 1987). Other research has shown that information coming after an event can shape memories of the event. Moreover, people can come to remember a *suggested* event as actually having occurred. Two useful reviews of this extensive research can be found in Henry Roediger's article on 'memory illusions' (Roediger, 1996) and Sydney

Brandon's report for the Royal College of Psychiatrists on recovered memories of childhood sexual abuse (Brandon et al., 1998).

Brandon and his co-workers concluded that when memories are 'recovered' after long periods of amnesia there is a high probability that the memories are false. However, they appear to accept the view that there could be a *dual* memory system, with 'a conditioned-emotional memory expressed through feelings, behaviours and images' that is independent of 'narrative-autobiographical memory, which emerges around four to five years of age and is accessible by intentional retrieval' (Brandon et al., 1998: 298). This is a welcome 'get-out' clause for psychoanalytic therapies in general and primal therapy in particular. It suggests that early childhood experiences might be registered by a 'perceptual-emotional memory'; these memories could be repressed or dissociated, and persist into adulthood. Although Brandon's team agree that there is no empirical evidence to support either repression or dissociation, they feel there is 'much clinical evidence for these concepts' (1998: 304).

Such an approach can easily accommodate Otto Rank's original thesis in 1929 that the repression of memories of birth trauma is a primary cause of adult neurosis. Referring to the psychoanalysis of neurotic patients, Rank wrote: 'The analysis finally turns out to be a belated accomplishment of the incompleted mastery of the birth trauma' (1957: 5). Rank did not advance any novel explanation of the mechanism of repression. He followed the Freudian model, in which unbearable psychic material is withdrawn from the conscious mind into the unconscious, from where it can perversely influence future behaviour. Freud regarded this material as forbidden sexual fantasies; for Rank and Janov it represented an emotional reaction to the physical trauma of birth. Contemporary advocates of primal therapy or its variants, such as Alice Miller, believe that childhood abuse (including even rigid parenting practices) is the source of repressed psychic pain.

In psychoanalytic theory, repression accounts for the occurrence of 'infantile amnesia', that is, the inability of adults to remember events from early in their lives. The intolerable thoughts or experiences of infants and young children, it is argued, are represented in memory but the individual cannot gain access to them. In fact, it is the premise of primal therapy that without the help of the therapist it is impossible to remove the defences which 'gate' primal pain and deal with the repressed emotions associated with it.

However, there is an inherent inconsistency in this concept of repression: infantile amnesia is not a selective phenomenon. Most of us cannot recall *any* experiences prior to our third birthday – pleasant, unpleasant, emotional or otherwise. We remember only a few events from three to five years, with recall increasing steadily after that.

This raises a further question: how do infants appreciate or evaluate sensory events as *painful* for the purposes of repression, given the paucity of their subjective experience (or its absence in the case of the newborn)?

One line of argument pursued by primal therapists is suggested by neo-natal research. Studies have demonstrated that newborn babies recognize familiar visual stimuli (Friedman, 1972), voices (DeCasper and Fifer, 1980) and smells (Cernock and Porter, 1985). Neonates also show imitation of facial expressions (Field et al., 1982; Meltzoff and Moore, 1983). These kinds of responses are cited as evidence that the newborn baby already possesses a nervous system with the capacity for memory and emotional feeling. However, this is somewhat misconceived. What is being described in this research are innate propensities for expressive actions and gestures in response to specific affective stimuli. These organized reflexes are the prerequisite for subsequent emotional development and they quickly begin to be conditioned by learning. Nevertheless, instinctual perception and recognition are not sufficient for either emotion or memory.

Emotion

Most theories of emotion stress that arousal, cognitive processes and feel-ing states are necessary for emotional experiences and responses. Cognitive processes include sensation, perception, images and ideas. Feeling states often involve autonomic reactions like changes in heartbeat, sweating and shaking. The *differentiation* of emotions (pain, anger, fear, joy) involves the cognitive component: that is, 'cognition arising from the immediate situ-ation as interpreted by past experience provides the framework within which one understands and labels' a feeling (Schachter, 1964: 50–1). These components and operations come together for the first time in babies at about four months. Only then does emotion emerge in its most rudi-mentary form.

Howard Leventhal's developmental model of emotion is quite useful in grasping these interactions. He distinguishes three levels of processing stimulus information:

> *Expressive-motor level*: an innate set of central neuromotor programmes for generating a distinct set of expressive reactions in response to specific stimuli in the newborn.
> *Schematic level*: an automatic processing system that codes emotional experiences in memory. 'It is not a memory about emotional reactions, it is an analog record of the reactions.' Schematic processing occurs around four months and produces stereotyped responses to sensory stimulation.
> *Conceptual level*: includes a set of abstract rules about emotional episodes and a set of rules for voluntary responses to emotional situations and emotions themselves. (Leventhal, 1984: 128)

The conscious conceptual system begins to operate from about 10 to 12 months of age, corresponding to the consolidation of cognitive abilities such as 'object permanence' and symbolic play. At this time, infants begin to distinguish between various adult reactions or attitudes and appreciate that these can be different from their own. It is only with the emergence of this elementary self-awareness that children can have *subjective* feelings. And it is only subjective emotional experiences that could conceivably have an impact on our subsequent emotional and social interactions.

Memory

The other prerequisite for feelings to have any longer term psychological consequence is that they are committed to memory in some way. Leventhal gives a good example of this when he considers 'phantom pain'. This is the phenomenon in which people who have had a limb amputated can experience a phantom limb, together with sensations and pain present prior to the loss. Phantom limbs and phantom pain are dependent on a reasonably mature memory system (a cognitive body imagery system) – they do not occur in children under the age of four to six years (Leventhal, 1984: 139–40).

In looking at memory in more detail, it is worth returning to the notion of a dual memory system discussed earlier. A perceptual-emotional memory was postulated to explain how unconscious 'memory traces' could survive into adulthood and affect adult behaviour. Writing about neonatal experiences, Arthur Janov says: 'What is amazing about these memories is that they remain absolutely pure and untouched by experience. They arrive at consciousness as though in freshly unwrapped gauze. The memory contains all of the details surrounding the trauma – no part of it is changed' (1993: 59). This conception of an enduring memory trace is inconsistent with current neuroscientific thinking. Neuroscientist Susan Greenfield points out that our neuronal circuitry is constantly changing as new connections are established in response to environmental and social influences – 'as more and more of the appropriate (that is, the most hardworking) neurons are connected to enable the most effective signalling' (Greenfield, 1997: 115). Underused connections and circuits become lost. This 'use it or lose it' rule accounts for the remarkable adaptability of the human brain during child development. At the risk of stating the obvious, an 'unconscious memory trace' is by definition underused.

The elaboration of these dynamic and transformative neurological processes is reflected in contemporary psychological theories of memory. Memory is understood as a *creative* process. When we remember, we use our conceptual understanding of a previous experience and link it to related knowledge or emotional memories in order to reconstruct the event. As psychological researcher Robyn Dawes puts it: 'We attempt to "make sense" out of our recall of bits and pieces of our past in terms of what we believe to be true of the world today, by "filling in the gaps"' (1996: 129).

Childhood memory

It seems evident that babies under 8 to 10 months have no memory. Their experiences are all in the immediate present. Developmental psychologist Margaret Donaldson believes that:

> [I]t is very likely that the baby in the first half-year of life at least, while having a sort of 'rolling' sense of movement from immediate past to immediate future, has no sense of an extended past in which specific events can be located and likewise no sense of a future filled with events yet to come. (1992: 54)

Around 8 to 10 months, babies start to show fear of strangers and of unfamiliar objects, suggesting they must anticipate that something is going to happen. They also become distressed if their carer goes away, indicating that they recall the person's presence. The related awareness of *object permanence* begins to emerge at this time. Infants will search for a toy hidden before their eyes and find it successfully. Again, unless they remembered that there was a toy they would not look for it.

To be able to recall things, we have to be able to *represent* them to ourselves. Visual imagery is one way this can occur, but it is predominantly through language that we give meaning to experiences, emotions and events. Some young children have the ability to remember highly detailed scenes as if they still had the actual scene before them. This so-called 'photographic' or 'eidetic' memory seems to be a type of 'visual persistence phenomenon' and the image can endure for days or even weeks (Wingfield and Byrnes, 1981: 361). The occurrence of eidetic images in preschool children and its extreme rarity in adults suggests that this form of memory is displaced by verbal thinking in older children. According to the eminent Soviet psychologists Lev Vygotsky and Alexander Luria, functions such as memory 'change abruptly as soon as speech begins to predominate in the behaviour of the child' and memory moves 'from the optical-graphic towards the verbal type'. Whereas eidetic memory is very limited in its scope and durability (because it depends on the existence of the external stimulus), the 'output' of memory rises sharply once children are able to use symbolic representation (and they can generate the stimulus internally themselves) (Luria and Vygotsky, 1992: 121, 143).

From the age of two years, children begin to talk about things which have happened or things that are going to happen. However, children younger than three seldom remember events occurring more than one or two days previously. Susan Greenfield highlights the fact that because children live in the present they tend not to dwell on pain. Although they usually overreact to a relatively trivial mishap, 'the tears are frequently banished by some distraction'. As soon as a new event in the external world arises, consciousness of the original pain vanishes (Greenfield, 1995: 182). Children's memories gradually improve with age and linguistic skill until 'by the age of five or six personal anecdotes and projections into the future become common' (Donaldson, 1992: 109).

It looks fairly obvious from this brief appraisal of emotional development and memory that primal therapy's basic proposition is not just unproven, it is frankly implausible.

Searching for a true self

Even if it were the case that we could retrieve infantile memories, why should we accept that early childhood experiences could have so disproportionate an impact on our lives compared with all subsequent influences? Attaching such importance to childhood trauma suggests a highly *deterministic* view of human behaviour. Sociologist Frank Furedi turns the question around very effectively:

> Why is it that people have managed to overcome the limits of their hormones and genes and their childhood experiences and exercise a measure of control over their lives? Why is it that many who experience a variety of abuses as children apparently grow up as reasonably aware, well-adjusted, non-abusive adults – usually without the benefit of expert intervention? The answer to these questions is provided by the rich experience of growing up, encountering new experiences and interacting with other people. (1997: 170–1)

A similarly degraded view of humanity is manifest in the belief that by searching in our primitive past for the source of our present misery, we shall discover our inner essence and *real* feelings. For Alice Miller, getting patients to experience and articulate their early traumas allows them to 'regain their lost ability to feel, for only on the path of feeling can they find their true self' (1998: 56). Arthur Janov agrees: 'Primal Therapy is a way of recapturing feelings' (1993: 284). As babies we quickly lose our own unique 'spark', according to Jacqueline James. She writes: 'At the age before the regimentation of school and the learning of pre-ordained ideas began to take effect, you were still in touch with your primal, unique self' (1996: 17).

Of course, suspending rational thought and yielding to strong emotion can be very satisfying on occasions. One could imagine that having casual sex or going skydiving might be just as therapeutic as a primal scream. But emotionalism *per se* is seldom a productive state of being. We are usually at our most creative when we combine rational thought with the full range and subtlety of our adult emotions – as evidenced by music, literature and art, feats of engineering and discoveries in science.

This elevation of the emotional and search for the 'inner child' tells us more about the relationship between the sufferer and the therapy than about the path to harmony and health. Whether you suffer from psychosomatic malaise, psychosocial disorder or plain discontent, you become an 'adult child' in therapy. Finding a 'damaged' inner child puts the blame for present problems on something or someone in your past. It ultimately legitimizes an abandonment of responsibility for what is happening in your life now.

There has been an exponential rise in the number of people with psychosomatic and neurotic disorders. This increased morbidity is clearly correlated with the major social, economic and demographic changes that have taken place over the past 20 years. Under these circumstances, we should be particularly wary of causal explanations that focus solely on *individual* psychology. A sceptical attitude seems all the more essential when 'psychosocial stress' is defined so widely as to include almost any form of social engagement or personal challenge, from marital strife and harassment at work to academic pressure and job insecurity.

In a climate which encourages people to see themselves as passive victims of their past, I think we need to reinvigorate the idea that 'discovering' ourselves is about realizing our full potential in the times ahead – through raising our expectations, stretching our minds and risking new experiences and relationships.

Notes

1. There are broadly three approaches distinguished: (i) *Primal therapy* – emphasizes regression and getting in touch with the original trauma; through re-experiencing the trauma, your pain can be discharged and current problems worked through in the light of new self-knowledge. (ii) *Primal integration* – aims to get in contact with a 'real self' that is split off from the persona, as a defence against intense childhood distress; the object of therapy is to integrate different aspects of your personality, body and mind. (iii) *Rebirthing* – involves 'self-conscious' breathing techniques that allow you to reach your earliest emotional experiences.

2. In fact, the scientific research referred to in Arthur Janov's *The New Primal Scream* (1993) does not scientifically evaluate or validate the efficacy of primal therapy as a treatment. Janov has estimated that primal therapy has a success rate of between 90 and 98 per cent. However, these estimates are entirely impressionistic. A questionnaire survey of 200 Primal Institute patients (reported in 1979) found a success rate of 79 per cent. These data were based on self-reports, a method now regarded as unreliable on its own. A Swedish study, using more exacting methods to determine therapeutic success, found a satisfactory outcome in 40 per cent of patients (Khamsi, 1988: 21).

3. From the early 1970s, the supply and possession of LSD was prohibited in Britain under the Misuse of Drugs Act 1971.

4. Caution should also be exercised in relation to reports of *forceps* marks reappearing during primal therapy. 'Patients reliving a birth sequence will again show the forceps mark on the forehead . . . or wherever else they originally left a mark' (Janov, 1993: 33, 60). Many of us have scars or blemishes on our scalp and face from a variety of causes (injuries, skin conditions like acne and eczema, and birth marks), and these will often become more prominent when we are emotional. Invariably attributing marks on the skin to forceps trauma (reappearing as a result of some as yet unexplained 'cellular memory') is simply an act of creative conjecture.

References

Brandon, S., Boakes, J., Glaser, D. and Green, R. (1998) 'Recovered memories of childhood sexual abuse: implications for clinical practice', *British Journal of Psychiatry*, 172: 296–307.

Cernock, J.M. and Porter, R.H. (1985) 'Recognition of maternal axillary odors by infants', *Child Development*, 56: 1593–8.

Dawes, R.M. (1996) *House of Cards: Psychology and Psychotherapy Built on Myth.* New York: Free Press.

DeCasper, A.J. and Fifer, W.P. (1980) 'Of human bonding: newborns prefer their mother's voice', *Science*, 208: 1174–6.

Donaldson, M. (1992) *Human Minds: An Exploration.* London: Allen Lane/ Penguin.

Field, T.M., Woodson, R., Greenberg, R. and Cohen, D. (1982) 'Discrimination and imitation of facial expressions by neonates', *Science*, 218: 179–81.

Friedman, S. (1972) 'Habituation and recovery of visual response in the alert human newborn', *Journal of Experimental Child Psychology*, 13: 339–49.

Furedi, F. (1997) *Culture of Fear: Risk-Taking and the Morality of Low Expectations.* London: Cassell.

Greenfield, S.A. (1995) *Journey to the Centers of the Mind: Toward a Science of Consciousness.* New York: W.H. Freeman.

Greenfield, S.A. (1997) *The Human Brain: A Guided Tour.* London: Weidenfeld & Nicolson.

James, J. (1996) *Reinvent Your Life.* London: Hodder & Stoughton.

Janov, A. (1993) *The New Primal Scream: Primal Therapy Twenty Years On.* London: Abacus.

Khamsi, S. (1988) 'A new look at primal therapy', *Aesthema, Journal of the International Primal Association*, 8: 11–23.

Lake, F. (1978) 'Treating psychosomatic disorders related to birth trauma', *Journal of Psychosomatic Research*, 22: 228–38.

Leboyer, Frederick (1975) *Birth Without Violence.* London: Wildwood House.

Leventhal, H. (1984) 'A perceptual-motor theory of emotion', *Advances in Experimental Social Psychology*, 17: 117–82.

Lewinsohn, P.M. and Rosenbaum, M. (1987) 'Recall of parental behaviour by acute depressives, remitted depressives and nondepressives', *Journal of Personality and Social Psychology*, 52: 611–19.

Luria, A.R. and Vygotsky, L.S. (1992) *Ape, Primitive Man, and Child: Essays in the History of Behavior.* Orlando, FL: Paul M. Deutsch Press.

Meltzoff, A.N. and Moore, M.K. (1983) 'Newborn infants imitate adult facial gestures', *Child Development*, 54: 702–9.

Miller, A. (1998) *Thou Shalt Not Be Aware: Society's Betrayal of the Child.* 3rd edn. London: Pluto Press. (1st edn, 1985.)

Pallister, M. (1998) 'Time of your lives', *The Herald* (Glasgow), 3 March, p. 14.

Rank, O. (1957) *The Trauma of Birth.* New York: Robert Brunner.

Roediger, H.L. (1996) 'Memory illusions', *Journal of Memory and Language*, 35: 76–100.

Schachter, S. (1964) 'The interaction of cognitive and physiological determinants of emotional state', in L. Berkowitz (ed.), *Advances in Experimental Social Psychology*, Vol. I. New York: Academic Press.

Wingfield, A. and Byrnes, D.L. (1981) *The Psychology of Human Memory.* London: Academic Press.

5   The trauma of birth

John Rowan

Otto Rank, in 1929, was the first person to deal seriously with the trauma of birth as possibly important for psychotherapy. His ideas (Rank, 1952) were welcomed by Freud at first, but were later discarded as a potential threat to the pre-eminence of the Oedipus complex. One of Rank's patients was Nandor Fodor (1949), who himself became a psychiatrist and focused his clinical attention on the formative experiences of birth. Francis Mott (1959), a British psychiatrist and a patient of Fodor's, wrote extensively on the mythological and dream content of prenatal and perinatal life, publishing several books on this between 1948 and 1964. Frank Lake (1980) was influenced by Mott's work, and was one of the first British psychiatrists to emphasize the effects of intra-uterine life, as well as the trauma of birth. Donald Winnicott (1958) recognized and worked with the impact of birth on his patients when circumstances warranted, and suggested that the body retained these impingements as memories. Bill Swartley (Rowan, 1988) was one of the founders of the International Primal Association, and introduced Primal Integration to Britain in the late 1970s. Winnicott supervised Ronald Laing (1976, 1982), who explored the fundamental significance of pre- and perinatal psychology in the structure of personality. One of the most important experimenters and theorists in this area is Stanislav Grof (1992), who is still alive and active, although his first work in this field started in the 1950s.

It was Stan Grof who discovered the four basic perinatal matrices, or BPMs. The first of these, which is called BPM1, is undisturbed life in the womb. Obviously it is possible for many bad experiences to be had in the womb, through accident, illness, drugs, and so forth, but let us assume that none of these have occurred. It is a good womb rather than a bad womb.

At this stage the person is, and feels, OK. It seems quite possible to regard this stage as a myth, in the sense of an unverifiable story which somehow makes sense of things. The essential thing is that this is a state before trauma. Somehow we all seem to have memories of such a state, and the sense of it has regularly been projected in the form of myths of a Golden Age, the Garden of Eden, the Primordial Paradise, and so on. I only postulate it because none of the rest seems to make sense unless we do start here.

At this stage there is nothing wrong. Whatever is needed is given, without the need to ask. The self is OK, and the world is OK, and there is no need to differentiate between the two. I do not need to be able to communicate my needs. It is peaceful and quiet (who ever heard of a noisy Utopia?), and when I do become aware of lights and sounds, they are filtered and muffled before they get to me. There is one sound which may become symbolic of this whole state of being – my mother's heartbeat. My body is relaxed and energy can easily flow in and flow out again. The energy is not trapped – I am open to the world. But it also indicates that I have no protection against harsh events which may occur. I assume that I am free, and even perhaps omnipotent. I am totally identified with myself. I am whole. This stage may be very far back, because the foetus is a very active creature and therefore such experience is possible.

Ken Wilber (1980) calls this the Pleroma stage, and points out how important it is not to confuse it with the later, more spiritual, stages of psychospiritual development. Many people have made this mistake, including Freud, Rank and others. Such lack of distinction Wilber calls the Pre/Trans Fallacy, because it confuses what is pre-personal with what is transpersonal.

At the beginning, we do not distinguish ourselves very well from our mothers. We are not quite sure where our mother ends and we begin; there seems to be an overlap, which is quite large at first. We are not even sure that we want to be separate, or have the right to exist as separate.

> It is an 'oceanic' state without any boundaries where we do not differentiate between ourselves and the material organism or ourselves and the external world. (Grof, 1992: 38)

All the strength, all the power, seems to be in the relation with the mother, the identity with the mother. Perhaps the mother and I are one. There may even be a feeling of omnipotence, of being all-powerful, because of this. Everything we do is right.

In order to move out of this unity, and become a separate body, something is necessary which threatens this power, this omnipotence. Harsh reality is going to have to tell us that we are not all-powerful, that we are not the mother, that we are little, and weak, and wrong.

Sometimes this is the trauma of birth (Janov, 1983). Sometimes it is an earlier trauma, or a later one. Sometimes it is just the experience of not getting what we want, when we want it. Sometimes it is the feeling of being abandoned. It may be actual insult or injury. But whatever it is, and however violent it may seem, the effect is the same. We split, in a primitive and almost instinctive way, into a hurt and vulnerable self that is hidden away, and a less sensitive self that is pushed forward. Winnicott (1958) has a good description of this, but many other people have described it quite independently.

At the same time, a notice is put up, as it were, which says: 'Do not enter; here be pain.' And so we carry on, improving the false self, and maybe even developing other false selves on the same model, to satisfy other, newer, situations. We do not go back.

It may be that this is the crucial move that made us different from the animals. There is no evidence at all that the consciousness of an animal splits in this way. Poets and other writers down the ages have told us that the appealing thing about animals is that they are simpler than we are, more direct, less tortured. Perhaps it is this fatal split that makes us the complex creatures that we are – creatures with an inner life that is just as important as our outer life, and often harder to cope with.

Let us just go back to the trauma of birth. It is important to understand this, and in recent years much new information has come from research and clinical experience. The basic point is that the foetus is well developed and quite experienced before the birth process begins, as Verny (1982) has well described. It is a person who is being born, not a ball of flesh that later becomes a person.

One of the curious things is that even a person who has brought some quite fresh thinking to the question of the early origins of neurosis, Daniel Stern (1985), has nothing to say about birth or foetal experience. He simply assumes that life starts at birth, and carries on from there. Extraordinary.

One of the best books to emerge about this is by David Chamberlain, an excellent researcher who has had papers published in some of the best journals in the field. He says:

> Perhaps the last big scientific barrier to full recognition of infants as persons will fall with acceptance of the possibility of complex personal memory at birth. Skeptical parents sometimes come to accept birth memory when they hear their two-year-olds spontaneously talking about it. Once we know that newborns are good at learning and that learning and memory go hand in hand, it is easier to accept birth memory. Some need no further convincing because they have discovered their own birth memories by one method or another. Others have discovered these memories under hypnosis or in a psychological breakthrough in therapy. (Chamberlain, 1988: xx–xxi)

One of Chamberlain's research projects was to correlate children's accounts of their birth with the mother's account of it. The mothers had to assure him that they had not spoken of their experience to the children. The children were aged between 9 and 23. He used open-ended questions and allowed the people to speak freely. Although there were one or two discrepancies, the vast majority of the descriptions tallied closely. In other words, the memories were on the whole extremely accurate.

The only reason more doctors and psychologists and counsellors and psychotherapists do not take this on board is that they are not aware of the burgeoning literature on infancy. I will come back to this shortly.

The primal split

At some point – maybe pre-birth, maybe during birth, maybe some while after birth – an event happens which indicates that I am not in control of my world. My assumption of freedom – and perhaps of omnipotence – is contradicted, and my total identification with myself is split.

The event which happens must be one which produces panic. I seem to be invaded by some aggressive force. It could objectively be said that I am being abused. But the way I take it, whether as foetus, neonate, infant or child, usually seems to be that I am wrong, and am being punished. How could I be hurt if I were perfect? But I am being hurt, therefore I am not perfect. In a state of panic, I resort to some kind of defensive tactic. At this stage I have no resources for dealing with trauma. I cannot cobble together any complicated defence. It seems as if I am faced with extinction, annihilation. In desperation, I split into two. I turn against my original OK self, and put in its place a self which has lost the notion of being perfect and whole. So now there is an OK-me (distanced and disowned) and a not-OK-me (fostered and put forward as the answer to the insult). This is the basic split, and of course splitting is a much more drastic defence than repression.

The non-OK-me, in order to repair itself and feel better about itself, may instantly adopt something salient from the invading and punishing entity, and incorporate it. After all, that is where the power is, and power is what it needs or lacks.

It is sometimes objected, in relation to this account, that something as early as the birth trauma cannot possibly be remembered, never mind events even earlier still. Yet the evidence accumulates each year, pushing back the limits further and further each time, that more is possible than we thought. For example, Janov (1977) has published photographs showing how bruises made in pre-verbal experiences may actually come to the surface as visible marks during psychotherapy. I have seen a video made with a heat camera by a gestalt therapist which shows very clearly the marks of early trauma becoming visible as the client relives the experience. It seems clear from all the evidence that we have to accept the possibility of muscular memory and cellular memory as well as the more common kinds of memory using the cerebral cortex.

This is not really very hard to understand. The great psychologist Jerome Bruner (1967) suggested that we actually have three distinct information-processing systems: the enactive (having to do with physical memories), the iconic (having to do with imagery) and the symbolic (which has to do with language). The enactive and iconic systems (which of course we still have as adults) come before language, and cannot be reduced to it.

Now this experience of trauma and splitting is a particularly powerful one, because it is only in this experience that I first become conscious that there is a 'me' at all, as distinguished from the world. My very first experience of being me is tied in with the first experience of being not-OK. We do not fully understand yet how this can happen with the foetus or with very young babies – it becomes more obvious about the three-year-old stage, as Duvall and Wicklund (1972) have described in detail – but somehow it does seem to occur. There may be a whole chain of such events, one of which may be more dramatic than the rest, and may come to symbolize the others: Grof has been clearer about this than most.

What Grof says is that there are four main stages at birth, four basic perinatal matrices. We have already mentioned the first one, BPM1, undisturbed life in the womb. BPM2 starts when the uterus starts contracting, and the cervix has not yet opened. For the baby about to be born, this is a situation of great pressure with no way out. If it is prolonged, or if the baby is already anxious for one reason or another, this can be traumatic.

I want to make it clear that some birth processes are quite all right, and may well induce a feeling of triumph as having made it into the world through all obstacles. It is not at all suggested that birth is always a trauma, but rather that there is always some kind of trauma which starts this process going. Balint (1968) calls this the 'basic fault'.

Frank Lake (1980) has been very specific about different levels of trauma and exactly how that makes a difference to how the trauma is taken and experienced. Partly it is a matter of how the mother and the other close and important figures react to various situations – the very young infant seems to be able to pick up emotional reactions very quickly.

Once this split has been established, it has effects which continue long afterwards. The trauma a psychotherapist is pitted against is often no longer the trauma of childhood but the cumulative traumas of a lifetime of repetition of the original in an attempt to master it. If the trauma is repeated indefinitely and mastery fails to evolve, it is like a series of reinoculations which come to exceed the original dose and restore the original disease in chronic and even more virulent forms.

And this links with the work of Alice Miller (1987), who has underlined the importance of early trauma and the way in which many analysts in the past have downplayed it and failed to do it justice. But if it is important, it must continue to be important, because the way of dealing with this first trauma will set the pattern for the way in which the person deals with the next trauma, and the next, and the next.

Infancy

The word 'infant' comes from a Latin word meaning 'unable to speak', and so, strictly speaking, we should save the word for this pre-verbal period of life; but of course in ordinary speech it is often used more widely. What are the facts about the kinds of experiences infants are capable of? In psychotherapy and counselling we often find clients going back to these early times, and we sometimes wonder if babies so young can have such complex experiences as seem to be revealed in this process.

Since psychologists gave up doing all their experiments on rats, there has been a tremendous amount of research on infants, and much more is known now than before. Goren and co-workers found that infants with an average age of nine minutes attended closest to a schematic face compared with a blank head shape, or one with scrambled features. Dziurawiec and Ellis found this hard to believe, repeated the experiment with improved methodology, and got the same results. It seems that the purpose of this face recognition is to aid in bonding (Goren et al., 1975; Dziurawiec and Ellis, 1986).

Wertheimer (1961) studied newborn babies in the delivery room, as soon as they were born. He worked only with those where there was no anaesthesia and no apparent trauma. He found that if he presented a series of sounds, placed randomly to left and to right, the baby looked in the direction of the sound source. There was no random looking about, just a direct look in the right direction.

Lipsitt (1969) did an experiment where newborn babies, just a few hours old, had to turn their heads to the right at the sound of a tone, and to the left at the sound of a buzzer. If they turned the right way they got a reward – a sweet taste in the mouth. It took them only a few trials to learn which way to turn their heads. Then the signals were reversed, and it took them only about 10 trials to unlearn the old task and learn the new one. Tom Bower says: 'The newborn can localize sounds. He can locate objects visually. He seems to know when he hears a sound, there probably will be something for him to look at, and that when an object approaches him, it probably will be hard or tangible' (1977: 24). Visually, the baby has size constancy from birth onwards: also shape constancy, form and colour perception, movement detection, three-dimensional and depth perception (Slater et al., 1983; Slater, 1990). After two days a baby will show a preference for the mother's face when this is shown side-by-side with a stranger's face (Bushnell, 1987).

There are similar findings in relation to the infant's ability to smell. Engen et al. (1963) found that infants only a few hours old will turn away from an unpleasant odour. And MacFarlane (1975) placed three-day-olds on their backs and then placed breast pads from their mothers on one side of their heads. On the other side he placed breast pads from other nursing mothers. The newborn reliably turned their heads towards their own mothers' pads, regardless of which side the pads were.

Several investigators in the 1970s found that babies less than a week old will imitate other people. If we stick our tongue out at the baby, the baby will begin to stick his or her tongue out too. If we stop this, and begin to flutter our eyelashes, the baby will flutter his or her eyelashes back. If we then open and shut out mouths, the baby will match us at the same speed. If we use a TV split-screen technique, showing the adult face and the baby's face side-by-side, we find close matching of one to the other, which by five weeks old becomes very accurate and very quick, so that real two-way communication is taking place. Even at 42 minutes old,

Meltzoff found the beginnings of this kind of response (Meltzoff and Moore, 1983).

Smiling is an interesting area. Bower (1977) says that babies smile at a conceptual age of 46 weeks, regardless of their age since birth. (Most babies are born 40 weeks after conception, but a range of 38 to 42 weeks is normal.) It very quickly becomes possible to see that there are actually four different smiles: the relief smile, when the baby realizes that an unexpected noise or movement is not threatening; the 'I want you to like me' social smile for strangers; the special smile for the mother or other very close person; and the 'got it, I've solved the problem' smile.

This last is the most surprising to many people. Papousek (1969) found that if he engineered a situation such that certain specific movements of a baby could effect a result, babies smiled when they worked out how to make this happen. The smiling, in other words, showed an intellectual pleasure in discovery and control. The actual characteristics of the event the baby was producing were quite unimportant. What was important was that there was a relationship between a given action and a given event in the external world. At this point there was vigorous smiling and cooing which was not directed at the event in particular, but rather seemed to reflect some internal pleasure.

Trauma

When something traumatic happens to the infant, therefore, whether during or after birth, there is a person there to experience and register it, and react to it.

Frank Lake (1980) argued that there are four levels of trauma, and what happens inside the individual depends very much on exactly what level of trauma is involved. He made no distinction between different causes of trauma. The first level is pain-free, and is the ideal state. The second level has to do with coping, and is where the stimulation is bearable and even perhaps strengthening, because it evokes effective and mostly non-neurotic defences. The third level involves opposition to the pain, but it is so strong that it cannot be coped with, and repression takes place. If the trauma happens in infancy or earlier, the defence will be splitting rather than repression, and some degree of dissociation will be experienced. The fourth level Lake calls transmarginal stress, and it is so powerful or so early, or both, that the person cuts off completely and may even turn against the self, wanting to die. Some recent work by Southgate and others suggests that many child accidents are in fact unconscious attempts at suicide, based on this fourth level of trauma (Southgate and Whiting, 1987). And if the trauma was actually a case of sexual or other abuse, and if the abuse is repeated or re-created somehow in later life, a real adult suicide may result, again possibly disguised as an accident. This has been seriously suspected in a number of cases.

Grof (1992) is very clear that early trauma can be very real and very important, and relates it particularly to the process of birth. He distinguishes four stages of birth, and says that adult neurosis is very frequently based upon traumas suffered at one or other of these stages. Lake (1980), in one of his charts, brings out the way in which his four levels of trauma can be related to Grof's four stages of birth to make a matrix of sixteen cells which account between them for many of the origins of many of the neuroses. And again, of course, many of the drastic things which happen in the lives of adults may result from repetitions of the original trauma in some direct or disguised form.

Recent research has shown that strict diagnostic criteria of post-traumatic stress disorder can be applied to very young children (in their first, second and third years), leading to the conclusion that

> a posttraumatic syndrome does appear to exist in infants and children exposed to traumatic events. The sequelae can be severely debilitating and last for years if untreated. Any lingering notion that infants cannot be affected by trauma because of their limited perceptual or cognitive capacities ought to be dispelled by these empirical findings. (Scheeringa et al., 1995: 199)

What we learn from this is that there is a logic of trauma, which can be understood and applied to sexual and other forms of abuse later in childhood, and can also be applied to adult trauma through earthquakes, floods, war, and so on. There is a direct link between the experience of the baby and the experience of the war veteran. This whole field is ripe for integration, and the primal work can help a great deal in understanding the phenomena of trauma generally.

References

Balint, M. (1968) *The Basic Fault: Therapeutic Aspects of Regression*. London: Tavistock.

Bower, T. (1977) *A Primer of Infant Development*. San Francisco: W.H. Freeman.

Bruner, J.S. (1967) 'Education as a social invention', in R.M. Jones (ed.), *Contemporary Educational Psychology: Selected Essays*. New York: Harper & Row.

Bushnell, I.W.R. (1987) 'Neonatal recognition of the mother's face'. Paper presented at the Annual Conference of the Developmental Psychology Section of the British Psychological Society, York.

Chamberlain, D. (1998) *The Mind of Your New-Born Baby*. Berkeley: North Atlantic Books.

Duvall, S. and Wicklund, R.A. (1972) *A Theory of Objective Self-Awareness*. New York: Academic Press.

Dziurawiec, S. and Ellis, A. (1986) 'Neonates' attention to face-like stimuli: Goren, Sarty & Wu revisited'. Paper presented at the Annual Conference of the Developmental Psychology Section of the British Psychological Society, Exeter.

Engen, T., Lipsitt, L.P. and Kaye, H. (1963) 'Olfactory responses and adaptation in the human neonate', *Journal of Comparative Physiology and Psychology*, 56: 73–7.

Fodor, N. (1949) *The Search for the Beloved*. New York: University Books.

Goren, C., Sarty, M. and Wu, P. (1975) 'Visual following and pattern discrimination of face-like stimuli by newborn infants', *Pediatrics*, 56: 544–9.

Grof, S. (1992) *The Holotropic Mind*. San Francisco: Harper.

Janov, A. (1977) *The Feeling Child*. London: Abacus.

Janov, A. (1983) *Imprints: The Lifelong Effects of the Birth Experience*. New York: Coward-McCann.

Laing, R.D. (1976) *The Facts of Life* Harmondsworth: Penguin.

Laing, R.D. (1982) *The Voice of Experience*. Harmondsworth: Penguin.

Lake, F. (1980) *Constricted Confusion*. Oxford: Clinical Theology Association.

Lipsitt, L.P. (1969) 'Learning capacities of the human infant', in R.J. Robinson (ed.), *Brain and Early Behaviour*. London: Academic Press.

MacFarlane, A. (1975) 'Olfaction in the development of social preferences in the human neonate', in *Parent–Infant Interaction* (CIBA Foundation Symposium 33). Amsterdam: Elsevier.

Meltzoff, A.N. and Moore, M.K. (1983) 'The origins of imitation in infancy: paradigm, phenomena and theories', in L.P. Lipsitt (ed.), *Advances in Infancy Research*, Vol. 2. Norwood, NJ: Ablex.

Miller, A. (1987) *For Your Own Good*. London: Virago.

Mott, F. (1959) *The Nature of the Self*. London: Allen Wingate.

Papousek, H. (1969) 'Individual variability in learned responses in human infants', in R.J. Robinson (ed.), *Brain and Early Behaviour*. London: Academic Press.

Rank, O. (1952) *The Trauma of Birth*. New York: Robert Brunner.

Rowan, J. (1988) 'Primal Integration', in J. Rowan and W. Dryden (eds), *Innovative Therapy in Britain*. Buckingham: Open University Press.

Scheeringa, M.S., Zeanah, C.H., Drell, M.S. and Laurien, J.A. (1995) 'Two approaches to the diagnosis of posttraumatic stress disorder in infancy and early childhood', *American Academy of Child and Adolescent Psychiatry*, 34: 191–200.

Slater, A.M. (1990) 'Infant development: the origins of competence', *The Psychologist*, 3 (3): 109–13.

Slater, A.M., Morison, V. and Rose, D. (1983) 'Perception of shape by the newborn baby', *British Journal of Developmental Psychology*, 1: 135–42.

Southgate, J. and Whiting, L. (eds) (1987) *Journal of the Institute for Self-Analysis*, 1 (1).

Stern, D. (1985) *The Interpersonal World of the Infant*. New York: Basic Books.

Verny, T. (1982) *The Secret Life of the Unborn Child*. London: Sphere.

Wertheimer, M. (1961) 'Psycho-motor coordination of auditory-visual space at birth', *Science*, 134: 1692.

Wilber, K. (1980) *The Atman Project*. Wheaton: Quest.

Winnicott, D. (1958) *Collected Papers: From Paediatrics to Psychoanalysis*. London: Tavistock.

6 False memories – a peripheral issue?

Roger Scotford

When discussing survivors of childhood sexual abuse, mental health professionals tend to push the problems of false accusations to one side as a peripheral issue of little concern. Some writers have even said that a few false accusations are the price we must pay for bringing out *real* cases and for finding the *real* perpetrators.

Many commentators present the so-called 'false memory syndrome' (FMS) as an artefact of a tiny minority of incompetent, undertrained therapists affecting only a few families. They argue that even if an accusation is false, it should be taken as a metaphor for the trauma generated in a dysfunctional family. This portrayal is, for the most part, accepted by mainstream mental health professionals specializing in sexual abuse, and is reflected in current textbooks (Dale, 1995; Sanderson, 1995).

The appropriation of FMS as little more than a rogue aberration tacked on to an otherwise unimpeachable body of knowledge is a convenient way for the psychological establishment to avoid taking responsibility for a major disaster that has arisen within its own profession. It is not simply a tiny minority who have helped clients 'recover memories'. As several British and American surveys conducted in the early 1990s have shown, the belief in 'massive or robust repression' of memories of childhood sexual abuse – in which *years* of extreme trauma are purportedly forgotten only to be recovered intact later in life – is widespread. Among British Psychological Society members ('highly experienced and well-qualified therapists who are well aware of the dangers of inappropriate suggestion and interpretation', BPS, 1995: 3), a survey revealed that 97 per cent of the polled sample believed in this highly questionable theory (Andrews et al., 1995).

Both the American False Memory Syndrome Foundation (FMSF) and the British False Memory Society (BFMS), whose scientific advisory boards include leading mental health professionals and memory researchers, have recognized the problem of false memories and false accusations as endemic to the beliefs held by a large number of trauma-search therapists (Weiskrantz, 1995; Weiskrantz and BMFS, 1995).

Rather than analysing the issues, a number of these therapists have attempted to hijack the term 'false memory syndrome' and, by reducing the debate to semantics, they hope to avert any examination of their beliefs and the disturbing techniques they use to 'help' clients recall mythical abuse.

Echoing a media stereotype, they, and their supporters, have issued contradictory edicts concerning the criteria for the application of FMS while simultaneously denying its very existence. An article in *The Psychologist* by Kay Toon et al. exemplifies this approach. 'FMS *only* applies to cases where an adult, who had no previous memories at all of the abuse, remembers sexual abuse which did not actually happen *and* is led to this by an unscrupulous or poorly trained therapist' (1996: 73, original emphasis). Rather than encapsulating the issues at stake, this caricature obscures the underlying truth and the far-reaching implications not just for mental health professionals, but for society at large.

False memories can arise without therapy at all. Many people have reported recovering massively repressed memories after reading books such as *The Courage to Heal* (Bass and Davis, 1988), or watching a television programme on the subject, or attending an 'incest survivors' group, or simply listening to a friend's story. Also, when a therapist *is* involved (as is usually the case), the therapist need not be – and usually is not – unscrupulous or poorly trained. One of the sad ironies of this phenomenon is that the therapists involved are usually well meaning and idealistic; they are devoted to helping their clients. They truly *believe* in this theory of repressed memories. Yes, they may be poorly trained in the science of human memory and suggestibility, but many therapists who help recover 'memories' hold advanced degrees – they are often 'well-trained' psychologists or consultant psychiatrists.

The issue is not just one of FMS, but of the validity of the whole concept of 'repressed memory'; the recovered memory therapy (RMT) techniques used to prompt and validate the claims and the beliefs of the therapists. Even the BPS Working Party's Report on 'recovered memories' fails to address this fundamental issue and reduces it to a footnote at the bottom of page 5 (BPS, 1995).

One of the reasons why the debate over false memories becomes so illogical and emotional is that many people misconstrue the intentions of those involved in examining the issues. They believe that those who call attention to false accusations are in some way denying the reality of real abuse, when such is obviously not the case. Child sexual abuse is a heinous crime. It violates a universal taboo and, when committed by a close relative, it betrays the trust we need to place in the family as a basic building block of a healthy society. Not only does such a crime deserve universal condemnation, but perpetrators must expect to be prosecuted and imprisoned. Against the background of public concern over the release of convicted paedophiles, it is obvious why those who have been falsely accused should so vigorously campaign for changes in the processes which led to the accusations.

But has the extent of these crimes been exaggerated and conflated with an ever-rising number of false memory cases? Retrospective surveys of adults' sexual experience as children indicate a wide variation in prevalence rates, but they universally indicate that the most serious and damaging forms of abuse, including incest, constitute only a small minority of the responses. Nevertheless, when adults claim to have *recovered* memories of abuse, *they* claim that they have been subjected to the most horrific forms of familial abuse (Gudjonsson, 1997a, b, c).

However psychologically damaging 'minor' incidents may or may not be, many adults appear to have little trouble in recalling them without measurable effort. Many others will have forgotten such 'nuisance' episodes – although these may be remembered accurately many years later, especially with the aid of a contextual cue. Genuine victims of sexual abuse, who continue to be haunted by the memory, may well wish to turn to therapy to alleviate their suffering. They have the right to expect appropriate treatment for abuse survivors. Equally, people with no prior memory of abuse deserve scientifically based therapy that does not lead them to believe in a childhood straight out of a horror picture. However, if therapists' preconceived beliefs lead to the 'validation' of such supposed 'memories' of abuse, the patient's treatment will be neither safe nor effective.

In the current climate of mistrust, many genuine victims may be wary of seeking help, and rightly so because there is no clear division between the treatment recommended for those who have always remembered their abuse, and for those who are believed, by the therapist or the client, to have memories which have been repressed. Evidence also exists to show that both groups may well experience various forms of suggestion – ranging from subtle body language to bullying persuasion – which can result in the creation of a confabulated narrative history causing further distress. In other words, many clients who have reported always-remembered childhood abuse have been treated in therapy as if those memories are *not enough* – there must be more, there must be some repressed memories.

What is FMS?

Coined in the United States, the term 'false memory syndrome' is defined by John Kihlstrom, professor of psychology at Yale, as 'a condition in which a person's identity and interpersonal relationships are centered around a memory of traumatic experience which is objectively false but in which the person strongly believes' (FMSF, 1998: 1). It classifies an epidemic of claims of hidden sexual abuse histories which previously unsuspecting adults suddenly, 'out of the blue', start making. The term itself was a riposte to an alleged 'repressed memory syndrome' which explained this process of sudden realization. What these people were describing were essentially delusional beliefs – as many retracting therapy victims have now testified. However, they were told and came to believe that their visions, dreams and hallucinations were actual memories and they were led to incorporate them into their consciousness as such (Crews, 1997). Characteristically, those affected appear to undergo a life-changing experience solely as a result of coming to believe that they had been abused. This reaction differs from those who have always remembered abuse, or who put a single incident to the back of their minds.

The upsurge of accusations did not occur in a cultural vacuum. On the contrary, putative 'victims' were encouraged to search for memories by the self-help recovery movement and its associated literature, most notably by the popular self-help book *The Courage to Heal* (Bass and Davis, 1988). The culture of victimhood, survival and renaissance became the stuff of magazines, television chat shows, pulp fiction and numerous Hollywood movies (Pendergrast, 1997). Underpinning this culture at one end of the spectrum were the ideological fixations of radical feminists and at the other, the cult-like influence of charismatic Christianity (Nathan and Snedeker, 1995).

The driving force, however, was the readiness of mental health and child abuse professionals to endorse and propagate the belief that childhood sexual abuse, of which the 'victim' was totally unaware, was the likely cause of their adult problems, usually involving fairly common symptoms such as troubled relationships, depression, panic attacks or eating disorders (Yapko, 1994; Ofshe and Watters, 1995).

There arose a theoretical linking between an inferred aetiology of sexual abuse and a pre-existing symptomatology, with long laundry lists that supposedly indicated that one must be a 'secret survivor', as one such book put it in its title (Blume, 1990).

One particularly unfortunate 'symptom' is supposedly an eating disorder. Many clients have been told that their anorexia or bulimia is a sure sign that they were sexually abused. While some anorexics will have suffered abuse, to suggest that anorexia, or any other symptom, is an indicator of abuse carries especial dangers. In fact, those with eating disorders have approximately the same likelihood of having suffered sexual abuse as the general population (Pope and Hudson, 1992).

By its very nature therapy creates a suggestible environment in which a sympathetic authority figure can sway a client's belief system. Those coming for therapy are, by definition, in a vulnerable frame of mind, seeking answers for their problems. They are likely to be suggestible, and a significant and lasting distortion of the truth can be created if, rather than dealing with current anxieties, the therapist implies that their problems must stem from 'something' in the past.

That is not to say that all therapists set out to try to induce 'false memories' of sexual abuse – that is a tendentious oversimplification of the argument. Although it appears that a substantial minority of therapists *were* engaged in recovered memory therapy during the height of this phenomenon, between 1988 and 1994, the practice has been severely curtailed because of legal and ethical issues, largely brought to the fore by the false memory societies, the media and the courts.

But the problem has by no means disappeared, largely because the theory of repression is fundamental to much therapy. It is likely that, in the current climate, both therapist and client entertain the possibility of childhood sexual abuse as being 'consistent' with the client's problem. The process of exploring this possibility may lead to an increasing acceptance of its likelihood which in turn leads to a conviction that abuse occurred. This belief invokes fear, and may give rise to images, dreams and anxieties which are then interpreted to be 'memories' of sexual abuse which confirm the original suspicion. It is this unwitting, circular process of make-believe which leads to the creation of 'false memories'.

Freud's 1896 seduction theory claims were based on a similar error (Israëls and Schatzman, 1993; Webster, 1995; Esterson, 1998). Freud originally believed that the somatic symptoms of patients he diagnosed as 'hysterical' were caused by repressed memories of sexual molestation in infancy. With the aid of his quasi-hypnotic 'pressure technique', he tried hard to force his patients to 'reproduce' the supposedly forgotten memories. Unfortunately, Freud's own inaccurate reports of these episodes many years later led readers to believe that most of his female patients had told him spontaneously that they had been sexually abused by their fathers (Rush, 1980; Masson, 1984). But in the 1896 seduction theory papers Freud explicitly states that it required a forceful application of his clinical technique to induce the recovery of the early 'memories' he believed his patients had repressed.

The foundation of false memory societies

The earliest autobiographical accounts of incest and childhood sexual abuse in the 1960s and early 1970s did not rely on repressed memories. These were people who had simply never spoken of their always-remembered trauma. Soon, however, some 'survivor' histories began to suggest the notion of frozen memories of abuse (Armstrong, 1978; Butler, 1978). The supposed existence of these hidden incest histories became conflated with the idea that therapists could heal the 'victims', and in the early 1980s this became formalized into a conscious search for abuse histories (Herman, 1981).

In 1988, following the publication of *The Courage to Heal*, the number of accusations based on newly 'recovered memories' of sexual abuse dramatically increased. In 1992, after an article on false accusations of abuse in the American press drew a huge response, a group of accused parents attended a meeting with professionals from the University of Pennsylvania and Johns Hopkins University and the False Memory Syndrome Foundation was formed. The appointment of a scientific advisory board led to a critical scrutiny of the social movement in which these therapeutic theories and practices were emerging. The rationale being offered by the therapists and their designated forms of treatment began to be challenged.

In Britain, the turning point was 1990, when the British edition of *The Courage to Heal* appeared and, following the American experience, a belief arose that 'repressed memories' of sexual abuse were commonplace. After an FMSF conference in the spring of 1993, accused parents who attended from the UK met and formed the British False Memory Society.

The response by therapists and mental health professionals was divided. On the one hand, there was great interest in the importance of the issues surrounding memory retrieval and a recognition of the powers of suggestion. On the other hand, there was staunch resistance to any critical analysis of the issues from those who believed in the pervasiveness of 'repressed memories'. Often this resistance was based not on argument, but was propagated by smear, innuendo and *ad hominem* attack (Orr, 1995; McGuire, 1997). External criticisms were brushed off as irrelevant, misinformed or, in the case of false memory societies, motivated by the vested interests of parents accused of childhood sexual abuse.

The arguments

Central to the concept of 'repressed memory' (a term distinct from 'repression') is the notion that whole personal histories of the most awful childhood abuse, repeated episodes over prolonged periods, can be hidden from consciousness, as they occur, often for decades. It is not that the subject fails to recognize the damage caused by these events, but that s/he has no awareness that the abuse had ever taken place. The idea that images of a traumatic past can suddenly emerge before the inner eye of a shell-shocked client has become commonplace, and there is now a widespread acceptance of the truth of such visionary revelations. Recovery episodes are accompanied by an immense release of emotional anger and pain. Despite the fact that neither detail nor emotional intensity guarantees the authenticity of these episodes, such catharses are viewed as evidence that repressed feelings have been released by the unlocking of the repressed memory cage. Paradoxically, these new-found beliefs, by the power of their narrative excitement, can sometimes be used to make sense of nagging problems in life, particularly if an authority figure validates them. Terms such as 'surfacing' and 'coming up', when applied to these experiences, capture the trance-like nature of the phenomenon, and the type of 'flashbacks' described are characteristics of delusional experiences seen in religious visions, or states of emotional excitement or exhaustion (Sargant, 1957). Dream diaries, journal writing, injunctions to believe and constant rehearsal in an environmental context where subtle suggestions act as unconscious cues all serve to reinforce the delusions to make them seem like 'memories' (Pendergrast, 1997).

So the real question is not whether false memories of abuse can occur, but what effect does the belief in 'repressed memories' have upon the associated therapy. This is the main point hammered home by the authors of the report into recovered memories commissioned by the Royal College of Psychiatrists (Brandon et al., 1998).

In the 1995 survey, 106 chartered BPS therapists, out of the 810 polled, believed they had worked with clients who had been genuine victims of satanic ritual abuse (Andrews et al., 1995). These exotic beliefs are the Achilles' heel of the 'recovered memory' movement. They tell us much about the mesmeric power of the narrative, the gullibility of clients, the influence of the therapist and the unconscious influence of popular culture on both parties (LaFontaine, 1998). The BPS survey also showed that 267 of their therapists believed that it was impossible to have a 'false memory' at all!

No-one suggests that suffering delusions of satanic abuse or alien abduction is an easy option for the client, but precisely because they are contrary to normal experience, they are shocking and deeply disturbing. Claims are now being made that it is significant that most 'recovered memories' do *not* involve implausible events (Andrews, 1997). But this misses the point: implausible 'memories' do call into question the authenticity of *all* 'memories' recovered in this way and it is precisely this form of wild excess which undercuts the scientific validity of recovered memory theory. Therapeutically supported satanic cult survivor or alien abductee testimony is generally as emotionally searing and vivid as recovered incest memories. Neither the existence of satanic cults nor the visitation of aliens can be definitively disproved, but whereas such testimony is usually regarded merely as a curious artefact, incest testimony shakes the world by implicating others in serious crimes.

Tellingly, those defending the validity of recovered memories resort all too readily to the fallacious circular logic of their own practice. Toon et al. write, 'the histories of those recovering memories are likely to be an indication of the effects of the sexual abuse, not an explanation for their disclosure' (1996: 75). Since almost *any* somatic or psychological symptom has been proposed as a consequence of childhood sexual abuse, this argument only serves to indicate that the authors are presuming the correctness of their position; they are not critically examining it.

Retractions

The fact that some 'false memory' victims retract their 'recovered memory' allegations has enormous significance. From a position of regained stability, they report their experiences as a period of obsessive delusion when they could 'call up' mental images of their worst fantasies which they mistakenly categorized as 'memories' (Goldstein and Farmer, 1993; Pendergrast, 1997). Child abuse guidelines, however, commonly warn against believing retractions because some people will be put under pressure to retract their true allegations of abuse (Islington Social Services, 1987). For this reason, Toon et al. (1996) argue that retractions do *not* indicate that the original disclosure was false. They seem to take no account, though, of the pressures not to retract which are put upon accusers who *do* come to realize correctly that their memories were false. To retract a serious allegation of sexual abuse against a parent takes enormous courage. It usually also entails a split from the therapist, who has an emotional, if not a professional, investment in the recovered memories and who will be discouraging such action. Retraction also means abandoning the support of like-minded peer groups who not only share the recovered memory beliefs but also provide emotional succour.

The allegations are devastating for all parties: they may have led to marriage and family break-up, police involvement, trial and false imprisonment and, in the extreme case, suicide. In some cases the accuser will have received a criminal compensation award, or civil damages, and, if a prosecution has taken place, he or she could face charges of perjury. In these circumstances it is not surprising that there appears little to gain and a lot to lose by retracting (Goldstein and Farmer, 1993), and yet still some do reject their false accusations.

Conclusions

Given the 'cycle of misinformation, distortion and repetition' (Tavris, 1993) which is proffered as knowledge in the recovered memory field, falsely accused families may be forgiven for distrusting the professionals involved, however well meaning the latter may be. Claims concerning studies purporting to show that memories can be repressed and recovered, or that such memories have been corroborated, will, no doubt, continue to appear in the academic press, but, given the methodological weaknesses of current research practice, such studies may well fail to withstand close critical scrutiny (Pope, 1997).

This pressing issue strikes at the heart of therapeutic theory and practice. Couching the controversy in terms of poorly trained therapists deliberately attempting to induce false memories is as misleading as it is dangerous. Though some fringe therapists have extended and reinforced mistaken beliefs and practices, they should not be held responsible for the emerging crisis of confidence in mental health services. As the article by Toon et al (1996) illustrates, the problems lie deep within the mainstream mental health system.

Talk of the false memory debate as a 'backlash' is to misunderstand the nature of the cultural phenomenon of false allegations. Worse, it ignores the reluctance of some professionals to examine their own beliefs and practices (Robbins, 1995). There is no evidence that 'recovered memory therapy', by searching for posited buried memories of abuse, is either safe or effective as a treatment for people, whether or not they have been sexually abused.

'False memory' is, in fact, a transitional term born out of a response to the belief in the reliability of recovered memories. 'Reinforced, delusional beliefs based on visions, dreams and hallucinations' more accurately describes the process of evolving psychological distress suffered by those entrapped in its thrall, and it is encouraging that the 'Brandon Report' (Brandon et al., 1998) now recognizes this. Some genuine victims of abuse may rightly fear that therapists may try to impose their own distorted interpretations of their clients' remembered abuse. Some will not want therapy at all and may never seek to disclose their experiences.

Financial compensation provides an additional motive to press recovered memory claims, but in the USA, the courts have, on a number of occasions, scrutinized the evidence for such claims and have found it wanting in scientific validity and therefore inadmissible (Supreme Court of New Hampshire, 1997). In other cases therapists have been successfully sued by ex-patients.

Prevalence figures have no bearing on the validity of 'recovered memory' histories, but it is surely of some concern that the vast majority of child sexual abuse histories in adult survivor literature seem to be drawn from the small minority of claims at the fringe of retrospective surveys. This imbalance creates a distorted impression which cannot be helpful.

For the good of their clients and patients and for the integrity and standing of the mental health profession, psychiatrists, psychologists, psychoanalysts, therapists and counsellors must adopt a critical stance, reviewing not only their current practice but also the source and reliability of the knowledge base upon which their practice has been founded.

References

Andrews, B. (1997) 'Forms of memory recovery among adults in therapy: preliminary results from an in-depth survey', in D. Read and S. Lindsay (eds), *Recollections of Trauma: Scientific Research and Clinical Practice*. New York: Plenum Press.

Andrews, B., Morton, J., Bekerian, D.A., Brewin, C.R., Davies, G.M. and Mollon, P. (1995) 'The recovery of memories in clinical practice: experiences and beliefs of British Psychological Society practitioners', *The Psychologist*, 8: 209–14.

Armstrong, L. (1978) *Kiss Daddy Goodnight*. New York: Simon & Schuster.

Bass, E. and Davis, L. (1988) *The Courage to Heal: A Guide for Women Survivors of Child Sexual Abuse*. New York: Harper & Row.

Blume, E.S. (1990) *Secret Survivors: Uncovering Incest and Its Aftereffects in Women*. New York: Ballantine.

BPS (British Psychological Society) (1995) *Recovered Memories: The Report of the Working Party of the British Psychological Society*. Leicester: BPS.

Brandon, S., Boakes, J., Glaser, D. and Green, R. (1998) 'Recovered memories of childhood sexual abuse: implications for clinical practice', *British Journal of Psychiatry*, 172: 296–307.

Butler, S. (1978) *The Conspiracy of Silence: The Trauma of Incest*. San Francisco: New Glide Publications.

Crews, F. (1997) *The Memory Wars: Freud's Legacy in Dispute*. London: Granta.

Dale, P. (1995) *Counselling Adults Who Were Abused as Children*. Rugby: British Association for Counselling.

Esterson, A. (1998) 'Jeffrey Masson and Freud's seduction theory: a new fable based on old myths', *History of the Human Sciences*, 11 (1): 1–21.

False Memory Syndrome Foundation (1998) 'Frequently asked questions'. Philadelphia, PA: FMSF.

Goldstein, E. and Farmer, K. (1993) *True Stories of False Memories*. Boca Raton, FL: SIRS Books.

Gudjonsson, G. (1997a) 'The members of the BFMS, the accusers and their siblings', *The Psychologist*, 10 (3): 111–15.

Gudjonsson, G. (1997b) 'Accusations by adults of childhood sexual abuse: a survey of the members of the BFMS', *Applied Cognitive Psychology*, 11: 3–18.

Gudjonsson, G. (1997c) 'Members of the BFMS: the legal consequences of the accusations for the families', *The Journal of Forensic Psychiatry*, 8 (2): 348–56.

Herman, J.L. (with Hirschman, L.) (1981) *Father-Daughter Incest*. Cambridge, MA: Harvard University Press.

Islington Social Services (1987) *Child Sexual Abuse – Policy and Practice Guidelines*. London.

Israëls, H. and Schatzman, M. (1993) 'The seduction theory', *History of Psychiatry*, 4: 23–59.

LaFontaine, J. (1998) *Speak of The Devil: Tales of Satanic Abuse in Contemporary England*. Cambridge: Cambridge University Press.

McGuire, A. (1997) *False Memory Syndrome: A Statement*. Research Study I. Rugby: British Association for Counselling.

Masson, J.M. (1984) *The Assault on Truth: Freud's Suppression of the Seduction Theory*. New York: Farrar, Straus & Giroux.

Nathan, D. and Snedeker, M. (1995) *Satan's Silence: Ritual Abuse and the Making of a Modern American Witch Hunt*. New York: Basic Books.

Ofshe, R. and Watters, E. (1995) *Making Monsters: False Memories, Psychotherapy and Sexual Hysteria*. London: André Deutsch.

Orr, M. (1995) 'Accuracy about abuse: the false memory syndrome debate in the UK', *Treating Abuse Today*, 5 (3): 19–28.

Pendergrast, M. (1997) *Victims of Memory: Incest Accusations and Shattered Lives*. London: HarperCollins.

Pope, H.G. (1997) *Psychology Astray: Fallacies in Studies of 'Repressed Memory' and Childhood Trauma*. Boca Raton, FL: Upton Books.

Pope, H.G. and Hudson, J.I. (1992) 'Is childhood sexual abuse a risk factor for bulimia nervosa?', *American Journal of Psychiatry*, 149 (4): 455–63.

Robbins, S. (1995) 'Wading through the muddy waters of recovered memory', *Families in Society: Journal of Contemporary Human Services*, 76 (8): 478–89.

Rush, F. (1980) *The Best Kept Secret: Sexual Abuse of Children*. Englewood Cliffs, NJ: Prentice-Hall.

Sanderson, C. (1995) *Counselling Adult Survivors of Child Sexual Abuse*. London: Jessica Kingsley.

Sargant, W. (1957) *Battle for the Mind: A Physiology of Conversion and Brain-Washing*. New York: Penguin.

Supreme Court of New Hampshire (1997) *The State of New Hampshire v. Joel Hungerford; The State of New Hampshire v. John A. Morahan*. 1 July.

Tavris, C. (1993) 'Beware of the incest-survivor machine', *New York Times Book Review*, 3 January, pp. 16–17.

Toon, K., Fraise, J., McFetridge, M. and Alwin, N. (1996) 'Memory or mirage? The FMS debate', *The Psychologist*, 9 (2): 73–7.

Webster, R. (1995) *Why Freud was Wrong: Sin, Science and Psychoanalysis*. London: Fontana Press.

Weiskrantz, L. (1995) 'Comments on the Report of the Working Party of the British Psychological Society on "recovered memories"', *The Therapist*, 2 (4): 5–8.

Weiskrantz, L. and BFMS Independent Advisory Board (1995) 'Further comment on recovered memories', *The Psychologist*, 8 (11): 507–8.

Yapko, M.D. (1994) *Suggestions of Abuse: True and False Memories of Childhood Sexual Traumas*. New York: Simon & Schuster.

7   Believing patients

Marjorie Orr

One has to know one's buried truth in order to be able to live one's life.
The 'not telling' of the story serves as a perpetuation of its tyranny. . . .
When one's history is abolished one's identity ceases to exist as well.

(Felman and Laub, 1992: 78, 82)

The re-emergence of childhood sexual abuse as a significant problem for psychotherapy has created a minefield of complexity and paradox. The accuracy of memory was never a major issue until recently, neither was the question of whether to believe or be sceptical about patients' childhood stories. Psychotherapy, with its inherent problem with reality testing, coped in the past by side-stepping external trauma. Childhood events related within the therapeutic session, whether real or fabricated, were assigned the same status, as symbols of inner conflict.

Now psychotherapy is faced with having to untie the Gordian knot and distinguish between (a) memories of real abuse, (b) pseudo-memories which have concretized as actuality the emotional undercurrents in an unhealthy family dynamic, and (c) the recent concept of 'false memories' which have no apparent basis in reality, emotional or physical. Faced by attack from two opposing, seemingly irreconcilable, pressure groups, the therapist is in a dilemma.

Increasing public disclosures from adults sexually abused as children and clinical studies indicating a high incidence of sexual abuse amongst the mentally disturbed, especially those in psychiatric care, suggest under-belief, not over-belief, is the problem. Approximately two-thirds of women inpatients report either physical or sexual childhood abuse; 50 per cent reported sexual abuse. The severely abused were five times more likely to be hospitalized, rising to 16 times more likely to be hospitalized, rising to 16 times more likely where intercourse had been experienced. Male inpatients were twice as likely to have been sexually abused as males in the general population. New Zealand psychologist John Read's international literature review of 'child abuse and psychosis' (1997) adds weight to Judith Herman's startling claim that 'many or even most psychiatric patients are survivors of child abuse' (1992: 122).

In his recent paper 'Child abuse and severity of disturbance among adult psychiatric inpatients' Read concludes: 'The pattern of findings emerging . . .

confirms the small but growing body of literature that child abuse is related not only to relatively mild or moderate dysfunction in adulthood but to the most severe levels of dysfunction' (1998: 364).

One study found that among patients with 'severe mental illness' 76 per cent of women and 72 per cent of men had been sexually or physically abused (Read, 1998: 360). Read refers to a New Zealand study which 'found that women whose childhood abuse involved intercourse were 16 times more likely than nonabused women to enter psychiatric hospital as adults' (1998: 365).

Read argues strongly that inpatients should be routinely asked about abuse histories. In one group only 6 per cent spontaneously reported abuse, whereas 70 per cent reported it after a direct question. 'Men may be particularly unlikely to disclose childhood abuse if not asked directly' (Read and Fraser, 1998: 357).

At the other end of the spectrum, the high-profile 'false memory' stories in the media counter-suggest that gullible or malign therapists have over-stressed the problem of child abuse and invented it where none existed. The polarization of the bitter 'memory wars' argument over the past five years (a splitting which in itself says a good deal about the intense emotional response to sexual abuse) has obscured the simple fact that this is a highly complex situation. Both may well be true. The key question then becomes: in what measure? – since there may be a danger in being too even-handed.

To date, almost 100 per cent of public attention has been focused on what may well be a small problem of 'false memories' of sexual abuse compared to a much larger problem of underreporting. In addition, 'false memories' in the form of 'false denials' from accused parents have come under very little scrutiny.

At the heart of therapists' double bind is the knowledge that in dis-believing patients, who may be forcing themselves to tell for the first time that they were sexually abused as children, they will be repeating the victimization pattern. As London analyst Brendan MacCarthy says in his paper 'Are incest victims hated?':

> A core conflict for every incest child is whether or not to tell, or more correctly to tell in such a way that the report cannot be brushed aside. . . . The dynamics surrounding secrecy are complex, but the key issue is the fear of not being believed. To be disbelieved is to be branded a liar, or mad, malicious, a destroyer of the family, a sexual pervert. (1988: 114)

There thus follows a series of questions which require answers. How accurate is memory of childhood events? Are pleasant pseudo-memories more likely to be created than unpleasant ones? Can people forget trau-matic experiences for periods of years? If so, how do recovered memories compare in reliability to continuous memories? Does forgetting necessarily imply that accurate recall is possible? Is there any point in remembering? What are the risks? Has it therapeutic value? Are traumatized individuals themselves more likely to produce hallucinations or 'false memories'? Should patients be directly asked about abuse histories? How suggestible are they? How frequent an occurrence is sexual abuse? In the absence of external corroboration, are there any reliable indicators, medical, psychological, or behavioural, of early abuse? Do therapists put themselves in professional danger by listening to and believing their patients' stories of childhood abuse?

Space being limited, I will outline the major studies which have attempted to throw light on these areas. Normal memory has its limitations, is subject to error and distortion, but the core generally contains 'a kernel of truth' (McGuire, 1997). Depressed psychiatric inpatients, often considered unreliable in their memories, are, according to psychologists Chris Brewin et al., less subject to bias then non-depressed individuals.

> [T]he central features of their accounts are likely to be reasonably accurate. Because the influences on memory serve mainly to inhibit recall or disclosure, it seems fair to conclude that reports confirming events should be given more weight than negative reports. (1993: 94)

Similarly British psychiatrist J.E. Oliver in his Wiltshire study of inter-generational abuse, looking at 50 abusive families through four generations, found the memory bias all in the direction of deleting unpleasant childhood experiences. He found:

> omission, confusion, irrationality, distortion and most bizarre of all – idealization in accounts of cruel, rejecting or neglectful grandparents by parents with rearing difficulties and/or ill-treated children. . . . [they] frequently gave bland or idealized pictures of their own biological parents which could be so incompatible with old written records that repeated checks were necessary to make sure we had the same family. (Oliver, 1993: 1320)

Maintaining the illusion of a protective parent appears to be a clear motivation for creating a 'false memory' which is better than the reality. Milton Erickson's 'Negation or reversal of legal testimony' provides a clear example: 'Ma wouldn't let anybody do these things' was the stout denial of two girls, 9 and 11 years old, who had been sexually assaulted over a period of months by patrons of their parents' brothel (Erickson, 1938: 549). At the time there were full confessions by the men, medical evidence of beatings, vaginal and rectal coitus, syphilis and gonorrhoea. On initial interview, the girls were fearful, anxious, resentful, expressed hate, shame and guilt. Two months later on re-interview, the details were minimized, denied and contradicted. The third interview two months on produced flat denials, especially of the more brutal assaults.

'Betrayal trauma' is the term and explanation offered by Jennifer J. Freyd as the logic to amnesia for childhood abuse: '[A]mnesia may allow a dependent child to remain attached to – and thus elicit at least some degree of life-sustaining nurturing and protection from – his or her abusive caregiver' (1996: 180).

Even abuse outside the family can be subject to burial within the child's mind. Swedish children involved in child pornography, interviewed after police uncovered the photographs and videos, were reticent to such a degree that the investigators concluded:

> [T]he children do not want to remember and sometimes mentally exclude their earlier experiences. . . . it is apparent that the greater number of questioning sessions that the children participate in, the more they are able to relate. It is as though they must 'digest the memories' before they can relate the events. The sessions are rather like an onion that is peeled; layer after layer is tentatively pulled away. (Svedin and Back, 1996: 64)

Not a single child told anyone unprompted of the abuse, which amongst the 10 children had gone on for an aggregate of 42 years.

Most adults abused as children remember their experiences, but it is clear from the growing number of recent studies that a substantial minority do 'lose' their memories for periods of time. The mechanisms, possibly several different ones, by which this occurs are not clear at present. Using terms such as 'repression' or 'dissociation' is not always helpful. Some adult survivors appear to use semi-conscious techniques, often drink and drug addictions or overworking, in order to push memories aside. For others the forgetting seems to have been a spontaneous process, outside their willed control, as indeed is often the reappearance of those memories, against their conscious wish not to know.

As memory disorder expert Michael Kopelman points out about amnesic offenders: 'The demarcation between "conscious" malingering and "unconscious" forgetting may not be clear-cut' (1997: 288). Some let the memory drift away; others think recollection would be too horrifying, though they retain a jumbled feeling of 'something in my mind'. He suggests the same could be true for amnesia over sexual abuse, where there can be a 'knowing without remembering'.

Twenty-five per cent of adult sexual abuse survivors reviewed in 1996 concluded that: 'Amnesia for childhood sexual abuse is a robust finding across studies using very different samples and methods of assessment. Studies addressing the accuracy of recovered memories show that recovered memories are no more or no less accurate than continuous memories for abuse' (Scheflin and Brown, 1996: 143). Psychotherapy was the least reported trigger for recovering memories. These studies from varied international research groups make interesting reading in the context of almost blanket media denial of the phenomenon of traumatic amnesia.

Dissociative identity disorder patients who recovered memories were in 68 per cent of cases able to find outside corroboration of the events. Richard Kluft, an American clinician, remarks: 'I had not anticipated that

85% of the confirmed retrieved memories would have been accessed with hypnosis, but I am not surprised that this proved to be the case. Hypnosis has been receiving a good deal of unwarranted "bad press"' (1995: 257). He also outlined instances in which inaccuracies in some recollections could be demonstrated.

Criminologists C.S. Widom and S. Morris (1998) found that there was 'substantial under-reporting of sexual abuse among known victims . . . this is particularly impressive since these are court substantiated cases' (1997: 34). A paper reviewing 36 studies by Charles Whitfield (1997) had reported similar conclusions – that periods of total or partial amnesia were relatively common amongst abuse survivors.

Documented individual cases of corroborated amnesia for childhood abuse are also increasingly being publicized. Susan Lees, a 38-year-old law student, found social work and medical records to validate memories which surfaced during therapy for depression and post-traumatic stress disorder (PTSD) in her early thirties. She was left at nine months old with her alcoholic father and subsequently with a known child abuser. When she went into care at four years old she was suffering from severe malnutrition, with evidence that she had been buggered and had her toes smashed with a hammer. Her memories started to resurface when she was listening to a radio news report from Bosnia and 'heard the screams of a young girl having shrapnel removed from her back without anaesthetic' (Johnston, 1997).

In addition, an Internet website set up by Ross Cheit (1998) lists civil and criminal court cases where recovered memories have been corroborated. Cheit himself was sexually abused as a child at summer camp, but only remembered in his late thirties. He tracked down other victims and witnesses, including a nurse who had seen one boy abused who when contacted as an adult did not recall the event. The abuser confessed. Ross Cheit sued the summer camp organizers successfully and gave the money to charity. He said: 'Long-lost memories of sexual abuse can resurface. I know because it happened to me. But I also know that I might not have believed this to be possible if [it] hadn't occurred to me' (Freyd, 1996: 6).

It is unclear why it has been so difficult in the heated professional arguments of recent years to establish that some people do block memories of unpleasant events, since it does not exclude the possibility of false memories occurring in other cases, nor indeed true and false memories occurring together in the same patient. Nor does it imply that memories can always be accurately or fully recalled. Hugh Thompson, an American helicopter pilot in Vietnam, recently honoured by Bill Clinton for his part in stopping the My Lai massacre of Vietnamese civilians by GIs 30 years ago, still cannot remember parts of the atrocities he witnessed. When he was interviewed two years later he remembered nothing except that he had been in Vietnam on the date in question. The events had all been documented at the time and with repeated questioning he was able to remember some but not all of the details (Mason, 1996).

Despite claims that combat veterans, torture, violent crime or disaster victims and Holocaust survivors never forget, there is clear evidence that a minority do lose memories. Brown et al., reviewing the literature in their considerable treatise *Memory, Trauma Treatment and the Law*, state: 'Traumatic amnesia and other memory deficits have been consistently documented for war trauma, including World War I . . . World War II . . . the Middle East War . . . and the Vietnam War.' Concentration camp survivors' memories appear on the whole to be remarkably 'consistent and accurate', but 'a sub-population of camp survivors failed after 40 years to recall memory for traumatic experiences . . . physical injury or threat of death was associated with memory loss' (1998: 156–7).

Neuroscientists working with Vietnam veterans and sexual abuse survivors are starting to provide scientific explanations for traumatic amnesia. 'Informed speculation is that the body responds to extreme stress by releasing a cascade of cortisol, adrenaline and other hormones that can damage brain cells, impair memory, and set in motion a long-lasting and worsening disregulation of the body's complex biochemistry' (Butler, 1996: 42). Three 1995 studies found significant reductions in the size of the hippocampus, one of the brain's memory-processing centres, in traumatized people compared to non-traumatized (Bremner and Marmar, 1998: 385). Those with the smallest hippocampi displayed most symptoms of PTSD and dissociation – the tendency to space out, feel detached from one's body and have unpredictable lapses in memory.

The neurobiology of trauma is now the focus of international attention. The extensive research findings well documented in *Trauma, Memory and Dissociation*, edited by Douglas Bremner and Charles Marmar (1998), and in *Traumatic Stress*, edited by Bessel Van der Kolk, Alexander McFarlane and Lars Weisaeth (1996), will do much to defuse the bitter polarities, once absorbed by the mainstream.

Suggestibility is central to arguments by critics of recovered memory, who believe that memories involving amnesia are *sine qua non* false, and are creations of treatment. The force of these arguments has tended to make therapists overwary when hearing stories of sexual abuse, whether always remembered or not. However, a recent study by Chicago psychologist Frank Leavitt (1997) indicates that patients who recover memories were remarkably less suggestible than patients in other psychiatric populations.

This was the conclusion of Sandor Ferenczi, as far back as 1933. Arnold Modell's commentary on his seminal paper 'Confusion of tongues between adults and children' points out that where a child is brought up with a conflicting view of reality from his or her own construction, the child will tend to reject the information offered. 'This may appear later as a resistance to learning from the analyst' (Modell, 1991: 227).

Horace Barlow, quoted in Lawrence Weiskrantz's *Consciousness: Lost and Found*, makes outside validation 'the crucial feature of consciousness': 'It requires a remembered partner for its introspection; consciousness is taught, awakened and maintained by interactions with other modelled minds' (Weiskrantz, 1997: 166).

That being precisely what is not offered within an abusive family, where denial tends to be the norm, the only choice for certain abused children may be to shut out the conflict of realities, by burying their 'knowing'. However, the knowledge remains either in the abused child's play (Terr, 1988), or in the body (Van der Kolk et al., 1996), in behavioural symptoms, self-harming (Babiker and Arnold, 1997), alcohol and drug abuse (Wilsnack et al., 1996; Wilson, 1997), eating disorders (Palmer et al., 1990); or suicidal behaviour (Read, 1998).

Bizarre reversals of reality occur frequently in arguments around child abuse. The 'false memory' concept is one. The problem is less one of brainwashing in 'foreign objects of fictitious abuse' from outside than in not providing a forum in which the adult survivor feels physically or psychically safe to 'know' unpleasant features of his or her history in the presence of another person. Abuse survivors need to know the therapist can tolerate what they themselves are often unable to bear.

Believing a patient who has been abused is a complex matter, requiring a capacity on the part of the therapist for holding high levels of anxiety, often suicidal depression and uncertainty over long periods of time. But too much passivity or fear on the part of the therapist will drive the abuse back underground or not allow it to surface. Abused patients do not wish forcing or intrusive techniques to be used. Diagnosis on the basis of presenting symptoms is unwise and irrelevant since patients who have forgotten will not benefit from a forced confrontation. They need, in the words of psychoanalytic psychotherapist Phil Mollon in *Remembering Trauma: A Psychotherapist's Guide to Memory and Illusion*, 'the space to feel and think and explore, without reaching for a premature conclusion' (1998: 195).

Buried memories, if they exist, will surface of their own accord, given time and trust, though not always accurately or coherently. Dori Laub, a Romanian psychiatrist and psychoanalyst who works with Holocaust survivors and torture victims, says: 'During massive trauma, fiction, fantasy and demonic art can become historical fact; this blurring of boundaries between reality and fantasy conjures up affect so violent that it exceeds the ego's capacity for regulation' (Laub and Auerhahn, 1993: 287).

Even Pierre Janet (1859–1947), whose approach to the therapeutic integration of memory forms the basis of modern treatments of post-traumatic stress, indicates that 'traumatic memory should . . . be considered as vulnerable to postevent modification'. Traumatic memories are 'not exact reflections of the original traumatic events'. Paul Brown and Onno Van der Hart, reviewing Janet's work in context with recent findings, describe real memory merging with fantasy elements, and 'distortions, when for example another person's trauma is "experienced" as if it were the subject's own'. Nevertheless, they do emphasize that 'traumatic memories are highly resistant to deliberate modification, for example by autosuggestion or therapist-induced suggestion' (Brown and Van der Hart, 1998: 1031–2).

Luckily therapists' hesitancy to commit prematurely to any conclusions about the accuracy of memories of abuse, forgotten or continuous, is mirrored in patients' own, often self-preserving, uncertainty. They cannot believe themselves, would much prefer to write it off as madness or perversion, than accept they have been abused, especially incestuously. As Phil Mollon in *Multiple Selves, Multiple Voices* says: '[I]t is misleading to suggest (as much of the FMS [false memory syndrome] literature does) that the idea of being abused as a child can be a comforting solution to mental distress. In my experience, recovering memories do not make people feel better – at least not initially' (1996: 80).

So why bother, if facilitating a patient's belief is going to lead, as some have suggested, to a disintegrating personality? Robert Krell, a Canadian psychiatrist working with child survivors of the Holocaust, writes:

> The most pervasive preoccupation of child survivors is the continuing struggle with memory, whether there is too much of it or too little. For the child survivor memory is a double edged sword. To achieve relief for symptomatic child survivors, the knowledgeable therapist elicits memories, assists in their integration, makes sense of the sequence and encourages [them] . . . to write their story. . . . (1993: 386)

Krell describes a latency period prior to the emergence of psychiatric symptoms, which often first appear after age 45.

With sexual abuse survivors equally there is a decline in long-standing problems of all kinds in long-term therapy. Catherine Cameron's study of amnesic and non-amnesic women found that anorexia and bulimia, drink/drug addictions disappeared almost altogether, negative self-perceptions were altered and depression became a background rather than suicidal concern: 'Depression (88%) and suicidal feelings (67%) were widespread in 1986. Six years later they had dropped to 52% and 22% respectively . . . even more impressive, the percentage using drugs or alcohol for coping was 35% in 1986 and only 2% in 1992' (Cameron, 1994: 129). Hypervigilance and compulsive eating were the strongest remaining effects. She also describes the crisis precipitated by the recall of memory in amnesic women. Many abused as children do over the course of time find the strength to seek and in many cases find full or partial confirmation from perpetrator confession, court records, other victims or family witnesses.

The other persuasive argument strongly indicating the benefits of an accurate understanding of early childhood events (where it can be tolerated) comes from Peter Fonagy et al.'s 'The ghost in the nursery' (1993). The study found that abused parents unable to face their own childhood deprivations are most likely to repeat the abuse. This echoes J.E. Oliver's conclusions that: 'The single most important modifying factor in intergenerational transmission of child abuse is the capacity of the child victim to grow up with the ability to face the reality of past and present personal relationships' (1993: 1322).

In the present state of extreme wariness in the therapeutic world in the wake of the 'false memory' furore and the threat of malicious professional complaints, described by me elsewhere as a 'culture of fear' (Orr, 1996), disbelief is easier than belief. Memory is uncertain, but not that uncertain. Traumatic amnesia without a shadow of a doubt occurs across a range of terrifying experiences, and was never controversial before sexual abuse appeared.

Therapists may quail at becoming the advocates (even silently) for sexually abused patients in a society which prefers almost unquestioningly to countenance the pleas of those who insist they are falsely accused. Professional uncertainties in the area of memory, some well-intentioned and misguided techniques used in the 1980s, and the existence of a few clearly unhinged fringe therapists have all been exploited as a way of trying to silence the voices of those who were abused as children. Society's coming to terms with child sexual abuse, especially incestuous abuse, is an erratic, painful process.

Therapy is caught between a rock and a hard place in the midst of this transitional phase, under attack on the outside, being forced on the inside substantially to rethink its theoretical underpinning. While premature belief or indeed a false belief in non-existent abuse is obviously damaging, disbelief can become just another way of side-stepping the problem of sexual abuse.

References

Babiker, G. and Arnold, L. (1997) *The Language of Injury*. Leicester: BPS Books.

Bremner, D.J. and Marmar, C.R. (eds) (1998) *Trauma, Memory and Dissociation*. Washington DC: American Psychiatric Press.

Brewin, C., Andrews, B. and Gotlib, I. (1993) 'Psychopathology and early experience: a reappraisal of retrospective reports', *Psychological Bulletin*, 113: 82–98.

Brown, D., Scheflin, A.W., Hammond, D.C. (eds) (1998) *Memory, Trauma Treatment and the Law*. New York: W.W. Norton.

Brown, P. and Van der Hart, O. (1998) 'Memories of sexual abuse: Janet's critique of Freud, a balanced approach', *Psychological Reports*, 82: 1027–43.

Butler, K. (1996) 'The biology of fear', *Networker*, July/August, pp. 39–45.

Cameron, C. (1994) 'Veterans of a secret war: survivors of childhood sexual trauma compared to Vietnam War with PTSD', *Journal of Interpersonal Violence*, 9 (1): 117–32.

Cheit, R. (1998) Recovered Memory Website. http://www.brown.edu/Departments/Taubman_Center/Recovmem/Archive.html

Erikson, M.H. (1938) 'Negation or reversal of legal testimony', *Archives of Neurology and Psychiatry*, 40: 548–53.

Felman, S. and Laub, D. (1992) *Testimony: Crises of Witnessing*. London: Routledge.

Fonagy, P., Steel, M., Moran, G., Steele, H. and Higgitt, A. (1993) 'The ghost in the nursery: the relation between parents' mental representations of childhood experiences and their infants' security of attachment', *Journal of the American Psychoanalytic Association*, 41: 957–90.

Freyd, J.J. (1996) *Betrayal Trauma: The Logic of Forgetting Childhood Abuse*. Cambridge, MA: Harvard University Press.

Herman, J. (1992) *Trauma and Recovery: The Aftermath of Violence from Domestic Abuse to Political Terror*. New York: Basic Books.

Johnston, L. (1997) 'Memories of child abuse spark lawsuit', *Observer*, 2 March, p. 3.

Kluft, R. (1995) 'The confirmation and disconfirmation of memories of abuse in DID patients: a naturalistic clinical study', *Dissociation*, VIII (4).

Kopelman, M. (1997) 'Anomalies of autobiographical memory: retrograde amnesia, confabulation, delusional memory, psychogenic amnesia, and false memories', in D. Read and S. Lindsay (eds), *Recollections of Trauma: Scientific Evidence and Clinical Practice*. New York: Plenum Press.

Krell, R. (1993) 'Child survivors of the Holocaust: strategies of adaptation', *Canadian Journal of Psychiatry*, 38 (6): 384–9.

Laub, D. and Auerhahn, C. (1993) 'Knowing and not knowing massive psychic trauma: forms of traumatic memory', *American Journal of Psychoanalysis*, 74: 287–302.

Leavitt, F. (1997) 'False attribution of suggestibility to explain recovered memory of childhood sexual abuse following extended amnesia', *Child Abuse & Neglect*, 21 (3): 265–72.

MacCarthy, B. (1988) 'Are incest victims hated?', *Psychoanalytic Psychotherapy*, 3 (2): 113–20.

McGuire, A. (1997) *False Memory Syndrome: A Statement*. Research Study I. Rugby: British Association for Counselling.

Mason, P. (1996) 'False memory syndrome v. lying perpetrator syndrome', *Post Traumatic Gazette*, 1 (4): 2–4.

Modell, A. (1991) 'A confusion of tongues or whose reality is it?', *Psychoanalytic Quarterly*, LX: 227–44.

Mollon, P. (1996) *Multiple Selves, Multiple Voices*. New York: John Wiley.

Mollon, P. (1998) *Remembering Trauma: A Psychotherapist's Guide to Memory and Illusion*. New York: John Wiley.

Oliver, J.E. (1993) 'Intergenerational transmission of child abuse: rates, research and clinical implications', *American Journal of Psychiatry*, 150 (9): 1315–24.

Orr, M. (1996) 'Culture of fear', *Counselling News*, March, pp. 14–15.

Palmer, R.L., Oppenheimer, A., Dignon, A., Chaloner, D.A. and Howells, K. (1990) 'Childhood sexual experiences with adults reported by women with eating disorders: an extended series', *British Journal of Psychiatry*, 156: 699–703.

Read, J. (1997) 'Child abuse and psychosis: a literature review and implications for professional practice', *Professional Psychology: Research and Practice*, 28: 448–56.

Read, J. (1998) 'Child abuse and severity of disturbance among adult psychiatric inpatients', *Child Abuse & Neglect*, 22 (5): 359–68.

Read, J. and Fraser, A. (1998) 'Abuse histories of psychiatric inpatients: to ask or not to ask?', *Psychiatric Services (NZ)*, 49 (3): 355–9.

Scheflin, A. and Brown, D. (1996) 'Repressed memory or dissociative amnesia: what the science says', *Journal of Psychiatry and Law*, 24 (2): 156–7.

Svedin, C.G. and Back, K. (1996) *Children Who Don't Speak Out*. London: Jessica Kingsley.

Terr, L. (1988) 'Case study: what happens to early memories of trauma? A study of twenty children under age five at the time of documented traumatic events', *Journal of the American Academy of Child and Adolescent Psychiatry*, 27 (1): 96–104.

Van der Kolk, B., McFarlane, A. and Weisaeth, L. (eds) (1996) *Traumatic Stress: The Overwhelming Experience on Mind, Body and Society*. New York: Guilford Press.

Weiskrantz, L. (1997) *Consciousness: Lost and Found.* Oxford: Oxford University Press.

Whitfield, C. (1997) 'Traumatic amnesia: the evolution of our understanding from a clinical and legal perspective', *Sexual Addiction & Compulsivity*, 4 (2): 3–34.

Widom, C.S. and Morris, S. (1997) 'Accuracy of adult recollections of childhood victimization: II. Child sexual abuse', *Psychological Assessment*, 19 (1): 34–46.

Wilsnack, S., Vogeltanz, N., Klassen, A. and Harris, R. (1995) *Childhood Sexual Abuse and Woman's Substance Abuse: National Survey Findings.* Rutgers, NJ: Rutgers University, Alcohol Studies Center.

Wilson, J. (1997) *The Connection: Proceedings of a Conference on Childhood Sexual Abuse and Adult Dependence.* September, Stirling University.

PART II

CLINICAL ISSUES

---

8   The ineffectiveness of psychotherapy

W.M. *Epstein*

The attraction of an inexpensive cure for social problems is irresistible. It would obviate the need for painful conflicts over the distribution of resources or for callous denials of claims for remediation; it would justify the preservation of comforting social relations and of the appearance at least that society is just and humane. Even the promise of an inexpensive cure has great appeal as a political symbol of hope and social progress. In this light, the debate over the effectiveness of psychotherapy transcends a truth-in-labelling issue between patients and psychotherapists to speak more generally to the conditions of citizenship for many members of society.

Many of the early challenges to talking cures for personal deviance, mental disease and emotional problems were themselves flawed (Eysenck, 1952; Rachman, 1971; Office of Technology Assessment, 1980), although Stuart (1970) anticipated many of the contemporary criticisms of the field. The controversy over the effectiveness of psychotherapy was not well developed until a number of reviews summarized the vast basic clinical evidence to reach ostensibly credible judgements of the field. These general statements first raised a few weak doubts about the effectiveness of psychotherapy, but then attempted to dispel scepticism through a series of intuitive analyses, box-score analyses and, finally, meta-analyses.

More recently, a few works have renewed scepticism, but customarily they still preserve claims for the effectiveness of some particular intervention, most frequently behavioural methods. Nevertheless, the typical mega-bookstore displays more than 270 shelf feet of books on self-help, psychology, and psychotherapy unrelieved by even a demurral to the power of professional helping or the plausibility of personal renewal.[1]

Yet the summaries rest upon the credibility of the individual studies from which they are constructed. Unfortunately, the basic clinical evidence is uniformly faulty: '[T]oday there is not one credible study conforming to the basic rules of objective proof that testifies to the effectiveness of any psychotherapeutic treatment' (Epstein, 1995: 1). In spite of its voiced commitments to the canons of science, the literature of psychotherapy remains proto-scientific and crypto-scientific, with the consequence that the effectiveness of psychotherapy is at best indeterminate. Moreover, there is evidence that psychotherapy may be ineffective and perhaps even harmful. The paradox of the field's curative weakness together with its persistence – indeed its continuing growth – begs for a search beyond the clinic for the vital social role of psychotherapy.

The contemporary summaries

In an age of doubt, Bergin (1971) published a mild reproach for which he seems to have spent the following decades in atonement and recantation. He had initially concluded that psychotherapy was only 'modestly positive', a conclusion whose capped enthusiasm seemed to confirm Eysenck's earlier suggestion that patient deterioration and spontaneous remission may have 'tempered' the effectiveness of the field. Subsequent editions of Bergin's influential review, however, retract any flavour of heresy (Bergin and Lambert, 1978; Lambert et al., 1986a, 1986b; Lambert and Bergin, 1994):

> [R]ecent outcome data look more favorable. A growing number of controlled outcome studies are analyzing a wide variety of therapies. These findings generally yield clearly positive results when compared with no-treatment, wait-list, and placebo or pseudotherapies. This may be the result of improvements in designs, but we believe that a major contributor to these newer findings is that more experienced and competent therapists have been used in recent studies. Our review of the empirical assessment of the broad range of verbal psychotherapies leads us to conclude that these methods are worthwhile when practiced by wise and stable therapists. . . . These considerations imply that psychotherapy is laden with nonspecific or placebo factors . . . but these influences, when specified, may prove to be the essence of what provides therapeutic benefit. (Bergin and Lambert, 1978: 179–80)

By 1986, there was no hesitation in claiming that the benefits of psychotherapy were long-lasting and related to the skill of the practitioner, thus endorsing both its market value and its social status as a profession:

> Many psychotherapies that have been subjected to empirical study have been shown to have demonstrable effects on a variety of clients. These effects are not only statistically significant but clinically meaningful. Psychotherapy facilitates the remission of symptoms. It not only speeds up the natural healing process but often provides additional coping strategies and methods for dealing with future problems. Psychologists, psychiatrists, and social workers, and marriage and

family therapists as well as patients can be assured that a broad range of therapies, when offered by skillful, wise, and stable therapists, are likely to result in appreciable gains for the client. (Lambert et al., 1986b)

The Bergin essays, employing largely intuitive methods of summary, were corroborated by similar works (Parloff, 1978; Gurman and Kniskern, 1986; Office of Technology Assessment, 1980). 'Box-score' analysis improved the consistency of the intuitive summaries by comparing the qualitative results of different studies, concluding that all therapies seem to be effective (Luborsky et al., 1975). Smith et al. (1980) and its numerous descendants greatly improved the rigour of the summaries by employing a statistical technique, meta-analysis, to compare the actual quantitative findings of different studies. Indeed, Smith et al. (1980) has become a 'citation classic' testifying to the effectiveness of the field.

Yet even on their own – without consideration of the quality of the clinical studies themselves – the summary reviews are flawed. The Bergin enterprise changed direction after experiencing an epiphany that placebo (non-specific) effects constitute true clinical cure and, therefore, grounds upon which to endorse psychotherapy. Yet the reverse is more appropriate for any clinical intervention: the positive effects of placebo treatment diminish the value of professional effectiveness which is intended as a rational improvement over the mere thought of cure. If placebos for psychotherapy are effective, then advanced university training is not needed and the field's status is reduced from the professional to the decorative.

The intuitive reviews as well as the box-score analyses largely accepted the reported findings of the studies themselves with little attention to their scientific quality. Pleas for greater methodological rigour were customarily made as suggestions for future research and did not intrude on the logic of the summaries themselves.

In spite of an entire chapter devoted to the value of the scientific method and the obligation of psychotherapy to adhere to its tenets, Smith et al. failed to live up to their own injunctions. They identified 475 outcome studies of psychotherapy that they judged to be reliable, controlled and in conformity with 'the acknowledged canons of experimental science' (1980: 8). However, many of these studies violated standard scientific practice. Smith et al. justified their inclusion by questioning previous reviews for arbitrarily imposing

'textbook' standards; these methodological rules, learned as dicta in graduate school and regarded as the touchstone of publishable articles in prestigious journals, were applied arbitrarily; for example, note again Rachman's high-handed dismissal on methodological grounds of study after study of psycho-therapy outcome. (1980: 8)

In the end, their meta-analysis concluded that psychotherapy was enormously effective: '[T]he average person who would score at the 50th percentile of the untreated control population, could expect to rise to the 80th percentile with respect to that population after receiving psychotherapy' (1980: 87–8). This conclusion is even more impressive since the maximum improvement was 50 percentage points. Moreover, they insisted that the screened research contained little evidence of negative results or deterioration. Yet they failed to subtract the reported placebo effects that accounted for more than 20 percentage points of improvement from their findings. With this adjustment, psychotherapy patients are only about 10 percentage points better off than controls. Moreover, on the basis of a reanalysis of the most credible portion of Smith et al.'s studies – the 32 studies that incorporated a placebo control – Prioleau et al. (1983) concluded that psychotherapy only confers a benefit of 6 percentage points. However, the small adjusted improvement of either 10 or 6 percentage points needs to be further reduced for the many likely biases of the basic clinical studies. With even small additional corrections for likely biases – and Rosenthal and Rubin (1978) would suggest a very large one solely for expectancy bias – the field is naked to the charge that it is routinely ineffective and perhaps even harmful.

Moreover, Smith et al. were far too quick to ignore the possibilities of both harm and deterioration. In particular, they reported effect sizes as though they were standard deviations when in essence they were more akin to standard errors (Epstein, 1984). In this case, the tightly dispersed outcomes of psychotherapy presented by Smith et al. become wildly variable, implying that many patients routinely deteriorate during therapy.

The research evidence

The heart of the problem with the summary judgements of psychotherapy's effectiveness rests with the scientific transgressions of the base of their studies. Credible clinical research needs to employ randomized, controlled trials along with other standard protections: multiple blinding, random selection of patients, reliable measures, and so forth (Meinert, 1986).[2]

The clinical studies characteristically utilize porous research designs that invite a multitude of biases. The studies rely upon patient reports. When the evaluators of the outcomes are not the very clinicians who provide the treatments, they are frequently not blind to whether the patient is in the control or the experimental group. Placebo controls are rarely used. Random assignment is not the universal practice; many studies utilize matched controls, waiting lists or simple before and after comparisons. Samples are tiny, frequently under 25. Evaluation instruments are unreliable. High subject attrition and great amounts of censored data are common. Treatment integrity, the assurance that the intervention is delivered in its described form, is not secured. Subjects for the studies are not randomly selected from the underlying populations of concern; rather, they are typically volunteers solicited from mass media announcements or they are recruited, frequently in acute states of their afflictions, from atypical clinical settings.

The temporary conditions of the studies and their highly motivated staffs probably produce demonstration effects that exaggerate the effectiveness of therapy. Much of the literature has been compiled from experiments in which presumably the best clinicians are delivering therapy under supervision. As a result, the reported outcomes, such as they are, probably fail to reflect the common setting, the typical patient or the usual therapist. The failure to evaluate representative conditions of psychotherapy is particularly problematic in light of recurrent criticisms of the field for tolerating many incompetent and unethical practitioners (Masson, 1988; Dineen, 1996).

These observations are becoming more frequently restated, although the little band of sceptics customarily redeems some small portion of psychotherapy from Epstein's universal indictment (1995). After devastating any rational basis for faith in Freudian psychoanalysis and seemingly talk therapy as well, Macmillan (1997) is able to retain some respect for psychotherapy generally, particularly the non-talk therapies (presumably including drug therapy) and a small number of behavioural interventions. Still, he glosses over the issue of measured effectiveness.

The most severe critics of the possibility of recovered memories maintain a belief in the efficacy of talk therapy (Pope, 1997). Dineen (1996) goes well beyond recovered memory to a diatribe against the business of psychotherapy, yet she retains a belief that appropriate practice has positive effects. While acknowledging that the results of psychotherapy are indeterminate, Kline (1988) believes that it prods people to take action against their problems. Dawes (1994) indicts professionalism, pointing out that the level of training has little to do with the effectiveness of the therapist, but retains a belief in the efficacy of a number of interventions.

Yet the sceptical tradition in psychotherapy profoundly fails to discipline the field's research. Psychotherapy's tatters of science fail to provide any credible evidence that psychotherapy is effective. The very best research – perhaps exemplified by the National Institute of Mental Health's Collaborative Research Program (CRP) and by the Second Sheffield Experiment (SSE) – is grievously flawed. The CRP relied upon patient self-report; interrater reliabilities were variable and frequently low; success in treatment was not consistent across measures; no non-treatment or placebo control was employed for psychotherapy; CRP suffered an average attrition of 38 per cent and consequently great censoring; and, most notably, the experimental groups did not perform better than the drug placebo group (Elkin et al., 1989; Imber et al., 1990; Sotsky et al., 1991). The SSE reported substantial clinical improvement. However, 'all of their outcome assessments were highly reactive to therapist expectations; the assessments were made either by committed therapists or by the patients themselves' (Epstein, 1995: 88). Moreover, their samples contained only 12 patients (Shapiro et al., 1990).

The most recent research, reported in the most prestigious of the field's journals, continues the pitfalls of the past, suggesting that the scholarship of psychotherapy has settled comfortably into a permanent scientific immaturity.[3] Eysenck's (1994) suspicions of psychotherapy might profitably be applied equally to the behavioural interventions he commends. Every claim for the efficacy of psychotherapy or behavioural methods can be alternatively explained in terms of methodological biases of one sort or another, placebo effects or spontaneous remission.

Social efficiency and the persistence of psychotherapy

Self-deception is the worst kind, and the field of psychotherapy has walled itself off from criticism of its own clinical weakness. Francher (1995) provides a typical illustration of the field's blind denial. After reducing psychotherapy to a series of 'cultures of healing' whose effectiveness defies empirical verification, Francher can still hold that 'mental health care is legitimate, but many of its claims to authority are not'. Yet he fails to identify the field's true claims to authority, although they seem to involve 'a wide variety of modes (not just scientific modes)' (1995: 14). In typical fashion, the pseudo-science of psychotherapy allows Francher access to the mystical each time that clinical practice requires resurrection.

In spite of desert conditions in the garden of its effectiveness, psychotherapy flourishes. Obviously its failed clinical role in curing emotional, social or mental problems cannot explain its popularity. Rather, psychotherapy finds profitable roles in fulfilling two different, separate functions. In the first place, it appeals to the vanity of many people (notably Gross's [1978] YAVIS syndrome) who have come to depend upon its reassurances. These people might well earn a more satisfying personal identity from the quotidian abrasions of civilization in the raw than the chain hotel personalities that psychotherapy attempts to confer. Civic life might also improve without so much professionally sanctioned narcissism.

The truly afflicted have apparently not benefited from psychotherapy. Yet the field's bogus evidence has retarded the search for effective remedies by hiding the enduring problems of personal and social deviance. Its role in making social problems invisible is knowingly performed. Thus, through the pursuit of its professional interests, psychotherapy has come to fulfil ideological, political and social functions that go far to explain its institutional buoyancy.

Psychotherapy is the apotheosis of social efficiency, the notion that social problems can be resolved inexpensively and without disrupting customary social relations. In essence, the psychotherapist promises to meliorate social problems that result from sustained cultural and economic deprivation with just a few inexpensive hours of benign treatment: no expensive restorations, no expensive preventative measures requiring greater social equality, none of the dislocations implied by greater taxes and changed social relations. Psychotherapy obviously places the burden of change on the shoulders of the patient, and by doing so ratifies both personal responsibility and a subcultural interpretation of social causation. As Kline comments, psychotherapy 'assumes that all is well in society and that if women feel depressed [as one example] there is something wrong with them. Listen to them, we can discover that perhaps there is something wrong with society' (1988: 147).

In these ways, false evidence of psychotherapy's effectiveness serves as propaganda for conservative political ideologies. As conservative dogma, the psychotherapeutic enterprise has travelled a long road from Freud's search for the pillars of civilization to apologize for social indifference. The field's institutionalized sin has been the distortion of science to advance the very forces that threatens socialization and civic cohesion. Yet it is too simple to clamour after business and profit as socially irresponsible when the attitudes that tolerate and reward the perverse creation of psychotherapy are so broadly embedded in society.

Notes

1. This finding is the result of field trips to the Bookstars in Las Vegas. Similar stores in London and New York, where life is grimmer than the tranquil oasis of Las Vegas, probably offer even more linear feet.

2. Moreover, alternatives to clinical research as methods for judging the effectiveness of psychotherapy are very suspect. Seligman's recent survey of *Consumer Reports* readers is a case in point. Both the criticisms of the survey and Seligman's response are presented in *American Psychologist* (1996).

3. This comment refers to the best of current research: Barkham et al. (1996), Shadish et al. (1997), Engels et al. (1993), Fairburn et al. (1993), Scholing and Emmelkamp (1993), Azrin et al. (1994), Mersch (1994), Reams and Friedrich (1994), Markowitz et al. (1995), Woody et al. (1995), Wiborg and Dahl (1996), Brent et al. (1997), Goenjian et al. (1997). These studies are methodologically indistinguishable from those reviewed in Epstein (1995). Perhaps because of recently constrained research budgets in the United States, they may even be somewhat weaker.

References

American Psychologist (1996) 51 (10).

Azrin, N.H., McMahon, P.T., Donohue, B., Besalel, V.A., Lapinski, K.J., Kogan, E.S., Acierno, R.E. and Galloway, E. (1994) 'Behavior therapy for drug abuse: a controlled treatment outcome study', *Behavior Research and Therapy*, 32 (8): 857–66.

Barkham, M., Rees, A., Shapiro, D.A., Stiles, W.B., Agnew, R.M., Halstead, J., Culverwell, A. and Harrington, V.M.G. (1996) 'Outcomes of time-limited psychotherapy in applied settings: replicating the Second Sheffield Psychotherapy Project', *Journal of Consulting and Clinical Psychology*, 64 (5): 1079–85.

Bergin, A.E. (1971) 'The evaluation of therapeutic outcomes', in A.E. Bergin and S.L. Garfield (eds), *Handbook of Psychotherapy and Behavior Change*. New York: John Wiley.

Bergin, A.E. and Lambert, M.J. (1978) 'The evaluation of therapeutic outcomes', in A.E. Bergin and S.L. Garfield (eds), *Handbook of Psychotherapy and Behavior Change*. New York: John Wiley.

Brent, D.A., Holder, D., Kolko, D., Birmaher, B., Baugher, M., Roth, C., Iyengar, S. and Johnson, B.A. (1997) 'A clinical psychotherapy trial for adolescent depression comparing cognitive, family, and supportive therapy', *Archives of General Psychiatry*, 54 (September): 877–85.

Dawes, R.M. (1994) *House of Cards: Psychology and Psychotherapy Built on Myth*. New York: Free Press.

Dineen, T. (1996) *Manufacturing Victims*. Montreal: Robert Davies.

Elkin, I., Shea, M.T., Watkins, J.T., Imber, S.D., Sotsky, S.M., Collins, J.F., Glass, D.R., Pilkonis, P.A., Leber, W.R., Docherty, J.P., Fiester, S.J. and Parloff, M.B. (1989) 'National Institute of Mental Health Treatment of Depression Collaborative Research Program: general effectiveness of treatments', *Archives of General Psychiatry*, 46 (November): 971–82.

Engels, G.I., Garnefski, N. and Diekstra, R.F.W. (1993) 'Efficacy of rational-emotive therapy: a quantitative analysis', *Journal of Consulting and Clinical Psychology*, 61 (6): 1083–90.

Epstein, W.M. (1984) 'Technology and social work 1: the effectiveness of psychotherapy', *Journal of Applied Social Sciences*, 8 (2): 155–75.

Epstein, W.M. (1995) *The Illusion of Psychotherapy*. New Brunswick, NJ: Transaction Publishers.

Eysenck, H.F. (1952) 'The effects of psychotherapy: an evaluation', *Journal of Consulting Psychology*, 16: 319–24.

Eysenck, H.F. (1994) 'The outcome problem in psychotherapy: what have we learned?', *Behavior Research and Therapy*, 32 (5): 477–95.

Fairburn, C.G., Jones, R., Peveler, R.C., Hope, R.A. and O'Connor, M. (1993) 'Psychotherapy and bulimia nervosa: longer-term effects of interpersonal psychotherapy, behavior therapy, and cognitive behavior therapy', *Archives of General Psychiatry*, 50 (June): 419–428.

Francher, R.T. (1995) *Cultures of Healing*. New York: W.H. Freeman.

Goenjian, A.K., Karayan, I., Pynoos, R.S., Minassian, D., Jajarian, L.M., Steinberg, A.M. and Fairbanks, L.A. (1997) 'Outcome of psychotherapy among early adolescents after trauma', *American Journal of Psychiatry*, 154 (4): 536–42.

Gross, M.L. (1978) *The Psychological Society*. New York: Random House.

Gurman, A.S. and Kniskern, D.P. (1986) 'Research on marital and family therapy: progress, perspective and prospect', in S.L. Garfield and A.E. Bergin (eds), *Handbook of Psychotherapy and Behavior Change*. New York: John Wiley.

Hartmann, M., Schulgen, A.G., Olshewski, M. and Herzog, T. (1997) 'Modeling psychotherapy outcome as event in time: an application of multistate analysis', *Journal of Consulting and Clinical Psychology*, 65 (2): 262–8.

Imber, S.D., Pilkonis, P.A., Sotsky, S.M., Elkin, I., Watkins, J.T., Collins, J.F., Shea, M.T., Leber, W.R. and Glass, D.R. (1990) 'Mode-specific effects among three treatments for depression', *Journal of Consulting and Clinical Psychology*, 58 (3): 352–9.

Kline, P. (1988) *Psychotherapy Exposed or the Emperor's New Clothes*. London: Routledge.

Lambert, M.J. and Bergin, A.E. (1994) 'The effectiveness of psychotherapy', in A.E. Bergin and S.L. Garfield (eds), *Handbook of Psychotherapy and Behavior Change*. New York: John Wiley.

Lambert, M.J., Christensen, E.R. and De Julio, S.S. (1986a) 'The assessment of psychotherapy', in A.E. Bergin and S.L. Garfield (eds), *Handbook of Psychotherapy and Behavior Change*. New York: John Wiley.

Lambert, M.J., Shapiro, D.A. and Bergin, A.E. (1986b) 'The effectiveness of psychotherapy', in A.E. Bergin and S.L. Garfield (eds), *Handbook of Psychotherapy and Behavior Change*. New York: John Wiley.

Luborsky, L., Singer, B. and Luborsky, L. (1975) 'Comparative studies of psychotherapies: is it true that "Everybody has won and all must have prizes"?', *Archives of General Psychiatry*, 32: 995–1008.

Macmillan, M. (1997) *Freud Evaluated*. Cambridge, MA: MIT Press.

Markowitz, J.C., Klerman, G.L., Clougherty, K.F., Spielman, L.A., Jacobsberg, L.B., Fishman, B., Frances, A.J., Kocsis, J.H. and Perry, S.W. (1995) *American Journal of Psychiatry*, 152 (10): 1504–9.

Masson, J.M. (1988) *Against Therapy: Emotional Tyranny and the Myth of Psychological Healing*. New York: Atheneum.

Mersch, P.P.A. (1995) 'The treatment of social phobia: the differential effectiveness of exposure in vivo and an integration of exposure in vivo, rational emotive therapy and social skills training', *Behavior Research and Therapy*, 33 (3): 259–69.

Meinert, C.L. (1986) *Clinical Trials: Design, Conduct, and Analysis*. Oxford: Oxford University Press.

Office of Technology Assessment (1980) 'The implications of cost-effectiveness analysis of medical technology', *Background Paper #3: The Efficacy and Cost of Effectiveness of Psychotherapy*. Washington, DC: Government Printing Office.

Parloff, M.B. (1978) *Assessment of Psychosocial Treatment of Mental Health Disorders: Current Status and Prospects*. Rockville, MD: Clinical Research Branch, Institutes of Mental Health.

Pope, H.G. (1997) *Psychology Astray*. Boca Raton, FL: Upton Books.

Prioleau, L., Murdock, M. and Brody, N. (1983) 'An analysis of psychotherapy versus placebo studies', *Behavioral and Brain Sciences*, 6: 275–310.

Rachman, S. (1971) *The Effects of Psychological Treatment*. Oxford: Pergamon Press.

Reams, R. and Friedrich, W. (1994) 'Efficacy of time-limited play therapy with maltreated preschoolers', *Journal of Clinical Psychology*, 50 (6): 889–99.

Rosenthal, R. and Rubin, D.B. (1978) 'Interpersonal expectancy effects: the first 345 studies', *Behavioral and Brain Sciences*, 3: 377–415.

Scholing, A. and Emmelkamp, P.M.G. (1993) 'Exposure with and without cognitive therapy for generalized social phobia: effects of individual and group treatment', *Behavior Research and Therapy*, 31 (7): 667–81.

Sexton, H. (1996) 'Process, life events, and symptomatic change in brief eclectic psychotherapy', *Journal of Consulting and Clinical Psychology*, 64 (6): 1358–65.

Shadish, W.R., Navarro, A.M., Crits-Cristoph, P., Jorm, A.F., Nietzel, M.T., Robinson, L., Svartberg, M., Matt, G.E., Siegle, G., Hazelrigg, M.D., Lyons, L.C., Prout, H.T., Smith, M.L. and Weiss, B. (1997) 'Evidence that therapy works in clinically representative conditions', *Journal of Consulting and Clinical Psychology*, 65 (3): 355–65.

Shapiro, D.A., Barkham, M., Hardy, G.E. and Morrison, L.A. (1990) 'The Second Sheffield Psychotherapy Project: rationale, design and preliminary outcome data', *British Journal of Medical Psychology*, 63: 97–108.

Smith, M.L., Glass, G.V. and Miller, T.I. (1980) *The Benefits of Psychotherapy*. Baltimore, MD: Johns Hopkins University Press.

Sotksy, S.M., Glass, D.R., Shea, T., Pilkonis, P.A., Collins, J.F., Elkin, I., Watkins, J.T., Imber, S.D., Leber, W.R., Moyer, J. and Oliveri, M.E. (1991) 'Patient predictors of response to psychotherapy and pharmacotherapy: findings in the NIMH Treatment of Depression Collaborative Research Program', *American Journal of Psychiatry*, 148 (8): 997–1008.

Stiles, W.B. and Shapiro, D.A. (1994) 'Disabuse of the drug metaphor: psychotherapy process–outcome correlations', *Journal of Consulting and Clinical Psychology*, 62 (5): 942–8.

Stuart, R.B. (1970) *Trick or Treatment*. Champaign, IL: Research Press.

Wiborg, I.M. and Dahl, A.A. (1996) 'Does brief dynamic psychotherapy reduce the relapse rate of panic disorder?', *Archives of General Psychiatry*, 53 (August): 689–94.

Woody, G.E., McLellan, A.T., Luborsky, L. and O'Brien, C.P. (1995) 'Psychotherapy in community methadone programs: a validation study', *American Journal of Psychiatry*, 152 (9): 1302–8.

9   It has been amply demonstrated that psychotherapy is effective

Stephen Saunders

Although most researchers have been convinced that the effectiveness of psychotherapy has been firmly established, others argue that research designs are flawed and that no satisfactory evidence yet exists. Psychotherapy is one of the most researched and scrutinized health care procedures ever invented, and this chapter will argue that there is a great deal of evidence indicating that it is effective. This chapter attempts to summarize the debate issue and argues that, from the perspective of scientific inquiry, psychotherapy has shown itself to be an efficacious and effective health care intervention.

A brief history of psychotherapy research

The roots of modern psychotherapy are usually traced to Sigmund Freud, who proposed that emotional symptoms could be relieved by having a particular type of conversation with a trained professional (for example, Freud, 1933/1964). Although Freud was satisfied that repeated clinical demonstrations (that is, case studies) sufficed, demands for empirical proof of the effects of psychoanalysis have endured (Freud, 1916/1963; Strupp and Howard, 1992). Eysenck reviewed 24 studies of psychotherapy and concluded that there was no evidence supporting the effectiveness of psychotherapy, and that there 'appears to be an inverse correlation between recovery and psychotherapy; the more psychotherapy, the smaller the recovery rate' (1952: 322). Both his methods and conclusions have been widely criticized (for example, Luborsky, 1954; Bergin, 1971). None the less, when the article came out, proponents of psychotherapy were forced to agree to the inescapable truth of Eysenck's observation that there was a need for better research (for example, Garfield, 1957). The report stimulated the field to evaluate, using rigorous scientific methodology, the hypothesis that there is a causal relationship between engaging in psychotherapy and mental health improvement.

Over the decades, hundreds of studies examined this issue. The science of this inquiry grew more sophisticated over the years. Initially, when treatments were compared, patients were assigned either to psychotherapy, to a no treatment group, or to a wait-list group. Assignment was typically made on the basis of whether the patient could wait for treatment (for example, Rogers and Dymond, 1954). This limited the validity and generalizability of the results. Research has become more sophisticated, many intractable problems of methodology have been overcome (Lambert and Bergin, 1992), and the conclusions to be drawn from it are both proper and justifiable.

The following will defend the status of psychotherapy research as a scientific enterprise. Evidence supporting the claim that psychotherapy is effective will be presented, and a summary of the major criticisms of this view will be reviewed and answered.

Psychotherapy research as scientific inquiry

Scientific inquiry starts with a theory, from which are derived hypotheses. To test hypotheses, constructs must be reliably and validly operationalized. Psychotherapy research has been criticized for being vague in its definitions of psychotherapy, of outcomes, and of the construct of mental health. Such criticisms are invalid.

Psychotherapy as a scientific theory

The theory that there is a causal relationship between psychotherapy and mental health improvement might be stated as follows:

> In the course of development, learning occurs at both the conscious and the unconscious levels. Learning encompasses ways of thinking about and behaving towards oneself and others. For some, early experiences establish unhealthy or maladaptive ways of feeling, thinking and/or behaving, causing *emotional problems*. Psychotherapy is a structured conversation that occurs within the context of an *empathic relationship*. Psychotherapy comprises a broad array of psychological *interventions* intended to assist the patient make or experience *changes* that will result in more healthy and adaptive ways of thinking or behaving.

According to this theory, the primary constructs of the enterprise of psychotherapy are: mental health problems; the psychotherapeutic relationship or therapeutic alliance, within which occur psychotherapeutic interventions directed at the client's understanding of self and others; and change or lack thereof in the person's mental health status. All have been scientifically operationalized.

The mental health construct

Mental health problems can be grouped into three general categories: unpleasant affective tone or general distress; symptoms related to specific disorders, such as anxiety or depression; and inability to fulfil important roles (cf. Mintz et al., 1992; Howard et al., 1993). There are numerous valid and reliable ways to measure all of these categories (Kramer and Conoley, 1992).

Psychotherapeutic alliance and interventions directed at change

The concept of the alliance has existed since the inception of psychotherapy, and there are numerous reliable and valid ways of measuring it (for example, Horvath and Greenberg, 1994). Researchers have also established reliable, replicable therapies aimed at changing negative emotions, cognitions and behaviours. For example, Luborsky (1984) developed a manual for psychoanalytic therapy, and cognitive-behavioural therapy manuals (for example, Beck et al., 1979; Steketee et al., 1982) are directed at changing maladaptive ways of thinking and behaving.

Change measurement

Methodology for evaluating change as a result of therapy continues to be improved. These include growth curve methodology, random regression modelling and clinical significance methodology (for example, Jacobson and Follette, 1985; Francis et al., 1991; Newman and Howard, 1991; Gibbons et al., 1993).

It can be seen that psychotherapy research meets the requirements of scientific inquiry. This methodology therefore allows investigation of the hypothesis, 'Psychotherapy causes positive change in a patient's mental health.'

Broad categories of psychotherapy research

Research into the effectiveness of psychotherapy can be broadly categorized into efficacy and effectiveness research (for example, Seligman, 1995; Howard et al., 1996).

Efficacy research

Efficacy research asks the question, 'Under controlled circumstances, does this particular procedure produce any particular effect above and beyond a comparison procedure?' The usual procedure for establishing efficacy is the randomized clinical trial (RCT).

In conducting an RCT, patients are randomly assigned to one of two or more interventions that are to be compared. One of these conditions may be a placebo-attention condition, wherein putative 'active ingredients' (for example, cognitive restructuring, behavioural activation) are withheld. More commonly, patients are assigned to competing psychotherapies (for example, cognitive therapy versus psychodynamic therapy). For example, Jacobson and colleagues (1996) partitioned cognitive-behavioural treatment (CBT) into cognitive restructuring and behavioural activation, and they compared therapies that emphasized either of these techniques.

In the usual RCT, patients are carefully selected to control for excessive patient variability. Therapists are trained to conduct a treatment that has been standardized (see above). By maximizing the integrity of putative therapeutic ingredients and minimizing variability of confounding variables, these experiments minimize threats to internal validity (Cook and Campbell, 1979; Kazdin, 1994).

Effectiveness research

The second broad category of psychotherapy research has been labelled 'effectiveness' research (Howard et al., 1996). It asks a related but important question: 'Can an intervention be conducted and produce an effect in the real world?' This methodology emphasizes external validity or generalizability. Psychotherapy is allowed to proceed in its typical, non-controlled manner (that is, a variety of patients, a variety of treatments, community-based settings), effects are monitored, and alternative explanations for observed changes are identified, evaluated and – if possible – eliminated.

When seeking to establish the validity of a health care procedure, both efficacy and effectiveness research are vital (Clarke, 1995). A procedure that works in the laboratory must be acceptable to patients and applicable by practitioners. The following review shows that both have been amply established.

Efficacy research

There are hundreds of studies confirming the efficacy of psychotherapy. This chapter reviews a prototypical and exemplary study and a recent meta-analysis of efficacy studies.

In the Treatment of Depression Collaborative Research Program TDCRP), depressed outpatients ($N = 239$) were randomly assigned to one of four treatment conditions. The primary aim was to compare the efficacies of two well-standardized psychotherapies for depression: cognitive therapy (CT; Beck et al., 1979) and interpersonal psychotherapy (IPT; Klerman et al., 1984). In an attempt to establish that the therapies were specifically responsible for any observed change, the researchers compared these to 'a standard reference condition' of known efficacy, the anti-depressant imipramine hydrochloride. Finally, in order to determine whether these 'active' treatments would produce change above and beyond enhanced hope and attention from a clinician, the fourth condition was a drug placebo plus clinical management, which included weekly sessions, with the psychiatrist, of general support and encouragement. These four conditions were explicitly specified in treatment manuals and were conducted by experienced therapists. Valid and reliable measures of depression, its associated cognitions and social functioning were collected across the course of the study (Elkin, 1994). Analyses of the TDCRP dataset (for example, Gibbons et al., 1993) indicated that patients improved in all four conditions, that the psychotherapies were not significantly different, that the psychotherapies were superior to placebo, and that the psychotherapies were not inferior to the drug treatment in reducing symptoms of depression (although therapy produced slower response rates than drug treatment).

Similar efficacy research has established the utility of numerous treatments for a variety of disorders, including anxiety disorders (for example, Barlow et al., 1989), bulimia nervosa (for example, Fairburn et al., 1993), marital problems (for example, Jacobson and Follette, 1985), sexual dysfunction (for example, LoPiccolo and Stock, 1986), obsessive compulsive disorder (for example, Steketee et al., 1982), borderline personality disorder (for example, Linehan et al., 1991), and a variety of childhood and adolescent disorders (for example, Kazdin et al., 1990).

The best way to summarize the plethora of efficacy research evaluating psychotherapy is through meta-analysis. Meta-analysis (cf. Glass, 1976; Rosenthal and Rubin, 1986) is a method for summarizing and integrating research. Numerous individual studies are quantified and coded so that they can be compared with one another. Typically, an effect size (ES) is calculated for each study, indicating the size of the difference between the treated and untreated groups. Smith et al. (1980) summarized 475 studies of psychotherapy and calculated an average ES of .85, indicating that the average treated person would have an outcome equal or superior to 85 per cent of the average untreated person. Hundreds of meta-analyses of psychotherapy have been conducted since then, and they vary according to whether they focus on a particular disorder (for example, Scotti et al., 1991), a particular type of treatment (Svartberg and Stiles, 1991), a particular patient group (for example, Weisz et al., 1987), or a particular type of study (for example, Greenberg et al., 1992). Most meta-analyses have reached the same conclusion: psychotherapy is effective in helping people change.

Lipsey and Wilson (1993) conducted what can only be described as a meta-analysis of meta-analyses of psychotherapy research. They examined 'the effects of treatments that are based on manipulation of psychological variables and are intended to induce psychological change, whether emotional, attitudinal, cognitive, or behavioral' (1993: 1182). They selected those 156 meta-analyses in which treatments were compared to control conditions. This requirement yielded a sample encompassing over 9,000 studies and more than one million patients. They calculated a mean ES of .47. This is considerably larger than the mean ES of a plethora of widely used, well-established medical interventions, such as heart bypass surgery, and they concluded that 'a strongly favorable conclusion about the efficacy of well-developed psychological treatment is justified' (1993: 1200).

Effectiveness research

High levels of experimental control over naturally occurring human interactions (such as psychotherapy) are difficult to achieve (Kline, 1992). Moreover, when such control is achieved, the resulting interaction may be highly unlike the naturally occurring event itself. Thus, efficacious treatments developed within the controlled environment of the psychotherapy research laboratory may not reflect psychotherapy as actually practised in everyday clinical settings. Efficacy must be translated into effectiveness within the uncontrolled, sometimes chaotic world of the practising clinician (Weisz et al., 1992, 1995). Effectiveness research is the necessary follow-up stage to efficacy research, as it asks: 'Does this new, experimentally validated treatment work in practice?'

There is little control exerted in effectiveness studies, in order to mimic, as closely as possible, actual practice (Clarke, 1995). As in actual practice, effectiveness studies follow the progress of patients who choose their treatment. There are few if any screening procedures, and many patients have more than one diagnosis. As in actual practice, therapy proceeds until the patient, sometimes in collaboration with the therapist, decides to terminate. In the absence of controlled conditions, it may be difficult to claim that the observed effect was due to the implemented procedure, that is, there are serious threats to internal validity. Such 'quasi-experiments' therefore need to be replicated to disqualify competing, alternative explanations of any observed results (Cook and Campbell, 1979).

In a type of meta-analysis of effectiveness studies, Howard and colleagues (1986) compiled and reanalysed data available from studies that included over 2,400 patients reported in studies covering a 30-year period. They found a lawful linear relationship between the number of sessions and the probability of patient improvement. To be specific, they reported that by about the eighth session, almost half of patients are measurably improved, and that by session 26, half of the remaining patients have improved. This 'dose–effect' finding has been replicated, and researchers have demonstrated that different disorders respond at different rates (for example, Horowitz et al., 1988; Kadera et al., 1996). For example, Kopta and colleagues (1994) found that over 75 per cent of chronically distressed patients are improved by session 52, whereas less than 60 per cent of characterologically disturbed clients are improved by then. These and other studies (for example,

Seligman, 1995) have established that psychotherapy as conducted in the real world is effective.

The interminable debate

Psychotherapy has been called upon, time and again, to defend itself (for example, Kline, 1992; Epstein, 1995). Researchers have done so with vigour and scientific clarity. None the less, many critics (for example, Dawes, 1994) contend that the question 'Does psychotherapy work?' has yet to be answered satisfactorily. Some of the most common criticisms of psychotherapy research are now reviewed and answered.

Psychotherapy is a placebo effect

Critics argue that being in treatment is enough of a 'placebo' for patients to get better. The placebo effect comprises expecting to feel better, feeling more hopeful, and experiencing a caring relationship. The placebo effect is powerful, but critics (for example, Kline, 1992; Epstein, 1995) are incorrect to state that it presents a problem for health care researchers. Indeed, to assert that placebo effects are problematic is to reveal a profound misunderstanding of the nature of health care.

The so-called 'placebo effect' is an integral aspect of all effective health care. Recent evidence from medical literature indicates that patients who adhere to treatment, even when that treatment is a placebo, have better health outcomes than poorly adherent patients. In other words, patients who comply with treatment because they trust that the treatment may work often obtain more benefit than patients given an active drug (see Horwitz and Horwitz, 1993). Outcomes of treatment – whether psychological or medical – depend on non-specific therapeutic effects, such as hope and the quality of the relationship between patient and clinician. This is reflected in the admonition to physicians to de-emphasize compliance and emphasize collaboration: 'It is not patients who should comply with their doctors' demands, but doctors who should comply with their patients' informed and considered desires' (Holm, 1993).

Even so, psychotherapeutic interventions have been shown time and again to be superior to placebo alone. The TDCRP (Elkin, 1994) included an attention-placebo condition that improved significantly, but the psychotherapy groups did better. Lipsey and Wilson (1993) explicitly explored the placebo effect in their meta-analysis and concluded that psychological interventions have an effect above and beyond the substantial placebo effect (see also Lambert and Bergin, 1994). Instead of demanding that it be eliminated, it is time to recognize that the so-called 'placebo effect' is, in fact, part and parcel of all effective treatments. Rather than having to eliminate it as a confounding variable in studying the effects of psychotherapy, it needs to be better understood, appreciated, explained and even manipulated (Wilkins, 1986).

Ruling out spontaneous remission

Critics (for example, Eysenck, 1952) argue that emotionally disturbed individuals will, in due time, get better all by themselves. This appears to be true, at least to some degree, for mild to moderate problems (Lambert, 1976). One feels compelled to point out, however, that being mentally ill is a miserable experience (for example, Wells et al., 1989), that serious mental illness can last for years or even a lifetime in the absence of intervention (for example, Keller et al., 1992), that many individuals suffer for many years before seeking help for their problems (Saunders, 1993), and that psychotherapy can achieve in two months what remits 'naturally' in two years (McNeilly and Howard, 1991).

All studies are flawed to some degree, therefore nothing can be known

Critics have argued that it is simply too difficult or even impossible to conduct the perfect psychotherapy study. Therefore, all studies are flawed and can tell us nothing about the effects of psychotherapy. Kline stated: 'I believe that, given these difficulties, it is exceedingly difficult to draw any conclusions concerning the effectiveness of psychotherapy' (1992: 98). Flowing from this argument comes a second argument: all studies are flawed, therefore meta-analyses of studies are worthless (for example, Epstein, 1995).

The absence of the perfect study, however, does not preclude the presence of proof. Tobacco sellers and their ilk in the US have argued that the absence of controlled experiments on human subjects precludes concluding that smoking is bad for one's health. Most reasonable persons are fairly well convinced of this none the less, however, as a plethora of various non-controlled, quasi-experimental and replicated research shows. In short, the evidence is not gathered in perfect experimental conditions, but such conditions are in fact rare in science, and such conditions are unnecessary for understanding nature. The same goes for psychotherapy research.

Concluding remarks

> Despite hundreds of studies and oft-repeated demonstrations that people who undergo psychotherapy of one form or another benefit from it, pervasive skepticism persists, and each additional study . . . is treated as if it were the first. (Strupp, 1996: 1017)

Summary of argument

This chapter, it is hoped, has demonstrated that the evidence for the effectiveness of psychotherapy as a health intervention is overwhelming. Hundreds of studies and countless reviews have all concluded the same thing, succinctly stated by Lambert and Bergin: 'Psychotherapy is effective at helping people achieve their goals and overcome their psychopathology at a rate that is faster and more substantial than changes that result from the clients' natural healing processes and supportive elements in the environment' (1992: 363).

None the less, there has been a seeming upsurge in all-out attacks on the validity of psychotherapy as a health intervention (for example, Dawes, 1994; Epstein, 1995) and on the superiority of medications to treat specific disorders (for example, Depression Guideline Panel, 1993). It may be impossible to convince sceptics, even if one were to point out that scientifically trained, sceptical individuals have repeatedly concluded that therapy works. It is hoped that the reader will be convinced, via a convergence of evidence that points to the same conclusion, that there is adequate empirical evidence supporting the efficacy and effect of psychotherapy for the treatment of a broad range of emotional disorders.

Further research directions

Despite effective treatments, substantial numbers of patients either fail to improve or improve to an inadequate degree. Understanding treatment failure and broadening the effectiveness of current treatments are critical agendas for the field (for example, Wilson, 1996). Psychotherapy researchers need to address issues of which treatment for which problem or client (for example, treatment matching), the issue of mediating versus moderating variables (for example, how does the therapeutic alliance work to allow or promote change), and the issue of further delineating the characteristics of effective versus ineffective treatments.

References

Barlow, D.H., Craske, M.G., Cerny, J.Z.A. and Klosko, J. (1989) 'Behavioral treatment of panic disorder', *Behavioral Therapy*, 20: 261–82.

Beck, A.T., Rush, A.J., Shaw, B.F. and Emery, G. (1979) *Cognitive Therapy of Depression: A Treatment Manual*. New York: Guilford Press.

Bergin, A.E. (1971) 'The evaluation of therapeutic outcomes', in A.E. Bergin and S.L. Garfield (eds), *Handbook of Psychotherapy and Behavior Change: An Empirical Analysis*. New York: John Wiley.

Clarke, G.N. (1995) 'Improving the transition from basic efficacy research to effectiveness studies: methodological issues and procedures', *Journal of Consulting and Clinical Psychology*, 63: 718–25.

Cook, T.D. and Campbell, D.T. (1979) *Quasi-Experimentation: Design and Analysis Issues for Field Settings*. Boston: Houghton Mifflin.

Dawes, R.M. (1994) *House of Cards: Psychology and Psychotherapy Built on Myth.* New York: Free Press.

Depression Guideline Panel (1993) *Depression in Primary Care, Vol. 2: Treatment of Major Depression* (Clinical Practice Guideline, No. 5; AHCPR Publication No. 93-0551). Rockville, MD: US Department of Health and Human Services, Public Health Service, Agency for Health Care Policy and Research.

Elkin, I. (1994) 'The NIMH Treatment of Depression Collaborative Research Program: where we began and where we are', in A.E. Bergin and S.L. Garfield (eds), *Handbook of Psychotherapy and Behavior Change* (4th edn). New York: Wiley.

Epstein, W.M. (1995) *The Illusion of Psychotherapy.* New Brunswick, NJ: Transaction Publishers.

Eysenck, H.J. (1952) 'The effects of psychotherapy: an evaluation', *Journal of Consulting Psychology,* 16: 319–24.

Fairburn, C.G., Jones, R., Peveler, R.C., Hope, R.A. and O'Connor, M. (1993) 'Psychotherapy and bulimia nervosa: longer-term effects of interpersonal psychotherapy, behavior therapy, and cognitive behavior therapy', *Archives of General Psychiatry,* 50: 419–28.

Francis, D.J., Fletcher, J.M., Stuebing, K.K., Davidson, K.C. and Thompson, N.M. (1991) 'Analysis of change: modeling individual growth', *Journal of Consulting and Clinical Psychology,* 59: 27–37.

Freud, S. (1916/1963) 'Analytic therapy', in J. Strachey (ed.) *The Standard Edition of the Complete Psychological Works of Sigmund Freud,* Vol. 16. London: Hogarth Press.

Freud, S. (1933/1964) 'New introductory lectures', in J. Strachey (ed.), *The Standard Edition of the Complete Psychological Works of Sigmund Freud,* Vol. 22. London: Hogarth Press.

Garfield, S.L. (1957) *Introductory Clinical Psychology.* New York: Macmillan.

Gibbons, R.D., Hedeker, D., Elkin, I., Waternaux, C., Kraemer, H.C., Greenhouse, J.B., Shea, M.D., Imber, S.D., Sotksy, S.M. and Watkins, J.T. (1993) 'Some conceptual and statistical issues in the analysis of longitudinal psychiatric data: application to the NIMH Treatment of Depression Collaborative Research Program dataset', *Archives of General Psychiatry,* 50: 739–50.

Glass, G.V. (1976) 'Primary, secondary, and meta-analysis of research', *Educational Researcher,* 5: 3–8.

Greenberg, R.P., Greenberg, M.D., Bornstein, R.F. and Fisher, S. (1992) 'A meta-analysis of antidepressant outcome under "blinder" conditions', *Journal of Consulting and Clinical Psychology,* 60: 664–9.

Holm, S. (1993) 'What is wrong with compliance?', *Journal of Medical Ethics,* 19: 108–10.

Horowitz, L.M., Rosenberg, S.E., Baer, B.A., Ureño, G. and Villasenor, V.S. (1988) 'Inventory of interpersonal problems: psychometric properties and clinical applications', *Journal of Consulting and Clinical Psychology,* 56: 885–92.

Horvath, A.O. and Greenberg, L.S. (eds) (1994) *The Working Alliance: Theory, Research, and Practice.* New York: John Wiley.

Horwitz, R.I. and Horwitz, S.M. (1993) 'Adherence to treatment and health outcomes', *Archives of Internal Medicine,* 153: 1863–8.

Howard, K.I., Kopta, S.M., Krause, M.S. and Orlinsky, D.E. (1986) 'The dose–effect relationship in psychotherapy', *American Psychologist,* 41: 159–64.

Howard, K.I., Lueger, R.J., Maling, M.S. and Martinovich, Z. (1993) 'A phase model of psychotherapy outcome: causal mediation of change', *Journal of Consulting and Clinical Psychology,* 61: 678–85.

Howard, K.I., Moras, K., Brill, P.L., Martinovich, Z. and Lutz, W. (1996) 'Evaluation of psychotherapy: efficacy, effectiveness, and patient progress', *American Psychologist,* 51: 1059–64.

Jacobson, N.S. and Follette, W.C. (1985) 'Clinical significance of improvement resulting from behavioral marital therapy components', *Behavior Therapy*, 16: 249–62.

Jacobson, N.S., Dobson, K.S., Truax, P.A., Addis, M.E., Koerner, K.K., Gollan, J.K., Gortner, E., Prince, S.E. (1996) 'A component analysis of cognitive-behavioral treatment for depression', *Journal of Consulting and Clinical Psychology*, 64: 295–304.

Kadera, S.W., Lambert, M.J. and Andrews, A.A. (1996) 'How much therapy is really enough? A session-by-session analysis of the psychotherapy dose–effect relationship', *Journal of Psychotherapy Practice and Research*, 5: 132–51.

Kazdin, A.E. (1994) 'Methodology, design, and evaluation in psychotherapy research', in A.E. Bergin and S.L. Garfield (eds), *Handbook of Psychotherapy and Behavior Change* (4th edn). New York: John Wiley.

Kazdin, A.E., Bass, D., Ayers, W.A. and Rodgers, A. (1990) 'Empirical and clinical focus of child and adolescent psychotherapy research', *Journal of Consulting and Clinical Psychology*, 58: 729–40.

Keller, M.B., Lavori, P.W., Mueller, T.I., Endicott, J., Coryell, W., Hirschfield, R.M.A. and Shea, T. (1992) 'Time to recovery, chronicity, and levels of psychopathology in major depression: a five-year prospective follow-up of 431 subjects', *Archives of General Psychiatry*, 49: 809–16.

Klerman, G.L., Weissman, M.M., Rounsaville, B. and Chevron, E. (1984) *Interpersonal Psychotherapy of Depression (IPT)*. New York: Basic Books.

Kline, P. (1992) 'Problems of methodology in studies of psychotherapy', in W. Dryden and C. Feltham (eds), *Psychotherapy and Its Discontents*. Philadelphia: Open University Press.

Kopta, S.M., Howard, K.I., Lowry, J.L. and Beutler, L.E. (1994) 'Patterns of symptomatic recovery in time-unlimited psychotherapy', *Journal of Consulting and Clinical Psychology*, 62: 1009–16.

Kramer, J.J. and Conoley, J.C. (eds) (1992) *The Eleventh Mental Measurement Yearbook*. Lincoln, NB: Buros Institute of Mental Measurements.

Lambert, M.J. (1976) 'Spontaneous remission in adult neurotic disorders: a revision and summary', *Psychological Bulletin*, 83: 107–19.

Lambert, M.J. and Bergin, A.E. (1992) 'Achievements and limitations of psychotherapy research', in D.K. Freedheim (ed.), *History of Psychotherapy: A Century of Change*. Washington DC: American Psychological Association.

Lambert, M.J. and Bergin, A.E. (1994) 'The effectiveness of psychotherapy', in A.E. Bergin and S.L. Garfield (eds), *Handbook of Psychotherapy and Behavior Change* (4th edn). New York: John Wiley.

Linehan, M.M., Armstrong, H.E., Suarez, A., Allmon, D. and Heard, H.L. (1991) 'Cognitive behavioral treatment of chronically parasuicidal borderline patients', *Archives of General Psychiatry*, 48: 1060–4.

Lipsey, M.W. and Wilson, D.B. (1993) 'The efficacy of psychological, educational, and behavioral treatment: confirmation from meta-analysis', *American Psychologist*, 48: 1181–209.

LoPiccolo, J. and Stock, W.E. (1986) 'Treatment of sexual dysfunction', *Journal of Consulting and Clinical Psychology*, 54: 158–67.

Luborsky, L. (1954) 'A note on Eysenck's article, "The effects of psychotherapy: an evaluation"', *British Journal of Psychology*, 45: 129–31.

Luborsky, L. (1984) *Principles of Psychoanalytic Psychotherapy: A Manual for Supportive-Expressive (SE) Treatment*. New York: Basic Books.

McNeilly, C.L. and Howard, K.I. (1991) 'The effects of psychotherapy: a reevaluation based on dosage', *Psychotherapy Research*, 1: 74–8.

Mintz, J., Mintz, L.I., Arruda, M.J. and Hwang, S.S. (1992) 'Treatments of depression and the functional capacity to work', *Archives of General Psychiatry*, 49: 761–8.

Newman, F.L. and Howard, K.I. (1991) 'Introduction to the special section on seeking new clinical research methods', *Journal of Consulting and Clinical Psychology*, 59: 8–11.

Rogers, C.R. and Dymond, R. (1954) *Psychotherapy and Personality Change*. Chicago: University of Chicago Press.

Rosenthal, R. and Rubin, D.B. (1986) 'Meta-analytic procedures for combining studies with multiple effect sizes', *Psychological Bulletin*, 99: 400–6.

Saunders, S.M. (1993) 'Applicants' experience of the process of seeking psychotherapy', *Psychotherapy*, 30: 554–64.

Scotti, J.R., Evans, I.M., Meyer, L.H. and Walker, P. (1991) 'A meta-analysis of intervention research with problem behavior: treatment validity and standards of practice', *American Journal on Mental Retardation*, 96: 233–56.

Seligman, M.E.P. (1995) 'The effectiveness of psychotherapy: the *Consumer Reports* study', *American Psychologist*, 50: 965–74.

Smith, M.L., Glass, G.V. and Miller, T.I. (1980) *The Benefits of Psychotherapy*. Baltimore, MD: Johns Hopkins University Press.

Steketee, G., Foa, E.B. and Grayson, J.B. (1982) 'Recent advances in the behavioral treatment of obsessive-compulsives', *Archives of General Psychiatry*, 39: 1365–71.

Strupp, H.H. (1996) 'The tripartite model and the *Consumer Reports* study', *American Psychologist*, 51: 1017–24.

Strupp, H.H. and Howard, K.I. (1992) 'A brief history of psychotherapy research', in D.K. Freedheim (ed.), *History of Psychotherapy: A Century of Change*. Washington, DC: American Psychological Association.

Svartberg, M. and Stiles, T. (1991) 'Comparative effect of short-term psycho-dynamic psychotherapy: a meta-analysis', *Journal of Consulting and Clinical Psychology*, 59: 704–14.

Weisz, J.R., Weiss, B. and Donenberg, G.R. (1992) 'The lab versus the clinic: effects of children and adolescent psychotherapy', *American Psychologist*, 47: 1578–85.

Weisz, J.R., Donenberg, G.R., Han, S.S. and Weiss, B. (1995) 'Bridging the gap between laboratory and clinic in child and adolescent psychotherapy', *Journal of Consulting and Clinical Psychology*, 63: 688–701.

Weisz, J.R., Weiss, B., Alicke, M.D. and Klotz, M.L. (1987) 'Effectiveness of psychotherapy with children and adolescents: a meta-analysis for clinicians', *Journal of Consulting and Clinical Psychology*, 55: 542–9.

Wells, K.B., Stewart, A., Hays, R.D., Burnam, A., Rogers, W., Daniels, M., Berry, S., Greenfield, S. and Ware, J. (1989) 'The functioning and well-being of depressed patients: results from the medical outcomes study', *Journal of the American Medical Association*, 262: 914–19.

Wilkins, W. (1986) 'Placebo problems in psychotherapy research: social-psychological alternatives to chemotherapy concepts', *American Psychologist*, 41: 551–6.

Wilson, G.T. (1996) 'Treatment of bulimia nervosa: when CBT fails', *Behavior Research and Therapy*, 34: 197–212.

10   The main change agent in effective psychotherapy is specific technique and skill

Albert Ellis

I shall perhaps be taking a peculiar or 'perverse' view in this chapter – namely that the relationships between the therapist and client is often, but definitely not always, a main change agent in effective psychotherapy *if*. If what? *If* the therapist has a specific theory and *if* he or she has workable techniques and skills, including social and persuasive skills, to bring to the therapeutic relationship.

Am I cavilling in taking this and/also rather than either/or position? I think not. For I doubt whether any either/or position, especially in a complex field like therapy, is adequate. As I have said for many years, therapy takes many guises (and disguises). It is exceptionally multifaceted and includes procedures overloaded with relationships – such as sessions where one client relates to two or more therapists; and such as group therapy sessions where one therapist intensely relates to eight or ten clients. It also – believe it nor not! – includes forms of therapy where clients, and sometimes a large number of clients, have no personal or human relationship with a therapist, but significantly change their thoughts, feelings and actions when they 'relate' to a book, an audio-visual cassette, a computer – or even to a guru who has been dead for 500 years!

Therapy, then, is almost infinitely varied. So are therapists! Thus, one therapist is cool, another cold, another warm, and another very warm. One says practically nothing for many months, another compulsively talks; one dialogues, another incessantly monologues. One therapist rigorously sticks to conversation; another discreetly keeps touching clients; still another has passionate sex with his or her clients. One therapist is overwhelmingly cognitive with almost all clients; another is exceptionally emotional; still another is one-sidedly behavioural.

What the devil, then, *is* psychotherapy? A good question! It is obviously many things to many different therapists – and to their clients. For what the given therapist does can easily be given widely different interpretations by different clients – or even by the same client on different occasions. Thus, when a therapist asks a client about her sex life, she may see this as nicely teaching her to become more orgasmic, as arousing her more than she wants to be aroused, as showing her that sex is shameful, or as revealing he's trying to sneakily seduce her.

Relationship itself has many different forms and meanings in therapy. Like Carl Rogers, I have always tried to give my clients unconditional acceptance, or what Rogers termed 'unconditional positive regard'. I therefore show them that I fully accept them as *persons* even when I deplore many of their behaviours. Some of my clients really see this and appreciate it. But others misinterpret what I am doing and wrongly conclude that I like or love them personally (which I rarely do); or that I hate their behaviour and therefore loathe them (which is definitely not true); or that I accept them because they are bright and competent (which is conditional acceptance, which I am definitely trying to avoid doing).

So it goes! Therapists use techniques, including relationship with their clients, because *they* think these will work. Clients interpret and for themselves use the therapist's techniques because of what *they* get – or think they get – out of them, and the twain often meet and produce 'effective' results. But even when this happens it is quite unclear why a particular method *sometimes* worked for *some* clients *some* of the time.

Just a few of the important variables to consider here are:

1   What the therapist says and how the client takes it.
2   What the therapist doesn't say – and how a client takes this omission.
3   What the client says and how the therapist takes it.
4   What the client doesn't say – and how the therapist takes it.
5   How the client reacts to how the therapist reacts to what the client says.
6   How the therapist reacts to how the client reacts to what the therapist says.

Et cetera!

Let me now address the main theme of this chapter and make a case for my theses: namely the main change in effective psychotherapy is specific therapeutic theory and the therapist's technique and skill to apply this theory.

History of the importance of therapeutic theory and technique

Early therapy – such as the philosophic therapies of the ancient Asians (especially Confucius, Gautama Buddha and Lao-Tsu) and of the ancient Greeks and Romans (especially Epicurus, Epictetus and Marcus Aurelius) – largely insisted that personality change stems from having a good theory of human disturbance and change and the teaching of effective techniques and skills so that people can use this theory to minimize their disturbances. Modern psychotherapy, beginning with Charcot, Janet and Freud, and continuing with Adler, Jung, Perls, May, Kelly, Ellis, Beck and others, largely continued this psychoeducational view of therapy; and it still is very important.

Many of the older therapists – especially Freud, with his emphasis on the transference – included important interpersonal and relationship elements in their theory and practice of therapy; but in the 1940s several therapists – such as Klein, Sullivan and Rogers – stressed them more than ever. Rogers (1957) went to extremes and insisted that a fairly close relationship between a therapist and her or his client is a 'necessary and sufficient' condition of therapeutic personality change.

During the last two decades a good deal of research has largely supported the position that the main change agent – or at least *a* main change agent – in effective psychotherapy is the relationship between therapist and client. Another body of research has also backed up Frank's (1985) suggestion that non-specific or common factors, including relationship factors, are significant ingredients in successful therapy.

Evidence against the theory that the main change agent in effective therapy is the client–therapist relationship

As I shall note later, although *a* main change agent in effective therapy is the client–therapist relationship, there is considerable evidence that it is often not *the* main agent, and certainly not – as Rogers claimed – a 'necessary and sufficient' condition for therapeutic change. Here is some of the evidence:

1   Probably millions of people over the centuries have made a remarkable personality change by listening to a lecture, a sermon, a teacher, a friend or an acquaintance, taking to heart the message received – yes, whether it was delivered emotionally or unemotionally.

2   Other millions have changed through reading a papyrus, pamphlet, article, book, computer messages or other written statement.

3   Millions of people today change by listening to audio cassettes, records, CDs, audio-visual cassettes, telephone messages, and so on.

4   Millions of people, over the centuries and in recent times, have significantly and sometimes radically changed by having some important, dramatic or even everyday experience, many of which do not involve other people. Thus, they experience an accident or illness, a near-death occurrence, a success or a failure, a view from a mountain top, a confinement, a visit to a museum, or any number of events that encourage them to see themselves and the world differently. People can be – and often are – constructive and creative in changing themselves: with or without help from others.

5   Rogers (1957) gives several specific conditions for clients to experience with therapists for therapeutic change to occur:

(a) Two persons must be in psychological contact.
(b) The client must be in a state of incongruence, being vulnerable or anxious.
(c) 'The therapist should be, within the confines of this relationship, a congruent, genuine integrated person' (1957: 828).
(d) The therapist must experience unconditional positive regard for the client.
(e) The therapist 'is experiencing an accurate, empathic understanding of the client's awareness of his own experience' (1957: 829).
(f) The client perceives, 'to a minimal degree, the acceptance and empathy which the therapist experiences for him' (1957: 829).

Granted that these six therapeutic conditions are usually desirable, obviously thousands of therapists have considerably helped their clients when several of these conditions – or even all of them – did not exist. In fact, points (c) and (d) in the foregoing list frequently don't exist, but I have seen many clients who benefited from their previous therapy sessions in spite of their therapists' lacking these traits.

6   Many therapists – not to mention mentors, teachers and religious leaders – consciously and unconsciously ignore Rogerian aspects of therapy and emphasize the other aspects – such as dogmatic moral teachings or Zen Buddhist critical and confusing tactics. None the less, some of their clients and students remarkably improve!

7   Many therapists, because of their own personalities or for other reasons, follow conditions and procedures which oppose Rogers' and which are almost opposite to what most therapists consider 'good' attitudes. Thus, they are in poor psychological contact with their clients; are severely disturbed; are incongruent and unintegrated; are often hostile to their clients; and are autistic and unempathic. I agree that such therapists usually do little good and much harm. But not always! I have seen some cases where they considerably helped their clients in these 'untherapeutic' ways.

Evidence for the theory that the main agent in effective therapy is the client-centred relationship

As noted above, a large number of research studies have indicated that the main agent in effective therapy is the client-centred relationship. Among other things, these studies have tended to show the following:

1   The process of therapy is shortened when good client–therapist relationships are achieved and maintained.
2   Various kinds of breaches of the client–therapist relationship block progress or help bring therapy to an end.

3   Therapy progress is deepened and extended when clients feel that they have a good therapeutic relationship.
4   As Frank (1985) has said, it is not so much what the therapist tells the client but the fact that he or she believes in a certain method and persuades the client to believe in it too that leads to therapeutic change. The *way* that the therapy is put across rather than the content that is put across is what really matters.

Why I disagree with the findings that a good therapeutic relationship leads to more effective therapy

I disagree with the findings for several reasons:

1   Practically all the many studies of therapy that have been done, as I said in 1972 (Ellis, 1972) and still continue to point out, ask clients how they *feel* better rather than probing to see if they actually *get* better. When they get better, I prejudicedly insist, they accomplish several things:

(a)   Reduce their main presenting symptom (for example, public speaking anxiety).
(b)   Reduce their related, though perhaps not as presenting, symptoms (for example, social anxiety and test-taking anxiety).
(c)   Maintain their reduced symptoms several years later.
(d)   Rarely experience severe symptoms again even when serious adversities occur in their lives.

2   If I am right about this, people fairly easily feel better – as Frank (1985) has noted – when they are carefully heard and fully accepted by a therapist, when this therapist is confident that his or her theory and practice is effective, and when he or she convinces the client that this particular therapy works. So this kind of therapeutic relationship quite often helps people feel better – even when therapists use radically different techniques.

3   In addition, because clients are usually over-focused on failures, rejections and discomforts, and also frequently overly concentrated on their disturbed feelings, many kinds of distraction therapies often help them feel better – including meditation, yoga, relaxation methods, biofeedback, sports, recreations, work and almost anything – including therapy itself – that they find absorbing. Relationships and distraction therapy, however, mainly cover up and side-track people from their basic disturbance-creating philosophies.

In terms of rational emotive behaviour therapy (REBT), disturbed individuals have several core absolute musts and demands which largely create their emotional-behavioural dysfunctioning: notably, 'I must do well at important tasks and win the approval of significant others or I am an inadequate person!' 'Other people must treat me kindly and fairly or they are rotten humans!' 'Conditions must give me what I really want and never seriously deprive me or else the world is awful, I can't stand it, and it will always be that rotten way!' Unless clients – and other people – see these musturbatory philosophies and work hard and persistently – cognitively, emotively and behaviourally – to replace them with preferences, they rarely will make themselves get better even though they manage to feel better on many occasions (Ellis, 1994, 1996; Ellis and Dryden, 1997; Ellis et al., 1997).

4 Relationship therapy – especially when it is Rogerian – is designed to help people unconditionally accept themselves *whether or not* they succeed in important areas of their lives and *whether or not* they are approved by significant others. This is what unconditional positive regard or unconditional self-acceptance (USA) means. Actually, it rarely accomplishes this. First, therapists rarely follow Rogers' rules and almost always give conditional acceptance. They respect, honour and like their clients largely because these clients have good traits: such as intelligence, niceness, persistence and hard work to accomplish therapeutic goals. Second – and perhaps more important – even when therapists are unconditionally accepting, as I think Rogers himself almost always was, practically all their clients wrongly jump to the conclusion that they are okay as persons *because* their therapist fully accepts them. They base their own acceptance *on* that of their therapist's respect. They then, of course, only achieve *conditional* self-acceptance!

USA is exceptionally hard for people to achieve, because it includes two ideas which humans are both biologically and sociologically prone to reject. The first idea is the existentialist notion that we have a choice in rating ourselves as persons and can decide to rate ourselves as 'good' when we do 'good' things and 'bad' when we do 'bad' ones. But that won't work very well because we are all very fallible humans, will often do 'bad' acts, and therefore will frequently view ourselves as 'bad' or 'worthless' people, and thereby depress ourselves. Therefore, a much more practical solution to the problem of human worth is for us to *choose* to say – and really *believe* – 'I am good because I am alive and human. I am good because I am me.' This is a decision that will work because if we think we are good because we are alive and human we will only be 'non-good' or 'bad' when we are dead. A pretty safe decision!

Even better than this philosophically – because it includes fewer assumptions or definitions – is the idea of human worth that REBT teaches and that we can all choose to follow: 'I *am* not "good" and I *am* not "bad", because these statements are overgeneralizations. I am a *person who* during my lifetime does many "good" things – which are my and my culture's chosen goals and purposes – and who does many "bad" things – which sabotage my and my culture's goals and purposes. So I will not give any global rating to my self, my being or my person, but shall keep rating my many individual thoughts, feelings and behaviours.'

These *chosen* philosophies of USA, I hypothesize, will work better for more people more of the time than the usual forms of self-rating that clients choose and that frequently lead them to self-denigration, self-hatred and depression. Therefore they appear to be excellent goals for effective therapy.

Can they be achieved without any form of therapy? Yes, for a few people seem to arrive at them on their own, largely through thinking about their life experiences. Can they be achieved through a therapist's modelling them and giving clients unconditional acceptance? Yes, because a few clients seem to conclude, 'Because my therapist fully accepts and respects me, I can do this for myself. So I will work at thinking through and acting on this unusual philosophy of unconditional self-acceptance.'

Can people achieve USA by learning about it, its value, and methods of achieving it, through educational means – books, articles, cassettes, lectures, sermons and workshops? Yes, and my guess is that this will ultimately prove to be the most efficacious and thoroughgoing way. Because, again, rating ourselves globally while also rating our 'good' and 'bad' behaviours seems to be the human condition – innate and learned. To do differently and to only evaluate what we think, feel and do, and acknowledge but refrain from rating our self, being, essence or personhood is most difficult and almost alien to human functioning.

Thus, in REBT sessions we therapists do our best to give all our clients unconditional acceptance. We actively teach its value and use many cognitive, emotive and behavioural methods of explaining and instructing our clients how to achieve it. We encourage them to employ a number of psychoeducational techniques, especially suitable pamphlets, books and cassettes. We give them in-session and out-of-session homework exercises and assignments to work toward USA. We do quite well with these modelling and active-directive therapy methods much of the time.

But hardly always! We have little trouble teaching the virtues of USA and helping most of our clients to acknowledge them. We actually succeed, I would say, teaching most of them to acquire considerably more self-acceptance than when they first began therapy – and often accomplish this in a few weeks or months. None the less, we still have trouble helping our clients to fully accept themselves, their personhood, *even* when they behave dysfunctionally; and we have more trouble helping them to only rate their specific thoughts, feelings and actions and to refrain from rating their *self* or *being* at all. As noted above, the mere unconditional acceptance by therapists of their clients doesn't quite work – because the clients then almost always accept themselves *conditionally*.

Unconditional self-acceptance is very difficult for most people to learn, truly believe in and consistently follow. So, according to REBT, are the other two major philosophies and actions that lead to clients' *getting* as well as *feeling* better: Unconditional other acceptance (UOA) and high frustration tolerance (HFT). All of us humans often are treated shabbily and unfairly by other people; and we frequently encounter serious frustrations and difficulties. To *get* better, therefore, we preferably should non-damningly accept other *people* even when their *behaviours* are abominable, and accept the potential goodness or enjoyment of life even when it is quite troublesome. Yes, *accept* many people and things that we do not *like*.

This is hard to do – by ourselves as well as with the kind and wise help of others. REBT therefore holds that to help people feel *and* get better, therapists preferably should have a good theory of what constitutes disturbance and improvement plus effective techniques of implementing this theory. Both! Teaching clients how they can make themselves less disturbed and less disturbable is important – but so is teaching them how to get there. It is fine to assume that *some* clients are bright and creative enough to largely help themselves as they dialogue with a therapist. But to assume that all or most clients are this way is highly unrealistic. Active-directive teaching of therapeutic theory and technique is probably desirable with most clients much of the time.

Active-directive therapy has its distinct limitations and hazards (Ellis, 1997). But so has passive therapy – especially considering that many clients, because of their own deficiencies or those accompanying their disturbances – got themselves into difficulties and, under their own power, are at first unable to resolve them. So their therapists had better be prepared to be persuasive teachers. This very much includes their subscribing to most of Rogers' conditions for effective therapy. Thus, they had better be in psychological contact with their clients; be a congruent, genuine integrated person; experience unconditional positive regard for their clients; and experience an accurate, empathic understanding of their clients' awareness of their own therapeutic experience. Fine! None of these traits are absolutely necessary – as I noted above – but all are highly desirable for therapists and, as Rogers himself pointed out, for teachers.

I can think of other important traits that an effective therapist can have to aid his or her effectiveness. For example: have a strong desire to help the client; be open-minded and non-dogmatic; be a creative problem solver; be highly ethical; be clear and understandable; have wide experience and knowledge; have high frustration tolerance; enjoy doing therapy; have a good sense of humour; be experimental; and so on. I doubt whether any of these characteristics or habits are necessary for good therapy. But they can probably help!

Unless a therapist in some ways adequately relates to her or his clients, the greatest theory and techniques may not help. Clients rarely intimately converse with or actively listen to therapists they dislike. So relating well to clients is an important *part* of a therapist's method. In regard to clients' *feeling* better, both during and after therapy, it may well be the most important part. In regard to their *getting* better, it is still important, but not crucial or necessary. I still maintain that the therapist's theory and methods are even more important. Now all that I – and other researchers – have to do is to back up or falsify this hypothesis!

A final word. When we talk about psychotherapy techniques, we usually mean those employed with what I call 'nice neurotic' clients and describe a variety of conversational methods that work with these individuals. We often fail to mention clients with severe personality disorders, such as phobic-avoidant personalities and obsessive-compulsive personality disorders. Such individuals, who constitute a fairly large percentage of our clients, often have biological deficits as well as psychological distortions and irrationalities. Many – perhaps most – of them are so fixed in their disordered behaviour that no amount of therapeutic conversation alone will help alter it. Consequently, it has been found that only behavioural techniques plus suitable medication will help them (Ellis, 1997). Unconditional positive regard may well encourage them to make the required behavioural changes and to take their medication, but in itself may do them little good. Oh, yes: if they do not change, relationship methods that help them achieve USA in spite of their continual behavioural deficiencies may help them feel much better. But without behavioural and medication intervention, they may still be sorely afflicted.

Why I believe this controversy is a crucial one

In the early years of therapy, theory and technique were of crucial importance, and may well have been overemphasized. Recently, there has often been a one-sided emphasis on relationship as the crucial element in therapy. I believe that a good therapeutic relationship is usually important to help people *feel* better, but to help them *get* better, theory and technique are more crucial. But not for all clients all of the time! A two-sided position will, I think, help more people feel better *and* get better. Again, let us do much more research and see if we can find out!

References

Ellis, A. (1972) 'Helping people get better rather than merely feel better', *Rational Living*, 7 (2): 2–9.

Ellis, A. (1994) *Reason and Emotion in Psychotherapy* (revised and updated edn). New York: Birch Lane Press.

Ellis, A. (1996) *Better, Deeper, and More Enduring Brief Therapy*. New York: Brunner/Mazel.

Ellis, A. (1997) 'Postmodern ethics for active-directing counseling and psychotherapy', *Journal of Mental Health Counseling*, 18: 211–25.

Ellis, A. and Dryden, W. (1997) *The Practice of Rational Emotive Behavior Therapy* (revised edn). New York: Springer.

Ellis, A., Gordon, J., Neenan, M. and Palmer, S. (1997) *Stress Counseling: A Rational Emotive Behaviour Approach*. London: Cassell; New York: Springer.

Frank, J. (1985) 'Therapeutic components shared by all psychotherapies', in M. Mahoney and A. Freeman (eds), *Cognition and Psychotherapy*. New York: Plenum.

Rogers, C.R. (1957) 'The necessary and sufficient conditions of therapeutic personality change', *Journal of Consulting Psychology*, 21: 95–103. (Reprinted *Journal of Consulting and Clinical Psychology* (1996), 60: 827–32.)

The main change agent in psychotherapy is the relationship between therapist and client

David Howe

The power of other people and the relationships we have with them to influence us for better or worse have been recognized in literature and journalism, film and television drama, folk psychology and the social sciences for a long time. However, over the last few decades, an unprecedented amount of formal research has gone into examining the extent to which the personal and interpersonal qualities that take place within relationships affect people's social experience. We might also add that people evaluate large tracts of their lives in terms of the quality of their relationships. Am I loved and liked? Am I socially effective? Can I sustain intimacy? Is my self-esteem low? Do I like myself? Am I in control of my life? Do I know how to relate to people in a relaxed, warm fashion? When the answer to such questions is no, people are likely to feel dissatisfied, distressed and unhappy. It is at this point that many will turn to others for help: friends, colleagues, priests, counsellors, psychotherapists.

If the help to which people turn is offered by professional psychotherapists or counsellors, it is reasonable to ask (scientifically, ethically and economically) whether or not the help given is effective. And if the help is effective, we might go on to investigate what makes the practice potent. It is at this point that different schools of treatment with their specific techniques weigh in with claims about the superiority of their product over others. Further fuel is added to the rivalry between therapies when yet other assessors celebrate the similarities and not the differences between the wide variety of helping practices.

In this chapter I shall review the psychotherapy outcome research, identify the ingredients of effective practice, and theorize why we might expect to find relationship-based qualities to be so widespread and fundamental across all effectiveness studies.

Psychotherapy outcome studies

Two basic findings have emerged repeatedly in outcome studies. The first reports that on the whole psychotherapy is effective (Smith and Glass,

1977; Luborsky et al., 1988; Matt, 1989). The second reports that across all types of therapy the success rate is similar – typically around 60–65 per cent (Luborsky et al., 1975; Smith and Glass, 1977; Luborsky et al., 1988). Thus, 'Everybody has won and all must have prizes', conclude Luborsky et al. (1975), quoting the verdict of the Dodo bird in Lewis Carroll's *Alice's Adventures in Wonderland*. These findings have also been dubbed the 'equivalence paradox' – the lack of differential effectiveness contrasted with the technical diversity sponsored by different schools of counselling and psychotherapy (Stiles et al., 1986).

> Despite volumes devoted to the theoretical differences among different schools of psychotherapy, the results of research demonstrate negligible differences in the effects produced by different therapy types. (Smith and Glass, 1977: 760)

The consistency of these observations has triggered the belief that there must be elements within the psychotherapeutic encounter that are common to most therapist–client relationships, independent of 'schools' and their specific treatment techniques. It is these shared factors that are responsible for the equivalence in effectiveness. Two aspects of these generic qualities have been developed: (a) the relationship; and (b) the helping (therapeutic) alliance. Close conceptual and empirical links exist between these two slants, for both tap into the social dynamics and competences of people in relationship.

The components of effective practice

However, further refinement of these early results recognizes that there *are* identifiable components of good-quality relationships and successful alliances, and it is the presence of these that is statistically correlated with successful outcomes (Horvath and Symonds, 1991). The converse is also true: that the absence of major components of competent interpersonal behaviour is associated with poor therapeutic outcomes. Thus, the original suggestion that interpersonal and relationships qualities were *non-specific* (that is, not associated with any particular style of counselling or therapy) turns out to be a misleading rendition of the research findings. The preferred view is that such qualities are *generic* in the sense that they underpin all successful practices, but nevertheless they are *specific* and they are necessary to the achievement of positive outcomes. In other words, research has allowed us to specify what features of the therapist–client relationships do contribute to successful counselling and psychotherapy (Gomes-Schwartz, 1978; also see Stiles et al., 1986, whose important review helps unravel many of the complex conceptual strands involved in effectiveness research).

Taking the views of clients as one measure of effectiveness, we might note that although psychotherapeutic techniques differ, the messages of consumers remain the same. It may be that the messages are pointing to a different type and deeper level of explanation. A particular therapy is really no more than a vehicle for carrying the important content of the encounter: a relationship in which people can talk, explore, reflect, interpret and make sense. What was previously thought of as the carrier is now in fact the carried. Clients strive to make sense of the meaning of their own experience in order to increase feelings of self-control and self-efficacy which in turn raise self-esteem. Whatever the techniques used by therapists to help clients 'make sense', the important generic factor is the ability itself to help clients make sense, even though the ideas used may be specific to therapists' particular brand of help (Howe, 1993).

The helping alliance recognizes that both the therapist and the client bring qualities and views to the relationship. It is the character of these specific qualities and their interaction that have a bearing on the psychotherapeutic outcome. The alliance is therefore more than the presence of general therapist factors – the 'necessary and sufficient conditions' of unconditional positive regard, accurate empathic understanding and openness formulated by Rogers (1957). It is produced by the mutual involvement and *collaboration* of both therapist and client. 'The helping alliance is an expression of a patient's positive bond with the therapist who is perceived as a helpful and supportive person' (Luborsky, 1994: 39). The ensuing relationship does most of the therapeutic work. Different schools of therapy merely provide a vehicle and framework for carrying the helping alliance. Recent work on identifying the ingredients that help form effective alliances includes:

(a) therapist qualities and characteristics as experienced by the client, including being warm, supportive, attentive, empathic, understanding, clarificatory, helpful, purposive, involved, collaborative, sensitive, having a good rapport; and
(b) client qualities and characteristics, including psychological security, good motivation, normal to raised affect, good self-disclosure, good IQ (Luborsky et al., 1988).

Psychosocial, developmental and relationship-based theories of psychotherapeutic effectiveness

We therefore know a number of interesting and important things about counselling and psychotherapy. In general terms, most clients seek help because they are experiencing difficulties, distress and dissatisfaction with themselves and the quality of their social relationships. People seek help by approaching and getting into relationships with other people. Clients use the everyday language of relationships to comment on and evaluate their experiences of being helped. They use the same language and vocabulary to evaluate different types of counselling and psychotherapy.

The 'equivalence paradox' observes that different brands of therapy and counselling appear to have broadly similar outcomes. The helping alliance is made up of behaviours and perceptions that are generic to relationships of many kinds, including both work-oriented and emotionally based relationships.

So, rather than be niggled and bothered by the perennial force of these observations; rather than be unsettled by findings which seem too commonplace, non-technical and ordinary; theoretically it might be more economical and fruitful to acknowledge the insistence of the research findings and wonder why it is that these interpersonal and relationship-based factors remain obdurately present in the world of empirical inquiry. Theories help organize what we know. Given the nature of what we know, developmental and relationship-based theories of personality and social behaviour seem strong contenders for organizing our observations.

Many developmental psychologists and social scientists recognise that the human self is a social self that forms within relationships (for example, Bowlby, 1988; Bakhurst and Sypnowich, 1995; Westen, 1996). In a very deep sense, the characteristics that make us human can only form as we relate with others throughout childhood. Within this perspective, the individual is no longer seen as someone who enters the world as an *a priori* psychologically discrete entity. Rather, the self and personality form as the developing mind engages with and tries to make sense of the world in which it finds itself. In so doing, it takes on many of the properties of the environment which it seeks to understand. Such a conception of the self is opposed to the Cartesian notion of the mind as a 'self-contained world of thoughts and experiences, essentially independent of the "external" world of people and things "outside" or "beyond" it' (Bakhurst and Sypnowich, 1995: 3). How we understand, think, feel, see and conceptualize, though influenced by our biological inheritance and make-up, is shaped by our social, cultural and linguistic experiences. Our consciousness and ability to self-reflect are not natural pre-givens. They emerge as the individual engages with society. 'Mind' and 'self' form within the 'communicative activity of the group' and through social experience (Mead, 1934). Individuality is therefore socially based, and personality forms as social understanding develops (Burkitt, 1991: 2). The 'socialness of self' recognizes the interplay between nature and nurture.

The psychological corollary of this line of thought also means that the *quality* of children's relationships affects their socio-emotional development. The poorer the quality of children's relationship history, the less robust will be their psychological make-up, emotional integrity and social competence.

It should not surprise us then that social relationships remain such a potent and compelling force within our lives, and that when we seek help and understanding, personal control and change, it is to other people and the relationships that they offer that we turn. And as language carries much of the information that helps us understand the self, others and one's cultural context, we might expect that 'talking cures'. The self originally formed and is therefore capable of re-forming within social relationships (Howe, 1993). Social competence depends on achieving positive self-esteem, self-efficacy and social understanding. When social and personal competence feel weak, entering into relationship with another who is willing to help feels natural and promising. But just as the quality of close relationships during early childhood can have either beneficial or adverse effects on personality development and social efficacy, the quality of the therapeutic relationship can have either a positive or negative impact on a client's sense of self and social proficiency. It is these positive and negative qualities that psychotherapy process and outcome research identifies. It is also the reason that many analysts suggest that the effective therapist is behaving, either consciously or unconsciously, as a skilled parent.

> The view of development as relationship based and the observation that the internalization of relationship experience is the product of interactions with parental caretakers have important implications for clinical theory and research. It seems to support, at least by implication, the vital role of the therapist–patient relationship as a curative agent in therapeutic treatments. (Jones, 1996: 5)

Effective parents help children develop a number of protective factors that allow them to cope with the rough and tumble of everyday social life. Such factors include good self-esteem, a sense of self-efficacy, emotional responsivity and social empathy. These factors are associated with the growth of personal resilience. 'Good enough' parents are emotionally warm, available, attentive, responsive, sensitive, attuned, consistent and interested in their children. Strategies which employ reciprocity (give and take), negotiation, reason and suggestion appear much more successful in helping children achieve impulse control, compliance and self-reliance. Parental sensitivity and responsibility promote secure attachments, self-confidence and problem-solving competence. Positive parental control strategies and semantic responses provide children with linguistic concepts that help them recognize, understand and cope with their own behavioural and emotional states. Within secure relationships, children learn to see themselves as loved, valued and of interest. They feel socially relevant and effective. They develop a positive model of themselves, others and social relationships (Howe, 1995).

It seems no coincidence that so many of the elements of the effective therapist–client relationship appear similar to the 'good enough' parent–child relationship. Henry et al. (1986) report that therapists in successful, high-change cases show more affiliative control (helping, teaching and protecting) and affiliative autonomy granting (affirming and understanding), while exercising less hostile control (blaming or belittling). Patients in good-outcome groups show significantly more friendly autonomy (open disclosure and expression) and are significantly less avoidant. Balance, consistency and complementary exchanges are also much higher in positive-outcome cases (Henry and Strupp, 1994: 65).

Secure psychosocial development witnesses children seeking *to make sense and control the meaning of their own and others' experience* within the context of early close relationships. The ability to make sense of other people is also the ability to make sense of one's self, and the ability to make sense of one's self is also the ability to make sense of other people (Frith, 1989: 169). Clients are people who feel that they are not understood, who have lost confidence in their ability to make sense of themselves and others, or who are not in control of the meaning of their own behaviour and experience (Howe, 1993). The loss of self-esteem and social efficacy may have its roots in either an adverse childhood or current traumatic and stressful life events. The effect of both experiences is to weaken people's resilience, leaving them vulnerable to social and environmental risks. The place to recover resilience and social competence is in good-quality relationships. Psychotherapists and counsellors who provide good-quality relationships help generate a therapeutic alliance in which clients are able to explore and develop psychological protective factors. These include good self-esteem, self-efficacy and semantic frameworks that help people recognize, understand and control emotional affect.

Similar conclusions have been reached by both psychotherapy and developmental researchers. Henry and Strupp (1994) develop the idea that the direct change mechanism is based on the theory of interpersonal introjection:

> People learn to treat themselves as they have been treated by important others early in life . . . we have come to conceptualize the therapeutic alliance as iso-morphic with these interpersonal transactions. That is, *the interpersonal process in the patient–therapist dyad is the therapeutic relationship or alliance*, and the alliance so conceived is a sufficient agent of direct therapeutic change underlying all psychotherapies. The function of interpersonal process in therapeutic change is both a specific *and* a common factor. (Henry and Strupp, 1994: 64, original emphases)

These observations are true for both patient and therapist. Indeed, the authors find 'a theoretically coherent link between early actions by parents toward the therapist, the therapists' adult introject state, vulnerability to countertherapeutic interpersonal processes with their parents, and differential outcome' (Henry and Strupp, 1994: 66). Dozier et al. (1994) also note that different outcomes are observed depending on the attachment history of the therapist as well as the client. This is another indication that *specific* relationships and personality factors offered by the therapist will differentially impact on *specific* relationship and personality attributes possessed by clients. This finding feeds into Stiles et al.'s (1986) discussion of Paul's (1967) paper on the 'specificity of effectiveness' – *what* treatment, by *whom*, is most effective for *this* specific problem, and under *which* set of circumstances? In practice, therefore we might expect that psychotherapists will be differentially effective with clients. Some therapists will get it wrong with most clients much of the time. Others will get it right with some clients, but not others, most of the time. And yet others will get it right with most clients more often than not.

In this sense, the helping alliance is redefined as an interpersonal process in which the characteristics and qualities of a developmentally sound parent–child relationship are present in an adult guise. The therapeutic power of an effective helping alliance is based on the ability of the psychotherapist to help clients shift their internal working models of the self, others and social relationships away from an insecure to a secure pattern. This is achieved by generating a relationship that allows the client to reformulate the self and others more positively. In the language of attachment theory, internal working mental models guide behaviour, influence social understanding, determine relationship styles and colour the way people cope with distress and anxiety. Internal working models form within relationships. Therefore relationships that disconfirm the internal working model's notion of how the self, others and relationships work (that is, the therapist breaks the client's assumptions of how others typically and predictably respond) can bring about changes in experience, behaviour and relationship patterns. Inner mental representations of the self, others and relationships become more positive and secure (Bowlby, 1988).

Therapists provide clients with a secure base from which to explore themselves and their relationships, including the way that interpersonal relationships are construed and conducted (Bowlby, 1977: 421). The therapist and client need to recognize how the therapeutic relationship is being perceived, handled and used by the client. This may reveal how the client typically handles his self or her self in relationship with others. Such understandings encourage clients cognitively to link past relationship experiences with current behaviours and emotions. Clients can then be helped to understand how their current mental representational models of self, others and relationships (formed within the context of past close relationships) can influence the conduct of present close relationships. This offers the opportunity to reconstruct mental models so that people can understand and handle themselves within relationships more competently. They strengthen the protective factors of self-esteem and self-efficacy which increase resilience. Increased psychological resilience helps people cope better with stress, risk and adversity.

'Therapy is beneficial', believe Henry and Strupp (1994: 71), 'because the patient experiences a relationship that is qualitatively different from early childhood relationships responsible for the maladaptive interpersonal patterns that ultimately led the patient to seek therapy.' And after more than 30 years, they conclude,

> our most recent research . . . continues to underscore the importance of ther-
> apists' personal qualities and the central role of the alliance in therapeutic change

processes. Our hope is that these studies of the alliance have ultimately demonstrated that concepts such as *personal qualities* and *relationship variables* are
indeed quite at home with scientific theory. (1994: 80, original emphases)

References

Bakhurst, D. and Sypnowich, C. (eds) (1995) *The Social Self*. London: Sage.

Bowlby, J. (1977) 'The making and breaking of affectional bonds: I. Aetiology and
psychopathology in the light of attachment theory', *British Journal of Psychiatry*,
130: 201–10.

Bowlby, J. (1988) *A Secure Base: Clinical Applications of Attachment Theory*.
London: Routledge.

Burkitt, I. (1991) *Social Selves: Theories of the Formation of the Personality*.
London: Sage.

Dozier, M., Kelly, L.C. and Barnett, L. (1994) 'Clinicians as caregivers: role of
attachment organization in treatment', *Journal of Consulting and Clinical
Psychology*, 62 (4): 793–800.

Frith, U. (1989) *Autism: Explaining the Enigma*. Oxford: Blackwell.

Gomes-Schwartz, B. (1978) 'Effective ingredients in psychotherapy: prediction of
outcome from process variables', *Journal of Consulting and Clinical Psychology*,
46 (5): 1023–35.

Henry, W.P. and Strupp, H.H. (1994) 'The therapeutic alliance as interpersonal
process', in A.O. Horvath and L.S. Greenberg (eds), *The Working Alliance:
Theory, Research and Practice*. New York: John Wiley.

Henry, W.P., Schacht, T.E. and Strupp, H.H. (1986) 'Structural analysis of social
behavior', *Journal of Consulting and Clinical Psychology*, 54 (1): 27–31.

Horvath, A.O. and Symonds, B.D. (1991) 'Relationship between working alliance
and outcome in psychotherapy: a meta-analysis', *Journal of Counseling
Psychology*, 38: 139–49.

Howe, D. (1993) *On Being a Client: Understanding the Process of Counselling and
Psychotherapy*. London: Sage.

Howe, D. (1995) *Attachment Theory for Social Work Practice*. Basingstoke:
Macmillan.

Jones, E.E. (1996) 'Introduction to the special section on attachment and
psychopathology: part I', *Journal of Consulting and Clinical Psychology*, 64 (1):
55–7.

Luborsky, L. (1994) 'Therapeutic alliances as predictors of psychotherapeutic
outcomes: factors explaining the predictive success', in A.O. Horvath and L.S.
Greenberg (eds), *The Working Alliance: Theory, Research and Practice*. New
York: John Wiley.

Luborsky, L., Singer, B. and Luborsky, L. (1975) 'Comparative studies of
psychotherapies: is it true that "Everybody has won and all must have prizes"?',
Archives of General Psychiatry, 32: 995–1008.

Luborsky, L., Crits-Cristoph, P., Mintz, J. and Auerbach, A. (1988) *Who Will
Benefit from Psychotherapy? Predicting Therapeutic Outcomes*. New York: Basic
Books.

Matt, G.E. (1989) 'Decision rules for selecting effect size in meta-analysis: a review
and reanalysis of psychotherapy outcome studies', *Psychological Bulletin*, 105 (1):
106–15.

Mead, G.H. (1934) *Mind, Self and Society: From the Standpoint of a Social
Behaviorist*. Chicago: University of Chicago Press.

Paul, G.L. (1967) 'Strategy of outcome research in psychotherapy', *Journal of
Consulting Psychology*, 31: 109–18.

Rogers, C.R. (1957) 'The necessary and sufficient conditions of therapeutic personality change', *Journal of Consulting Psychology*, 21: 95–103. (Reprinted *Journal of Consulting and Clinical Psychology*, 60 (1992): 827–32.)

Smith, M.L. and Glass, G.V. (1977) 'Meta-analysis of psychotherapy outcome studies', *American Psychologist*, 32: 752–60.

Stiles, W.B., Shapiro, D.A. and Elliott, R. (1986) 'Are all psychotherapies equivalent?', *American Psychologist*, 41 (2): 165–80.

Westen, D. (1996) *Psychology: Mind, Brain and Culture*. New York: John Wiley.

12   Deconstructing diagnosis: psychopathological practice

Ian Parker

This century has seen a relentless psychologization of society and the proliferation of diagnoses of forms of unhappiness. The increasing popularity of psychotherapy and counselling is both a symptom of and response to this process. As social problems become located more firmly inside individuals, each of us then experiences our distress as something intensely personal which must be addressed. Perhaps this is not necessarily a bad thing, and we do need to be able to develop a response to social problems which works at the interface of the personal and the political instead of pretending that society is something separate from us. While some of us may participate as clients or providers in psychological services with this progressive purpose in mind, however, we are always also faced with the more reactionary side of the problematic, where forms of expert knowledge are used to identify psychopathology and so to specify what we should feel as normal or abnormal. This psychopathological practice, which increases distress at the very moment it defines it, finds its quintessential expression in the activity of 'diagnosis'.

Diagnosis transforms the varieties of ways in which we might achieve and enjoy mental health into a bewildering range of categories of dysfunction and mental illness. People living in varying degrees of discomfort or unhappiness are themselves transformed into categories, and modes of behaviour and thinking are then prescribed and proscribed for them. Prescription follows ineluctably from the diagnosis when certain expectations about what patients should do, what they have done and what they might be expected to do in the future are elaborated. Proscription accompanies this normalizing of states of health and illness when certain experiences and feelings are consigned to the realm of illness. Until the early 1970s these included kinds of sexual orientation, and nowadays they still include the hearing of voices, for example. It would seem from social and psychiatric trends in North America that even mild states of depression that all of us sometimes experience will soon be suppressed with drugs. Diagnosis brings with it dehumanization, labelling, the pathologization of many human activities, and iatrogenesis (Illich, 1976). Here, the career path of those who have been subjected to the sometimes well-meaning attempts to comprehend exactly what they 'have' or what they 'are' often leads them into more profound distress as they undergo treatment, or struggle to understand what professional logic governs the treatment.

Histories of the presenting problem

Diagnosis has become more prevalent as modern life has become more complicated, and its practitioners have had to become more creative to counter the many attempts to shake them off. Diagnosticians are convinced that they can see exactly what is wrong with other people, or that one day they will be able to do this. They function as parasites upon the unhappy, dependent on the very complexity and mutability of the unhappiness that sustains and frustrates them. There have been many attempts to understand the way that the obsession with making diagnosis is itself a form of psychopathological practice, and what tormented certainties afflict the diagnosticians.

The anti-psychiatry movement in the 1960s, for example, was inspired by Laing's (1965) insistence that despite his medical and psychoanalytic training he could not agree that the person sitting with him in a session was a collection of symptoms. The removal of homosexuality from the *Diagnostic and Statistical Manual of Mental Disorders* (*DSM*) in the 1970s would not have been possible if the gay liberation movement had not refused to accept that they suffered from a condition that could and should be cured, and lesbian activists are still at the forefront of radical critiques of psychiatric reasoning (Kitzinger and Perkins, 1993). Feminists have challenged the ways in which diagnostic systems pathologize women's experience, and the rise of counselling and psychotherapy has, in part, been a result of the involvement of feminists in mental health practice as an alternative to psychiatry (Ussher, 1991). There have been many forms of resistance to the treatment of the experience of cultural minorities by white psychiatry, and this has entailed the rejection of approaches which reduce the person to a diagnostic type or to being an exemplar of a certain community marked by distinct exotic forms of pathology (Littlewood and Lipsedge, 1989).

There have always been alternatives to diagnosis. Within the broad domain of counselling and psychotherapy, systemic family therapists have always attempted to understand how the 'index' patient carries and expresses a collective pathology, and their implicit resistance to the diagnostic response of a family to conflict has become more explicit recently in the emergence of narrative therapies which see images of pathology as carried by kinds of discourse in the surrounding culture (Monk et al., 1997). The Hearing Voices Network has emerged to challenge the way the hearing of voices is usually treated as if the voices were necessarily pathological 'auditory hallucinations' and so a first-rank symptom of schizophrenia, and it has been building supportive environments for coping with or celebrating voice hearing instead of diagnosing it as a symptom of something else (Romme and Escher, 1993).

Sometimes the very attempt to resist diagnosis is treated as a symptom which must be located in a diagnostic system, and each of these attempts to escape psychiatric reasoning has also succumbed at some point as personnel trace a career path into counselling or psychotherapy and take it too seriously.

Deconstructing psychiatric power, and resistance

Each of these different movements employs a theoretical framework to make sense of diagnosis, to understand how diagnosticians come to believe that it works, and to challenge the way it is implemented. A framework that has been particularly useful recently has been a form of 'practical deconstruction' which reverses the priority given to certain concepts, locates those concepts in certain relations of power, and supports resistance on the part of those subjected to them (Parker et al., 1995).

With respect to the first aspect, the form of reasoning that diagnosis employs can be turned against itself, as I have already done. Those who are so intent upon fixing pathology in others can themselves be 'diagnosed' as suffering from an obsession with order and with arranging people in a set of a categories (Lowson, 1994). The relationship between diagnoser and diagnosed can thus be reversed. However, this kind of simple reversal is only the first step in a deconstruction, and we then need to develop an analysis of the way 'diagnosis' operates independently of the wishes of any particular person, whether professional or client. Deconstruction as a particular form of conceptual analysis and theory of meaning has always been attentive to the way we try to find anchoring points where meanings seem to be 'present', self-sufficient and independent of context, and to the way this attempt to fix meanings unravels under a little pressure. To understand how meanings of symptoms appear to us as if they were signs of something else, as if they were the natural expression of diagnostic categories, we have to look at how the diagnostic texts, in the *International Classification of Diseases* (*ICD*) and *DSM*, for example, have been structured.

The ability of diagnosticians to impose their own stereotypical distinctions on others is made possible by the wider systems of power that weave counselling, psychotherapy, psychology and psychotherapy together as a dense network of theories and practices, termed by some critics the 'psy-complex' (Ingleby, 1985; Rose, 1985). At this point we need to go beyond simple 'deconstruction' as such – the kind of deconstruction one finds in much contemporary liberal literary theory – and locate diagnostic texts in the psy-complex. The psy-complex contains prescriptions and proscriptions for the behaviour of mental health professionals as much as it does for their clients, so that when a counsellor or psychotherapist rejects diagnosis they may face disapproval or even sanctions from disciplinary professional organizations (Mowbray, 1995; House and Totton, 1997).

A practical deconstruction is not satisfied with the academic game of juggling conceptual oppositions and identifying the ways they work in relations of power; rather, we should always look to forms of resistance. This is all the more necessary because resistance to diagnostic categories functions in such a way as to construct alternative moral-political communities, and these provide points of reference for people with problems to see that they may be able to live without their problems. The disciplinary side of the psy-complex which fixes people in their place and sees them as the source of distress is complemented by a confessional side in which each individual feels themself to contain that distress and believes that they will only find relief by speaking about it within certain acceptable forms of expert discourse (Parker, 1998). Resistance may indeed include the right to speak about abusive or oppressive experiences and to work with others to develop a collective voice on such matters, but this means speaking out of turn and outside existing systems of categories. Examples of this resistance also provide evidence that diagnostic systems may not be necessary at all.

Diagnostic culture and its contradictions

Diagnostic systems are fragile things without systems of power to hold them in place. The underlying assumptions about cognition and emotion that must be made by diagnosticians for them to make sense are easily dissolved if we step back and look at them in cultural context. It would be a mistake to say that diagnostic systems like *DSM* and *ICD* are 'arbitrary', but they are certainly contingent on quite narrow local historical, cultural and subcultural conventions.

The sense of self as an internal delimited entity coterminous with the physical duration of a body is wedded to common sense in Western culture, but it has not always been like this (Heelas and Lock, 1981). Seemingly fundamental emotions also seem to be quite recent, and other descriptions of emotion, in medieval England for example, simply do not make sense to us now. Other cultures are structured around different notions of 'self', if that should even be employed as the appropriate term for individuated experience in those contexts, and different patterns of emotion are made possible by different forms of description (Harré, 1986). If present-day Western assumptions about self and emotion have not always applied and do not apply around the world, then how can diagnosis proceed? It could be argued that these gross historical and cultural differences can be bracketed out, but this is a desperate and dangerous move for it must then either ignore the existence of people from different cultures – and this has tended to be the way in white psychiatry (Fernando, 1988) – or introduce additional diagnostic procedures to identify special patterns of pathology in minority cultural groups – and this has tended to be the option favoured by psychiatrists interested in 'transcultural' approaches (Mercer, 1986). Either way, anyone different is pressed into a diagnostic system. The problem is worse than this in practice, however, for no culture is homogeneous. It is always fractured at least by age, class, ethnicity, gender and sexuality.

It has been within the contradictions between official and unofficial knowledge which are made possible by such fractures in society that alternative 'deconstructive' therapeutic practices have developed. We see this, for example, in the activities of 'deconstructive' or 'postmodern' narrative or discursive therapists who explore the way the 'problem' has become storied into being and internalized by the client (White, 1991). The 'externalizing' of the problem in this work is a profoundly anti-diagnostic process, reversing the ways in which a person has been made into the problem and helping them treat the problem as the problem, using deconstruction with and against psychotherapeutic power (Parker, 1999).

Deconstruction of pathological practice is not simply a negative 'destructive' refusal of all that has been learned by those labouring in the psycomplex. Counselling and psychotherapy which employs deconstructive analysis as part of the therapeutic process is in some ways a quite 'constructive' activity. What makes it so different is that this anti-diagnostic activity is constructed with the client as part of the process of emancipating the client from the problem (and they may then deconstruct the problem), and it must of necessity operate against the efforts of the diagnosticians who construct and implement the *DSM* or *ICD* in such a way as to subject the client to the problem (by which they then ruthlessly reconstruct the problem).

Diagnostic systems would, perhaps, be less dangerous if they rested on sound empirical foundations and if the allocation of individuals to the categories could be made smoothly and logically. Unfortunately, counsellors or psychotherapists who employ diagnosis are drawn into a system and process of application that has little foundation in reality and which mystifies those who attempt to make use of it. Studies of the contradictions and gaps in research on 'psychotic language', for example, have concluded that the discourse in which such impossible and untenable distinctions are made is itself 'psychotic' (Parker et al., 1995). There is little agreement between observers of behaviour deemed to be pathological as to which categories are relevant. Psychiatric patients thus find themselves placed in a confused overlapping series of different categories, and confusion on the part of the psy-complex is then projected deeper into the patient as further confirmation of their pathology.

Tactics and ethics

This does not mean that it is not sometimes necessary to use diagnostic labels. In some settings we use a label to enable communication between professionals, and between professionals and clients. In other settings we may play with labels precisely to show how mutable they are.

When the psychiatric hospital of San Giovanni in the northern Italian city of Trieste was closed down as part of a wide-ranging reform of mental health provision in the 1980s, for example, personnel in the new community mental health centres had to continue using some of the *ICD* diagnostic categories (Ramon and Giannichedda, 1989). This was primarily because European Community funding was predicated on the existence of certain mental health problems and community provision for ex-patients, and returns had to be made to the project organizers about the prevalence of certain kinds of symptomatology among the users of the health centres. On the one hand, then, the ideology of the reforms was driven by an attempt to dissolve the distinction between the 'psychiatric' patients and the wider disparate community of the 'emarginated' (the homeless, the youth, the unemployed). On the other hand, if a homeless person were to apply for a bed for the night at a community 'mental health' centre, they would have to display a recognized diagnosable psychiatric complaint. It is in such a fashion that counsellors and psychotherapists often communicate with psychiatrists. Similar tactical moves have to be made by those who want to keep diagnosis intact but reframe it in terms of 'risk' and 'risk prediction'. Diagnostic categories can be useful to display the effects of racism, sexism and poverty on mental health, turning them against the very system that employs them. Even those using radical 'deconstructive' approaches may have to speak the same language as diagnosticians, but their task is to help their client speak many other languages as well as that one, and to be able to understand how that language as diagnostic discourse works to mislead their client about what and where the problem is.

When members of the Hearing Voices Network participated in an academic conference on theories of voice hearing in Manchester in 1994, the 'practical deconstruction' of diagnostic categories that this meeting invited entailed a deliberate excessive flood of diagnoses so that many different systems could be brought to bear on voice hearing by voice hearers themselves. Not only was this meeting a festival of explanations, then, but it was also a festival of diagnosis. Psychiatrists and psychologists were permitted to rehearse their categories and theories but now alongside speakers who explored shamanism, spiritualism and telepathy as diagnostic and anti-diagnostic tools. There have been many other initiatives of this kind since (Coleman, 1997).

In either case, however, those who use diagnosis are doing so tactically, and with a view to encouraging critical reflection on the categories and the procedures by users of services rather than luring us into the illusion that we are tapping some deep enduring truth about forms of psychopathology.

Diagnosis as psychopathology

Diagnosis is a crucial issue for counsellors and psychotherapists, for they are brought face to face with a moral-political choice about where their allegiance should lie. If we agree that diagnosis captures forms of underlying pathology, then we may well find ourselves on the side of the psy-complex and we will reproduce all the assumptions and relations of power that underpin it. This is dangerous on three counts.

First, hierarchies of expertise inside the psy-complex are reproduced. Diagnosis of any kind threatens to do this, for psychiatric systems, with the *DSM* and *ICD* as the key examples, define how other psychotherapists and counsellors categorize people, and so these professionals who are lower down on the diagnostic pecking order are themselves subject to a good deal of mystification as they implement elaborate abstract stereotypical judgements on the real people they are trying to work with. Often counsellors and therapists use diagnostic systems after thinking through why, and deciding that they are simply doing it for pragmatic tactical reasons, usually to please the bureaucrats who like official records organized around certain categories. The *DSM* and *ICD* can now be read simply as detailed descriptions of symptoms rather than a guide to the discovery of underlying disease states, and 'symptomatology' has even been posed as an alternative to diagnosis (Bentall, 1992). There are even quite a few psychiatrists involved in therapeutic work who know that the diagnostic categories are a *post-hoc* representation of a problem, and the structure of power in the mental health system is such that they have a freer reign to voice their uncertainties about such matters. The worst cases are those psychiatrists and their hangers-on who are enthusiastic about diagnosis; for them it serves as a form of control, often to control their own anxiety about being in the presence of distress, and these people are as much a danger to themselves as to others.

Second, hierarchies of emotional ability are reproduced amongst the client population. Psychotherapists can sometimes be tempted to find security in alternative institutional or home-spun diagnostic categories, and these too can serve to fix people in place as firmly as do the *DSM* and *ICD*. Lacanians, for example, make a strict distinction between neurosis, perversion and psychosis and between hysteria and obsessional neurosis, and see diagnosis of these clinical structures as tapping something laid down very early in childhood and as not susceptible to change (Evans, 1996). A more widespread, softer and, for that, more pernicious diagnosis psychotherapists and counsellors are encouraged to make is as to the level of 'psychological-mindedness' and so the extent to which a client might be expected to engage with and benefit from therapeutic work (Coltart, 1988). Not only does this often smuggle assumptions about race and class into professional perceptions of those unsuitable for treatment, but it also prevents those diagnosed as 'schizophrenic' from receiving therapeutic support. Psychological-mindedness here is often assumed to include the client having a notion of an unconscious, something that many narrative therapists (for example) would not even sign up to.

Third, hierarchies of soft and hard truth are reproduced. We find ourselves on the slippery slope of deference to psychiatry and the illusion that there is a hidden hard truth under the soft stories we learn in our own counselling and psychotherapeutic practice. Not only is this mystifying, but it also legitimizes terrible abuses of power on the part of those who seem to be dealing with the hard stuff. Here the terrible practices of drug 'treatment' and ECT await as options for people who are not deemed suitable subjects for therapeutic intervention (Coleman, 1998). Diagnosis gives warrant for these things too, practices which many counsellors and psychotherapists have devoted their lives to encouraging people to avoid as they help people to help themselves.

To refuse diagnosis is to take the side of the client and to challenge the relationship between those who think they know and those who are attempting to become experts on their own lives, and in the process we can deconstruct psychopathological practice.

Acknowledgement

I would like to thank Erica Burman, Eugenie Georgaca, David Harper, Mark Stowell-Smith and Terence McLaughlin for their helpful comments on an earlier version of this chapter.

References

Bentall, R. (1992) 'Reconstructing psychopathology', *The Psychologist: Bulletin of the British Psychological Society*, 5 (2): 61–5.

Coleman, R. (1997) *From Victim to Victor: Hearing Voices*. Runcorn: Handsell.

Coleman, R. (1998) *The Politics of the Madhouse*. Runcorn: Handsell.

Coltart, N.E.C. (1988) 'The assessment of psychological-mindedness in the diagnostic interview', *British Journal of Psychiatry*, 153: 819–20.

Evans, D. (1996) *An Introductory Dictionary of Lacanian Psychoanalysis*. London: Routledge.

Fernando, S. (1988) *Race and Culture in Psychiatry*. London: Tavistock.

Harré, R. (ed.) (1986) *The Social Construction of Emotion*. Oxford: Blackwell.

Heelas, P. and Lock, A. (eds) (1981) *Indigenous Psychologies: The Anthropology of the Self*. London: Academic Press.

House, R. and Totton, N. (eds) (1997) *Implausible Professions: Arguments for Pluralism and Autonomy in Psychotherapy and Counselling*. Ross-on-Wye: PCCS Books.

Illich, I. (1976) *Limits to Medicine: The Expropriation of Health*. Harmondsworth: Penguin.

Ingleby, D. (1985) 'Professionals as socializers: the "psy complex"', *Research in Law, Deviance and Social Control*, 7: 79–109.

Kitzinger, C. and Perkins, R. (1993) *Changing Our Minds: Lesbian Feminism and Psychology*. New York: New York University Press.

Laing, R.D. (1965) *The Divided Self: An Existential Study in Sanity and Madness*. Harmondsworth: Penguin.

Littlewood, R. and Lipsedge, M. (1989) *Aliens and Alienists: Ethnic Minorities and Psychiatry* (2nd edn). London: Unwin Hyman.

Lowson, D. (1994) 'Understanding professional thought disorder: a guide for service users and a challenge for professionals', *Asylum*, 8 (2): 29–30.

Mercer, K. (1986) 'Racism and transcultural psychiatry', in P. Miller and N. Rose (eds), *The Power of Psychiatry*. Cambridge: Polity.

Monk, G., Winslade, J., Crocket, K. and Epston, D. (eds) (1997) *Narrative Therapy in Practice: The Archaeology of Hope*. San Francisco: Jossey-Bass.

Mowbray, R. (1995) *The Case Against Psychotherapy Registration: A Conservation Issue for the Human Potential Movement*. London: Trans Marginal Press.

Parker, I. (1998) 'Constructing and deconstructing psychotherapeutic discourse', *European Journal of Psychotherapy, Counselling and Health*, 1 (1): 77–90.

Parker, I. (ed.) (1999) *Deconstructing Psychotherapy*. London: Sage.

Parker, I., Georgaca, E., Harper, D., McLaughlin, T. and Stowell-Smith, M. (1995) *Deconstructing Psychopathology*. London: Sage.

Ramon, S. and Giannichedda, M. (eds) (1989) *Psychiatry in Transition: The British and Italian Experiences*. London: Pluto.

Romme, M. and Escher, A. (1993) *Accepting Voices*. London: MIND.

Rose, N. (1985) *The Psychological Complex: Psychology, Politics and Society in England 1869–1939*. London: Routledge & Kegan Paul.

Ussher, J. (1991) *Women's Madness: Misogyny or Mental Illness?* Hemel Hempstead: Harvester Wheatsheaf.

White, M. (1991) 'Deconstruction and therapy', *Dulwich Centre Newsletter*, 3: 21–40.

13 Psychopathology is a reality and psychodiagnosis is a necessity

Norman D. Macaskill

Heat rather than light is almost invariably the sole end result of any debate characterized by dichotomous thinking, which leads to an overriding wish to defend the cherished position rather than explore the validity and value of the viewpoint of one's opponent.

Therefore, in writing an essay in defence of psychiatric classification and its value in assessing and treating patients effectively, it is important that I clarify the precise position I wish to defend and not be drawn into defending what I believe is a caricature and misinterpretation of modern psychiatric classification systems such as *Diagnostic and Statistical Manual of Mental Disorders*, 4th edition (APA, 1994), and their practical usage in day-to-day clinical and therapeutic practice. The caricature I do not wish to defend is that of psychiatrists/diagnosticians who believe that each and every time they make a diagnosis by eliciting and defining experiences of personal distress and dysfunctional behaviour, they are delineating a distinctive and biologically based illness which will respond to an appropriate biological intervention. These psychiatrists, while acknowledging that as yet there are no specific diagnostic tests to confirm the medical basis of that diagnosis, are none the less confident that in the future research will produce such tests and terminate the unnecessary, irritating and uncomfortable debate with scientific and philosophic critics both within and without their profession about the real and biological nature of all so-called 'mental illnesses'. The intellectual and conceptual view which informs psychiatric diagnostic practice is much greyer, and more uncertain, pragmatic and empirically driven. It is multi-factorial, multi-axial, multi-theoretical and multi-interventionist. It is not surprising if, as a way of transcending this complexity and uncertainty, one response is to narrow the world view to one dominant system, be it biological, psychodynamic, cognitive behavioural or sociocultural.

However, the position that I wish to argue is the view of psychiatric classification and its value in treatment as seen by the non-doctor and the psychiatrist/diagnostician and the view enshrined in major psychiatric classification systems such as *DSM-IV*.

DSM-IV is the product of over 40 years of debate, research, opinion and clinical consensus about the most helpful way of ensuring that psychiatrists can provide their patients with the most effective psychiatric treatments that are available currently. For those who are not familiar with *DSM-IV*, there are several key features worth drawing attention to.

1 There is an explicit acknowledgement that there is no current satisfactory definition which specifies precise boundaries for the concept of mental disorder (APA, 1994: xxi). *DSM-IV* acknowledges that the concept of mental disorder lacks a consistent operational definition that covers all situations.
2 There is no assumption that each category of so-called 'mental disorder' is a completely discrete entity with absolute boundaries dividing it from other mental disorders or from no mental disorder.
3 There is no assumption that all individuals described as having the same mental disorder are alike in all important ways.
4 Making a *DSM-IV* diagnosis is only seen as the first step in a comprehensive evaluation for treatment planning.
5 *DSM-IV* states that the highest priority has been given to provide a helpful guide to clinical practice. Its aim is to be practical and useful for clinicians.

The text of *DSM-IV* indicates that the aetiology of many disorders is unknown, treatment indications are sometimes imprecise and the status of many disorders as diagnostic categories is uncertain, and is the subject of revision as a result of ongoing research. Accompanying the *DSM-IV* diagnostic manual are companion guides which provide the empirical data supporting the validity of each mental disorder. It is explicit that with further research there will be changes in the diagnostic categories and a need for further revisions of *DSM*.

What is most striking in all this is the degree to which *DSM-IV* acknowledges that it is a pragmatic classification system with limitations in its fundamental, intellectual and clinical constructs. *DSM-IV* is not designed as an edifice from which to defend the concept of mental illness, nor to argue for any fundamental reality to the construct of psychopathology. *DSM-IV* therefore is fundamentally to be seen and judged as a clinical tool. It is from this point of view that the remainder of this essay will argue for the value of classification of human distress and dysfunction as psychopathology and the ordering of this psychopathology into coherent patterns called mental disorders.

Psychiatric diagnosis in action

Why do I think that psychiatric assessment and diagnosis is important and potentially very helpful for the psychotherapist and his/her patient? I will try to illustrate this by briefly describing three case examples where I think a psychiatric diagnostic perspective had an important effect on treatment selection and outcome. I will then go on to describe in the next section in some detail the various benefits that can accrue for the patient and the therapist from utilizing a psychiatric diagnostic perspective.

Case example 1

Mary was a 35-year-old secretary, married with two children, referred to me by a psychiatrist for assessment for cognitive therapy because of long-term problems with depression, panic and low self-esteem dating back to her teenage years. At the time of referral she had been treated unsuccessfully with antidepressant medication and had completed two years of weekly group therapy with little improvement overall in her symptoms and functioning.

When I assessed her she described multiple episodes of low mood, insomnia and lethargy generally lasting three months, since her early teens. She reported that some of these episodes appeared to be triggered by upsets, others appeared to arise for no reason. She felt that her main problem was that she was inadequate and unable to cope with life's problems.

When I interviewed Mary's mother to obtain a collateral history she also gave a similar picture of recurrent episodes of depression and low mood, and reported that Mary at times appeared impulsive, spent excessively, appeared giddy and excitable and over-confident. When I re-interviewed Mary on the basis of this additional information, she did acknowledge that at times in her life, sometimes for days or weeks on end, she felt confident and optimistic and made plans which she later felt were unrealistic. On the basis of this history I suggested to Mary it was possible that she suffered from a mood disorder and, after reviewing her history over a period of several weeks during which this proposition appeared to be supported, Mary agreed to a trial of lithium carbonate, a specific mood stabilizer. Over a period of six to eight months Mary's mood swings gradually reduced and over the following five years she remained free of significant periods of depression.

Case example 2

Helen was a 25-year-old teacher referred with long-term problems of low self-esteem and social isolation which had not responded to a course of group therapy and individual dynamic psychotherapy over one year. On assessment she told me that she had no confidence in herself and believed that she was ugly. She described with some distress her preoccupation with the shape of her nose, the size of her eyes, and the texture of her skin. Because of her preoccupation with these perceived blemishes, she told me that she would not look in any mirrors, she kept her bedroom in darkness, and would spend hours putting on her make-up each day to try to conceal her supposed flaws. As a child she had been teased frequently at school for being overweight, and her mother had compared her unfavourably with her more attractive sister.

At the end of my assessment I suggested to Helen that she was describing a typical dysmorphophobic problem, and that this could be ameliorated significantly through intensive exposure-based sessions of cognitive-behavioural therapy. Mary was initially very sceptical and apprehensive about this, but did agree to try this approach. Over a period of four weeks she had six three-hour long sessions of exposure therapy, where she was gradually encouraged to tolerate looking at her face in a mirror at home and helped to cope with the distress and self-critical thoughts that accompanied this. Her partner was present during these highly charged sessions and was able over the following weeks to help her carry out some of this work without my presence. After six weeks Helen felt less withdrawn and depressed, and tentatively began to arrange to work at school. She was able to do so successfully, and over the following six months reported that her preoccupation with her appearance only marginally interfered with her daily life.

Case example 3

John was a single, 22-year-old, unemployed male, living with his parents, referred to me for cognitive therapy after he had returned home to live with his parents following a period of intensive inpatient behaviour therapy for severe obsessive-compulsive disorder characterized by severe fears of contamination with chemicals and dirt. Shortly after his return home he had become very depressed and angry; his preoccupation with contamination had recurred and his parents became very distressed by his behaviour, including his attempts to extract reassurance from them that he was not contaminated.

At my assessment he described intense obsessional fears, an inability to stop asking his parents for reassurance, feelings of hopelessness, insomnia, marked feelings of tiredness, poor concentration and loss of interest. I indicated to John and his parents that, while he undoubtedly had gained some benefit from his period of inpatient behaviour therapy, he was currently profoundly depressed and too disabled to be expected to overcome this problem using his behavioural self-help techniques. I recommended that he have a trial of antidepressant medication with a view to recommencing his behaviour therapy once his depression had remitted. With considerable reluctance, largely because of his fears of contamination with chemicals, John accepted a trial of medication, and over two months improved dramatically in terms of both his obsessions and his depression. He was then able to recommence his self-help behavioural techniques, and after four months moved out of his parents' home into a flat where he was able to live independently, although still partially handicapped by obsessions.

Discussion

These three cases indicate in different ways the benefits of a psychiatric diagnostic assessment and treatment planning in patients explicitly referred for psychotherapy. In the first instance a simple biological treatment, namely lithium, was suggested on the basis of a history of periods of mood elevation as well as periods of depression. The patient herself did not recognize these mild periods of mood elevation, and without the collateral history from her mother this problem would have been missed.

In the second case a diagnosis of dysmorphophobia resulted in successful treatment with brief but intensive exposure-based behaviour therapy. Failure to elicit this problem prior to previous therapy had resulted in two failed therapies.

In the third case, recognition of a concurrent depression complicating an obsessive-compulsive disorder led to a recommendation for medication, which improved the depression and allowed the patient to continue to benefit from self-help techniques previously learned in therapy.

In each of these three cases I would argue that failure to be aware of and search systematically for specific psychiatric symptomatology led to failed psychotherapeutic treatments. In each of these instances specific psychiatric assessment and diagnosis would have led to more effective treatment selection. This is one of the arguments made for the value of psychiatric diagnosis and assessment and will be returned to later in this chapter. However, I would now like to outline some of the more general benefits to be gained from maintaining a psychodiagnostic approach when assessing patients for psychotherapy.

Benefits of diagnostic labelling

While the critics of diagnostic labelling (for example, Szasz, 1961; Laing, 1965; Parker et al., 1995), have eloquently and vigorously rehearsed the potential disadvantages or even dangers of diagnostic labelling and treatment prescription, the potential advantages and benefits for patient, therapist and society have rarely been argued or acknowledged.

Why could diagnostic labelling be just as likely to be a helpful as harmful process?

First, a diagnosis gives a name to what for many patients is a frightening, confused and unfamiliar experience of distress and dysfunction. For the patient a diagnosis by organizing apparently unconnected and distressing symptoms and behaviours into a coherent and meaningful pattern reduces the fear of the unknown, and by implication also suggests that something can be done to alleviate the distress. Frank, in his classic treatise *Persuasion and Healing* (1973), pointed out that giving patients a coherent framework in which to conceptualize their problem was an important factor in reducing demoralization and inducing hope and the expectation of improvement

Second, a diagnosis gives the patient the sense that his or her symptoms and behaviours are not unique. Patients often feel enormously relieved to know that others suffer from a similar disorder and that they are not some bizarre phenomenon or human freak. Universalization – the process of becoming aware that 'others are in the same boat' – has long been recognized as a powerful psychotherapeutic factor (Yalom, 1970).

Third, the provision of a diagnosis undercuts the tendency of many patients to attribute their symptoms and behavioural problems to some moral, spiritual or characterological weakness. This reattribution process is a powerful guilt-reducing factor and is not only consciously utilized by psychiatric diagnosticians, but also used extensively in cognitive therapy (Beck et al., 1979) and interpersonal psychotherapy (Klerman et al., 1994).

Fourth, the processes of diagnostic labelling provides patients with a degree of detachment and objectivity regarding their symptoms and behaviour which facilitates their collaboration in the psychotherapeutic process (Beck et al., 1979).

Fifth, a careful and systematic approach to eliciting and classifying the symptoms and signs of patients' distress often enhances the empathic bond which forms the core of any successful therapeutic relationship. Patients respond positively to the awareness that their psychiatrist or therapist has a keen and thorough grasp of their experiences and the impact of these on their lives and those around them.

Sixth and finally, the process of diagnostic labelling not only can facilitate patients working collaboratively with the therapist, but also potentially puts the patient in an empowering position. As a result of being ascribed a diagnosis, the patient potentially has access to a wide source of knowledge and therapeutic resources within that framework. For example, a diagnosis can lead to access to a vast literature on self-help, peer support groups and local and national organizations which among their many functions have a destigmatizing and championing role.

In addition to the above potential benefits for patients, a systematic knowledge of psychopathology and diagnosis has a number of benefits for the psychiatrist or therapist. These are outlined briefly below.

First, a thorough knowledge of psychopathology can enhance the therapist's credibility with the patient and lead the patient to feel thoroughly understood. The capacity to organize a range of personal experiences and distress into a coherent pattern increases the therapist's sense of confidence and helps provide a focus and direction to the therapeutic encounter. This reductionist function of diagnosis, while often decried, is used positively in psychiatry, cognitive therapy and interpersonal therapy to facilitate the treatment process and improve treatment outcomes.

Second, a thorough knowledge of psychopathology and diagnostics helps the therapist to be alert for common problems which may not be explicitly articulated by patients as their main concern, but which may none the less have a significant impact on treatment outcome. For example, patients who present with problems of anxiety and panic frequently have concurrent depressive disorder, which, unless explicitly searched for, may remain undetected and impair response to treatment of the presenting problem unless treated itself (Macaskill and Macaskill, 1999).

Third, a thorough knowledge of psychopathology and diagnostics can also alert the therapist to search for symptoms which patients may deliberately conceal for fear that they may be labelled 'insane'. For example, many patients with obsessional symptoms who are plagued with fears about aggressive thoughts or impulses may conceal these from the therapist and talk only about their feelings of depression and anxiety. If the basic obsessional nature of their problems is not uncovered and this problem addressed directly, for example with behavioural therapy, the patient's symptoms of anxiety and depression may remain unresponsive to treatment.

The fourth benefit to derive from a thorough knowledge of psychopathology and of classification systems such as used in *DSM-IV* is that the diagnostician is encouraged not only to be thorough about eliciting patients' symptoms of distress and dysfunction, but also to explore thoroughly the patient's normal functioning across all domains of his or her life, with a view to establishing whether any particular behavioural traits or patterns are sufficiently disruptive and disabling to jeopardize the therapeutic relationship and compromise the efficacy of any treatment provided such that a poorer outcome and likely recurrence of the problems may be predicted. This rigorous attention to the assessment of personality functioning and its impact across the patient's life and in response to treatment is an important aspect of modern classification systems (Gelder et al., 1989).

The fifth and final advantage of diagnostic classification of patients' distress and dysfunction is that it leads to effective treatment planning. One of the most powerful and frequently cited arguments for the value and necessity of diagnosis is that an accurate diagnosis will inevitably lead to the prescription of a specific effective and efficient treatment. This is in fact a proposition that few psychiatrists or diagnosticians would defend in such an extreme form, possibly much to the surprise and chagrin of those who would wish to have a relatively easy target to demolish. Most psychiatrists would instead put forward the following views on the place and value of diagnosis in treatment planning:

1 The relationship between diagnosis and treatment planning is complex in most situations and can only be decided on after consideration of a wide range of factors of which diagnosis is but one. *DSM-IV* is explicit about this, saying that in general a diagnosis alone is insufficient to determine a treatment plan.

2 A diagnosis can often be very beneficial in proscribing certain treatments for certain problems: for example, a diagnosis of obsessive-

compulsive disorder predicts that psychotherapies other than behaviour therapy will be ineffective for this problem; a diagnosis of schizophrenia would predict that treatment with any form of psychotherapy on its own would be ineffective.

3   A diagnosis may lead to the selection of specific treatment as the treatment of choice: for example, neuroleptic medication in schizophrenia; mood stabilizers such as lithium in bipolar affective illness; behaviour therapy in obsessive-compulsive disorder or phobia.

4   The power of diagnosis in predicting treatment selection is enhanced when combined with an assessment of the severity of disability and distress caused by the disorder. For example, mild to moderate forms of depression respond equally well to antidepressants, cognitive-behavioural therapy or interpersonal therapy (Elkin et al., 1989). However, at more severe levels of depression, antidepressant medication is more effective on its own than either form of psychotherapy (Elkin et al., 1989). For more severe depression a combination of medication and psychotherapy is often the best treatment option (Macaskill, 1999). Similarly, for obsessive-compulsive disorder, a combination of medication and behaviour therapy is the optimum treatment, whereas mild to moderate levels of obsessive-compulsive disorder respond equally well to medication or behaviour therapy (Sperry, 1995).

5   The complexity inherent in the symptomatology of the ordinary patient often does not allow a simple generalization to be made from research findings on treatment and outcome even though these studies have utilized pure research diagnostic tools and been well conducted. Many patients require multiple interventions either sequentially or combined to provide optimum outcomes. The power of diagnosis to predict treatment selection and to predict treatment response is limited in many disorders, particularly when the problem is of relatively mild severity, by the finding that the quality of the therapeutic alliance has a powerful general effect and accounts for a large amount of the variance in outcome. This finding holds true not just for psychotherapeutic intervention but for biological interventions such as medication as well.

The above list indicates that, while diagnosis can be a powerful aid in treatment planning, it also has significant limitations.

Disadvantages of diagnostic labelling

As well as having significant limitations, diagnostic labelling can have the following disadvantages. It can be stigmatising, dehumanizing and coercive of patients. It can lead to an abuse of power by psychiatrists and to an invalidation of patients' experience. It can lead away from a focus on patients' lives and their problems to a focus on symptoms, and render the patient more helpless, dependent and excessively reliant on biological treatment. In over 20 years of working with patients as both a psychiatrist and a therapist, I have had the painful feedback from patients that on occasion my diagnostic and classifying efforts have been unhelpful in one or more of the ways I have outlined above. I have yet to meet a psychiatrist who can honestly recount that he or she has not had similar experiences. Szasz (1961), Laing (1965) and Parker et al. (1995) undoubtedly have a powerful point to make about the disadvantages of diagnostic labelling and assessment. I think, however, that their case is weakened by overgeneralization and their solution weakened by dichotomous thinking. While I agree with them that diagnosis *can* be unhelpful in the many ways mentioned above, personal experience, the result of patient treatment satisfaction studies, and the effective use of diagnostic labelling in major approaches to psychotherapy such as behavioural, cognitive and interpersonal therapy would argue against the problem being as pervasive as they imply.

The solution offered by Szasz to this putatively pervasive problem has been to argue for the abandonment of current classification endeavours and the whole process of thinking behind them. This approach misses the point entirely. My argument has been that the process of diagnosis and classification is not in itself intrinsically helpful or unhelpful: it is a tool that can be used well or badly. Like all tools, it is best when used with a thorough knowledge of how the tool works, its limitations and potential disadvantages. The way forward is to continue refining the tool and teaching those who use it how to do so in the best interests of their patients. The first objective is best achieved by the slow and painful process of systematic research. The second goal of ensuring that the classification system is used helpfully can only be achieved through thorough training in its use, coupled with a readiness to explore on a day-to-day basis with our patients the impact of our diagnostic and assessment interventions on their experience of themselves and their problems.

This is an evolutionary rather than revolutionary approach to the limitations both practical and theoretical of current psychiatric classification systems such as *DSM-IV*. Critics of the theory, purpose and effects of current psychiatric classification systems, such as Parker et al. (1995), would I think be less than satisfied with this conservative proposition. In their recent text *Deconstructing Psychopathology*, Parker et al. (1995) put forward an argument for a radical alternative mental health movement. In so doing they are at pains to answer the criticisms of the anti-psychiatry movement as being angry, negative, destructive and impractical. This awareness of an attempt to distance themselves from earlier and dogmatic proponents of the anti-psychiatry movement, for example Szasz and Laing, does much to facilitate the potential for genuine dialogue and understanding between the diagnostic classifier and the deconstructionist.

Approaching the deconstructionist alternative in the light of these reassuring self-reflections, what does the diagnostician make of the alternative radical mental health movements which are offered as exemplars of the deconstructionist approach to psychopathology in action?

The nature of the supporting evidence cited for the deconstructionist movement immediately highlights the gulf between the diagnosticians and the deconstructionists on what they present in evidence. The former approach emphasizes controlled clinical trials as the ultimate arbiter of the practical, clinical value of treatment supplied within its theoretical framework. The latter, by contrast, relies primarily on descriptive accounts unfettered by the methodological criteria of good, quantitative, clinical research. This epistemological chasm has a very unfortunate result. Little of the clinical evidence cited by the deconstructionists to support their view, for example the Italian anti-psychiatry movement of the 1980s and the radical psychiatric approaches in the United States following the writings of Szasz (1961) and Holzman (1995), can be accepted as legitimate evidence by researchers from conventional diagnostic approaches. It is difficult to see how this methodologically driven stalemate can be transcended unless a new collaborative spirit of joint research begins to permeate an intellectual debate dominated by outdated rhetoric and polemics.

References

Beck, A.T., Rush, A.J., Shaw, B.F. and Emery, G. (1979) *Cognitive Therapy of Depression*. New York: Guilford Press.

APA (1997) *Diagnostic and Statistical Manual of Mental Disorders*. 4th edn. Washington, DC: American Psychiatric Association.

Elkin, I., Shea, M.T., Watkins, J.T. and Imber, S.D., Sotsky, S.M., Collins, J.F., Glass, D.R., Pilkonis, P.A., Leber, W.A., Docherty, J.P., Fiester, S.J. and Parloff, M.B. (1989) 'The National Institute of Mental Health Treatment of Depression Collaborative Research Program: general effectiveness of treatments', *Archives of General Psychiatry*, 46: 971–82.

Frank, J.D. (1973) *Persuasion and Healing*. 2nd edn. New York: Schocken.

Gelder, M., Gath, D. and Mayou, R. (1989) *Oxford Textbook of Psychiatry*. 2nd edn. Oxford: Oxford University Press.

Holzman, L. (1995) 'Newman's practice of method completes Vygotsky', in I. Parker and R. Speads (eds), *Psychology and Marxism: Co-existence and Contradiction*. London: Pluto.

Klerman, G.L., Weissman, M.M., Makkowitz, J.C., Glick, I., Wilner, P.J., Mason, B. and Shear, M.K. (1994) 'Medication and psychotherapy', in A.E. Bergin and S.L. Garfield (eds), *Handbook of Psychotherapy and Behavior Change*. 4th edn. New York: John Wiley.

Laing, R.D. (1965) *The Divided Self: An Existential Study in Sanity and Madness*. Harmondsworth: Penguin.

Macaskill, N.D. (1999) 'Combined psychotherapy with pharmacotherapy to optimize treatment outcomes in psychiatric disorders', *Advances in Psychiatric Treatment* (in press).

Macaskill, N.D. and Macaskill, A. (1999) 'Failure to diagnose depression in patients referred to psychotherapy', *International Journal of Social Psychiatry* (in press).

Parker, I., Georgaca, G., Harper, D., McLaughlin, T. and Stowell-Smith, M. (1995) *Deconstructing Psychopathology*. London: Sage.

Sperry, L. (1995) *Psychopharmacology and Psychotherapy: Strategies and Optimizing Treatment Outcomes.* New York: Brunner/Mazel.
Szasz, T. (1961) *The Myth of Mental Illness.* New York: Harper & Row.
Yalom, I. (1970) *The Theory and Practice of Group Psychotherapy.* New York: Basic Books.

14   The limitations of boundaries

Derek Gale

Doesn't it strike you as strange that the rules governing boundary issues in virtually all types of psychotherapy today are based on the ideas of an elderly misanthropist living in turn-of-the-century Vienna and that this man, Sigmund Freud, himself broke every rule he ever invented, especially the rule that the therapist should be a *tabula rasa* onto whom the patient can project?

It is my contention in this chapter that the all-pervading influence of Freud's ideas has driven psychotherapy and counselling into an intellectual straitjacket which restricts therapy both as an intellectual process and also as a practical process. These restrictions are expressed in terms of boundaries and I suggest that if we were less keen on boundaries and more keen on change, our therapeutic endeavours would be far more successful.

Given the remit of putting my argument in 3,000 words I shall not be able to develop it as thoroughly as I would have wished and do not have the space to explain how the case for strict boundaries stems from Freudian theory, which is itself highly questionable on human, scientific and intellectual grounds.

Instead, I propose in my chapter to adapt a letter I wrote to a therapist in training in the analytic tradition who showed me an essay she had written on 'The Frame'. It may seem to some readers that I am a therapist without boundaries, but as one of my clients said recently: 'It's not that you don't have boundaries – in fact your boundaries are very strict – it's just that your boundaries are much wider and more flexible than other therapists. This of course puts more responsibility on you, but you seem to be able to handle it.'

The frame

It is fortuitous that I was sent this essay just as I was starting to think about this chapter, so my letter was in the form of a first draft of my thinking. I mention this lest you should think that laziness has caused me to merely shove in a pre-existing piece of writing. I was interested in the essay for two reasons. First, the author is very intelligent and a good essay writer who I was sure would have produced a very good digest of the issues. This view was shared by her tutor. However, a more important reason for wanting to read her essay was that she is deeply in psychodynamic therapy and holds to her belief in the value of the frame with a passion.

Dear . . .

I know you didn't want to tell me that you had upped your therapy to three times a week and that my enthusiasm for your increased commitment surprised you. But if I wanted to have therapy in this tradition I should most emphatically insist that it was done properly and that all the trappings were observed. In parenthesis I should add that I submitted to three years of analytical psychotherapy after the death of my mother, so I do know what it is like to lie on the couch two or even three times a week.

I am not therefore arguing that these trappings are wrong in terms of a psychoanalytically based therapy, because without them analysis would not be analysis. It would be like complaining that ice cream would be very nice if it weren't so cold. What I do argue is that for myself, I found analysis cold, laborious and slow, and that being held in the tight boundaries did not have the benefits promised.

I have looked at your essay carefully and I noted two things which worried me: first, you write in a quite infantilized style; and, second, your analysis is purely internal and takes account of no other viewpoints. I think strict boundaries encourage infantilization of the client and I think this is happening to you.[1] One of the things which worries me about the frame is how difficult it is for the client to grow up. Strict boundaries strike me as being like school rules: something which keeps you in your place. Proponents of strict boundaries don't tend to accept criticism, as Jeffrey Masson found to his cost. My own experience was that my analytic therapist was very good at interpreting, which often felt like criticism, and very poor at acknowledging progress, which rarely felt like praise. This left me feeling unsupported, which is strange as the couch and the other boundaries are supposed to give a feeling of support and safety.

You could quite easily dismiss my ideas and responses as being from someone who is from a different discipline and who quite simply doesn't understand. However, the real thing is that most psychotherapy only accepts internal criticism, and therefore we just either accept the dogma or have a dialogue of the deaf.[2] There is no real discussion between approaches, and such discussions, when they do occur, generally founder on the boundary issues. I find that proponents of strict boundaries find it impossible to discuss looser boundaries, and, more disturbing, led by psychoanalysts they take the high moral ground on this, stating that their viewpoint is the only one which can help the patient. What interests me is the shock with which I am often greeted when I speak of a part of my own practice which breaks a boundary espoused by my interlocutor. I am rarely asked why I adopt such a practice, I am just told that it is incorrect, because it breaks a boundary. This holds true as far as I can tell for psychotherapists of all persuasions, and I notice that each has different boundaries, so that what is acceptable behaviour to one is unacceptable to another.

As a humanistic psychologist, my boundaries are very different from yours, and I probably run wider boundaries than most humanistic psychologists. This does not mean that I work without boundaries or limits; what it does mean is that I and my clients feel safer in a much wider relationships which is based on authenticity both in the client and in myself. I probably see therapy as more a moral activity than anything else. This is much more difficult for me as the therapist because it leaves my own behaviour open to question, but this is a challenge I accept, as I believe therapy is about learning to live and the best teacher teaches by example. I do not think there is much of an example in a *tabula rasa* therapist.

Now let's look at some of the specific boundary issues you raise.

Neutrality

I think all therapists should be neutral, but I am realistic enough to know that it is impossible. It is like the *tabula rasa*: it's an interesting goal, but not an achievable one. Richard Stevens (1987) in his book on Freud points out that Freud actually rewards and punishes free association by responding to some associations with interpretations and ignoring others.

Neutrality is about not forcing your ideas on another person; it is not about having no ideas yourself, and as you will see from what follows, I keep on coming back to the fact that there can be no such things as a value-free relationship between two human beings. As I see this neutrality as being impossible, I think it is more beneficial and more honest to be up front about my values and preferences while at the same time allowing the client to have his or her own views. As I am far less dogmatic and less authoritarian than most analysts, I can handle these differences better.

You may wish to keep politics, class and money out of therapy, but you can't, as the following simple example makes clear. You see your therapist at home, so you see how she decorates her home and where she lives and you know how much she charges. On the basis of this, consciously or unconsciously you cannot fail to make some pretty shrewd guesses about her views, social class and lifestyle. She, on the other hand, takes an absurd position if she tries to argue that you can be understood only in terms of your unconscious processes, which are not inextricably linked with your own social class, politics and financial position.

I sometimes ask a client who has spent a long time trying to make a difficult decision which side he or she thought I was on, and generally think I have done a good job if they say, 'I don't know, but I think you may have thought . . .' Having views of my own does not force the client to agree with them, but refusing to have views can make the client feel that he or she has to try and 'suss out' my views and appear to agree with them – which follows on nicely to your next point.

Anonymity of the therapist

OK. Let's get the gloves off. 'Anonymous I ain't' and I don't see it doing any harm. Classically the argument is based directly in Freud's thinking on the subject, which is that if the analyst is not anonymous, the patient will not be able to make a transference on to him or her. Empirically my practice shows me that this is not the case and my clients, despite my lack of anonymity, manage to project and to transfer on to me with no difficulty at all. Furthermore, I think there are advantages in the therapist not being anonymous and therefore I think my looser boundary has advantages over the strict boundary proposed by the frame. I want to offer you a simple example which I think speaks volumes. We all have experiences of having been helped by a bit of personal sharing by the therapist. Once in therapy with my analytic therapist, who gave very little away, I asked her if buying shoes for a young child wasn't the worst thing on earth. Her reply, although very circumspect, implied a shared experience which brought me closer to her and made it easier for me to trust her and to think of her as a human being, not a cold and remote therapist.

One of my clients said to me recently when I mentioned a small personal problem, 'But Derek you are human after all . . .' Her tone of voice made it clear that this helped her, and some interesting discussion followed on why and how she created a perfect image of me and how that was what she had done with her father.

Like many people in therapy, I have feared hurting my therapist, and although at the time I may have argued that this was because I knew she was having a hard time in her life, the reality is that I was engaging a defence mechanism to do with my own unwillingness to express my anger; not her perceived vulnerability. I was frightened of the power of my anger and of the damage it could do, so I did the classic thing of not facing the fear and excusing myself on the grounds that I could not be angry with her when she was vulnerable herself. The rationalization was clear and became clear to me when her personal problems were resolved and I still could not be angry with her. Clearly I had big difficulties with being really angry with women. I had just as much trouble confronting my analytic anonymous therapist as I did confronting her predecessor. The problem I had finally to realize was in me and not in the orientation of the therapist.

I think clients make real progress when they say, 'I don't care about you, I want to speak about me', because it is a real test of their trust in the therapy and therefore a real chance to increase their trust in themselves. This is a very difficult thing to do, and no psychotherapeutic structure that I have come across makes it any easier.

Refraining from physical contact

As for refraining from physical contact, well I wouldn't know how to do my work if I didn't touch people, but then I wouldn't know how to do my life if I didn't touch people. I see my job as making people more comfortable with normal human contact and giving access to a wider range of actions, not a narrower one. My clients often ask for a hug, and I don't think they would be helped by or be very pleased with a suggestion that they analyse their need rather than satisfying it. It might be hard to believe, but even if a session starts with a hug and a cry, the painful feelings can still be worked through and may even be worked with deeper and more effectively than in a more boundaried form of therapy.

There is a very interesting example given in Patrick Casement's *On Learning from the Patient* (1985), in which he goes to great lengths to explain why it would have been counterproductive to hold a patient's hand (as she had asked him to do) while she recounted a dreadfully painful experience. While I am sure Casement's motives were pure, his behaviour strikes me as simply inhumane and also based on a mistaken assumption that his making the recall easier for the client would have somehow made the recall less therapeutic.

Of course the body-oriented therapies often involve a lot of touch, and I have tried Postural Integration and found it very helpful. I realize that this sort of thing is anathema to analysis, but I found twelve sessions over nine months of taking all my clothes off in front of a not unattractive woman and engaging in a quite painful form of deep tissue massage incredibly helpful on a deep therapeutic level.

Confidentiality

I don't see how any therapy can take place without complete confidentiality, and I have even worked with a therapist who thought that what she said was confidential. So there seems to be no disagreement here. However, I do think there is a great deal to be gained from people being able to share what they have worked on in therapy, but this of course must be their own choice.

I noted in your essay some uncertainty about whether you would feel obligated to report a client who admitted a crime to the police. On this point it seems that my boundaries are stricter than yours, because I see myself as a healer and not a policeman or judge, and therefore while I might encourage someone to give themself up, I would not see it as my duty to report them.

When I worked in mental hospitals I worked with some real criminals, so this is an issue to which I had to give a lot of practical thought.

The fixed location

I see the fixed location as more a matter of organizational convenience than dogma, and I think if we make a fuss about it, it is just giving clients something to complain about. I didn't have therapy in a fixed location for years and it never bothered me. More to the point, I don't see why it should, and if it does there is something to discuss which might be fruitful for the client. I can see how this can be difficult in an analytic setting, but that's a problem that strict boundaries create for themselves. I can't see how teaching people to demand an unreal situation teaches them to act authentically in the real world. I have given therapy in some weird locations: a café, a bar, even my hotel room or on a walk, and while I tend to shy away from doing this, clients seem to benefit from it.

Therapists are not parents

Well of course not, but they are in a way!

I think I would argue that by trying to institutionalize this idea by making it a boundary issue the analyst is trying to do the impossible, because the role of the therapist is to act the good parent that the client never had. While I do not see it as being the therapist's job to be indulgent to the client, an act of indulgence can be of enormous help in moving a client on. I once made an omelette for a client and she told me, after finishing therapy, that it was the most helpful thing I had ever done for her. As with all boundary issues, what worries me about the position described in the frame is that flexibility is lost, implying that all people are somehow the same and require the same response. This is an attitude which is clearly damaging in the rearing of children and is no less so in therapy.

The fee

You say the fee, once set, should not be altered. This strikes me as twaddle. I agree that if there is to be a change of fee it should be discussed with the client, but fees change for all sorts of reasons: I find the sight of a therapist seeing people for peanuts, because they have been seeing them for so long, ridiculous. You make Gray's (1994) point that therapists are not parents, yet on the question of the fee you seem to expect them to be indulgent. I see as good reasons for changing the fee: inflation, the client getting a significant increase or decrease in salary.

In my experience fee issues are usually more the therapist's problem than the client's, and I have been banging on for years about how little therapists value their work and time in money terms. I think people should pay what therapy is worth and not get it on the cheap, and if they can afford to pay more they should. If I take someone on as a poor single parent at one fee and her kids leave home and she gets a well-paid job, I don't see why the fee shouldn't increase.

I think you understand how important money is in therapy as you describe a problem with paying the bill. I guess we've all left our cheque books at home. I even once made the cheque out to Derek Gale!!

The fixed time

I can't really see that this matters so much, although it is convenient for both sides in terms of organization. Perhaps this is because I had my own therapy at all sorts of times. The fixed time seems to me just a bit of psychoanalytic hocus-pocus and a creation of an even more unreal experience. What strikes me as important is that the client knows that he or she is important to the therapist and that the time is not changed at whim. Furthermore, I work with people who work shifts and have irregular timetables for other reasons and who would be disenfranchised by a demand that they come at the same time every week. So there you have it. I am in favour of boundaries which keep the therapist and the client safe, but I am not in favour of boundaries which limit and cramp the therapy.
Yours,
Derek

The vexed question of Brian Thorne's having taken his clothes off

The editor of this book has asked me if I would be willing to comment on the therapeutic process in the late 1970s and early 1980s, during which one of Brian's clients sometimes removed her clothes and on one unique occasion he removed his. By chance, I happen to own the rights to the book in which a description of these sessions was published (Dryden, 1984), and know that if there is ever a second edition of this book, Brian has asked for certain amendments to be made to his original text in order to make it crystal clear that this was a unique case of exceptional challenge with exceptional characteristics and can in no way act as a model for other therapists. He also notes that it was conducted before the introduction of the British Association for Counselling's Code of Ethics and Practice and its particular interpretation of what constitutes 'sexual behaviour'. I therefore have no hesitation in taking this opportunity to commend Brian for his courage, first in allowing his client to do what she needed to do, and second in describing what had happened, in the public domain. I do not know Brian personally, but I have only heard colleagues and past clients speak well of him.

I believe the client was helped by the experience and continues all these years later to regard it as central to her continuing psychological well-being.

Clearly Brian sailed very close to the wind in his work with this client, but he experienced the relationship at great depth and decided that he could contain the brief naked encounter within the boundary of the therapeutic session, which came very near the end of a process lasting almost four years.

Brian recognized that a boundary in psychotherapy is something which exists on three parallels: first, that which the therapist is able to manage; second, that which the client can manage; and third, that which they can both agree on. I see this in direct contrast to Casement's view, mentioned above. Thorne's approach is what I call 'boundaried therapy'. In my opinion those who wish to criticize Brian for what he did would be better employed in commending him for his courage and self-control and his ability to observe boundaries in what must have been a very difficult and tempting situation. He was therefore able to put the needs of his client first, something which the frame's inflexibility does not allow.

I assume he would not again do what he did then, not because he thought it was wrong, but because the rule makers are in the ascendancy. I sincerely hope that I do not open an old wound in mentioning this subject. Brian's experience clearly shows that obsession with boundaries, rules and professionalization does deprive the client of something, because we all have to operate at the speed of the slowest. This kills innovation and provides no space for genius. So in trying to protect the client from the unscrupulous, we deprive him or her of genius. I wish I knew how this paradox could be resolved.

Notes

1. Needless to say this comment caused her great offence when she read the first draft, for which I am genuinely sorry, but I still hold to my observation.
2. This point is emphasized by the correspondence I have had with the author of the essay, who seems unable to engage in dialogue about the issues on which we disagree. Clearly I am criticizing something which is far too personally important for her to be able to hear it dispassionately. In her case this is understandable, but surely experienced therapists should be able to have such discussions. The current debate about who can be a member of The United Kingdom Council for Psychotherapy highlights this problem.

References

Casement, P. (1985) *On Learning from the Patient*. London: Tavistock/Routledge.
Dryden, W. (ed.) (1984) *Key Cases in Psychotherapy*. London: Croom Helm.
Gray, A. (1994) *An Introduction to the Therapeutic Frame*. London: Routledge.
Stevens, R. (1987) *Freud and Psychoanalysis*. London: Croom Helm.

15   Maintaining boundaries in psychotherapy: a view from evolutionary psychoanalysis

David Livingstone Smith

I have been asked to write a chapter defending the thesis that strictly maintaining boundaries is essential to the responsible practice of psychotherapy. As the title implies, I will approach the subject from an evolutionary psychoanalytic perspective. Although the first part of my discussion may strike the reader as somewhat arcane and remote from the practical and ethical issues of psychotherapy, the initial sections lay the groundwork for a clinically focused discussion in the latter half of the chapter.

The rules of the game

What makes a game, for instance the game of chess? It isn't the physical equipment, an eight-by-eight black and white matrix and a set of chess pieces. Chess could be played using a red and purple matrix and seashells. We can even play abstract chess on a virtual chessboard using virtual pieces, only specifying coordinates such as P–K4. Like any other game, chess is defined by its rules. Abstract non-physical chess, standard chess and red and purple seashell chess all share identical rules. If we change a rule we change the game. Like chess, psychotherapy too is constituted by its rules (Mooij, 1982). Different rules, implicit and explicit, differentiate one form of psychotherapy from the next.

Games can tell us much about the world. Biologists have turned to a discipline called 'game theory' to understand the game of life, that is, to understand the principles governing the way that organisms interact. In particular, biologists have used game theory to come to grips with the problem of explaining altruism.

Altruism is at first glance biologically puzzling. After all, Darwinian theory claims that individual reproductive success drives evolution. Why should any creature sacrifice its own advantage for the benefit of another? It makes biological sense for a creature to make personal sacrifices for the benefit of its blood relations. A mother making personal sacrifices for her offspring enhances the likelihood that her offspring will live to reproduce and thereby cause her own genes, which they have inherited, to proliferate. Biologists call this form of altruism 'kin altruism'.

But what about altruism between unrelated creatures? How might this have evolved? Self-sacrifice for the sake of a neighbour may benefit an individual if there is an actual or potential *exchange* implied. The principle of 'I scratch your back, you scratch mine' applies literally in the case of mutual grooming amongst primates. Apes exchange roles grooming one another's backs, an area that is out of reach for a lone ape left to its own devices. Biologists call such patterns of cooperation 'reciprocal altruism'.

Reciprocal altruism inevitably involves elements of instability and uncertainty. Although it may be very advantageous for me to cooperate with you to our mutual benefit, it is unfortunately even *more* advantageous for me to pull the wool over your eyes and take from you without paying my full dues, thus *defaulting* on our contract. One way to do this is to 'take the money and run'. If you and I agree that you will buy the first round of drinks and I will buy the next, I can drink my beer and leave the pub without keeping my part of the bargain. This strategy only works if I don't want to have anything more to do with you. If I need more favours from you, defaulting will be to my disadvantage. I know that you won't want to do business with me again, and I will be deprived of the desired benefits of our cooperation.

If I am going to default I had better *cheat*. I had better *deceive* you into thinking that we are equal partners, whereas I am actually taking more than my fair share. It has been argued (Trivers, 1985) that human beings are evolved cheaters. Criminality, deceit and infidelity are human universals. Vast effort and resources are dedicated to the tasks of policing and penalizing cheaters on local, national and even international scales.

Most people seem prepared to concede that criminality and dishonesty are pervasive. However, we tend to point the finger at *others* rather than ourselves. Not one person whom I have asked about the prevalence of dishonesty in the human species has said to me, 'Yes, you should have seen how I screwed my business partner!' or, for example, 'I told my husband that I was out shopping when I was actually with my lover in a hotel room.' It is always *somebody else* who is doing the cheating.

Perhaps it is just part of human nature to avoid coming to grips with our own potential for exploitativeness and we all tend to deceive ourselves about the extent to which we deceive others. Trivers (1976, 1985) argues that there are evolutionary reasons why we might be inclined to keep our own treachery a secret from ourselves. Being conscious of our own duplicity causes discomfort. Our discomfort leaks out in spite of efforts to appear sincere. Insincerity is betrayed by our tone of voice, facial expression and involuntary body movements (Ekman, 1988).

The problem of inadvertent self-incrimination thus confronted Mother Nature with an engineering problem: how can we lie to others without emitting any of the tell-tale signs of deception? One way of accomplishing this is to keep oneself unaware of what is going on. If you remain *unconscious* of your own deceitfulness you can consciously lie in good faith!

> Biologists propose that the overriding function of self-deception is the more fluid deception of *others*. That is, hiding aspects of reality from the conscious mind also hides these aspects more deeply from others. An *unconscious* deceiver is not expected to show signs of the stress associated with consciously trying to perpetrate deception. (Trivers, 1988: vi, original emphasis)

The evolution of language would have provided us with a new and potent technology of deception. Language enables us to lie.

> With the advent of language in the human lineage, the possibilities for deception and self-deception were greatly enlarged. If language permits the communication of much more detailed and extensive information . . . then it both permits and encourages the communication of much more detailed and extensive misinformation. A portion of the brain devoted to verbal functions must become specialized for the maintenance of falsehood. This will require biased perceptions, biased memory, and biased logic; and these processes are ideally kept unconscious. (Trivers, 1981: 35)

There is even evidence that capacities for deception and deception-detection are hard-wired into the architecture of the human central nervous system (Lockhard and Mateer, 1988; Gazzaniga, 1992; Badcock, 1994).

It is widely acknowledged that the psychotherapeutic situation is potentially and all too often actually abusive. Freud (1916–17/1964) was apparently the first person to note that there is always a strong element of suggestion (and suggestibility) in psychotherapy. He believed that psychotherapy patients are inclined to idealize their therapists and uncritically accept their views. To make matters worse, the psychotherapeutic situation is full of temptations for the therapist.

> One way or another, the analyst's temptation is to use the analytic work to get otherwise unavailable gratifications, support faltering defences, enhance grandiose fantasies, and, in the end, to *use* the analysand rather than *work for* him or her. (Schafer, 1983: 25, original emphasis)

All of this is normally included under the rubric of 'countertransference' – the therapist's residual psychopathology that interferes with the work. According to an evolutionary perspective, the tendency to unconsciously exploit one's patients is not essentially an expression of psychopathology (although this can come into it): it is an expression of human nature. When we covertly exploit our patients we are behaving in a 'healthy' fashion. We are doing what Mother Nature designed us to do. Therapists' 'empathic resonance' with their patients is inevitably biased in favour of their own self-interest. Those who believe that their training and personal psychotherapy has immunized them against these tendencies are dangerously self-deceived. They have deceived themselves about the degree of their own self-deception. It is perhaps useful to understand self-deception as just another vector of deception. The deception-producing module need not know *who* it is that is being deceived, just so long as the act of deception provides some evolutionary advantage.

How, in the face of our evolved nature, can we make sure that we are working for our patients? We need something that transcends the treacherous and opaque waters of our own subjectivity. We need a clearly articulated set of ground rules to keep us in line, and to which we must strive to subordinate our personality. However, these guidelines must not be arbitrary or dogmatic dicta. They must be derived from a real understanding of the causal processes at work in human interactions.

Working for the patient requires discipline. Those therapists who balk at the necessity for intense self-discipline should find another field. Good-enough therapists must have the humility to accept that they are inclined to exploit their patients and to accept that they will mainly be unconscious of this. The required degree of altruism comes neither easily nor naturally, and can be sustained only with the help of the most exacting vigilance.

The evolution of unconscious communication[1]

At this point in the argument we confront a new problem: which ground rules should therapists use? Controversy has raged over this matter for decades. Psychotherapists of different theoretical persuasions advocate very different approaches, and even within a single tradition there can be considerable disagreement about the rules for appropriate therapeutic conduct. In light of the argument already presented, it seems likely that each of us will be attracted to that psychotherapeutic approach which is most consistent with our own characteristic mode of interpersonal exploitation.

> Ultimately one of the major ways in which therapists fail their patients revolves around the therapist's use of self-deceptive strategies for protecting or enhancing his or her interests . . . in a fashion that is cast in terms of the interests of the patient. (Slavin and Kriegman, 1992: 254, original emphasis)

So, once again we are in a position of requiring some standard of judgement external to our biased subjectivity. I will develop the argument that we have just such an independent standard in the unconscious subjectivity of our patients, who, as Little (1951) memorably described it, 'hold up a mirror' to us. The patient, although no less biased and self-interested than the therapist, is none the less able to provide a corrective to the therapist's point of view.

Trivers (1976), Alexander (1979) and others suggested that the evolution of unconscious exploitation might provoke an evolutionary 'arms race' promoting development of more and more sophisticated forms of deception-detection. In other words, if you and I both tend to unconsciously exploit one another, I can get the 'edge' on you if I am sensitive to the very subtle signals that betray your intentions. Refined detection mechanisms would then beget the natural selection of more effective deceptive strategies until after a number of cycles the 'arms race' would reach a point of equilibrium. The evolution of self-deception was a crucial step in this progression.

There is reason to suppose that our minds have evolved in such a way that we remain largely unconscious of the ability to detect deceit in others. Badcock argues that

> it is in your own self-interest to deceive yourself about others' self-interest because then the others can all the more easily be pressured into acting against their self-interest. . . . In other words, self-deception about others' self-interest serves our own selfishness because it makes it easier for us to exploit others, expecting them to pay while we benefit. . . . After all if we would never suspect George of free-riding, why should we suspect ourselves? Like our personal consciousness, our social consciousness could be cryptic and could hide, not merely our own selfish and anti-social motives, but those of others too. (1994: 74–5)

If we follow Badcock's line of reasoning we are led to the conclusion that *deception-detecting abilities would be advantageous if they operated outside of consciousness.* Sophisticated neural deception-detecting technology would then co-exist with conscious naïveté, allowing us the best of both worlds. But what possible use are purely unconscious perceptual sensitivities? Such capacities would be of use if they impacted constructively on our behaviour in such a way as to help us escape exploitation. As far as is known, however, this does not occur (Langs, 1995). Alternatively, the capacity for unconscious deception-detection would be of use if it enabled us to influence the behaviour of the person or persons attempting to exploit us, that is, if we were able to unconsciously *signal* our awareness to the very person attempting to mislead us. With such a communications system in place we could converse simultaneously on two separate levels. A relatively defensive stream of conscious communication could co-exist with a far more psychologically incisive unconscious 'conversation'.

The idea that human beings unconsciously communicate such messages does not contradict the clear and obvious fact that human beings vary considerably in their capacity to *consciously* detect and communicate about such things. The model that I have derived from the work of the evolutionary psychologists does not rely on the broadly Freudian principle that unconscious mental states are actively excluded from awareness because we find their presence unbearable. Rather, it argues that human beings have been designed by evolutionary pressures to remain unconscious of certain forms of engagement with their fellows. There is no psychological *motive* causing our awareness of cheating to remain unconscious: our unconsciousness is an aspect of what Slavin and Kriegman (1992) have called the 'adaptive design of the human psyche'.

If true, this would mean that psychotherapy patients unconsciously monitor their therapists' behaviour, unconsciously perceive their therapists' exploitative and self-serving actions, and unconsciously communicate these perceptions to their therapists in the unconscious hope of influencing them to stop. Were therapists able to decode these communications, they would no longer be puzzled about which ground rules to follow, because their patients would unconsciously *tell* them. Therapists could use their patients' evolved capacity to detect exploitation as a way of monitoring and evaluating their own behaviour, thus escaping the inevitable bias of their own subjective viewpoint.

The communicative approach

The work of Robert Langs has corroborated these evolutionary speculations. Langs' *communicative approach* to psychotherapy revolves around patients' unconscious awareness of therapists' boundary violations. Langs (for example, 1992a, 1992b) holds that all of us possess an unconscious ability to rapidly draw extremely incisive conclusions about the implications of human interactions, and our unconscious insights never become directly accessible to consciousness (Langs, 1988).

According to Langs, we communicate our unconscious awareness of one another only in an indirect, encoded fashion. We express our unconscious awareness only in the form of *narratives*. Narratives encode unconscious meaning. A narrative is an account of a real or imaginary event or situation. Narratives are vivid and concrete: they can be *pictured* by the listener. Non-narrative communication is reflective and abstract. A person talking about 'the meaning of life' is engaged in non-narrative discourse, whereas a person recounting the plot of a film that he or she has recently seen is narrating. A number of psychologists and cognitive scientists have distinguished between the two modes of thinking and communicating (for example, Tulving, 1983; Bruner, 1986; Donald, 1991; Bucci, 1997).

Psychotherapy patients often narrate during sessions. According to Langs, these narratives virtually always provide a running commentary on the therapy. They spell our the raw implications of the therapist's behaviour. Perhaps an example will make this clear. A psychoanalytic therapist began the hour by suggesting to his patient that she increase the frequency of sessions from once to twice a week, basing this recommendation on the way that the work had been deepening. The patient replied that she would give it some thought. She then went on to describe a recovered memory of huddling in her bedroom as a small child listening to her parents violently argue. Her mother was shouting in anger at her father for not earning the amount of money that she wanted. She remembered being frightened that her mother would abandon them and go to find a wealthier man.

Communicative psychotherapists interpret narratives in light of their *triggers* (those acts of commission or omission by the therapist that have evoked the narrative). This is accomplished by abstracting the *themes* of the narratives. In this example, the trigger is the therapist's suggestion that the number of sessions be increased. The narrative is the patient's memory of her parents' argument. The themes are 'Somebody wants more money from somebody else' and 'Somebody may abandon somebody else for the sake of more money'. According to the communicative view, the memory encodes the patient's unconscious awareness of the exploitative implications of the therapist's suggestion that they increase the frequency of sessions. The patient unconsciously feels that the therapist wants her to provide him with more money (by paying for more frequent sessions) and has concluded that unless she complies the therapist may terminate the therapy and replace the patient with someone who will pay her more. This leads to a hypothesis about a ground rule: *the therapist should refrain from unilaterally recommending a change in the frequency of sessions.* This hypothesis could be tested against further clinical examples to determine whether it reliably holds. If it does, then something has been learned about the appropriate ground rules for psychotherapy. A conclusion will have been reached based on patients' unconscious responses rather than therapists' ideologies.

Langs found that there is a reliable, lawful relationship between the behaviour of therapists and the thematic content of patients' responsive narratives. All psychotherapy patients seem to unconsciously want their therapists to strictly adhere to a set of fundamental ground rules. Although many of these ground rules contradict widely advocated psychotherapeutic practices, Langs argues that their violation will regularly and predictably evoke negative narrative responses from patients. The ideal ground rules include the following:[2]

1 The therapy should be totally private.
2 The therapy should be totally confidential.
3 The therapy should take place at a fixed location.
4 There is a set time for each session.
5 Each session lasts for the same number of minutes.
6 There is a set fee for each session.
7 The patient is responsible for paying for all scheduled sessions.
8 The therapist is responsible for attending all scheduled sessions.
9 The therapist is responsible for explicitly setting out the ground rules of therapy.
10 The therapist should intervene in accord with the rule of neutrality.
11 The therapist should not unilaterally terminate the therapy.
12 The therapist should subordinate his or her personality to the task of understanding the patient.
13 The therapist should silently listen for most of the time.
14 The therapists' verbal interventions should be mostly interpretative.
15 The therapist should conduct the therapy in a manner in accord with the patient's unconscious communications.

16 The therapist should refrain from physical contact with the client.
17 The therapist should have no contact with the client outside therapy sessions.
18 The therapist should not accept referrals from the patient.
19 The therapist should not accept friends or acquaintances of the patient into therapy.
20 Gifts should be neither given nor received.
21 The therapist should take full responsibility for his or her failure to comply with these ground rules.

These are the rules that psychotherapy patients unconsciously want their therapists to follow, irrespective of their conscious preferences. They appear to be *universal* rules that are relatively immune from either individual or cultural variation.[3] Every time a therapist deviates from these ground rules, the patient unconsciously feels violated and will express this in negatively toned narratives spelling out the deceitful and exploitative implications of the deviation. By the same token, when the therapist rectifies some aspect of the therapy in response to the patient's unconscious recommendations, the therapist will be rewarded with an *encoded validation*. The patient will produce a positively toned narrative involving such themes as altruism, care, understanding and self-discipline.

Because I advocate this method of psychotherapy, I have often been accused of being 'rigid' and 'dogmatic'. These are appropriate epithets for someone who clings stubbornly to a set of assertions and practices in the absence of supporting evidence and who rejects evidence-based criticism of their position. The beauty of Langs' approach is its reliance on observation and scientific reasoning in place of the vacuous *a priori* arguments and rationalized preferences that have hitherto dominated the field. Langs' claims about the ideal ground rules are based on a sophisticated clinical methodology with clear criteria for falsification. I have on several occasions spelled out the ways that these propositions can be objectively evaluated (Smith, 1991, 1996, 1999).

Langs' work has often provoked intense and irrational responses from the psychotherapeutic community, and very little in the way of sober and informed criticism (Smith, 1991). If my evolutionary hypothesis is correct, this is entirely comprehensible. If we are all inclined to exploit our patients, and to deceive both ourselves and them about what we are doing, it is small wonder that Langs' insistence on maintaining therapeutic boundaries has caused many in our field to feel trapped, anxious and angry and to intemperately reject communicative psychoanalytic principles. The communicative approach enjoins us to do something deeply unnatural and antagonistic to our evolved character. It charges us to allow our deceptive and self-serving strategies to be laid open by our patients, and to abide by the ground rules that they unconsciously lay down. Doing this we can truly *work for* our patients. Ignoring it, we are condemned to use them for our own aggrandisement.

Notes

1. For a very different approach to this issue, see Langs (1996).
2. This list is not exhaustive.
3. If true, this implies that patients' unconscious secured-frame criteria are a product of hominid evolution. As the human mind evolved many millennia before the advent of psychotherapy, secure frame criteria must have evolved in order to meet other, more fundamental kinds of social interaction.

References

Alexander, R.D. (1979) *Darwinism and Human Affairs*. Seattle: University of Washington Press.

Badcock, C.R. (1994) *PsychoDarwinism: The New Synthesis of Darwin and Freud*. London: HarperCollins.

Bruner, J. (1986) *Actual Minds, Possible Worlds*. Cambridge, MA: Harvard University Press.

Bucci, W. (1997) *Psychoanalysis and Cognitive Science: A Multiple Code Theory*. London: Guilford.

Donald, M. (1991) *Origins of the Modern Mind*. Cambridge, MA: Harvard University Press.

Ekman, P. (1988) 'Self-deception and detection of misinformation', in J.S. Lockhard and D.L. Paulhus (eds), *Self-Deception: An Adaptive Mechanism?* Englewood Cliffs, NJ: Prentice Hall.

Freud, S. (1916–17/1964) 'Introductory lectures on psycho-analysis', in J. Strachey (ed.), *The Standard Edition of the Complete Psychological Works of Sigmund Freud*, Vols 15–16. London: Hogarth Press.

Gazzaniga, M.S. (1992) *Nature's Mind: The Biological Roots of Thinking, Emotions, Sexuality, Language and Intelligence*. London: Penguin.

Langs, R.J. (1985) *Madness and Cure*. Emerson, NJ: Newconcept Press.

Langs, R.J. (1988) *A Primer of Psychotherapy*. New York: Gardner Press.

Langs, R.J. (1992a) *Science, Systems and Psychoanalysis*. London: Karnac.

Langs, R.J. (1992b) *A Clinical Workbook for Psychotherapists*. London: Karnac.

Langs, R.J. (1995) *Clinical Practice and the Architecture of the Mind*. London: Karnac.

Langs, R.J. (1996) *The Evolution of the Emotion-Processing Mind*. London: Karnac.

Little, M. (1951) 'Countertransference and the patient's response to it', *International Journal of Psycho-Analysis*, 32: 32–4.

Lockhard, J.S. and Mateer, C.A. (1988) 'Neural bases of self-deception', in J.S. Lockhard and D.L. Paulhus (eds), *Self-Deception: An Adaptive Mechanism?* Englewood Cliffs, NJ: Prentice Hall.

Mooij, A. (1982) *Psychoanalysis and the Concept of a Rule: An Essay in the Philosophy of Psychoanalysis*. London: Springer.

Schafer, R. (1983) *The Analytic Attitude*. London: Hogarth Press.

Slavin, M.O. and Kriegman, D. (1992) *The Adaptive Design of the Human Psyche*. London: Guilford.

Smith, D.L. (1991) *Hidden Conversations: An Introduction to Communicative Psychoanalysis*. London: Routledge.

Smith, D.L. (1996) 'Should psycho-analysts believe what they say?', *British Journal of Psychotherapy*, 13 (1): 64–75.

Smith, D.L. (1999) *Approaching Psychoanalysis*. London: Karnac.

Trivers, R. (1976) Introduction to R. Dawkins, *The Selfish Gene*. Oxford: Oxford University Press.

Trivers, R. (1981) 'Sociobiology and politics', in E. White (ed.), *Sociobiology and Human Politics*. Lexington, MA: Lexington Books.

Trivers, R. (1985) *Social Evolution*. Boston: Addison-Wesley.

Trivers, R. (1988) Introduction to J.S. Lockhard and D.L. Paulhus (eds), *Self-Deception: An Adaptive Mechanism?* Englewood Cliffs, NJ: Prentice Hall.

Tulving, E. (1983) *Elements of Episodic Memory*. Oxford: Clarendon.

PART III

PROFESSIONAL ISSUES

---

16   Personal therapy as a training requirement: the lack of supporting evidence

Ann Macaskill

The requirement for personal therapy in the training of psychotherapists has a long history. It was Freud (1910/1957) who first suggested that a personal analysis should be the core part of training which would enhance the efficiency of analysts in their practice. Later, Freud (1937/1964) reiterated this claim, stating that the ideal qualification for the psychoanalyst was a training analysis. In this paper Freud in fact goes further and suggests that periodic reanalysis may also be desirable, if not indeed necessary, for practising therapists. At this point it is pertinent to note that Freud did not have the experience of didactic analysis himself. He conducted a self-analysis at an early stage of his career, but although advocating regular recurrent reanalysis for psychoanalysts throughout their careers, he did not pursue this for himself even when other suitable trained analysts were available. Despite this inconsistency, there has been a long history of psychoanalysts claiming the necessity of a personal analysis as a core component of training (Fromm-Reichman, 1949, 1950; Racker, 1953, 1957; Bion, 1955; Ticho, 1967; Baum, 1970; Nierenberg, 1972; Guntrip, 1975; Wampler and Strupp, 1976; Rachelson and Clance, 1980; Lomas, 1981; Caligor, 1985; Deutsch, 1985; Clark, 1986; Norcross and Prochaska, 1986).

This position has not been held universally, however, and over the same period there have been significant numbers of practitioners arguing that there is no necessity for personal therapy in training (Coleman, 1946; Mowrer, 1951; Sanderson, 1954; Appell, 1963; Altucher, 1967; Truax and Carkhuff, 1967; Leader, 1970; Wolberg, 1977; and Watkins, 1983). Other practitioners, such as Kelley et al. (1978), have argued its necessity only if the trainee is experiencing significant psychological dysfunction at the commencement of his or her training. This is a somewhat controversial position as many training courses would exclude any trainees displaying significant psychological dysfunction and advise the prospective practitioners to seek help prior to embarking on a formal training course.

The debate has tended to focus on the perceived benefits which the experience of personal therapy is thought to bring to the trainee. These benefits are considered to be twofold, in that it is suggested that it will increase the effectiveness of the therapist and also significantly help to maintain the psychological well-being of the therapist while undergoing the practice of therapy, which is increasingly recognized as being a stressful activity. These putative benefits have been discussed widely in the literature (Fromm-Reichman, 1950; Strupp, 1955; Ford, 1963; Nierenberg, 1972; Garfield and Kurtz, 1975; Wampler and Strupp, 1976; Caligor, 1985) and they will be summarized below.

Personal therapy will:

(a) enhance the sensitivity and empathic awareness of the therapist by having the experience of being a client;
(b) improve the therapist's self-awareness by facilitating a better understanding of his or her own personality dynamics, which it is claimed will reduce personal bind spots;
(c) improve own psychological well-being;
(d) reduce levels of personal symptomatology;
(e) increase the trainee's awareness of his/her own problems and areas of conflict, which will then allow the recognition and appropriate handling of countertransference;
(f) lead to the resolution of personal conflicts;
(g) result in increased mastery of the techniques used via the close observation of an experienced therapist in action:
(h) lead to an increased conviction about the validity of the therapeutic model being used;
(i) lead to an increased conviction about the validity of the techniques being practised, as the trainee will have had personal demonstrations about how the actual process works.

This emphasis on self-exploration as a major focus of training has been adopted by many schools of therapy and counselling. Its prevalence in the training of family therapists was demonstrated by Guldner (1978), Forman (1984) and Francis (1988); in clinical psychologists by Garfield and Kurtz (1975) and Guy et al. (1988); in group therapists by Salvendy (1985); and even in behaviour therapists by McNamara (1986). This area has been briefly reviewed by McEwan and Duncan (1993), although it needs to be noted that the vast majority of the literature refers to the practice in North America. In the United Kingdom the training of psychoanalysts always involves extensive personal therapy, and for other dynamic therapists some form of mandatory personal therapy is probable and is a requirement for membership of the British Confederation of Psychotherapists. The United Kingdom Council for Psychotherapy have always viewed personal therapy positively, although mandatory hours are not specified. With counsellor training, the British Association for Counselling now requires counsellors seeking accreditation to have had a minimum of 40 hours of personal development or therapy. This is becoming similar to the position in the United States, but there, in addition, a survey by Wampler and Strupp (1976) of the 87 clinical psychology training programmes approved by the American Psychological Association reported that in 4 per cent of courses personal therapy was obligatory, 67 per cent of courses encouraged it and the remainder had no stated position. This is in contrast to the British position where personal therapy is not a requirement for any of the British Psychological Society approved courses. The experience of personal therapy is thus much more prevalent amongst therapists in the United States, with Guy et al. (1988) indicating that 70 per cent of the American Psychological Society members working in clinical psychology, psychotherapy and independent practice have experienced personal therapy as part of their training.

The crucial question, however, is whether it can be demonstrated that the experience of personal therapy does in fact produce more effective therapists. Several additional questions can also be asked. Are the benefits claimed to emanate from personal therapy known to be necessary skills and qualities for an effective therapist? If they are, then is personal therapy necessarily the only or the most effective way of training these skills? These questions will be addressed in turn using data from a survey of the research literature where appropriate.

Personal therapy and therapist effectiveness as measured by therapy outcome studies

As Meltzoff and Kornreich (1970) point out, there are very few studies which directly address the effect of personal therapy on therapist effectiveness measured via patient outcome. Holt and Luborsky (1958) looked at psychiatric residents in therapy training and took the judgements of their supervisors as a measure of the trainees' effectiveness as therapists. It appeared that personal therapy was not obligatory but could be requested by trainees; however, the request was not necessarily granted. Results indicated that there were three distinct groups of trainees. The first group had few significant psychological problems and had not requested personal therapy as part of their training. This group were judged by their supervisors to be developing appropriately and making good progress as therapists, despite having had no personal therapy experience. The second group had requested and been given personal therapy, and this group were also judged by their supervisors to be making suitable progress. The third group had requested personal therapy but it had not been provided, and this was the group judged to be most problematic and making least progress as therapists. Holt and Luborsky suggest that this demonstrates that the issue is not so much about developing therapy skills but about getting help with personal problems. They appear to conclude that to benefit from training, prospective therapists need either to be in good mental health from the outset, or, if they have problems, to receive personal therapy to help resolve their problems so that they can then focus on developing skills as therapists. This is a position which is adopted by many training courses based on past experience and clinical knowledge. The study does not demonstrate that there are any other benefits to be gained from the experience of personal therapy or that those without the experience are deficient in any way in their development as therapists. This is soft data, however, based as it is on the subjective judgements of the trainees' supervisors. Katz et al. (1958) reported that patient improvement in therapy was unrelated to whether the therapist had experienced personal therapy. The significant factor which they found related to patient improvement was the experience of the therapist. The most experienced therapists were most successful in obtaining improvement in their therapy patients.

Derner (1960) asked senior therapists to rate therapists in training on an annual basis over four consecutive years. For his sample he selected the two highest-rated and the two lowest-rated trainees in each of the years, giving him two groups of eight trainees overall, one a highest-rated group of trainee therapists and the other, the lowest-rated group. When their experience of personal therapy was examined, he found that half of each group had personal therapy and the other did not. While acknowledging the small sample size, Derner concluded that therapists can be effective both with and without personal therapy.

McNair et al. (1963) explored the issue of early patient termination in therapy to see whether therapists who had personal therapy as part of their training had fewer clients who terminated early. Early termination was defined as ceasing treatment against advice within 16 weeks of commencement. There were no differences found with regard to early cessation of treatment by clients between therapists with personal therapy experience and those without it. McNair et al. (1964) looked at patient outcome after at least 16 weeks of therapy, comparing patients of therapists with personal therapy with patients of therapists without personal therapy. No significant differences were found in patient outcome between the two groups. The only difference reported in this study between the groups was that therapists with personal therapy treated their patients for significantly longer times than therapists without therapy.

Garfield and Bergin (1971) also looked directly at client outcomes. This is one of the more systematic studies using objective measures of client change rather than relying solely on the clinical judgement of the therapist. These measures were the MMPI Depression Scale and K (Correction) Scale and also therapist ratings of disturbance on a five-point scale at the beginning and end of treatment. The numbers in the study were relatively small, however, with 18 therapists and 38 clients. In terms of experience of personal therapy there were three groups of therapists, one group with no personal therapy experience, another with 175 hours or less and a third group with more than 175 hours of personal therapy. The results demonstrated that clients of therapists with no personal therapy showed most positive change after therapy on all the measures. Therapists with most experience of personal therapy had clients who demonstrated least improvement after therapy. The group of therapists with less than 175 hours of therapy were in an intermediate position, with clients doing better than the group with most therapy but not as well as those clients of therapists with no personal therapy. That personal therapy was negatively related to outcome was considered to be a very provocative finding and other explanations were sought. Additional analysis examined the mental health of the therapists in the study but no significant differences in levels of mental health between the three groups of therapists were found. They did report that the personal adjustment of the therapist did appear to be positively related to patient outcomes but not to whether the therapist had personal therapy. This does not support the claim that personal therapy promotes the psychological well-being of the therapist.

The six outcome studies reviewed suggest no positive relationship between the experience of personal therapy by the therapist and patient outcomes; indeed, the Garfield and Bergin (1971) study demonstrates a negative relationship between the two. There are two studies in the literature which are not in line with these findings. Kernberg (1973) reported that greater patient improvement was achieved by experienced therapists who had received personal therapy than by inexperienced therapists who were still undergoing personal therapy. He did not, however, have a comparison group who had not undergone personal therapy. The findings are inconclusive as it could be that experience is the crucial factor or alternatively that undergoing personal therapy may have a temporary disruptive effect on the therapy process and hence affect outcome. More recently Greenspan and Kulish (1985) reported lower rates of early termination of therapy for therapists with personal therapy compared with therapists without personal therapy. This contradicts the findings of McNair et al. (1963) discussed previously. Further research with larger numbers is required on this aspect.

To answer the question, namely whether the experience of personal therapy does in fact produce more effective therapists, the research literature would suggest that there is no evidence to suggest that it does. There appear to be good therapists who have undergone personal therapy and good therapists who have not had personal therapy, and the converse is also true: there are bad therapists both with and without the experience of personal therapy. However, these studies have produced some interesting and important results aside from the issue of personal therapy. Katz et al. (1958) demonstrated the importance of experience in achieving good therapy outcomes, with a positive correlation between positive therapy outcomes and the levels of experience of therapists. Holt and Luborsky (1958) demonstrated the necessity of good mental health to function effectively as a therapist, reporting positive correlations between good outcomes from therapy and the positive mental health of the therapist. McNair et al. (1964) indicated that therapists with personal therapy treated their patients for longer than therapists without personal therapy. The outcomes were no different between the two groups of therapists but there are obvious differential resource implications both for services and clients from this finding.

The role of personal therapy in the development of effective therapists

The second question posed relates to the therapy process and whether the benefits claimed to emanate from personal therapy are known to be the necessary skills and qualities required in an effective therapist. The therapist who has devoted most attention to the question of what constitutes necessary skills for therapists is Carl Rogers. Rogers (1957) states that empathy, unconditional positive regard, genuineness or congruence in the therapist role and the ability to convey these qualities are the essential requirements for an effective therapist. There is a reasonable level of consensus among practitioners about the importance of these factors in creating a good therapeutic alliance with clients which is necessary to facilitate positive change in the therapy setting. These factors and relevant research will be used as a baseline against which to judge the claims for personal therapy in the training of therapists as outlined earlier. The third question, namely whether personal therapy is the only or most effective way to develop the skills and qualities which are known to be necessary for effective therapists, will also be addressed when appropriate.

(a) Personal therapy enhances the sensitivity and empathic awareness of the therapist by having the experience of being a client

There is consensus in the literature, both with Rogers and with other schools of therapy, that empathy is an important contributor to the therapeutic alliance. It is argued that having the experience of being a client during training via personal therapy will enhance the sensitivity and empathic understanding such therapists then demonstrate with their clients. The research most relevant to address this question comes from experimental studies by Strupp (1958) where therapists who had received more than 500 hours of personal therapy were compared with therapists having less than 500 hours. There were no differences in the empathy ratings given to therapists in each group. In other words, increases in personal therapy experience did not result in increasingly empathic therapists. Strupp (1973) in another experimental study found that therapists without personal therapy experience were more likely to reveal their negative attitudes to clients than were therapists who had received personal therapy. Strupp interprets this as demonstrating that therapists with personal therapy express higher levels of empathy than therapists without personal therapy, but this raises a question about genuineness, another of Rogers' therapist qualities. Is it not possible for therapists to demonstrate empathic under-standing of clients' behaviour even when they do not approve of that behaviour? Indeed sometimes is it not crucial that clients are made aware of the unacceptability of some of their actions? The author would argue that this is the case, that negative attitudes towards a client's behaviour do not preclude empathic understanding of that behaviour and its precursors by the therapist. Therapists working, for example, with offenders or with parents who have abused their children can testify to this. The Strupp (1973) findings would thus be interpreted not as supporting personal therapy as producing more empathic therapists, but rather as encouraging an uncritical focus on the relationship between client and therapist and ignoring the realities of the external social world in which the client will ultimately have to function and where behaviour is frequently perceived negatively. Experimental studies such as these are also problematic in that while they provide good control over the information being judged, using either videos or written accounts of therapy and then getting therapists to make responses at predetermined points in the interview, it is unclear how well these therapists' responses transfer to real therapy sessions.

However, Peebles (1980) reported evidence unequivocally in support of personal therapy developing empathy in practitioners. Using independent observers to rate empathy in taped therapy sessions, he found a positive relationship between the numbers of hours of personal therapy the ther-apist had experienced and their ability to display empathy with clients. Wogan and Norcross (1985) found that therapists with personal therapy focused more heavily on their relationship with their client than did ther-apists without personal therapy, who were more technique-oriented. This would be cited as positive evidence for psychodynamic practitioners but not for more cognitive-behavioural approaches to therapy. Contradictory evidence comes from Wheeler (1992), who measured empathy as a con-stituent of the therapeutic alliance counsellors had with their clients. A negative relationship was found between the level of therapeutic alliance counsellors had achieved with clients and the hours of personal therapy counsellors had experienced. Macaskill and Macaskill (1992), in a survey of UK therapists who all had personal therapy as part of their training, reported that only 33 per cent of the sample claimed to have experienced increases in empathy as a result of their personal therapy.

On the basis of current research it cannot be concluded that the experience of personal therapy increases empathy in therapists. The evidence is inconclusive, even although intuitively it would seem that having the experi-ence of being a client is a valuable aspect of training. Personal therapy, however, is not the only way to get this experience, and many training programmes use sessions of peer counselling and role play as alternatives. Truax and Carkhuff (1967) have shown that empathy, genuineness and warmth can actually be taught via individual and group exercises in training programmes. This work has several replications with a variety of populations (Truax and Mitchell, 1971; Carkhuff, 1972; Strupp and Hadley, 1979), and it would seem that this provides a demonstrably more reliable and cost-effective way of promoting empathic understanding in therapists than does personal therapy.

(b) Personal therapy improves self-awareness by facilitating a better understanding of therapists' own personality dynamics, which it is claimed will reduce personal blind spots

Positive support for this contention has come from Macaskill and Macaskill (1992), where 76 per cent of the therapists surveyed reported increases in self-awareness as a result of their personal therapy. Intuitively practitioners have accepted this as a necessary skill, but there is no real evidence in the research literature.

(c) Personal therapy improves own psychological well-being

Only Garfield and Bergin (1971) included a direct measure of psychological well-being in their study, but they found no differences in psychological health between therapists with no personal therapy and those with moderate or extensive amounts of personal therapy in their training. Buckley et al. (1981), in a survey of therapists who had all had personal therapy as part of their training, found that 47 per cent of their sample reported a moderate improvement in self-esteem after therapy. The same result was reported by Macaskill and Macaskill (1992). Thus less than half of the sample had improved in these studies and no evidence for the superiority of personal therapy emerged from the Garfield and Bergin study. There is consensus from practitioners and studies such as Holt and Luborsky's that positive mental health in the therapist facilitates the therapy process, but many practitioners would argue that training as a therapist is stressful enough *per se* and that trainee therapists with significant psychological problems should resolve them before undertaking therapy training. These comments also relate to the following three items, which also focus on the mental health of therapists.

(d) Personal therapy reduces levels of personal symptomatology

The Buckley et al. (1981) study reported that 73 per cent of their sample experienced decreases in symptomatology but only of a moderate nature. Macaskill and Macaskill (1992) found less support, with only 43 per cent of their sample reporting reductions in symptomatology. Here again the evidence is unclear.

(e) Personal therapy increases the trainee's awareness of his/her own problems and areas of conflict, which will then allow the recognition and appropriate handling of countertransference

Only one study has examined this directly. This was an experimental study by McDevitt (1987). Therapists were given a questionnaire of therapy vignettes with forced-choice answers from four alternatives which represented different styles of therapist intervention. Positive correlations were found between the use of countertransference-oriented solutions and the length of personal therapy the therapist had experienced. Not all therapists having personal therapy had high countertransference (CT) scores; rather, extensive personal therapy correlated with high CT scores. As the authors point out, the relationship is not necessarily a causal one; it could be due to the personality of the therapist, for example, with trainees who opt for extensive personal therapy being more introspective than those who have briefer personal therapy. As this question was not resolved, this study cannot be taken as supporting the proposition, although it provides useful insights for future research.

(f) Personal therapy leads to the resolution of personal conflicts

An indirect measure of this was found in two studies where therapists were asked to judge if their personal therapy had affected their personal relationships. Buckley et al. (1981) reported improved relationships as an outcome of personal therapy for 86 per cent of their sample. Macaskill and Macaskill (1992) found that this held for only 43 per cent of their sample, despite this being the second most important aim of personal therapy as far as the trainees were concerned. Again the evidence is inconclusive.

(g) Personal therapy results in increased mastery of the techniques used via the close observation of an experienced therapist in action

This aspect was not directly evaluated in any of the studies reviewed. The only related insight came from Buckley et al. (1981), where 86 per cent of the sample reported that they functioned better at work as a result of their personal therapy. Exactly which aspects of work the improved functioning relates to is unclear.

As proposition (h) and (i) are closely related and there is a dearth of evidence in the literature dealing with these aspects, they will be dealt with together.

(h) Personal therapy leads to an increased conviction about the validity of the therapeutic model being used

(i) Personal therapy leads to an increased conviction about the validity of the techniques being practised, as the trainees will have had personal demonstrations about how the actual process works

Macaskill and Macaskill (1992) reported that 83 per cent of respondents maintained or increased their levels of enthusiasm for therapy as a treatment method after their own personal therapy. This finding replicated an earlier result from McDevitt (1987), who found that 82 per cent of his sample of therapists felt that personal therapy was valuable. He found that the more personal therapy therapists had the more highly they valued it. While these are very supportive findings, they are open to different interpretations. They are based on consumer evaluations of their own therapy, and this is problematic. Trainees invest a lot of time, energy and finance in obtaining personal therapy, and this investment predisposes them to evaluate the activity positively, otherwise they are likely to experience significant amounts of cognitive dissonance. That the experience of personal therapy is stressful in terms of financial costs and time commitments was attested to by 50 per cent of the sample in the Macaskill and Macaskill study. Overall 38 per cent of the therapists in this study reported some negative effects from personal therapy, but many rationalized this with comments of the 'no pain, no gain' variety.

Summary

The research studies fail to demonstrate that having the experience of personal therapy produces more effective therapists. Indeed there is no evidence to support that some of the putative benefits of personal therapy claimed by its supporters are indeed necessary skills for effective therapists. Even in areas where some supportive evidence exists, such as in the development of empathy skills, there are other less expensive and demonstrably more effective ways of developing these skills. Self-reflective diaries are used to assist trainees to explore their own personalities, personal conflicts and symptomatology as well as become more self-reflective. In consultation with supervisors and mentors many of these issues can be resolved without the need for in-depth personal therapy. Experience of being a client can be obtained via peer counselling and role plays, and the video-taping of sessions can provide both role models of other therapists and detailed feedback on the trainees themselves as therapists. The claim that personal therapy increases the therapist's confidence in the validity of the model and its techniques smacks somewhat of indoctrination. The scientific method sets out to argue a case by presenting research evidence, and there is a dearth of this on this topic. In 1948, Balint pointed out that there was a great veil of secrecy about the process of personal therapy and that independent research has been discouraged. This has not changed over the years. Despite the huge growth of research on other topics, Fleischer and Wissler (1988) point out that there is still a marked reluctance amongst therapists to examine a core aspect of their training and to allow for an effective evaluation of its effectiveness.

References

Altucher, N. (1967) 'Constructive use of the supervisory relationship', *Journal of Counselling Psychology*, 14: 165–70.

Appell, M. (1963) 'Self-understanding for the guidance counsellor', *Personnel and Guidance Counselling Journal*, 42: 143–8.

Balint, M. (1948) 'On the psychoanalytic training system', *International Journal of Psycho-Analysis*, 29: 163–73.

Baum, O.E. (1970) 'Countertransference', *Psychoanalytic Review*, 56: 621–37.

Bion, W.R. (1955) 'Language and the schizophrenic', in M. Klein, P. Heimann and R.E. Money-Kyrle (eds), *New Directions in Psychoanalysis*. New York: Basic Books.

Buckley, P., Karasu, T.B. and Charles, E. (1981) 'Psychotherapists view their personal therapy', *Psychotherapy: Theory, Research and Practice*, 18: 299–305.

Caligor, L. (1985) 'On training analysis or sometimes analysis in the service of training', *Contemporary Psychoanalysis*, 21: 120–9.

Carkhuff, R.R. (1972) *The Art of Helping*. Amherst, MA: Human Resource Development Press.

Clark, M.M. (1986) 'Personal therapy: a review of empirical research', *Professional Psychology*, 17: 541–3.

Coleman, J. (1946) 'The teaching of basic psychotherapy', *American Journal of Orthopsychiatry*, 17: 625–7.

Derner, G.F. (1960) 'An interpersonal approach to training in psychotherapy', in N.P. Dellis and H.K. Stone (eds), *The Training of Psychotherapists*. Baton Rouge: Louisiana State University Press.

Deutsch, C.J. (1985) 'A survey of therapists' personal problems and treatment', *Professional Psychology: Research and Practice*, 16: 305–15.

Fleischer, J.A. and Wissler, A. (1988) 'The therapist as patient: special problems and considerations', *Psychotherapy*, 22: 587–94.

Ford, E. (1963) 'Being and becoming a psychotherapist: the search for identity', *American Journal of Psychotherapy*, 17: 472–82.

Forman, B.D. (1984) 'Family of origin work in systemic/strategic therapy training', *Clinical Supervisor*, 2 (2): 81–6.

Francis, M. (1988) 'The skeleton in the cupboard: experiential geneogram work for family therapy trainees', *Journal of Family Therapy*, 10: 135–52.

Freud, S. (1910/1957) 'The future prospects of psychoanalytic therapy', in J. Strachey (ed.), *The Standard Edition of the Complete Psychological Works of Sigmund Freud*, Vol. 11. London: Hogarth Press.

Freud, S. (1937/1964) 'Analysis terminable and interminable', in J. Strachey (ed.), *The Standard Edition of the Complete Psychological Works of Sigmund Freud*, Vol. 23. London: Hogarth Press.

Fromm-Reichman, F. (1949) 'Notes on personal and professional requirements of a psychotherapist', *Psychiatry*, 12: 361–78.

Fromm-Reichman, F. (1950) *Principles of Intensive Psychotherapy*. Chicago: University of Chicago Press.

Garfield, S.L. and Bergin, A.E. (1971) 'Personal therapy, outcome and some therapist variables', *Psychotherapy: Theory, Research and Practice*, 8: 251–3.

Garfield, S.L. and Kurtz, R. (1975) 'Clinical psychologists: a survey of selected attitudes and views', *The Clinical Psychologist*, 28 (3): 7–10.

Greenspan, M. and Kulish, N. (1985) 'Factors in premature termination in long-term psychotherapy', *Psychotherapy*, 22: 75–82.

Guldner, C.C. (1978) 'Family therapy for the trainee in family therapy', *Journal of Marriage and Family Counselling*, 4 (1): 127–32.

Guntrip, H. (1975) 'My experience of analysis with Fairbairn and Winnicott', *International Journal of Psycho-Analysis*, 2: 145–56.

Guy, J.D., Stark, M.J. and Poelstra, P.L. (1988) 'Personal therapy for psychologists before and after entering professional practice', *Professional Psychology*, 19: 474–6.

Holt, R.R. and Luborsky, L. (1958) *Personality Patterns of Psychiatrists*, Vol. 1. New York: Basic Books.

Katz, M.M., Lorr, M. and Rubenstein, E.A. (1958) 'Remainder patient attitudes and their relation to subsequent improvement in psychotherapy', *Journal of Consulting Psychology*, 22: 411–13.

Kelley, E.L., Goldberg, L.R., Fiske, D.W. and Kilowski, J.M. (1978) 'Twenty-five years later', *American Journal of Psychiatry*, 137: 32–5.

Kernberg, O. (1973) 'Psychotherapy and psychoanalysis: final report of the Menninger Foundation's Psychotherapy Research Project', *International Journal of Psychiatric Medicine*, 11: 62–77.

Leader, A. (1970) 'The argument against required personal analysis in training for psychotherapy', in J. Meltzoff and M. Kornreich (eds), *Research in Psychotherapy*. New York: Atherton.

Lomas, P. (1981) *The Case of a Personal Psychotherapy*. London: Oxford University Press.

Macaskill, N.D. and Macaskill, A. (1992) 'Psychotherapists in training evaluate their personal therapy: results of a UK survey', *British Journal of Psychotherapy*, 9 (2): 133–8.

McDevitt, J. (1987) 'Therapists' personal therapy and professional awareness', *Psychotherapy*, 24: 693–703.

McEwan, J. and Duncan, P. (1993) 'Personal therapy in the training of psychoanalysts', *Canadian Psychology*, 34: 186–97.

McNair, D., Lorr, M. and Callahan, D.M. (1963) 'Patient and therapist influences on quitting psychotherapy', *Journal of Consulting Psychology*, 27: 10–17.

McNair, D., Lorr, M., Young, H., Roth, I. and Boyd, D.R. (1964) 'A three-year follow-up of psychotherapy patients', *Journal of Clinical Psychology*, 20: 258–64.

McNamara, J.R. (1986) 'Personal therapy in the training of behaviour therapists', *Psychotherapy*, 23: 370–4.

Meltzoff, J. and Kornreich, M. (eds) (1970) *Research in Psychotherapy*. New York: Atherton.

Mowrer, O.H. (1951) 'Training in psychotherapy', *Journal of Consulting Psychology*, 15: 274–7.

Nierenberg, M.A.C. (1972) 'Self-help first', *International Journal of Psychiatry*, 10: 34–41.

Norcross, J.C. and Prochaska, J.O. (1986) 'Psychotherapist heal thyself – I: The psychological distress and self-change of psychologists, counsellors and other lay persons', *Psychotherapy*, 23: 102–14.

Peebles, M.J. (1980) 'Personal therapy and ability to display empathy, warmth, and genuineness in psychotherapy', *Psychotherapy: Theory, Research and Practice*, 17: 258–62.

Rachelson, J. and Clance, P. (1980) 'Attitudes of psychotherapists towards the 1970 APA standards for psychotherapy training', *Professional Psychology*, 11: 261–7.

Racker, H. (1953) 'A contribution to the problem of countertransference', *International Journal of Psycho-Analysis*, 34: 313–24.

Racker, H. (1957) 'The meanings and uses of countertransference', *Psychoanalytic Quarterly*, 26: 303–57.

Rogers, C. (1957) 'The necessary and sufficient conditions of therapeutic personality change', *Journal of Consulting Psychology*, 21: 95–103.

Salvendy, J.T. (1985) 'The making of the group therapist: the role of experiential learning', *Group*, 9 (4): 35–44.

Sanderson, H. (1954) *Basic Concepts in Vocational Guidance*. New York: McGraw-Hill.

Strupp, H.H. (1955) 'The effect of the psychotherapist's personal analysis upon his techniques', *Journal of Consulting Psychology*, 19: 197–204.

Strupp, H.H. (1958) 'The psychotherapist's contribution to the treatment process', *Behavioural Science*, 5: 34–67.

Strupp, H.H. (1973) *Psychotherapy: Clinical Research and Theoretical Issues*. New York: Jason Aronson.

Strupp, H.H. and Hadley, S.W. (1979) 'Specific versus non-specific factors in psychotherapy: a controlled study of outcome', *Archives of General Psychiatry*, 36: 1125–36.

Ticho, G. (1967) 'Self-analysis', *International Journal of Psycho-Analysis*, 48: 308–19.

Truax, C. and Carkhuff, R. (1967) *Toward Effective Counseling and Psychotherapy: Training and Practice*. Chicago: Aldine.

Truax, C.B. and Mitchell, K.M. (1971) 'Research on certain therapist interpersonal skills in relation to process and outcome', in A.E. Bergin and S.L. Garfield (eds), *Handbook of Psychotherapy and Behavior Change: An Empirical Analysis*. 1st edn. New York: John Wiley.

Wampler, L.D. and Strupp, H.H. (1976) 'Personal therapy for students in clinical psychology: a matter of faith', *Professional Psychology*, 7: 195–201.

Watkins, C.E.C. (1983) 'Counsellor acting out in the counselling selection: an exploratory analysis', *Personality and Guidance Journal*, 6: 417–23.

Wheeler, G. (1992) *Gestalt Reconsidered: A New Approach to Contact and Resistance*. New York: Gardner.

Wogan, M. and Norcross, J. (1985) 'Dimensions of therapeutic skills and techniques: empirical identification, therapist correlates and predictive utility', *Psychotherapy*, 22: 63–74.

Wolberg, L. (1977) *Techniques of Psychotherapy*, Vol. 2. New York: Grune & Stratton.

17   In defence of therapy for training

Valerie Sinason

The history

> Madness in great ones must not unwatch'd go.
>
> (Shakespeare, *Hamlet*, Act III, Scene 1)

> Physician, heal thyself!
>
> (Luke 4: 23)

From self-analysis

Over 100 years ago Sigmund Freud found that a 'self-analysis', particularly in interpreting his own dreams, was an indispensable tool in the development of psychological understanding. This self-analysis was important for any individual who wished to understand more about human nature in general as well as personal psychology in particular. It was also viewed by Freud as an essential prerequisite for an individual who wished to treat others. In 1910 he comments:

> [N]o psychoanalyst goes further than his own complexes and internal resistances permit; and we consequently require that he shall begin his activity with a self-analysis and continually carry it deeper while he is making his observations on his patients. Anyone who fails to produce results in a self-analysis of this kind may at once give up any idea of being able to treat patients by analysis. (Freud, 1910/19: 145)

(The full details of Freud's painstaking self-analysis can be found documented by Anzieu [1975].) The biblical injunction 'Physician, heal thyself!' in a new setting.

However, whilst self-analysis led to the creation of psychoanalysis, and whilst self-analysis as a process of reflection and commitment to self-understanding continued (and continues) to be seen as a crucial task, Freud became aware that it could not take the place of being analysed by another. Hence 'one learns psychoanalysis on oneself by studying one's own personality. . . . Nevertheless there are definite limits to progress by this method. One advances much further if one is analysed oneself by a practising analyst' (Freud, 1916a: 19). Freud's correspondence with Fliess (rather like his earlier correspondence with Martha, whilst she was his fiancée) revealed the way in which, through a dialogue with an external other, internal conflicts could be externalized and perceived somewhat more clearly. As he wryly comments: 'Genuine self-analysis is impossible; otherwise there would be no illness' (Freud, 1916b: 19). For me, the title of Bruno Bettelheim's book *When Love Is Not Enough* speaks to a similar issue. Whilst love, friendship and self-analysis can help self or other progress, there is a point where treatment is needed.

Training analysis

As the concept of a training analysis grew, Freud praised the Zurich School for 'the demand that everyone who wishes to carry out analyses on other people shall first himself undergo an analysis by someone with expert knowledge' (1912: 116). It would be in 1922 at the Congress of the International Psychoanalytical Association that a training analysis would be instituted as a compulsory aspect of training.

This requirement was particularly endorsed by Ferenczi. He made clear that a training analysis was primarily a personal one, but with the added proviso that the clinician's need for adequate self-knowledge was even greater because of the responsibility he carried for vulnerable patients: 'The analyst himself . . . on whom the fate of so many other people depends, must know and be in control of even the most recondite weaknesses of his own character; and this is impossible without a fully completed analysis' (1927: 84). It is worth noting that an average analysis at this period, which Ferenczi was not happy with, was only a year!

However, together with the biblical 'Physician, heal thyself!' we can add Shakespeare's sentient comment in *Hamlet*: 'Madness in great ones must not unwatch'd go.' The more power and authority one individual carries over another, the more there is a need for understanding in how that is exercised.

In other words, the idea of a personal treatment as part of training came through learning from experience. It was a pragmatic decision based on clinical hypotheses that were validated clinically.

As Bader comments:

> The analyst has no choice but to generate and test hypotheses and to develop and use criteria for deciding if the intervention was on the mark. The constructivist might believe, in principle, that the 'mark' is not ultimately verifiable in the sense that positivist science would have it. It might be a hermeneutic mark, an intersubjective mark, a co-constructed mark, or a mark in analytic space. Nevertheless, it is a physically real experience for which the analyst is reaching and for which effort he or she needs markers or confirmatory clinical guideposts. (1998: 9)

Freud and Ferenczi were both aware from their own personal experiences of the limits of self-analysis. The concept of these limits is perennially retested. Whilst it is indeed possible that some training schools try to rigidify the revolutionary meaning of analysis into something as bland as a 'requirement', others continually question what it is that is needed. For example, the adult psychoanalytic psychotherapy training at the Tavistock Clinic's Adult Department does not require further psychoanalysis from qualified child psychotherapists who have completed a previous psychoanalysis in conjunction with their primary training and do not feel the need for a further one.

With several hundred kinds of psychotherapy available in the UK from several thousand practitioners, most, outside of cognitive and behaviour therapy, include personal therapy for the trainee of some kind and duration. Indeed, an increasing number of cognitive therapists are seeking either therapy or group support. This is not surprising when we consider the powerful impact patients and their narratives have on clinicians. Whilst it could be argued that professionals are capable of seeking out support that is iatrogenically harmful and that the desire to both damage and repair is closely balanced, the intrinsic message of learning from experience is that a hard-pressed professional will not voluntarily seek, from a range of alternatives, something that does not provide further illumination. Indeed, Jones and Pulos (1993) point to the dynamically oriented techniques that behaviour therapists have been bringing into their work, whilst Ablon and Jones (1998) have shown that experienced psychodynamic and cognitive practitioners had a high level of agreement in a Q-set questionnaire concerning ideally conducted therapy. All therapists share a boundary around the meaning of time and space and have the relationship between therapist and patient as the primary tool (aided by music, art, dance, sandplay, drama, in the creative therapies).

Regardless of the exact nature of the therapy or counselling, a large number of contemporary psychotherapies could be seen as grandchildren of psychoanalysis in that many of the tenets concerning the need for theory, supervision and personal treatment are shared.

A *personal rationale*

Whilst undertaking the child psychotherapy training, I had to enter a personal psychoanalysis with a psychoanalyst. Initially, it was twice a week for a few months, then three times a week, and after a year it was a full psychoanalysis of five times weekly. That experience was a very useful one in helping me understand as a consumer the different experience that frequency brought. Additionally, when a trainee psychoanalyst, I also had a further training analysis.

I agree with Ferenczi that a training analysis is a personal one. I also agree that in order to do as well as possible for patients or clients it is crucial to be able to know yourself as well as you can.

The pre-clinical component of the Tavistock Clinic Child Psychotherapy training requires some work with disturbed children. As a qualified teacher I took a job in an inner London school to run nurture groups for such children. For this pre-clinical first component, analysis was not compulsory. During one group session near a summer break there was a sudden explosion of violence with chairs thrown and tables kicked. For a moment I was paralysed with fear. The fear was of my lack of knowledge. In that moment I did not know if I was frightened because it was understandable to be frightened in a group who were behaving violently; I did not know if I was frightened because they had projected their fear into me so I would feel it for them; and finally I did not know if I was scared of my own potential violence if they did not stop their destructive behaviour.

In that one slow-motion moment I realized that without psychoanalysis I would not be able to work with such violent children adequately. I could recognize that whilst I had some resources, experience and talent that served me well with disturbed children without any psychotherapy or psychoanalysis, there were certain areas that would not be able to develop through self-analysis, reading or supervision.

Nearly 20 years on from that moment, having supervised therapists from many orientations I find I have some conclusions.

1   There are likely to be some emotionally insightful people who are endowed with more good inside them than others will gain after intensive treatment of whatever kind.
2   There are likely to be some emotionally insightful people who would have a positive clinical effect on anybody they had any dealings with without any personal therapy of any kind.
3   There are likely to be some people who, despite lengthy personal therapy or analysis, fail to deal with certain crucial problems.

However, even when taking into account those three factors – which so often cause hurt when they are not acknowledged but which also cause damage when they are not adequately contextualized – I consider that the profession of psychotherapy across the board – United Kingdom Council for Psychotherapy (UKCP) and British Confederation of Psychotherapists (BCP) – requires treatment to accompany training. When the resource is your self and you are encountering a vulnerable 'other', you need to have the key tool of your trade as honed as possible.

Attachment, identification, introjection and learning from experience

The setting was a fifth-form school-leavers' classroom in a noisy comprehensive at the end of a summer term. I was giving a talk on 'transitions' to open up discussion about the impending move from school to the workplace. I asked the students about the work experience they currently had and whether that was informing their choice. Tracy and John were two class members who would be moving into full-time work with the placements that already employed them on a weekend basis.

Tracy, aged 16, commented:

> I am going to be a hairdresser, a stylist. But you have to start as a junior and I am doing that now anyway. You do all the sweeping first but then you get to do the shampooing and so you move on. I get good tips from the way I do it because one of the juniors did my shampoo last week – my neck really hurt and the water temperature wasn't right so I always check those things out properly. When you know what it feels like on the other side you get much better at your work.

John, a 16-year-old would-be car mechanic, agreed.

> The last boss at my weekend job just yelled at me. It didn't matter if there were customers there or not. He did not think about it. But the new boss is really different. Not that he lets you get away with things, but things run well because of the standard and the mood he sets, you know. When I have my own garage I would be like him I hope.

Tracy and John are being involved in a training. Through identification, attachment and through evaluating their own experiences they are honing into a philosophical attitude a theory of mind, a theory of the other. They have been able to learn through experience, through negative moments as well as positive. This intersubjective understanding is where empathy comes from, an ability to emotionally be in the shoes of the other. Charles Kingsley's *The Water Babies* included the figure of Mrs Do-as-you-would-be-done-by.

Through a treatment that is both personal and connected with a training, there is a taking in of experience. You know what you feel like after your first holiday break and that allows you to lend yourself out to what your first patient feels like after a break.

How does a child become an adult, and what kind of adult do they become? So long as there is adequate nutrition and freedom from gross impingements, public health, attachment and medicine take care of physical growth. However, just the act of growing does not determine the kind of adult someone becomes. The field of child development has shown that we grow through attachment and identification with those who have brought us up, with a sprinkling of help from our internal genetic endowment. We know what it was like being the child of our families, and our own parenting has hopefully improved on the model we received in a few places thanks to our transformation of that knowledge. Medical students learn what an injection feels like when they tend to each other. Apprenticeships of all kinds are based on a similar developmental model.

Psychotherapy and counselling, whether for training or personal use only, are usually aiding a part of the person that did not get a chance to grow up adequately at the time. Obviously, a bad or mismatched therapy will on the whole have an adverse effect. If such a treatment were intensive and lasted for a longer duration, the iatrogenic damage would be more likely to be exacerbated. However, of course, even with a mismatch some trainees can learn from experience. As Jeffrey Masson told me:

> The intensity of that kind of scrutiny is always a good thing. Merely the fact that one can lie down 5 times a week for 5 years and talk about oneself and be able to free associate is a good thing and I think paying that amount of attention to dreams . . . you come out of those things with a certain awareness. I know what I would never do as an analyst. You either think I suffered it so they will – or you decide not to. I decided not to. (Personal Communication, 1996)

However, that point is true of all professional behaviour. A poor or downright bad teacher/doctor/police officer/childminder/religious figure/nurse will increase the level of suffering his or her recipient experiences according to how long he or she remains in negative contact. Nevertheless, the fact that poor teachers and doctors exist does not lead to many concerted professional or lay attacks on the actual existence of their subject. Psychoanalytic and psychotherapy organizations, like other professions, have ethical committees available to consider the difficult subject of damaging practice.

Where psychoanalysis or psychoanalytic psychotherapy is unusual, however, is that its very existence as a body of knowledge, let alone as a treatment or training, remains a perennial source of such conflict.

It says something for the enormous power of Freud as a thinker and theoretician that passionate brilliant people continue to argue with him directly as if he were still alive. The need to fight 'father' persists, regardless of the changes in psychoanalytic treatment in the last 100 years. The yearly publication of books which are advertised as 'completely demolishing the whole foundations of psychoanalysis' continue unabated and probably always will. Human insight and communication and the power of unconscious impulses are threatening topics.

I am also curious as to whether the increased movement towards bottle-feeding (you can measure exactly what a baby has drunk, get away from bodily intersubjectivity and internal sense of validation and measurement) and away from breast-feeding (unscientific) reflects the current societal need for simplistic proof.

This is not to imply that I completely agree with the postmodern perspective that 'psychoanalytic experience isn't "knowable" in the same sense that one can "know" the weight of a table' (Bader, 1998). I consider, as Bader does, that the psychoanalyst/psychotherapist is following myriads of minute hypotheses and testing them and learning from them sentence to sentence.

Indeed, I consider it an important development interprofessionally that there is now a large body of research outcome results (Milton, 1996; Roth and Fonagy, 1996) showing the beneficial impact of treatment. It is often overlooked that the trainee therapist/psychoanalyst is also a patient. The describing term 'training' in 'training therapy' can sometimes euphemistically and defensively disguise the inevitable emotional vulnerabilities and difficulties of the trainee. As a human being, the trainee therapist is also struggling with different levels of functioning.

Psychodynamic psychotherapy does not have any better outcome than other treatments, so why should therapists need a training therapy? They could have something else as an alternative.

Many roads lead to Rome. Those who do not see any value in psychotherapy for anyone (let alone trainees) can sometimes build up a straw opponent to attack. The superb Finnish study on treatment of schizophrenic patients (Alanen et al., 1991) showed an integrated model in which family work, individual psychotherapy and drug treatments were combined with the patients' needs uppermost. Trainee therapists, whilst sharing human vulnerability and problems with all other groups, are not in the throes of schizophrenic pain. Certain problems would counter-indicate the ability to counsel others. However, the point I am making is that to consider a training therapy is needed for trainee therapists does not mean that other kinds of treatments are being seen as ineffectual. Whilst there are important research issues to look into as to what is the best treatment for what kind of problem (Roth and Fonagy, 1996), there can also be a sibling rivalry in evidence.

Some of the research that is used to show that behaviour therapy (which does not require any training therapy) has as good an outcome as or a better one than analytically oriented therapy is flawed. For example, in comparing short-term and analytic and behaviour treatments, Sloane et al. (1975) found that one year and two years after the initial assessment all groups were equally and significantly improved. However, brief treatment models favour cognitive-behavioural treatment and there is no real equivalence. Additionally, how do we evaluate improvement? Different professions ascribe different meanings. A child who suddenly does well at school after years of failing could be misperceived as a therapeutic success. The internal meaning of doing well could represent an attack of enormous dimensions.

In tests in which the same clinician offers two alternating treatments (Crowe, 1978; Shapiro and Firth, 1987), there is an inherent bias as there would be a primary professional skill in the clinician's own favoured mode of work. Therapists do best when working in a mode they are experienced in and favour (Luborsky et al., 1986). Second, from a psychoanalytic point of view, the same person offering two treatments is a transference figure and attachments build up. How then can the results be examined?

Mental health service users (Rogers et al., 1993) favour talking therapies, which they largely see as 'confirming and validating'.

Psychodynamic treatments might improve patients, but the clinicians do not need to have had personal therapy or analysis.

It is certainly true that if all kinds of psychotherapy cause improvement in patients because of attachment, treating people's pain with courtesy and seriousness, then some clinicians can help some patients improve without having had therapy themselves. We then come to the complex problem I mentioned before as to how improvement is measured. A referral symptom that disappears might seem like a proof of improvement to one professional but represent something less healthy to the therapist. Finally, since all trainings work on the tried and tested threesome of theory, practice and treatment, removing one element to test the possible difference would be experienced as deeply unethical to all the clinicians who 'know' how much their craft depends on it.

Conclusions

Many different therapy trainings offer hope and help to citizens burdened by mental pain. Each of those within the UKCP and BCP do their best to plan trainings that will adequately help their trainees. There are now major authors (Holmes and Lindley, 1989) who have looked into the varieties of trainings available, the key attacks on therapy and the key answers to it. What I would like to emphasize is that here is a craft and all of us who are learning it from different schools of psychotherapy are nevertheless united in considering that without personal therapy our ability to deliver a service would be infinitely smaller. One hundred years after Freud's painful and rich self-analysis began, new students have the chance of undertaking this powerful journey. The huge proliferation of psychoanalytic journals and clinical papers provides the clinical testimony of change. This change can be reflected noticeably in external functioning and relationships but also internally through changes in defensive constellations that are no longer needed. However, Freud as a researcher would also appreciate the interface with other disciplines which learn more through proof than from emotional experience.

References

Ablon, J.S. and Jones, E.E. (1998) 'How expert clinicians' prototypes of an ideal treatment correlate with outcome in psychodynamic and cognitive-behavioural therapy', *Psychotherapy Research*, 8 (1): 71–83.

Alanen, Y.O. et al. (1991) 'Need adapted treatment of new schizophrenic patients: experiences and results of the Turku project', *Acta Psychiatrica Scandinavica*, 83: 363–72.

Anzieu, D. (1975) *Freud's Self-analysis*. London: Hogarth Press (International Psychoanalytic Library no. 118).

Bader, M. (1998) 'Postmodern epistemology', *Psychoanalytic Dialogues*, 8 (1): 1–32.

Crowe, M. (1978) 'Conjoint marital therapy: a controlled outcome study', *Psychological Medicine*, 8: 623–36.

Ferenczi, S. (1927/1994) *Final Contributions to the Problems and Methods of Psychoanalysis*. London: Karnac Books.

Freud, S. (1910) in J. Strachey (ed.), *The Standard Edition of the Complete Psychological Works of Sigmund Freud*, Vol. 11. London: Hogarth Press.

Freud, S. (1912) in J. Strachey (ed.), *The Standard Edition of the Complete Psychological Works of Sigmund Freud*, Vol. 12. London: Hogarth Press.

Freud, S. (1916a) in J. Strachey (ed.), *The Standard Edition of the Complete Psychological Works of Sigmund Freud*, Vol. 15. London: Hogarth Press.

Freud, S. (1916b) in J. Strachey (ed.), *The Standard Edition of the Complete Psychological Works of Sigmund Freud*, Vol. 15. London: Hogarth Press.

Holmes, J. and Lindley, L. (1989) *The Values of Psychotherapy*. Oxford: Oxford University Press.

Jones, E.E. and Pulos, S.M. (1993) 'Comparing the process in psychodynamic and cognitive-behavioural therapies', *Journal of Consulting and Clinical Psychology*, 61: 306–16.

Luborsky, L. et al. (1986) 'Do therapists vary much in their success? Findings from four outcome studies', *American Journal of Orthopsychiatry*, 56 (4): 501–13.

Masson, J.M. (1996) Personal communication.

Milton, J. (1996) *Presenting the Case for Psychoanalytic Psychotherapy Services: An Annotated Bibliography*. London: APP and the Tavistock Clinic.

Rogers, A., Pilgrim, D. and Lacey, R. (1993) *Experiencing Psychiatry: Users' View of Services*. London: Macmillan and MIND.

Roth, A. and Fonagy, P. (1996) *What Works for Whom? A Critical Review of Psychotherapy Research*. New York: Guilford.

Shapiro, D. and Firth, J. (1987) 'Prescriptive v. exploratory psychotherapy', *British Journal of Psychiatry*, 151: 790–9.

Sloane, R., Staples, F., Cristol, A. and Yorkston, N. (1975) 'Short-term analytically orientated psychotherapy vs behaviour therapy', *American Journal of Psychiatry*, 132: 373–7.

18   Becoming an effective psychotherapist or counsellor: are training and supervision necessary?

Jim McLennan

At first glance, the title of this contribution to discussion of current controversies in psychotherapy and counselling may seem absurd. After all, nobody would question the need for electrical engineers or veterinary surgeons to be highly trained before being permitted to offer their services to the public. Is it not self-evident that the same principles must apply to psychotherapists and counsellors? Notwithstanding, I will demonstrate that *evidence* supporting the necessity for high levels of academic training in psychotherapy and counselling is conspicuously lacking. I suggest that psychotherapy/counselling is quintessentially a *human* interpersonal activity, the effectiveness of which is, at most, only weakly related to current academic systems of training psychotherapists and counsellors. To become an effective counsellor or psychotherapist, one must immerse oneself in the craft and *practise* it intensively.

Reservations about the need for high levels of training in order to produce good counsellors were raised almost two decades ago by no less a figure than Carl Rogers:

> I think of the 'hot-line' workers whom I have been privileged to know in recent years. Over the phone, they handle bad drug trips, incipient suicides, tangled love affairs, family discord, all kinds of personal problems. Most of these workers are college students or those just beyond this level, with minimal intensive 'on-the-job' training. And I know that in many of these crisis situations they use a skill and judgment that would make a professional green with envy. They are completely 'unqualified', if we use conventional standards. But they *are*, by and large, both dedicated and *competent*. (Rogers, 1980: 245, original emphases)

Before proceeding, it is necessary to establish a framework, even though some of my starting assumptions are themselves topics of controversy elsewhere in this book: any discussion has to begin somewhere! First, I do not believe that it is useful to distinguish between psychotherapy and counselling. In the present context I will treat the terms as being synonymous for most practical purposes. I define both as referring to purposeful conversation intended explicitly to help troubled individuals manage more effectively some hitherto personal-problematic aspect of living. These troubled individuals concerned may, of course, be relationship partners, members of a family or participants in some group activity. Second, I take it as having been amply demonstrated that psychotherapy and counselling are generally effective. I realize that psychotherapy bashing remains a perennial sport for sophisticated social critics, such as Masson (1988). However, I suggest that anyone who is persuaded by evidence, rather than seduced by sophisticated rhetoric, need do no more than read Seligman (1995) or Lambert and Bergin (1994). The vast majority of individuals who seek help from psychotherapists or counsellors report favourably on their experience. An overwhelming number of soundly conducted research studies have demonstrated that most psychotherapy and counselling clients are helped measurably. I accept that not everyone who presents for counselling or psychotherapy is helped. Elsewhere I have proposed an account of the circumstances under which therapeutic failures are most likely to occur (McLennan, 1996): namely such failures are most likely when the personal qualities of the counsellor do not match the needs of the client.

The lack of evidence supporting the necessity for high levels of training

I begin by referring to a paradoxical aspect of the general research finding noted above that counselling and psychotherapy are demonstrably effective. The paradox was first highlighted by Luborsky et al. (1975), and subsequently articulated further by Smith et al. (1980) in their seminal meta-analytic review of psychotherapy outcome research studies: all the major theoretical approaches to counselling and psychotherapy (for example, psychodynamic, cognitive-behavioural, phenomenological) are equally effective on average, despite fundamental differences in both orienting concepts and specific intervention techniques. This has been confirmed by subsequent studies (for example, Shapiro and Shapiro, 1982): the several issues involved in the so-called 'equivalence paradox' have been discussed comprehensively by Stiles et al. (1986). For the purposes of the present discussion, the paradox has two alternative implications for claims as to the necessity of training in counselling and psychotherapy. The first – optimistic – implication is that any form of psychotherapy training is as efficacious as any other. The second – pessimistic – alternative is that no form of psychotherapy training makes any appreciable contribution to therapist effectiveness. The body of comparative therapy outcome efficacy research literature cannot help us to decide between these two alternative interpretations of the paradox and we must turn to research focused more directly on the utility of counselling and psychotherapy training.

The necessity for high levels of formal academic training in counselling and psychotherapy became a serious issue of controversy within the field with the publication of Durlak's (1979) review of research comparing the effectiveness of *professionally trained* therapists and counsellors (defined as psychologists, psychiatrists, social workers and psychiatric nurses who had completed formal, post-bachelor degree training in psychotherapy or counselling) with the effectiveness of *relatively untrained* helpers (or 'para-professionals', in Durlak's terminology). Durlak reviewed 42 comparative effectiveness studies and concluded that 'the clinical outcomes parapro-fessionals achieve are equal to or significantly better than those obtained by professionals' (1979: 89). This claim was disputed by Nietzel and Fisher (1981), who argued that methodological deficiencies in many of the studies used by Durlak eroded any claim that the effectiveness of professionally trained helpers was not demonstrably superior to that of paraprofes-sionals.

Hattie et al. (1984) replicated and extended Durlak's original study using quantitative meta-analytic procedures which took into account the kinds of objections raised by Nietzel and Fisher (1981). Hattie et al. noted that it was quite possible that professionals may be more likely than paraprofessionals to be referred 'difficult' cases with poorer prognoses. Taking this into account, they concluded that 'the average person who received help from a paraprofessional was better off at the end of therapy than 63% of persons who received help from professionals . . . these data support Durlak's suggestion that paraprofessionals are comparable to – and often more effective than – professional helpers' (1984: 536). Hattie et al. also noted that 'the more experienced the paraprofessionals, the greater their effec-tiveness as compared with professionals' (1984: 540). Such an observation is consistent with recent findings concerning the acquisition of expertise in a complex cognitive skill: the major determinant of expertise is the amount of time engaged in the self-reflective practice of the skills in question, not *learning about* the skill in a classroom (Ericsson and Lehmann, 1996).

The issue of professional versus paraprofessional therapeutic effectiveness was revisited by Stein and Lambert (1984) and by Berman and Norton (1985). Both teams of investigators, independently, replicated Hattie et al.'s (1984) work, while excluding studies deemed to be poorly designed and incorporating several other methodological refinements. Notwithstanding these improvements (relative to Hattie et al.), both teams found that there was no evidence that professionally trained therapists were more effective than paraprofessionals. Stein and Lambert also reported that 'differences in outcome were most likely to occur when there was a large discrepancy in experience between the therapists offering treatment within a study' (1984: 186).

The question of the necessity for high levels of academic training in psychotherapy and counselling re-emerged as a controversial issue in the mid-1990s in both North America (VandenBos, 1996) and the United Kingdom (Mowbray, 1995), in the context of (a) a US Congressional discussion of national mental health insurance coverage and (b) discussion of the necessity for the regulation of psychotherapy practice, respectively.[1]

The most up-to-date comprehensive review of research concerning the need for high levels of academic training in counselling and psychotherapy which could be located (Stein and Lambert, 1995) reported evidence that, on average, therapists with postgraduate training in psychotherapy or counselling (a) had slightly lower rates of premature termination by clients; (b) received slightly higher satisfaction ratings by clients (by a magnitude of approximately one-fifth of one standard deviation unit);[2] and (c) evidenced somewhat greater objective evidence of client improvement (also by a magnitude of approximately one-fifth on one standard deviation unit). However, Stein and Lambert acknowledged that in almost all the studies examined, level of postgraduate training was inextricably confounded with amount of practical experience as a counsellor. They identified only two studies where this was not the case, those of Strupp and Hadley (1979) and Stolk and Perlesz (1990).

Strupp and Hadley (1979) compared the average effectiveness of a group of highly trained and experienced therapists with that of a group of untrained university academic staff members who each had a well-established reputation over the course of several years for being approachable and helpful. The two groups saw a total of 31 university student clients who were experiencing a range of emotional and social difficulties. Strupp and Hadley reported that there was no overall difference between the trained and the untrained therapists in effectiveness. However, closer inspection of the data shows that client ratings of improvement favoured the *untrained* therapists, though the difference was small (slightly less than one-fifth of one standard deviation unit).

Stolk and Perlesz (1990) reported a longitudinal study of the effectiveness of postgraduate trainees undertaking a family therapy training programme who saw a total of 176 family members over the two-year course. On average, the trainees were *less* effective at the end of their second year of training than they were during their first year of training! The outcome measure was satisfaction rating by family members, and the magnitude of the (apparent) deterioration in effectiveness associated with the additional year of training was slightly greater than two-fifths of one standard deviation unit. Stolk and Perlesz tentatively offered as an explanation that with the additional training, trainees became more preoccupied with theoretical models and purity of technique at the expense of their inherently helpful personal attributes, such as warmth, empathy and spontaneity.

I concede that I have selected for discussion only two studies out of the total of 36 covered by Stein and Lambert's (1995) very thorough and scholarly review. However, these two studies provide the most clear-cut tests of the effectiveness of more- versus less-trained therapists. I find myself in complete agreement with Stein and Lambert in their conclusion that

> A substantial challenge to graduate training programs in psychology, psychiatry, and social work remains. Programs have yet to systematically demonstrate (a) whether the skills they teach relate directly to year-by-year increases in the

successful number or quality of therapy among the patients of trainees or (b) that specific didactic or practicum experiences affect dropout rates over time. (1995: 193)

It should be noted that (a) in the majority of the studies surveyed by Stein and Lambert, the less highly trained therapists had undertaken some basic training in counselling, and (b) in all the studies, the less highly trained therapists had some practical experience as counsellors. I suggest that what we can conclude from this body of research is that the contribution of high levels of academic training to therapeutic effectiveness, additional to that which results from basic training in counselling skills plus some practical experience, is marginal at most.

I acknowledge that the research which I have drawn upon does not include any of the considerable number of 'private' – that is, non-university-based – formal training courses in the theory and practice of particular forms of psychotherapy and counselling (psychoanalytic, experiential, existential, family-systemic, Gestalt, transactional analysis, and so on) which have proliferated over recent years. Proponents of such training programmes may well wish to assert that *their* graduates are superior in therapeutic effectiveness to individuals otherwise engaged in psychotherapy or counselling practice who have not received comparable levels of training. However, asserting is a long way removed from demonstrating. As the doyen of therapeutic effectiveness research Sol Garfield (1986) observed succinctly: 'No comparison, no conclusion!'

The lack of evidence supporting the necessity for high levels of supervision

While the evidence for the necessity of high levels of academic training to ensure therapeutic efficacy is largely negative, or at least well short of being compelling, the evidence for the positive contribution of supervision is almost non-existent! It is, of course, very difficult for researchers to separate training from supervision: supervision of practice is a component of most graduate-level therapy training programmes, while supervisees bring very disparate levels of prior training with them into supervision. Nevertheless, it is surely a matter of concern that in spite of the considerable body of published research about the process of supervision (for example, Holloway, 1992), only two studies have, apparently, investigated *client outcomes* in relation to therapist supervision. Dodenhoff (1981) found that supervisees who were given direct instructional feedback by their supervisors were more effective with their clients than were supervisees who received general supportive supervision. Steinhelber et al. (1984) found that the amount of supervision was unrelated to level of client improvement from pre-therapy to post-therapy.

The importance of supervision in order to ensure the efficacy of – particularly novice – therapists seems to be an article of faith for most counsellor and therapist educators. Yet, as Holloway and Neufeldt noted, 'there is no research on standardized and empirically validated training programs for supervisors' (1995: 211). Only one supervision training manual is known to have been developed (Neufeldt et al., 1996).

The overwhelming impression created by the considerable literature on the counselling and psychotherapy supervision process is that supervision is absolutely essential to protect both client and counsellor. However, there is absolutely no sound evidence that this is the case. Certainly, perusal of complaints made about psychologists to regulatory bodies demonstrates starkly that supervision does not ensure ethical practice, nor does it guarantee protection of clients!

If not high levels of training, what?

The empirical evidence presently available is not supportive of any claim that high levels of academic training are important determinants of therapeutic effectiveness. (The evidence simply has not been gathered in relation to the necessity for high levels of supervision.) We might ask what this state of affairs implies about the nature of the therapeutic process. An answer to this question requires us to step back from our narrow Western, post-World War II understanding of the essential nature of counselling and psychotherapy. The first systematic account of training in counselling and psychotherapy was published in 1947 (Blocksma and Porter, 1947).[3] To claim that, prior to this, effective counselling and psychotherapy did not occur because nobody had been systematically trained as a counsellor or psychotherapist would be manifestly absurd! Throughout human history, individuals with social and emotional difficulties have benefited from talking with a sympathetic 'other' perceived as being able to offer words of comfort and sound counsel either because of recognized inherently helpful personal qualities, or by virtue of his or her role in the community. In Western society, prior to the Industrial Revolution, such 'counselling' took place within the matrix of everyday social interaction in (mostly) stable rural communities. With the urbanization of Western society, individuals' stable social supports were weakened and the counselling function in society has become increasingly specialized and professionalized as a societal response to the personal problems of individuals living in a complex, technologically based society (Gerstl, 1968; Lewis, 1970). However, even in today's world, the vast majority of individuals who are experiencing psychological distress do not seek help from trained and credentialled professional counsellors and therapists: they obtain relief by talking to individuals untrained in counselling or psychotherapy. These untrained helpers range from trusted relatives to hairdressers, and they are approached on the basis of perceived personal qualities and their social role (Cowen, 1982). In the words of Emory Cowen:

> For society at large, and even more in certain of its sectors, most distressed people look first towards accessible, parsimonious, well-understood, trusted sources of help that are minimally costly or stigmatizing. Those 'specs' do not typically define mental health professionals; indeed, in most cases family, friends, neighbours, support networks, and informal care givers fill the bill much better. (1982: 394)

Many writers have sought to describe the fundamental character of the interpersonal helping process (for example, Frank, 1971; Torrey, 1986; Strupp, 1989). When these accounts are inspected, a consistent picture emerges. The helper provides an accepting, understanding and sympathetic context in which the troubled individual can converse. The helper listens carefully and maintains a stance of attentive interest and reasonableness, in spite of any attempts by the troubled individual to provoke the helper into behaving in a punishing or rejecting or defensive or exploitive or over-protective manner. Judiciously, the helper will offer information, suggestions and advice concerning the issues of relevance to the individual and his or her difficulties. (The information, suggestions and advice may be quite explicit, or they may be implicit, as is the case with interpretations as to the 'real' underlying causes of the individual's difficulties.) High levels of academic training in counselling and psychotherapy are not necessary in order to effectively provide the kind of interpersonal relationships described above. Nor are high levels of academic training in counselling and psychotherapy *sufficient* to ensure such an interpersonal relationship (McLennan, 1996).

Is there any expected benefit from any training in counselling and psychotherapy? Effective counselling and psychotherapy are complex interpersonal skills. Expertise in a skill is acquired by immersive, intensive practice of the whole skill, not by being 'trained' in a classroom (Ericsson and Lehmann, 1996). I suggest, on the basis of sound evidence, that brief, direct, skills-based training in facilitative communication can rapidly equip a trainee to commence helping clients, thus beginning the process of learning how to be an effective counsellor or therapist (Baker and Daniels, 1989; Baker et al., 1990; McLennan, 1994). Assuming a beginner counsellor has an adequate pool of life experiences to draw upon, brief direct training in facilitative communication skills (such as that described by Ivey, 1988), in ethical behaviour as a counsellor and in risk assessment will be sufficient in most cases for him or her to help clients who have been carefully screened as appropriate for an inexperienced helper. The beginner's interviews should be audio- or video-recorded as a matter of routine and reviewed by the beginner, with feedback input from an experienced instructor. On an ongoing basis, the experienced instructor should help the beginner to identify and remedy evident knowledge-gaps, skill-deficits and dysfunctional emotional responses to client material. If we want the public to take us seriously as professional counsellors and psychotherapists, then we need to ensure that we train beginning counsellors and psychotherapists directly in *doing* effective counselling and psychotherapy, as distinct from *talking about* counselling and psychotherapy.

Notes

1. In Australia, there has been no serious consideration of restricting the *activity* of counselling or psychotherapy. However, in all Australian states and territories there are restrictions on who may claim to have a particular professional *qualification* (for example, medicine, psychology, social work, nursing) as the basis for counselling and psychotherapy practice.

2. Because studies employ different outcome measures, it is now usual for reviewers to convert raw client improvement scores into what are called effect sizes. Effect sizes are calculated by (usually) subtracting the mean of paraprofessional therapists' client improvement scores from the mean of professional therapists' client improvement scores, and dividing this difference by the standard deviation of the paraprofessional therapists' client improvement scores.

3. I do not believe that the method by which an individual typically became (becomes?) qualified in psychoanalysis – a personal analysis, reading seminars and supervision (without any direct observation, or audio or video-taped replays of therapeutic sessions) – should be dignified by the term 'training'. Such a process resembles nothing less than attempting to learn to be a neurosurgeon by reading *Gray's Anatomy* and operating on one's own brain while receiving occasional advice over a telephone.

References

Baker, S.B. and Daniels, T.G. (1989) 'Integrating research on the microcounselling program: a meta-analysis', *Journal of Counseling Psychology*, 36: 213–22.

Baker, S.B., Daniels, T.G. and Greeley, A.T. (1990) 'Systematic training in graduate-level counselors: narrative and meta-analytic reviews of three major programs', *The Counseling Psychologist*, 18: 355–421.

Berman, J.S. and Norton, N.C. (1985) 'Does professional training make a therapist more effective?' *Psychological Bulletin*, 98: 401–6.

Blocksma, D.D. and Porter, E.H. (1947) 'A short-term training program in client-centered counseling', *Journal of Consulting Psychology*, 11: 56–60.

Cowen, E. (1982) 'Help is where you find it: four informal helping groups', *American Psychologist*, 37: 385–95.

Dodenhoff, J.T. (1981) 'Interpersonal attraction and direct–indirect supervisor influence as predictors of counselor trainee effectiveness', *Journal of Counseling Psychology*, 28: 47–62.

Durlak, J.A. (1979) 'Comparative effectiveness of paraprofessional and professional helpers', *Psychological Bulletin*, 86: 80–92.

Ericsson, K.A. and Lehmann, A.C. (1996) 'Expert and exceptional performance: evidence of maximal adaptation to task constraints', *Annual Review of Psychology*, 47: 273–305.

Frank, J.D. (1971) 'Therapeutic factors in psychotherapy', *American Journal of Psychotherapy*, 25: 350–61.

Garfield, S.L. (1986) 'The effectiveness of psychotherapy'. Paper presented at the Austin Hospital, Melbourne, July.

Gerstl, J.E. (1968) 'Counseling and psychotherapy today: role specialization and diversity', in D.A. Hansen (ed.), *Explorations in Sociology and Counseling*. Boston: Houghton Mifflin.

Hattie, J.A., Sharpley, C.F. and Rogers, H.J. (1984) 'Comparative effectiveness of professional and paraprofessional helpers', *Psychological Bulletin*, 95: 534–41.

Holloway, E.L. (1992) 'Supervision: a way of teaching and learning', in S.D. Brown and R.W. Lent (eds), *Handbook of Counseling Psychology*. New York: John Wiley.

Holloway, E.L. and Neufeldt, S.A. (1995) 'Supervision: its contribution to treatment efficacy', *Journal of Consulting and Clinical Psychology*, 63: 207–13.

Ivey, A.E. (1988) *Intentional Interviewing and Counseling: Facilitating Client Development*. 2nd edn. Pacific Grove, CA: Brooks/Cole.

Lambert, M.J. and Bergin, A.E. (1994) 'The effectiveness of psychotherapy', in A.E. Bergin and S.L. Garfield (eds), *Handbook of Psychotherapy and Behavior Change*. 4th edn. New York: John Wiley.

Lewis, E. (1970) *The Psychology of Counseling*. New York: Holt, Rinehart & Winston.

Luborsky, L., Singer, B. and Luborsky, L. (1975) 'Comparative studies of psychotherapies', *Archives of General Psychiatry*, 32: 995–1008.

McLennan, J. (1994) 'The skills-based model of counselling training: a review of the evidence', *Australian Psychologist*, 29: 79–88.

McLennan, J. (1996) 'Improving our understanding of therapeutic failure: a review', *Counselling Psychology Quarterly*, 9: 391–7.

Masson, J.M. (1988) *Against Therapy: Emotional Tyranny and the Myth of Psychological Healing*. New York: Atheneum.

Mowbray, R. (1995) *The Case against Psychotherapy Registration: A Conservation Issue for the Human Potential Movement*. London: Transmarginal Press.

Neufeldt, S.A., Iversen, J.N. and Juntunen, C.L. (1996) *Supervision Strategies for the First Practicum*. Alexandria, VA: American Counseling Association.

Nietzel, N.T. and Fisher, S.G. (1981) 'Effectiveness of professional and paraprofessional helpers: a comment on Durlak', *Psychological Bulletin*, 89: 555–65.

Rogers, C.R. (1980) *A Way of Being*. Boston: Houghton Mifflin.

Seligman, M.E.P. (1995) 'The effectiveness of psychotherapy: the *Consumer Reports* study', *American Psychologist*, 50: 965–74.

Shapiro, D.A. and Shapiro, D. (1982) 'Meta-analysis of comparative therapy outcome studies: a replication and refinement', *Psychological Bulletin*, 92: 581–604.

Smith, M.L., Glass, G.V. and Miller, T.I. (1980) *The Benefits of Psychotherapy*. Baltimore, MD: Johns Hopkins University Press.

Stein, D.M. and Lambert, M.J. (1984) 'On the relationship between therapist experience and psychotherapy outcome', *Clinical Psychology Review*, 4: 1–16.

Stein, D.M. and Lambert, M.J. (1995) 'Graduate training in psychotherapy: are therapy outcomes enhanced?', *Journal of Consulting and Clinical Psychology*, 63: 182–96.

Steinhelber, J., Patterson, V., Cliffe, K., and LeGoullon, M. (1984) 'An investigation of some relationships between psychotherapy supervision and patient change', *Journal of Clinical Psychology*, 40: 1346–53.

Stiles, W.B., Shapiro, D.A. and Elliott, R. (1986) 'Are all psychotherapies equivalent?', *American Psychologist*, 41: 165–80.

Stolk, Y. and Perlesz, A.J. (1990) 'Do better trainees make worse family therapists? A follow-up study of client families', *Family Process*, 29: 45–58.

Strupp, H.H. (1989) 'Psychotherapy: can the practitioner learn from the researcher?' *American Psychologist*, 44: 717–24.

Strupp, H.H. and Hadley, S.W. (1979) 'Specific versus nonspecific factors in psychotherapy: a controlled study of outcome', *Archives of General Psychiatry*, 36: 1125–36.

Torrey, E.F. (1986) *Witchdoctors and Psychiatry: The Common Roots of Psychotherapy and Its Future*. New York: Harper & Row.

VandenBos, G.R. (1996) 'Outcome assessment of psychotherapy', *American Psychologist*, 51: 1005–6.

19 Training and supervision make a difference

Mary Connor

Of course training and supervision must make a difference. But are we asking the wrong question? Perhaps the real controversy is about the sort of difference training makes to the counsellor and supervisor. Is training helpful or harmful? Could it be helpful to the trainees but harmful to their clients? Or could it be discomforting for the trainees and helpful to their clients? Or is it helpful to both trainee and client?

Before I became a trained counsellor I was a well-intentioned helper who had thought that if I really cared about people I could counsel them. I learned the hard way that not only was I naïve in thinking that I could manage 'on my own', but that by not being aware of my own limitations as a helper I was in danger of harming both my clients and myself. At that time I worked in an inner-city secondary school. A young, approachable, caring teacher. Youngsters started coming to see me with their problems: staying out late, getting into drugs, leaving home, getting pregnant, wanting an abortion. Of course I could listen to them and show that I cared. That part was easy. I was also good at solving problems. But what I knew nothing about was how to manage the helping relationship, how to maintain confidentiality when there were others in the parent or *loco parentis* role, and how to work within a network of helping with proper support and monitoring. I applied for counsellor training after two particularly difficult experiences: one concerning a 14-year-old girl who was pregnant and wanted me to help her to get a back-street abortion; and one concerning a skirmish with the police over confidentiality and a missing person. Training gave me confidence in both my strengths and my limitations. It prepared me for issues which I had never previously considered. It helped me to know myself better and to understand others more sensitively and accurately. It most of all gave me the realization that counsellor training and supervision are for life and that they must be ongoing processes of learning and development, because the more I know, the more I realize I do not know.

Lambert and Bergin (1994) looked at studies which compared the effectiveness of professional versus paraprofessional and experienced versus inexperienced therapists. The literature did not supply clear evidence for the superior therapeutic effectiveness of trained professionals. But then the research designs had several weaknesses. They noted that controls, criteria and follow-up lacked rigour and that often the samples were not truly representative. 'We are not observing substantial therapeutic effects in the usual kinds of cases' (1994: 171). Some interesting findings emerged when using meta-analytic reviews of the relationship between experience of the therapist and therapeutic outcome. In work with children, trained professionals were found to be equally effective with all age groups, whereas paraprofessionals were more effective with younger clients. Weisz et al. (1987) also found that with particular client problems, that is, phobias and shyness, effectiveness increased with the amount of formal training, but with problems such as aggression and impulsion the level of training did not make a significant difference. However, they make an important observation about variables which may affect research outcome. They note that the so-called 'paraprofessionals' 'were selected, trained, and supervised by professionals in techniques that professionals had designed' (1987: 548, in Lambert and Bergin, 1994: 170). If the reader is to make any sense of research findings about the effects of training and professionalism on counsellors and therapists, the research must be completely clear about definitions of 'professional', 'paraprofessional' and 'training'.

There appears to be broad agreement that what Rogers referred to as the core conditions are necessary for therapeutic change. More recently, writers have elaborated on the centrality of congruence, respect and empathy in the development of 'bonds' in the working alliance (Bordin, 1975) and in the different levels of the therapeutic relationship (Clarkson, 1995). If the qualities of the helping relationship are the most important indicators of client change, then several writers argue that these can be offered as effectively, if not more effectively, by spontaneous helpers who have not been contaminated by training and professionalism. Masson (1990) vociferously denounces the way in which therapists masquerade behind the professional façade, arguing that therapy, by its very nature, is harmful. So is it not true that some people are natural counsellors, born that way? And are counselling and therapy just trying to rationalize a process that already exists in good and loving relationships? And if so, training, supervision and the professionalisation of helping will militate against the very genuineness and spontaneity that they seek to develop.

I do not believe that anyone is born with the ability to communicate congruence, respect and empathy effectively. I do believe that some people have a greater natural capacity for sensitive and perceptive interpersonal communication than others. However, this capacity is nurtured and developed through early significant relationships, including observations of the other, responses to the other, responses of the other, and the learning that occurs when making sense of these responses – learning which reinforces or extinguishes certain thoughts, feelings and behaviours. In other words, training is occurring, even in infancy, both overtly and covertly, consciously and unconsciously. There is no such thing as a totally spontaneous effective helper who has not 'learned' about helping, even though this learning may have been implicit rather than explicit. If this is the case, then research into the effectiveness of training is research into explicit training. The question then is: what effect does explicit training have upon the therapist or helper? Mearns (1997) notes that Rogers 'was fond of pointing out' that it was the personal and relational qualities of the counsellor which made a difference and it would be possible to find someone who had these qualities without having been trained:

> Unfortunately, for every person for whom this may be true there are a thousand who believe it to be true of themselves. Personally, I have never met this fictional person who needed no training. The danger of working with insufficient training is that the approach involves highly volatile elements such as empathy, therapeutic congruence, working within the client's existential world, a deep relational connection and a kind of loving. With powerful elements such as these, there is a danger of lightly trained practitioners using the person-centred approach as a licence for their own disorder rather than a disciplined professional way of working. (Mearns, 1997: x)

Mearns argues that, contrary to popular belief, the person-centred approach probably requires more intense training than other approaches because of the crucial elements of personal development. He also makes the case for an extended 'training period' after initial training in order to offer support and challenge for the continuing personal development of the counsellor. If this is important for counsellors, it is even more crucial for psychotherapists. Clarkson (1994) highlights the different demands upon counsellor and therapist made by the *evolutionary* focus on developmental change in counselling, and the *revolutionary* focus on personality restructuring in psychotherapy.

> It has now been agreed by all the organisations of UKCP [United Kingdom Council for Psychotherapy] that entry to psychotherapy training must be at postgraduate level and have an academic content roughly equivalent to a masters degree, in addition to supervised clinical practice. It has also been agreed that each psychotherapy training must show that it has adequate arrangements for the trainee to become aware of and manage appropriately their own personal contribution to the kind of psychotherapy being practised. For the psycho-analytically based and humanistic/existential or integrative psychotherapies, these arrangements will continue to be the personal training psychotherapy or psychoanalysis. All require ongoing supervision. (Clarkson, 1994: 23)

The problem with explicit training for any profession is that it may make people feel more incompetent, in the process of helping them to become more competent. Some trainee counsellors and supervisees never recover from this. They choose to be helpers or counsellors, and indeed they are selected for training, because they already possess some of the necessary

characteristics. During training and supervision they move from unconscious competence to conscious incompetence as they discover more about
what they have been doing. It is to be hoped that they learn new ways of
relating and of being and at this point they move to conscious competence. It
is at this point that the client may experience more harm than good from the
trainee, and, indeed, some counsellors and therapists never get beyond this
point. They are the ones who are caricatured by Masson and other sceptics,
because they appear to be operating as therapy-robots, at best appearing
parrot-like, at worst appearing to be distant and abusive. It is the responsibility of the training programme to ensure that trainees move beyond this
point, to that of unconscious competence. It is at this point that the client is
likely to experience beneficial effects from the counselor who acts with
integrity within the therapeutic relationship, as 'he or she is' rather than as a
clone of some theoretical approach or model.

Let us now turn to particular aspects of counselling which may be affected
by training and supervision. Ridge (1997) has researched the effects on the
client of conscious identification in the counsellor. She defines this as 'a
process of differing levels of cognitive and emotional recognition and identification within the counsellor (ranging from a brief cognitive recognition of
a similarity through to an overwhelming feeling of over-identification, or
cognitive distraction), the precise level of which is dependent upon intra-,
inter-, and extrapersonal factors' (1997: 211). Her research showed that
newly trained counsellors were more likely than more experienced counsellors to report experiences of conscious identification. She found that when
clients completed the Barrett–Lennard Relationship Inventory after sessions
where the counsellor reported an experience of conscious identification,
clients rated counsellors lower than the counsellors rated themselves on the
communication of the core therapeutic qualities. The sample was small, but
the results are worthy of further research. Training and supervision help
counsellors to become aware of, to reflect upon and to decide appropriate
action in relation to their internal experiencing during client encounters. The
untrained, unsupervised counsellor, well meaning though he or she may be,
could be thrown off-balance by certain disclosures made by the client, and as
a result could be experienced as uncaring, or distant, or punitive, or abusive
or unethical. What training and supervision do is to prepare the counsellor
so that forewarned is forearmed. Such preparation helps to guarantee a
baseline of quality for the client, rather than the hit and miss approach of
using well-meaning but not necessarily well-informed helpers.

What is the problem with being well meaning? It is the problem of possibly
also being misguided and misinformed. If counsellors were involved in
making widgets, such a possibility may have unfortunate consequences, but
because counselling can involve life and indeed death decisions, being
misguided or misinformed can have disastrous consequences. Once a helping
relationship moves away from a family or friendship relationship it becomes
a 'fiduciary relationship', one that is held or given in trust and therefore
one which depends on public confidence (Connor, 1994). For this reason,

professional standards must be set and training must prepare counsellors to act competently and ethically within such standards. Ethical principles will guide the behaviour of the counsellor or therapist:

> Fidelity assumes that we are faithful to promises made. Justice ensures that benefits are distributed fairly. Beneficence implies that we work for the good of the other. Nonmaleficence expects that we do no harm to the other. Autonomy encourages the exercise of maximum choice. When it comes to counsellor training I hear it said, 'the bottom line is this: will this trainee do any harm to clients?' (Connor, 1994: 188)

Baron (1996) reports on the findings of a public tribunal (VAT) which had to decide whether the British Association for Counselling (BAC) was 'a professional association' or 'an association whose primary purpose is the advancement of a particular branch of knowledge or the fostering of professional expertise'. BAC submitted that it was the latter. The ruling of the commissioners stated that 'counselling was simply an advanced form of communication skill', but Baron quotes the panel members as saying that neither

> that description, nor the fact that it may be a form of knowledge or skill that can be acquired to a high level by intelligent people through practice and the normal experience of life, precludes it from being an area, form or branch of knowledge that can clearly be more deeply, and probably much more quickly, learnt with proper teaching and instruction. (1996: 19)

Training provides counsellors with useful frameworks and perspectives which broaden their options for working with a range of clients and a range of client problems. Wheeler and Izzard (1997) train counsellors using a psychodynamic orientation. In an article which explains how they focus upon ways in which sexual identity, race and culture are integrated in the course, they show how they provide an opportunity for trainee counsellors to challenge themselves, and to challenge traditional psychoanalytic interpretations of homosexuality and heterosexuality. They conclude that counsellor training can 'provide a positive approach to sexual orientation and counselling across cultures'. They note that 'in clinical seminars attention must be paid to the implications of working with radically or culturally different, gay or lesbian clients, particularly the impact on the countertransference of homophobia or racism' (1997: 415). Can we imagine what may happen when the untrained or unsupervised counsellor has not explored his or her own attitudes and beliefs in relation to sex, race, religion and culture? Can we imagine how limited the untrained counsellor will be if he or she has not explored case material with other trainees and practised approaches, skills and strategies in the safe, experimental space of the training programme?

The BAC has identified key elements in training that will make a difference to the effectiveness of counsellors, and these need to be offered at a satisfactory level in order to gain accreditation for the course. These include: personal development; theory; skill development; client work and supervision. From almost 20 years of experience as a counsellor trainer I have developed an integrative model (Connor, 1994) which has at the centre the counsellor and client in relationship. Intrapersonal and interpersonal development are at the heart of the model and contributing to this are the four stages of learning: exploring attitudes and values; gaining knowledge and skills; engaging in client work and supervision; reflecting upon that experience and evaluating learning. The aim of this integrative model is to produce both reflective and competent counsellors. How do we know whether such an intentional way of developing counsellors makes any difference? One trainee, Helen, records in her learning journal what she has learned from having her counselling skills assessed, using video-recording and feedback:

> Give clients more space, tone down the flow and eagerness of my own speech, offer less in the way of information-giving. I feel this may be to do with my own level of anxiety and enthusiasm. (Connor, 1994: 176)

Not only has she identified four areas for development here, but she is also realizing how her intrapersonal dynamics are affecting her way of being with clients. If she had not had the opportunity to see and hear herself on video and receive honest and supportive feedback from peers and tutors, how many clients would have experienced these shortcomings, whilst she was oblivious to them? One of the problems in counsellor training is the difficulty of not being able to access easily the trainee at work with real clients. However, good professional training requires regular supervision of client work, and within the model I have developed I see it as essential that there is communication between the course and the supervisor in the form of a joint learning statement agreed between the trainee and the supervisor and sent to the course tutor at the end of each year. This moves us one step closer to the actual experience of the client, rather than just relying on self-reflection and assessment.

Rod was a trainee who reflected on his learning from supervision and Andy, his supervisor, wrote:

> Rod's awareness of transferential and countertransferential issues arising in counselling interactions has increased substantially. He appears to have developed the appropriate antennae for listening out for relevant cues. . . . Regarding the balance of dialogue between Rod and the client, there has been an improvement, but on occasions Rod's natural exuberance threatens to overwhelm some clients. The use of appropriate silence may be something he could profitably work on. . . . My perception is that he is a safe and effective practitioner who has demonstrated a combination of refined core conditions, developing interpersonal skills and a growing knowledge base. (Connor, 1994, p. 183)

Such an honest and supportive statement from the supervisor highlights areas where Rod will need help and development. It is only within formal training arrangements and within accreditation procedures that such developmental monitoring can take place. Even if an untrained counsellor is receiving regular supervision, there is no guarantee that reflections and insights gained in supervision can be turned round into different ways of behaving. This leads us on to research evidence which indicates that skills can be developed successfully, using microtraining approaches. Competent counselling involves the judicious use of skills in order to establish rapport, develop the therapeutic relationship, and help the client to bring about desired change. The microcounselling approach developed initially by Ivey involves the instruction, demonstration and practice of specific skills with feedback. Ivey and Authier (1971) admitted that preliminary evidence concerning the generalization and retention of microcounselling skills was mixed, but encouraging. They found that if, during training, trainees were given specific learning criteria, if there was follow-up later, and reinforcement in the practice setting, then there was an influence on the retention of skill. Baker and Daniels (1989) did a meta-analysis of 81 studies of microcounselling and found that learning counselling skills in this way did make a difference. There is plenty of evidence for effectiveness in 'basic' listening skills (Kurtz et al., 1985), but still more research is needed into whether training makes a difference in relation to some of the 'higher order' skills such as immediacy and confrontation. A recent study reported the effect of training on client-perceived rapport. Sharpley and McNally note that: 'Data indicated that the higher level trainees produced higher mean levels of client-perceived rapport per minute than the lower level trainees' (1997: 449).

Training and supervision are not without their problems., The professionalization of counselling brings both opportunities and pitfalls. It could be argued that a poorly trained counsellor, or a trained poor counsellor, is worse than an untrained counsellor. What the well-meaning, untrained counsellor brings to the client is, at best, unvarnished and spontaneous. The paradox is that, by not knowing more, that counsellor can be more immediately and spontaneously 'with' the client, or, more accurately, with 'the person' being helped. This genuine and 'real' quality in the relationship is what makes all of us approach certain friends, family members or colleagues for help. And which of us, from time to time, has not chosen such a person for wise counsel, rather than choosing a trained counsellor? But, as Gerard Egan (1998) has often remarked, which of us, if we had to have surgery, would be happy to look up from the operating table and be told that the person about to 'open us up' had not been trained as a surgeon? The analogy is obvious. I am aware, as a counsellor, that every time a person comes to see me to tell me his or her story, it feels like he or she is 'opening up' with all the vulnerability and exposure that is implied in that experience. Even if we go no further than that, I have a responsibility to help that person to preserve his or her integrity, to remain whole. The responsibility is both awesome and invigorating because I know that if I can help that person to gain insight and make changes, the effect upon his or her life could be profound. If the surgeon needs training for physically opening up, surely the counsellor needs training for the vastly more complex psychological and emotional opening up that can occur through even just the first sentence spoken by the client: 'I wonder if you can help me . . .?' I wonder.

References

Baker, S.B. and Daniels, T. (1989) 'Integrating research on the microcounseling program: a meta-analysis', *Journal of Counseling Psychology*, 36: 213–22.

Baron, J. (1996) 'The emergence of counselling as a profession', in R. Bayne, I. Horton and J. Bimrose (eds), *New Directions in Counselling*. London: Routledge,

Bordin, E.S. (1975) 'The working alliance and bases for a general theory of psychotherapy'. Paper given at the Annual Meeting of the American Psychological Association, Washington, DC.

Clarkson, P. (1994) 'The nature and range of psychotherapy', in P. Clarkson and M. Pokorny (eds) *The Handbook of Psychotherapy*. London: Routledge.

Clarkson, P. (1995) *The Therapeutic Relationship*. London: Whurr.

Clarkson, P. and Pokorny, M. (eds) (1994) *The Handbook of Psychotherapy*. London: Routledge.

Connor, M. (1994) *Training the Counsellor*. London: Routledge.

Egan, G. (1998) *The Skilled Helper*. 6th edn. Pacific Grove, CA: Brooks/Cole.

Ivey, A.E. and Authier, J. (1971) *Microcounseling*. Springfield, IL: Charles Thomas.

Kurtz, P.D., Marshall, E.K. and Banspach, S.W. (1985) 'Interpersonal skill training research: a twelve-year review and analysis', *Counselor Education and Supervision*, March.

Lambert, M.J. and Bergin, A.E. (1994) 'The effectiveness of psychotherapy', in A.E. Bergin and M.J. Lambert (eds), *Handbook of Psychotherapy and Behavior Change*. 4th edn. New York: John Wiley.

Masson, J.M. (1990) *Against Therapy: Emotional Tyranny and the Myth of Psychological Healing*. London: Fontana.

Mearns, D. (1997) *Person-Centred Counselling Training*. London: Sage.

Ridge, S. (1997) 'Conscious identification within the counsellor and its impact upon the counselling relationship'. Unpublished doctoral thesis, Manchester Metropolitan University, Manchester.

Sharpley, C.F. and McNally, J. (1997) 'Effects of level of academic training on client-perceived rapport and use of verbal responses modes in counselling dyads', *Counselling Psychology Quarterly*, 10 (4): 449–60.

Weisz, J.R., Weiss, B., Alicke, M.D. and Klotz, M.L. (1987) 'Effectiveness of psychotherapy with children and adolescents: a meta-analysis for clinicians', *Journal of Consulting and Clinical Psychology*, 55: 542–9.

Wheeler, S. and Izzard, S. (1997) 'Psychodynamic counsellor training – integrating difference', *Psychodynamic Counselling*, 3 (4): 401–17.

20 Against and beyond core theoretical models

Colin Feltham

If the unconscious is that which does not fit in, why has it been so difficult to sustain non-compliant versions of psychoanalysis?

(Phillips, 1995: xv)

The session becomes a pretext for decipherment, the need for theoretical coherence and symmetry appears, linked to professional communication, discussion and comparison. This distortion is then played back into further sessions as theory guides practice.

(Heaton, 1993: 114)

Continued use of nebulous labels seriously hinders our efforts to achieve open enquiry, informed pluralism and intellectual relativism. In the final analysis, unless therapists stop hiding behind labels, and are able and willing to state precisely what they do, and don't do, to and with their clients at specific choice points . . . psychotherapy will continue to be guided by faith rather than fact.

(Lazarus, 1989: in Dryden, 1991: 186)

In a previous article (Feltham, 1997a), I argued that the insistence by professional bodies on core theoretical models in training was misplaced. An article by Adams (1984) demonstrates that this controversy is not in fact new, nor confined to British soil; nor is there evidence of any progress since that time. In this chapter I briefly summarize my original argument, I underline the problem of theory in counselling and psychotherapy generally, and go on to develop certain options for future consideration.

Professional bodies like the British Association for Counselling (BAC) and the United Kingdom Council for Psychotherapy (UKCP) promote, and to some extent insist on, the tradition of brand-name therapies in training. To some extent there is a recognition of integrationism and eclecticism but experience seems to suggest that single-model therapies (for example, person-centred and psychodynamic counselling) are more easily accredited than newer, creative, eclectic models. The argument supporting this revolves ostensibly around the concepts of coherency (all elements of a training reflecting its core philosophy) and professional competency development (the belief that mature adult trainees must master steps and principles in a linear, non-polemical, arguably kindergarten-like, ABC fashion).

Dire warnings are generally sounded about the dangers of poorly trained practitioners, and these are bolstered by playing up the complexities of core theoretical models and their associated competencies. The idea of training courses being based on sceptical dialogue, open-ended inquiry or empirical evaluation (Adams, 1984), for example, is not entertained at all, as far as I am aware. Whenever the emotive terms 'coherency', 'competency', 'skill', 'knowledge', 'ethics', and so on, are trotted out in arguments like these, we should guard against the mesmerizing affect generated by such rhetoric. After all, where will the competency imperative end? I have not yet heard it suggested that in two of the most responsible areas of life people should have to undergo rigorous competency-based training for fear that they will otherwise wreak havoc. But just consider what dire need it could be argued there is for parents and government politicians to undergo systematic competency-based training!

I have argued that core theoretical models in our field are untenable, for a number of reasons. We appear to have over 400 different therapeutic models to choose from, much research appears to suggest that their outcomes are more or less equivalent, and few if any practitioners or spokespersons for professional bodies are willing to publicly single out any theoretical orientations as outstandingly poor or excellent. (*Privately*, of course, it's another matter.) Advocates of each approach – particularly founders or others with vested emotional or financial interests in them – tend to believe passionately in the competency of their approach to deal positively with almost any client concern. If Roth and Fonagy (1996), and in turn the research sources they have cited, are to be believed, we should all be deserting the humanistic approaches, embracing the cognitive-behavioural approaches, and reserving the psychoanalytic approaches for a few cases of obviously interpersonal or intra-familial distress. That is unlikely to happen because therapy is such a subjective and traditional business, generating fierce attachments. Also, what is either novel or evidence-based today tends mysteriously but assuredly to become stale or ineffective tomorrow.

There are no strong, rational grounds for choosing one core theoretical model over another unless we believe and follow the likes of Roth and Fonagy, but even here we can criticize the research criteria and methods cited. We might, instead, fashionably, opt for the kind of 'normative cognitive pluralism' advocated by Stich (1990). Personally, however, I think that the dozens of rather hastily organized schools of therapy belonging to the twentieth century probably have little more to offer than previous centuries of systems of ultimately wrongheaded religion and philosophy. I think there is good reason to believe that we construct, support and irrationally defend particular systems of thought based on their emotional necessity to us. This kind of subjectivity is understandable in the matter of private aesthetic preferences but highly problematic when we decide to inflict systems of thought and their accompanying practices on others. In general, this is exactly what we do in counselling and psychotherapy, as trainers (who dictate the syllabus), as trainees (who eventually become the objects of clients' hopes and often major influences on their lives) and, most worryingly, as agency policy makers (who sometimes arbitrarily and cultishly organize an entire service around their own theoretical preferences).

If clients value most highly the simple components of acceptance, being listened to, being believed, having someone interested in them, and so on (Howe, 1993), and many practitioners in retrospect value most highly what they have learned from their actual work with clients and from reflecting on it in formative supervision (Dryden and Spurling, 1989), then why do we not make these our areas of focus, instead of the many arcane or far-fetched theories we espouse in training? Why is the open secret – that many practitioners freely practise their own idiosyncratic version of what they were trained in, and do not teach what they practise – kept so secret, except for one or two notable exceptions (Corbett, 1995; interview with Richard Wessler in Dryden, 1997: 77–89)?

The answer to these questions may have something to do with the expropriation of lucrative training markets by the universities, and attendant distortions (Berry and Woolfe, 1997); but independent institutions too tend to promote questionable traditions of lengthy mandatory therapy for trainees, coverage of unnecessary and tedious theory (official canon), and so on. Indeed, in response to my original article (Feltham, 1997a), a number of trainees and practitioners wrote to me saying how frustrating they found the shackles of their model-bound, autonomy-denying training.

Surprisingly for a profession that places such weight on the principle of autonomy (Holmes and Lindley, 1989), training norms typically suppress or postpone trainees' autonomy instead of nurturing autonomous thinking (Kramer, 1990). Our training norms are unfortunately canon-centred, not truth-seeking, student-centred or discovery-oriented. Even those courses attempting admirably to take seriously a person-centred philosophy are, I think, perhaps unhelpfully stuck with already dated Rogerian terminology and concepts (and I suspect that Rogers might have agreed). Since the common reality is that all practitioners (mythical, robotic manualized therapists aside) must and do interpret received theory generally, from session to session and throughout their career, in congruence with their own personality, should we not fully acknowledge and nurture this 'pragmatic blending' and 'interpretative free play' (Halgin, 1989; Owen, 1996) in training?

My original article also argued that our current monolithic models are based on hierarchical, patriarchal assumptions and practices, being almost entirely the result of the great thoughts of white, Western, male founders. All our core theoretical models are incurably predicated on the notion that great psychic explorers (Freud, Jung, Perls, Berne, Rogers, Beck, Ellis et al.) have heroically or inspirationally charted totally new psychic territory, handed on precious findings to scribes and disciples and founded important institutions whose self-reinforcing traditions must be revered. Clients who happen to find themselves in front of a diehard Freudian, enthusiastic Gestaltist, committed person-centred therapist or dedicated cognitive therapist will inevitably get some variant of what their therapist has been trained to give them, regardless of whether this is in their best interests.

All core models also inevitably perpetuate the uncritical and untenable assumption that human life is or should be orderly, can be understood analytically, and that our individual problems in living can be addressed systematically, or scientifically, but above all coherently. Coherency is a *sine qua non* of the psychotherapy world (and the cornerstone of the core theoretical model position), but is a concept sorely in need of analysis and challenge. I have argued elsewhere (Feltham, 1998) that therapists' theories and their actual experiences often do not correlate well, because human life is subject to chaos, chance and macro-social processes much more than we care to admit (Dean, 1997). Also, we delude ourselves by imagining that theories which could have some consistency and predictive capability in natural science will similarly apply to human beings in complex, social and open systems (Pilgrim, 1997). We jump prematurely to conclusive theories of order instead of patiently experiencing and reflecting on human life as the elusively orderly chaos it is.

Ways forward

I want now to focus this argument by offering four options for ways forward:

1 Insistence on core theoretical models may be accepted as desirable for one reason or another, and they should therefore remain the norm, at least for the time being.
2 Defenders of the core theoretical model position should concede that this is a pluralistic field, and yield to those who have argued for pluralism in training (House and Totton, 1997).
3 The possibility of a consensually agreed, standardized model of training, based on common interests, good practice and empirical research findings, cannot be ruled out.
4 The argument that in this field of human suffering and meaning seeking no theory is or ever can be adequate may take us in new, atheoretical or post-conceptual directions.

In terms of expediency, (1) is likely to predominate, having the best chance of ensuring practitioners short- to mid-term survival in economically harsh times. In terms of passionate opposition and unofficial practice, (2) is likely to remain highly influential and may even eventually expand in line with postmodern, millennially agitated theorizing. Since this field is so very riven by numerous competing helping professions as well as theoretical models, (3) is probably a non-starter, unless funders and consumers apply even greater pressure. And attachment to traditions and fear of perceived nihilism is likely to render (4) a highly unlikely option, unless, again, millennial anxiety and meaning seeking exert an influence.

However, my guess is that once such options are out of the bag, and as the field of psychotherapy and counselling becomes somewhat more sophisticated in terms of reflexive self-criticism, all four (and any other) options will be simultaneously influential to some degree. I hesitate to attribute this to any postmodern inevitability, but we do indeed seem locked into such relativities. Also, I cannot know without a temporal periscope what unexpected technological or cultural developments may lie around the corner which could simply overturn and transform all four options.

Unpacking the core theoretical model case

Let us begin to unpack all this by critiquing the first option in a little depth. Since Prochaska and Norcross have posed a succinct defence of core theoretical models, I cite a crucial part of their text here for analysis:

> Without a guiding theory or system of psychotherapy, clinicians would be vulnerable, directionless creatures bombarded with literally hundreds of impressions and pieces of information in a single session. Is it more important to ask about color preferences, early memories, parent relationships, life's meaning, disturbing emotions, environmental reinforcers, thought processes, sexual conflicts, or something else in the first interview? At any given time, should we empathize, confront, teach, model, support, question, restructure, interpret, or remain silent in a therapy session? A psychotherapy theory describes the clinical phenomena, delimits the amount of relevant information, organizes that information, and integrates it all into a coherent body of knowledge that prioritizes our conceptualization and directs our treatment. (1994: 3–5)

Prochaska and Norcross have a case, certainly, and it would only be fair to mention that they qualify this statement later by arguing against dogma and for due flexibility. However, a little micro-analysis serves to expose flaws in their core theoretical model case.

First, they present the therapeutic encounter as bewildering, exaggerating for dramatic effect the plight of the poor 'creature' of the allegedly atheoretical therapist subjected to many simultaneous decisional dilemmas. They seem to imply that the choice of what to ask is something like a life-and-death, now-or-never, surgically precise matter, and that an incorrect choice could be disastrous. They go on to spell out the wonderful benefits of a psychotherapy theory, which will reliably describe, delimit, organize, integrate, prioritize and direct 'treatment'. This will apparently integrate all this bewildering information into a coherent body of knowledge. I would say, rather, quasi-coherent; and I certainly dispute the easy appellation of 'body of knowledge'. In what way is a psychotherapy system knowledge rather than a mass of opinions, best guesses and selected experiences organized into one belief system among dozens of competing and conflicting others by partisan practitioners? It is more honest and accurate to say, I think, that psychotherapy systems resemble competing narratives (McLeod, 1997). And what guiding system or theory of truth is available to assist the vulnerable creature (you and me) who is bombarded by literally hundreds of competing psychotherapy systems or narratives (Feltham, 1997b)?

Second, Prochaska and Norcross choose to disregard inconvenient alternative interpretations of their scenario. For example, I doubt that many encounters are actually completely atheoretical, since most of us have some guiding system or implicit theory composed of inferences from life experiences, personal suffering, close relationships, common sense, intuition and liberal education, not to mention the extent to which therapeutic discourse has seeped into everyday consciousness. Call all or most of this 'folk psychology' if you will, but on philosophical grounds we have to make a place for such reasoning (Richards, 1996).

In addition, recalling the evidence that psychotherapy training does not necessarily lead to better clinical results than no training at all (see McLennan's chapter in this book), we had better allow that even some laypersons might not in fact feel totally bombarded and directionless, as suggested by Prochaska and Norcross. Furthermore, exactly how are trained clinicians better equipped to know whether to ask about early memories, life's meaning, and so on? Certainly a schooling in one system will lead you to ask clients certain questions and neglect others, and this will appear to resemble coherence: you may feel and look as if you know what you're doing and where you're going. But as I have pointed out already, clinicians first have to choose quite randomly, apparently, between about 400 different systems of psychotherapy.

Third, Prochaska and Norcross also choose to ignore the possibility that meaningful and helpful atheoretical encounters may actually take place. Although it is a longstanding dogma of psychology that we are incapable of unmediated experience, mystics have long argued that this is not only possible but perhaps essential for human survival, since it may be our very entrapment in familiar thought patterns and associated habitual practices that leads to action-postponement, divisiveness, misunderstanding, combative nationalism, and so on (Bohm, 1992). In more familiar therapeutic terms, it may be that Carl Rogers' (1986) commendation of the therapeutic power of *presence* and Jung's admonition to 'learn your theories as well as you can, but put them aside when you touch the miracle of the living soul' (1928: 361) imply the same possibility and even necessity of atheoretical human encounter. Kahn (1991: 159) too argues that therapists at their best offer and elicit a moment-to-moment 'readiness to be surprised' that is 'as important to them as their theory'. Many if not most new theories have sprung from clinical encounters which therapists have not been able to fit into existing theories; another alternative would be to resist (usually self-aggrandizing) theory building and to embrace more fully the actual exploration of presence. We do not *have to* construct theories and write books!

Incidentally, one can come to Rogerian or Jungian conclusions without reading Rogers or Jung, and one may agree with aspects of their theories without agreeing with an entire opus or even without studying them any further. It is an irony too seldom contemplated that simple truths of actuality, presence, self-discovery and wholeness, as advocated by many mystics and philosophers through the ages, are packaged into systems and procedures that mystify such truths, by those who wish to have their cake and eat it; that is, who wish to claim that the truth is under your nose for you to claim as a birthright, and yet only, or most reliably, available from their own publications, procedures and institutions (for example, Perls et al., 1977). The extent to which published wisdom is assumed to be superior to psychological wisdom found in everyday settings is an interesting and under-researched area.

On the theme of presence, Tudor and Worrall assert that

> presence, in this transpersonal, almost mystical sense, arises out of the solid practice of developed counselling skills, including congruence, over years. It is significant that Rogers wrote about presence, and that tentatively, after over fifty years of practice. Presence describes a quality of relationship which we sometimes reach, and is not a substitute for the diligent and committed building of relationship on which the person-centred approach is based and for which it stands. (1994: 205)

Such a statement clearly endorses the core theoretical defence and in particular conveys a deep respect for tradition, where the virtues of diligence, commitment, rigour, and so on, are preconditions of therapeutically potent presence. The logic of this would seem to imply that presence can only be achieved following years of hard-won study and skill development. It does not necessarily follow in fact that Rogers himself attained greater presence *because of* his 50 years of practice; he may have been barking up the wrong tree for 50 years until finally finding a simpler and more profound truth. This may sound irreverent or facetious, but is intended rather to point out that we do tend to respect, if not revere, our own heroes and traditions and to dismiss contradictory theses. It is on record that Thomas Aquinas experienced a revelation a year before he died which led him to declare that by contrast all his theological writings now appeared 'as so much straw'. Not only mystics but untrained 'innocents' frequently argue that presence can and often does arise spontaneously rather than after 50 years of toil. It may take 50 years for some, but only a moment for others, to get to the point, and perhaps some people are simply more therapeutically gifted than others.

Indeed it is also argued that many of our traditions themselves are responsible for epidemic mental and social distress since they commit us to procrastinatory, presence-diminishing attitudes and practices. The tension between tradition and presence is immanent in the biblical division between the Old and the New Testaments, between history and law, and the good news of forgiveness and the end of history. Analogously, in therapy we have continuous tension between the concepts of development, theoretical canon and therapeutic process, on the one hand, and autonomy, presence and indeterminacy, on the other. It is not insignificant that the history of therapy, like that of religion, is characterized to date by charismatic founders, faithful followers and ever-erupting sects and cults, all representing rhythms of apparent revelation, reification, repression and revolution.

To return to Prochaska and Norcross's thesis: in spite of their disclaimer – that they advocate flexibility not dogma – they perhaps do not appreciate the extent to which any guiding theory of human distress must logically distort what is perceived. All such theories are partial, all emphasize one human characteristic over another (cognition, emotion, behaviour, unconscious conflict, spirituality, interpersonal systems, and so on), and all are bound more or less to fit (one might say, uncomfortably, 'shrink') clients to pre-existing expectations. Theories of psychotherapy do not neutrally *describe* the clinical phenomena, as implied here; rather, they *construct* clinical phenomena. It should be obvious to us by now that patterns of human behaviour and suffering are deeply rooted yet diverse, always changing somewhat from culture to culture and from age to age, and that theorists can self-servingly cut this cake in as many different ways as they choose, *ad infinitum*. This is indeed what is done, with ostensibly novel interpretations being presented and appropriated at regular intervals.

Underlying Prochaska and Norcross's case, and that of most other defenders of core theoretical models, is a commitment to respect or to appear to respect mainstream clinical schools; and furthermore to speak of these as if no other attitude is possible. But if our main concern is to address human suffering, we are not at all bound to respect such schools of thought simply because they exist. It does not follow that I must assume the greatness of Freud or those who followed him, or that I must be uncritically impressed by self-styled scientific psychotherapists and their theories. When reading about the life and work of Lacan, for example, I am bound to ask myself what sense it makes, whether it really makes sense at all, and whether – as parts of Lacan's biography suggest – it may not ultimately be exploitative nonsense (Roudinesco, 1997).

In fact it is obvious from ordinary conversations with colleagues that one person's grail is another's mumbo-jumbo, fairy tale, rip-off or simply something not to his or her taste. In this sense, we might talk less grandly of core theoretical models and more realistically of provisional working models or hypotheses, or even of transient interest groups, although this would of course undermine aspirations to professional status. In the context of constructivist research, Schwandt (1994) declares a preference for the term 'persuasions' instead of 'models', and it may be that in counselling and psychotherapy serious analysis is required of what exactly our canonical positions have a right to be called.

In conclusion

In a sense, options (1) and (2) above are in their own ways thriving already, as establishment and anti-establishment practices. Option number (3) is worth consideration, in part because of its ironic neglect. In an age of anxious and sometimes absurd competency construction, it is strange that few have apparently suggested or constructed a standard theoretical model, or national therapeutic curriculum. This would not be hard to do; there are some logical, central items, such as professional ethics, which are pretty common to all approaches. It would not require too much work to weed out redundant theoretical waffle and instead present the key concepts of major schools of thought, along with their core practical skills. Provided that hysterical defence of the unfounded idea – that techniques detached from their theoretical moorings will brain-damage clients – can be quashed, there is a clear pathway to rational curriculum building.

In my view we need exposure to a selection of highly condensed traditional theories, plus perhaps training in the most useful techniques, a concentration on relationship factors, but above all room to think, study and engage in dialogue on human suffering in history, culture and in ourselves. As the dialogical psychotherapist Hycner puts it: 'It is not the therapist's theoretical orientation that is as crucial in the healing process, as is the wholeness and availability of the self of the therapist' (1991: 12–13). Now, a new training programme cannot come about, apparently, because we are all so fiercely partisan. Few if any of us are concerned enough about seriously addressing human suffering to want to find the best mix of pragmatism, cooperation, dialogue, creativity and necessary selflessness. The quest appears as doomed as Esperanto or a committee-created non-oppressive world religion.

Recently a certain amount has been done to attempt to clarify the nature of theory and theorizing in counselling and psychotherapy (Horton, 1996; Cramond, 1997). These are very welcome advances, but we also have a great deal of soul searching to do, by which I mean sincerely asking the necessary big – and often inconvenient and threatening – questions. Theoretical anchorage is perhaps useful at times, but is also frequently misleading and deadening. We have yet to learn to use and discard theories wisely; mostly we are still lived, used and deadened by our own theories and traditions (Bohm, 1992).

Carl Rogers suggested that consciousness of theory in therapeutic encounters themselves was *irrelevant* and *detrimental*: 'if theory is to be held at all, it seems to me that it should be held tentatively, lightly, flexibly, in a way which is freely open to change, and should be laid aside in the moment of encounter itself' (Rogers in Rogers and Stevens, 1973: 186). As far as I know, neither Rogers nor anyone else has convincingly explained the need for theoretical preparation at all if theory has no place in therapy itself. That theory may be interesting, even reassuring, for some does not logically mean that it is essential or useful. In addition, Pilgrim (1997) argues that psychotherapeutic theory is typically 'wise after the event' (not predictive) and is not demonstrably superior to common-sense explanations.

Perhaps what therapists and ordinary citizens alike need is not yet further models, theories or persuasions, but a core radical communitarian concern for exploring mental and social health. This might partly entail provisional theorizing and dialogue in the manner of Bohm (1992), a shift from cognition to activity (Newman and Holzman, 1996) or a revolution against the oppression of our bodies and emotions by our intellects. As Bohm points out, human thought and its products have not had much success in bringing about a sane society, and it seems unlikely that core theoretical models of counselling will have much further impact. But whatever form it takes, I believe this implied new direction implicitly transcends the immaturity of our many centuries of superstitious and divisive religions, philosophies and psychotherapies *and* the currently ascendant glamour of cerebral postmodernism. Life is, and we are, far bigger and more vital than the ultimately flimsy, hero-worshipping thought systems and prized ingots of intellectual property with which we habitually weigh ourselves down. Institutions institutionalize us. Core theoretical models infantilize and zoologize us and our clients – that is, deny us our autonomy, cage, shrink and dehumanize us. At least, that's my theory – for now!

References

Adams, H.E. (1984) 'The pernicious effects of theoretical orientations in clinical psychology', *The Clinical Psychologist*, 37: 90–3.

Berry, M. and Woolfe, R. (1997) 'Teaching counselling in universities: match or mismatch?' *British Journal of Guidance and Counselling*, 25 (4): 517–25.

Bohm, D. (1992) *Thought as a System*. London: Routledge.

Corbett, L. (1995) 'Supervision and the mentor archetype', in P. Kugler (ed.), *Jungian Perspectives on Clinical Supervision*. Einsiedeln, Switzerland: Daimon.

Cramond, J. (1997) 'The nature and role of theory', in I. Horton and V. Varma (eds), *The Needs of Counsellors and Psychotherapists*. London: Sage.

Dean, A. (1997) *Chaos and Intoxication: Complexity and Adaptation in the Structure of Human Nature*. London: Routledge.

Dryden, W. (ed.) (1997) *Therapists' Dilemmas*. Rev. edn. London: Sage.

Dryden, W. and Spurling, L. (eds) (1989) *On Becoming a Psychotherapist*. London: Routledge.

Dryden, W. (ed.) (1991) *The Essential Arnold Lazarus*. London: Whurr.

Feltham, C. (1997a) 'Challenging the core theoretical model', *Counselling*, 8 (2): 121–5. (Reproduced in R. House and N. Totton (eds), *Implausible Professions: Arguments for Pluralism and Autonomy in Psychotherapy and Counselling*. Ross-on-Wye: PCCS Books, 1997.)

Feltham, C. (1997b) *Which Psychotherapy? Leading Exponents Explain Their Differences*. London: Sage.

Feltham, C. (1998) 'Doubt, discrepancy and dishonesty in counselling'. Paper presented to the 46th Conference of the International Association for Educational and Vocational Guidance, Tampere, Finland, 5 February.

Halgin, R.P. (1989) 'Pragmatic blending', *Journal of Integrative and Eclectic Psychotherapy*, 8 (4): 320–8.

Heaton, J.M. (1993) 'The sceptical tradition in psychotherapy', in L. Spurling (ed.), *From the Words of My Mouth: Tradition in Psychotherapy*. London: Routledge.

Holmes, J. and Lindley, R. (1989) *The Values of Psychotherapy*. Oxford: Oxford University Press.

Horton, I. (1996) 'Towards the construction of a model of counselling: some issues', in R. Bayne, I. Horton and J. Bimrose (eds), *New Directions in Counselling*. London: Routledge.

House, R. and Totton, N. (eds) (1997) *Implausible Professions: Arguments for Pluralism and Autonomy in Psychotherapy and Counselling*. Manchester: PCCS Books.

Howe, D. (1993) *On Being a Client: Understanding the Process of Counselling and Psychotherapy*. London: Sage.

Hycner, R.H. (1991) *Between Person and Person: Toward a Dialogical Psychotherapy*. Highland, NJ: Center for Gestalt Development.

Jung, C.G. (1928) 'Analytical psychology and education', in *Contributions to Analytical Psychology*. London: Trench Trubner.

Kahn, M. (1991) *Between Therapist and Client: The New Relationship*. New York: Freeman.

Kramer, D.A. (1990) 'Conceptualizing wisdom: the primacy of affect–cognition relations', in R.J. Sternberg (ed.), *Wisdom: Its Nature, Origins and Development*. Cambridge: Cambridge University Press.

Lazarus, A.A. (1989) 'Why I am an eclectic (not an integrationist)', *British Journal of Guidance and Counselling*, 17: 248–58.

McLeod, J. (1997) *Narrative and Psychotherapy*. London: Sage.

Newman, F. and Holzman, L. (1996) *The End of Knowing: A New Developmental Way of Learning*. London: Routledge.

Owen, I. (1996) 'Are we before or after integration? Discussing guidelines for integrative practice via clinical audit', *Counselling Psychology Review*, 11: 12–18.

Perls, F., Hefferline, R.F. and Goodman, P. (1977) *Gestalt Therapy*. New York: Bantam.

Phillips, A. (1995) *Terrors and Experts*. London: Faber & Faber.

Pilgrim, D. (1997) *Psychotherapy and Society*. London: Sage.

Prochaska, J.O. and Norcross, J.C. (1994) *Systems of Psychotherapy: A Transtheoretical Analysis*. Pacific Grove, CA: Brooks/Cole.

Richards, G. (1996) 'On the necessary survival of folk psychology', in W. O'Donohue and R.F. Kitchener (eds), *The Philosophy of Psychology*. London: Sage.

Rogers, C.R. (1986) 'A client-centered/person-centered approach to therapy', in I. Kutash and W. Wolf (eds), *Psychotherapist's Casebook*. San Francisco: Jossey-Bass.

Rogers, C.R. and Stevens, B. (1973) *Person to Person: The Problem of Being Human*. London: Souvenir.

Roth, A. and Fonagy, P. (1996) *What Works For Whom? A Critical Review of Psychotherapy Research*. New York: Guilford.

Roudinesco, E. (1997) *Jacques Lacan*. Cambridge: Polity Press.
Schwandt, T.A. (1994) 'Constructivist, interpretivist approaches to human inquiry', in N.K. Denzin and Y.S. Lincoln (eds), *Handbook of Qualitative Research*. Thousand Oaks, CA: Sage.
Stich, S.P. (1990) *The Fragmentation of Reason*. Cambridge, MA: MIT Press.
Tudor, K. and Worrall, M. (1994) 'Congruence reconsidered', *British Journal of Guidance and Counselling*, 22 (2): 197–206.

21   Training in a core theoretical model is essential

Sue Wheeler

This chapter is written drawing on my experience of working with the British Association for Counselling (BAC) Courses Accreditation Group, latterly as the Co-Chair of the group and inevitably on my experience as a counsellor trainer. Contrary to Colin Feltham, who has argued both in this book and elsewhere (Feltham, 1997a) against the need for a core theoretical model for counselling or psychotherapy training, I support the notion that such courses should define and then adhere to a coherent model that influences all aspects of the training, but I am not prescriptive about what that model should be. In developing my argument in favour of a core theoretical model, I shall take a pragmatic approach, presenting a realistic appraisal of the art of the possible. I will also argue that the core theoretical model will evolve as a function of the staff team, which may or may not be coherent. This will lead to a discussion about the development of an appropriate core theoretical model. My personal allegiance and professional experience has been with the British Association for Counselling. In many instances I see the words 'counsellor', 'therapist' and 'psychotherapist' as being interchangeable and I would argue that both counselling and psychotherapy training courses should adhere to a core theoretical model. However, as I am more familiar with training described as 'counsellor' training and the requirements for BAC Accreditation, most of this chapter will refer to counsellor training specifically.

Counsellor training in Britain

Various studies of counsellor training in Britain reveal that there are probably more integrative or eclectic training courses than any other. In response to a survey of counsellor training courses (Wheeler, 1997), 39 courses supplied information which revealed that 9 were described as person-centred, 9 as psychodynamic, 2 adhered to another single model and 19 were either integrative or eclectic. Counting the current courses accredited by the BAC (1999), 47 in total, 13 are person-centred, 12 are psychodynamic, 2 are other single models and the remaining 20 are integrative and eclectic.

Hollanders surveyed counsellors, asking about their training and subsequent practice, and found a substantial interest in eclecticism/integration: 'The evidence gathered in this study is both clear and strong, showing a reported preference by a great majority of the participating practitioners for working with concepts and techniques that span a number of orientations and approaches' (1997: 455). Hunt (1995) collected prospectuses of counsellor training courses in the North-West of Britain and reported that the majority seemed to be person-centred, many were described as integrative, although 38 per cent of the publicity material produced about courses failed to indicate what theoretical model was being offered.

Theoretical creativity and diversity are therefore integral to the counsellor's profession and there is no evidence to suggest that traditional purist mono-theory courses are the norm nor that they dominate the list of courses that have gained BAC accreditation. However, experience of working as a consultant to courses seeking accreditation suggests that counsellor training courses that present an integrative or eclectic model probably have to do more soul searching and preparation for the accreditation process than those that adhere to a model that is supported by a body of literature.

Definition of a core theoretical model

> Most approaches or models of counselling have in some way been spawned by one of the broad psychological schools of personality and are often regarded as synonymous with them.
>
> (Dryden et al., 1995: 26)

Approaches to the understanding of personality vary widely and provide diverse explanations for the way in which psychological problems occur. Some theories have given rise to associated methods and techniques for treating distressed clients that have become known as psychotherapeutic interventions and are organized in schools of thought such as Rogerian or Kleinian, named after the prime protagonist for that school. The practice of counselling in Britain has been influenced by psychoanalytic theory, humanistic and person-centred theories and the behavioural school (McLeod, 1993). A theoretical base for counselling might be labelled as an orientation, a school or model and describes the nature of the theory, including theory of personality that informs practice. Indeed Mahrer (1989) suggests that it is the understanding of personality that is of prime importance for counsellors rather than the skills they use in the therapeutic process.

A narrow view of a core theoretical model would be one that was based on one of the three predominant paradigms, humanistic, psychoanalytic or cognitive-behavioural, made even more specific by being aligned with one of the major writers within these groups such as Carl Rogers, Sigmund

Freud or Aaron Beck. A broader view of a core theoretical model (and indeed the one embraced by BAC course accreditation) is one that accepts that integration of theory and skills is possible., providing that the integrative process has been fully considered and documented.

The core theoretical model should be reflected in all aspects of a course, from theory to skills training, methods of and criteria for assessment, supervision and personal development, as well as the inclusion of 'equal opportunities' issues. It can be just as difficult to incorporate some of these elements into a mainstream core model as into an integrative model. Integrating an approach to race, culture and sexual orientation issues into a mainstream psychodynamic course, bearing in mind the classic psychoanalytic interpretation of homosexuality as a perversion (Davies and Neal, 1996) and that tradition's complete disregard for social issues (Thomas, 1992), is a challenging prospect (Wheeler and Izzard, 1997). An integrative model is less hampered by dogma and has the potential to be more creative in adopting an approach to cross-cultural counselling.

The BAC course accreditation scheme demands that 'there should be enough counselling theory, drawing on relevant social science disciplines to enable students to make explicit the underlying assumptions, basic principles and elements, concepts, strategies and techniques of the core theoretical model' which the course espouses as well as the therapeutic process and principles and mechanisms of change (BAC, 1996: 13). Elsewhere the recognition booklet states that 'the core theoretical model would be reflected not just in theory, skills and practice of the students but also in the way the course is structured, assessed, taught and administered' (1996: 3).[1] In other words the core theoretical model is evident throughout the course, providing coherence and internal consistency. This emphasis does not mitigate against eclectic or integrative courses, but it does demand that such courses regard their eclectic or integrative nature as their core theoretical model, exploring fully its philosophical, theoretical and practical implications. The model must have a rationale for the nature of psychological difficulties, a theoretical basis for understanding human growth and development, the nature of the therapeutic relationship and the change process, as well as an explanation for the way in which counselling techniques are employed to bring about change. Horton (1996) details the components of a model of counselling under the broad headings of process structures and themes, general principles of change, process of change and mechanisms of change.

The development of counselling in Britain

It is noteworthy that one of the foremost and longest established journals for the counselling profession in Britain is called the *British Journal of Guidance and Counselling*. Established in 1973, the title reflects the role and the function of counselling as it was imported from the USA in the 1960s.

In the USA counsellors often have a guidance function, working in schools and colleges assisting students with all aspects of their personal, academic and career development, what might be described as broad welfare roles. 'Mental health counsellors' with a specific training profile are more likely to be doing similar work to that which counsellors in GP surgeries, mental health resource centres or even student counselling centres do in Britain today, working psychotherapeutically with a broad range of emotional disturbance. 'Any gathering of counsellors, particularly those in agencies where there is no filtering of clients, will these days be a forum for discussion of the severity of disturbance that they are called upon to hear about' (Noonan, 1997: 249). Hence when we look across the Atlantic to see what is happening in counsellor training there, it is not surprising that the nature of many courses is different, adopting a requirement for training to be broad-based and to span a minimum number of theoretical models. We are not comparing like with like, as our counselling profession has taken a route that embraces mental health work rather than guidance. Indeed, perhaps the time has come for the title of that journal to change? The Counselling Psychology Division of the British Psychological Society (BPS) in Britain prescribes that counselling psychology courses should teach two contrasting models in depth (Allen, 1990). This decision by the BPS is perhaps a sign of progress as this requirement now means that psychologists traditionally wedded to the cognitive-behavioural school are prepared to look beyond that to what other models of counselling have to offer.

Reasons why counsellor training courses should adhere to a core theoretical model

Time

The minimum number of taught hours for a counsellor training course to be accredited by the BAC is 400. Applicants for individual BAC accreditation need to have completed 450 hours of counsellor training. The average number of taught hours for diploma level counsellor training courses is approximately 353 (Wheeler, 1997). Given the amount that there is to learn to take on the responsible role of professional counsellor, perhaps even 400 hours are far too few. Some institutions offer more hours of training, but there are strong market forces, and courses need to be economically viable to recruit. So time is limited. While it may be desirable that attention is paid to the question of 'What treatment suits what kind of client best?' and that all students are able to turn their hand to the preferred model or technique for a particular complaint, how realistic is it that competence can be achieved in a broad range of counselling approaches in such a short time? Surely it is preferable that, given time limitations, students develop skills that fit within an identifiable framework within which they feel confident to practise, even if it means that they cannot meet everyone's needs all of the time.

Assessment

> Student assessment should be congruent with the core theoretical model.
>
> (BAC, 1996: 14)

It is only fair that students embarking on a course of study know what is expected of them and how they will be assessed. An assessment procedure should be comprehensive and reflect all aspects of a student's learning (Wheeler, 1996). They also need to know the criteria by which they are to be assessed, which will include criteria developed to determine whether they meet the required standard of the course in maintaining a counselling relationship, creating a climate of understanding conducive to bringing about change, interacting with a client to bring about change, and understanding the process of change. In other words, reflecting on Horton's components of the counselling model, it is about whether they have achieved competence in the model. If there is a lack of clarity in what the model is, this will be reflected in the criteria for assessment, which in turn leaves students unclear about what is expected of them. Excessively broad outcome statements about competence will now be put to shame by the publication of National Vocational Qualification (NVQ) draft standards (AGC and PLB, 1995), developed over five years using the skill and expertise of hundreds of counsellors and therapists. While the NVQ scheme for awarding qualifications in counselling is subject to considerable criticism and scepticism (Frankland, 1996), the competency statements are both clear and comprehensive across a range of counselling models and will almost certainly be adopted by counselling trainers for use as assessment tools on courses. Clarity about the core theoretical model will then be even more important.

Supervision

Supervision of clinical work has often been described as the forum in which the most powerful learning about practice takes place (Carroll, 1996). Courses will engage or work alongside a number of supervisors providing supervision for their students. Unless there is some coherence to a core theoretical model, how can students best use their supervisory experience to achieve the competence that the course requires? While psychodynamic supervisors may provide help and support to trainees, if the course is antithetical to psychoanalytic ideas, how will students be assessed if they have adopted ways of thinking about their work in tune with their supervisors? Inskipp and Proctor (1994) argue that if a working contract is agreed between therapist and supervisor, a mismatch of theoretical orientation is possible, but supervisors must know what students are expected to achieve by the end of their course. If the objectives related to the model are clear, then supervisors can decide whether they are suited to working with the course and can provide appropriate feedback to their supervisees.

Stance of the therapist and relationship with the client

One of the crucial ways in which theoretical models differ is reflected in the stance that the therapist takes with the client. This might mean, for example, that in a person-centred model the therapist exhibits warmth and empathy towards the client and perhaps sometimes discloses things about him- or herself. In a psychodynamic model, the therapist takes a more neutral role and holds back from self-disclosure. Using a behavioural model, the therapist will be quite directive with the client and suggest activities that may help to alleviate symptoms, which is quite different from an approach that expects clients to develop through self-actualization. The similarities and differences between psychodynamic and person-centred counsellors are debatable (McLeod and Wheeler, 1996), and there is a suggestion that one behaves like a companion on a journey and the other like Sherlock Holmes on a case. Students need clarity about how they are expected to be with clients and how they are expected to behave, which a coherent model provides. Kahn (1991) is optimistic that a 'new harmony' can be brought about in providing a relationship that can be therapeutic yet not entrenched in the dogma of traditional models, but that can only happen as a result of painstaking work on the process of integration.

Staff are more likely to work as a cohesive team

The development of a counselling or psychotherapy training course is an interesting phenomenon. A training course is designed by the staff engaged to teach it, often with constraints imposed by the institution they work in, which might include finance, staffing, accommodation, existing courses within the institution, the mission statement of the organization, or with regard to local competition from other counselling courses, or even local employment opportunities. Some courses are developed by individuals who 'grow' an organization to support the training that they design. The staff group may choose each other, based on their prior acquaintance and knowledge of their professional interests, or they may be thrown together with little or no regard for their compatibility. Hence sometimes courses are conceived with a shared vision of an ideal training course, but more often they are created with the ideas generated by individuals that are modified and transmuted as others join the team. Consequently counselling courses reflect the knowledge and belief systems of the people who design them, which works well as long as those people stay in post, but becomes more problematic when they move on. When new staff are appointed, either they must fit in with the course as it is or be proactive in bringing about change that creates greater job satisfaction through congruence with their competence and expertise. In essence the core theoretical model will be influenced by the people teaching it, who will provide a more consistent training for their students if they are in harmony.

The core theoretical model is a personal choice

Larsen (1996) claims that all psychological theories can be viewed as stories which reflect the life experiences of their authors. Counsellors and therapists are influenced by their own experience or story as they develop or adopt their theoretical stance. It is interesting to trace how many of the therapeutic theoreticians have been influenced by the environment that fostered their development: Freud was influenced by Charcot and began to develop his theories of the unconscious from his experience of hypnotism; Rogers was influenced by his psychologist background to use an experimental approach to understanding the helpful aspects of the therapeutic relationship (McLeod, 1993); Perls, Berne and others (Feltham, 1997b) rejected their analytic training and developed new models to take account of aspects of human experience that they did not find in analytic theory. Counselling or psychotherapy trainers are similarly influenced by their life experience, training, environment, friends and colleagues, as well as responding to demands from students and employers which may or may not harmonize and synthesize into a coherent whole when a package of training is offered. A theoretical model may stretch to accommodate individuals, or may be distorted by individuals. Hence it could be argued that it will be easier to recruit staff to teach a course that has a well-known and well-documented core theoretical model about which there will be some level of agreement. On the other hand, from a diverse and creative staff group, particularly one that has ample time for developmental activities and discussion, an innovative and comprehensive new and unique core model may evolve.

Objectives for a counsellor training course

Given a training course of about 450 hours of face-to-face teaching, such as might be eligible for BAC course accreditation (BAC, 1996), the objectives will vary, but may include something like the following. By the end of the training course students will:

(a) be competent to practise as counsellors in an agency that offers counselling to a generic client group;

(b) be able to distinguish between those clients for whom counselling as practised by the student is appropriate and potentially helpful and those for whom it is not;

(c) be able to make appropriate referrals to other agencies, having knowledge of other services available;

(d) be competent to manage the therapeutic frame for counselling with due regard to the *Code of Ethics for Counsellors* (BAC, 1990);

(e) be aware of cross-cultural, disability, sexual orientation, gender, age and social class/economic issues that affect clients and settings, and be able to interact with clients appropriately;

(f) be able to manage the boundary between their own interpersonal and intrapersonal processes and those of the clients;

(g) have a clear understanding of the theoretical background to their practice;

(h) be able to monitor and evaluate their own practice;

(i) be willing and able to engage in a supervisory relationship with an appropriately experienced and qualified practitioner who will be involved with the continuing professional development of their practice.

A lot is required from a relatively short course to meet such objectives. A curriculum that incorporates theory, practical skills training, ethics and professional practice, social awareness, personal awareness, understanding and cooperation with other helping agencies, research and evaluation, specific issues related to client groups and contextual issues, supervision, preparation for assignments, community meetings, and so on, as well as methods of assessment and criteria for assessment, is a challenge. The therapy literature is rich, counselling models proliferate, and for those enthralled by therapeutic process, the attraction to incorporate a wide range of diverse theories and ideas is great. It is like being confronted with a sumptuous feast. The choice is whether to eat as much as possible, with its inevitable consequences, or whether to choose a discreet amount that is complementary and digestible. Curriculum development is a complex and skilled process. Making choices about what should be included in the syllabus to ensure that the learning objectives are met and that competent counsellors emerge is an exacting task. Time must be carefully allocated to ensure that all crucial aspects of counsellor training are covered. A core theoretical model provides a framework for the syllabus, within which all the elements of training can be contained.

Integration of theory and practice

Given the discussion about the amount of time available to deliver a viable course, it follows that the most important consideration is that trainees are provided with an experience that meets the aims and objectives of the course. The onus is on the trainers to put together a package that best meets that need. Students need a comprehensive and digestible model that provides a foundation for their practice. This may be an integrative model, but the BAC accreditation criteria require that the integration is clarified by the staff offering the training rather than left to the students. Of course counsellors evolve and develop their own integrative style of working with experience, but the initial training should provide clear guidelines about how pieces fit together. It is this that is so often lacking in courses that apply for accreditation, not the fact that they claim to be integrative *per se*.

There are integrative models that are well documented and comprehensive providing detailed information about theory and practice (Kohut, 1984; Ryle, 1990; Prochaska and DiClemente, 1992; Egan, 1998). Egan is a popular choice for courses in Britain. Integrative models that are more questionable are those idiosyncratic ones that evolve largely as a result of the mix of current or previous staff teaching the course. At best, an integrative course has been rigorously thought-through and documented. Attention is given to an understanding of human growth and development, development of psychological problems, therapeutic and theoretical frame, the nature of the therapeutic relationship, skills and techniques, assessment of client difficulty, congruent means of pursuing personal development and complementary methods of organizing the course and assessing progress and final competence. At worst, the course is constructed around what staff are available and what they are best qualified to teach. In such instances dialogue about the theoretical model between staff is potentially problematic and students are given conflicting messages. Assessment procedures are woolly because there is no internal consistency. The rationale sometimes offered for such a course is that students can make of it what they will and find their own style.

Ideally a course should offer students a map of the journey they are about to embark on. The map should not be rigidly drawn so that no deviations from the path can be made, but needs to be colourful enough to provide opportunities to stop and admire the view on the way, or to take minor detours. The journey is time-limited, however, and cannot include too many deviations or the ultimate destination will not be reached. The journey needs to be planned in such a way that the trainees arrive at the destination feeling stimulated and rewarded by their travel, enriched and matured through the experience and hungry for more, but feeling adequately equipped to manage the tasks that a professional counsellor faces. Students need to be able to articulate how their interventions and strategies in working with clients are rooted in their theoretical understanding. A spirit of adventure and creativity should unite the trainers rather than pull them in opposite directions.

Eclecticism

Defining eclecticism in the context of counselling as a collection of techniques from different theoretical models, there is no reason why a training course should not offer training in two or more models, providing that sufficient time (probably in excess of 400 hours) is given to the training.

The problem arises when an eclectic course offers a taster of a range of distinct models, applying none of them in any depth. Students may then be expected to draw on their skills in a particular model to work with a relevant client, or to synthesize the training into a coherent whole, a lot to ask of inexperienced trainee therapists. Another way in which an eclectic model might be acceptable would be if it is offered as an established model such as multi-modal therapy (Lazarus, 1992). At least there is some documentation to refer to that explains the rationale for the model. One course accredited by the BAC offers a parallel psychodynamic and person-centred training. Two trainers are present at all sessions and pose the perspective of both models throughout the course. Students tend to choose one model or the other, while consistent dialogue takes place and Kohut's work is discussed as a possible point of integration. Perhaps this offers some hope for eclectic courses that seek BAC accreditation, but there is probably a book to be written about how the theory and the practice taught on each course hang together and constitute a training of sufficient depth.

Conclusion

Counselling and psychotherapy training could be compared to the process of growing up. Consistent parenting that provides a containing environment in which the child feels nurtured and safe is a blueprint for healthy emotional development (Winnicott, 1986). Children thrive when they know where they are and what is expected of them. Parents provide some kind of life map and set of rules that guide and provide security. They cannot provide children with specific knowledge to deal with every situation they meet, but they can provide a template for thinking about and managing life. Good parenting provides a good foundation on which a child can build his or her own identity. It is not infinitely malleable and flexible. Parents adhere to their values and beliefs and pass them on to their children. As young people mature they hold these in mind while experimenting with new ideas and making adjustments to their beliefs. This seems like a helpful metaphor for training as a therapist, a process of growing and developing intellectually, emotionally and professionally, with a sound core theoretical model. The model provides the framework in which the learning takes place, a secure base to which the counsellor can return, or from which new paths can be explored.

Note

1. The BAC course accreditation scheme was called the 'recognition' scheme until 1997. The official BAC publication describing the scheme still uses the title *Recognition of Counsellor Training Courses*.

References

AGC and PLB (Advice Guidance, Counselling and Psychotherapy Lead Body) (1995) *First Release of Standards*. Welwyn.

Allen, J. (1990) 'Counselling psychologists and counsellors: new challenges and opportunities', *British Journal of Guidance and Counselling*, 18 (3): 321–5.

BAC (British Association for Counselling) (1990) *Code of Ethics for Counsellors*. Rugby: BAC.

BAC (British Association for Counselling) (1996) *Recognition of Counsellor Training Courses*. Rugby: BAC.

BAC (British Association for Counselling) (1999) *BAC Accredited Counsellor Training Courses*. Rugby: BAC.

Carroll, M. (1996) *Counselling Supervision: Theory Skills and Practice*. London: Cassell.

Davies, D. and Neal, C. (eds) (1996) *Pink Therapy*. Buckingham: Open University Press.

Dryden, W., Horton, I. and Mearns, D. (1995) *Issues in Professional Counsellor Training*. London: Cassell.

Egan, G. (1998) *The Skilled Helper*. 6th edn. Pacific Grove, CA: Brooks/Cole.

Feltham, C. (1997a) 'Challenging the core theoretical model', *Counselling*, 8: 121–5.

Feltham, C. (ed.) (1997b) *Which Psychotherapy? Leading Exponents Explain Their Differences*. London: Sage.

Frankland, A.M. (1996) 'Accreditation and registration', in R. Bayne, I. Horton and J. Bimrose (eds), *New Directions in Counselling*. London: Routledge.

Hollanders, H. (1997) 'Eclecticism/Integration among counsellors in the UK in the light of Kuhn's concept of paradigm formation'. Unpublished PhD thesis, University of Manchester.

Horton, I. (1996) 'Towards the construction of a model of counselling', in R. Bayne, I. Horton and J. Bimrose (eds), *New Directions in Counselling*. London: Routledge.

Hunt, P. (1995) 'Regional training audit: a survey of counselling, psychotherapy and related trainings within Merseyside and adjacent regions' (unpublished and obtainable from the Administrator, Merseyside Psychotherapy Institute, c/o 26 Barchester Drive, Liverpool L17 5BZ, UK).

Inskipp, F. and Proctor, B. (1994) *Making the Most of Supervision*. Twickenham: Cascade.

Kahn, M. (1991) *Between Therapist and Client: The New Relationship*. New York: Freeman. Co.

Kohut, H. (1984) *How Does Analysis Cure?* Chicago: University of Chicago Press.

Larsen, D.J. (1996) 'Eclecticism: psychological theories as interwoven stories'. Paper given to the IRTAC Conference, Vancouver, Canada, May.

Lazarus, A.A. (1992) 'Multimodal therapy: technical eclecticism and minimal integration', in J.C. Norcross and M.R. Goldfried (eds), *Handbook of Psychotherapy Integration*. New York: Basic Books.

McLeod, J. (1993) *An Introduction to Counselling*. Buckingham: Open University Press.

McLeod, J. and Wheeler, S. (1996) 'Person-centred and psychodynamic counselling: a dialogue', in S. Palmer, S. Dainow and P. Milner (eds) *Counselling: The BAC Counselling Reader*. London, Sage.

Mahrer, A.R. (1989) *The Integration of Psychotherapies: A Guide for Practicing Therapists*. New York: Human Science Press.

Noonan, E. (1997) 'Editorial', *Psychodynamic Counselling*, 3 (3): 245–50.

Prochaska, J.O. and DiClemente, C.C. (1992) 'The transtheoretical approach', in

J.C. Norcross and M.R. Goldfried (eds), *Handbook of Psychotherapy Integration*. New York: Basic Books.

Ryle, A. (1990) *Cognitive-Analytic Therapy: Active Participation in Change: A New Integration in Brief Psychotherapy*. Chichester: John Wiley.

Thomas, L. (1992) 'Racism and psychotherapy: working with racism in the consulting room – an analytical view', in J. Kareem and R. Littlewood (eds), *Intercultural Therapy: Themes, Interpretations and Practices*. Oxford: Blackwell Scientific.

Wheeler, S. (1996) *Training Counsellors: The Assessment of Competence*. London: Cassell.

Wheeler, S. (1997) 'Issues and trends in professional counsellor training'. Paper presented to the BAC Counselling Research Conference, Birmingham, June.

Wheeler, S. and Izzard, S. (1997) 'Training counsellors: integrating difference', *Psychodynamic Counselling*, 3 (4): 401–17.

Winnicott, D.W. (1986) *Home Is Where We Start From*. Harmondsworth: Penguin.

22   Professionalization of therapy by registration is unnecessary, ill advised and damaging

Richard Mowbray

In *The Case Against Psychotherapy Registration* I concluded that

> the case against statutory psychotherapy registration is, firstly, that the case *for* it is so poor. 'The case for' fails to stand up to close scrutiny. . . . Secondly, the case against psychotherapy registration is that the effects of it would, on balance, actually be negative and represent a deterioration of the existing situation. This 'treatment' would be worse than the 'disease'. (Mowbray, 1995: 213, original emphasis)

In this chapter, I will summarize the reasons for this assessment.

Statutory registration, also known as licensing, especially in North America, refers to the legal protection of an occupational title (Title Act) or practice (Practice Act) and is the crowning event in the formation of an established profession. This 'legally enshrined closure' (Saks, 1995: 73) confers state-endorsed monopoly powers with all the economic and status advantages that can bring for the recipients.

Where I use the term 'registration', I will be referring to statutory registration unless the term is otherwise qualified. However, the arguments that follow are relevant to both statutory and voluntary registers in so far as the latter are intended as preludes to the former or may become *de facto* equivalents.

The arguments are also as relevant to 'counselling', 'personal growth work' and 'psychology' as to 'psychotherapy', since the use of terminology in this area is highly ambiguous and there are no clear or agreed boundaries between these activities. For example, psychotherapy is regarded as a form of psychology in many countries and title usage or practice restricted to licensed psychologists (and medical practitioners).

The assumptive nature of the 'case for'

Whilst bearing a seductive plausibility, arguments in favour of registration in this field frequently amount to little more than taken-for-granted assumptions that the registration of psychotherapists is *necessary, beneficial, preferable* (to any other means of regulation available) and in any case probably *inevitable*.[1]

The purported benefits of licensing and their means of achievement

Statutory registration is invariably argued for on the grounds that such legislation is necessary to protect the public from harm resulting from the practice of the occupation in question. This protection is supposed to be achieved first through a process of accreditation which establishes restrictive entry requirements for practice or title usage. This represents a form of what is known in economics as the 'input regulation' of a market for goods or services. It is a form of regulation which is particularly prevalent in professional markets in which the costs of incompetent supply for the consumer or third parties are particularly high and yet the consumer cannot reasonably be expected to make an informed choice as to who is competent. This is because competence to practise such occupations depends upon the mastery of a body of professional knowledge which is not readily open to lay understanding and which can be acquired only by long and arduous training (Trebilcock, 1982).

In addition to screening out the incompetent at the entry stage, codes of ethics and practice are promulgated and complaints and disciplinary procedures established in order to provide a means of deterring and addressing subsequent 'malpractice' or 'unprofessional conduct' by licensed practitioners.

Finally, under a system of statutory registration, unlicensed practice or title usage becomes a crime, and prosecutions, when they occur, will usually be initiated by the regulatory authority.

Failure to deliver the benefits

However, the claimed benefit of enhanced public protection through statutory registration 'has not been a proven consequence of such laws' (Alberding et al., 1993: 34). Why not?

As with psychotherapy in the UK, it is usually the occupation itself which is the main source of pressure for professionalization and statutory recognition, often in competition with or emulation of other occupations. Whilst claims of client protection are invariably the rallying cry for this, there are sound reasons for doubting that such altruism is the primary motivation (Mowbray, 1995: 28–34; Saks, 1995).

Once established, the profession typically dominates, either directly or indirectly, both the accreditation system and the disciplinary system. This ensures that when the system does work, it tends to do so more for the profession's benefit than for that of the public.

With regard to accreditation, professions in general have been inclined to raise the barriers to entry under the banner of 'raising standards' by the promotion of compulsory prerequisites for practice which enhance professional 'closure' but not necessarily client safety.

With regard to disciplinary procedures, these tend to be more concerned with preserving the public image and status of the profession than the ethical significance of the offence. Thus the extent to which violations receive publicity or notoriety that would negatively impact on the public image of the profession tends to be the determining factor in the responsiveness of the procedures (Hogan, 1979a; Mowbray, 1995, 1997b).

As to the prevention of unlicensed practice or title usage, when enforcement of legislative powers occurs, 'it is frequently aimed at curbing economic competition, not dangerous practices' (Hogan, 1979b: 2).

Both the Foster and Sieghart reports (which were early inspirations for movement towards psychotherapy registration in the UK) made claims for statutory registration as this 'well-tried method' (Sieghart, 1978: 5) which has 'worked excellently in the past' (Foster, 1971: 178). These enthusiastic claims were not, however, substantiated in those reports and appear to have been unsound. As the conclusions of Pfeffer indicate, the prevalence of licensing systems is not a testament to their publicly beneficial nature:

> It must be concluded that the outcomes of regulation and licensing are frequently not in the interests of the consumers or the general public. It is difficult to find a single empirical study of regulatory effects that does not arrive at essentially this conclusion.
>
> . . . There is evidence that administrative regulation and licensing has actually operated against the public interest; and that rather than protecting the public from the industry, regulation has frequently operated to protect and economically enhance the industry or occupation. . . . Even if quality differences are observed, the question remains as to whether they are worth the cost. (Pfeffer, 1974: 474, 478)

The harmful side-effects of statutory registration

Not only does statutory regulation often fail to deliver the purported benefits of public protection, it is also likely to be detrimental as well. The potential liabilities of legislated regulation are 'facts of life to political scientists, economists, and sociologists' (Alberding et al., 1993: 37). Licensing tends to have the following negative side-effects:

(a)   unnecessarily restricting the supply of practitioners by introducing monopolistic factors into the market such as higher than necessary and irrelevant entry requirements;

(b) decreasing the geographic mobility of practitioners;

(c) inflating the cost of services;

(d) making it difficult for paraprofessionals to perform effectively;

(e) stifling innovations in the education and training of practitioners and in the organization and utilizing of services through accreditation systems, disciplinary provisions and ethical standards based on what is currently acceptable by the majority of practitioners rather than empirical evidence of effectiveness;

(f) discriminating against minorities, women, the poor and the aged by raising entry requirements in terms of time, cost and academic prerequisites;

(g) promoting unnecessary and harmful consumer dependence and hence vulnerability (Hogan, 1979a: Vol. 1, 238–9; 1979b: 2; Mowbray, 1995: 86–8).

In sum, '[The] weaknesses of an occupational licensing system are formidable' (Trebilcock and Shaul, 1982: 99).

Preconditions for licensing: valid criteria for the establishment of a statutory profession

The deleterious public impact of these unintended side-effects of licensing must be compared with the *actual* rather than claimed benefits in order to establish the overall balance of risk and benefit that the licensing of a particular occupation would produce: 'the preferred policy is to protect the public from harm in general, whether or not incurred by a practitioner' (Hogan, 1979a: Vol. 1, 239).

As a basis for assessing this balance, Hogan offers the following *preconditions for licensing* – criteria which need to be met if the overall impact of statutory registration is to be beneficial rather than detrimental:

1 The profession or occupation being regulated must be mature and well established.

2 The profession being regulated must have a clearly defined field of practice adequately differentiated from other professions.

3 The profession must have a significant degree of public impact.

4 The benefits of licensing must outweigh the negative side-effects cited above.

5 Simpler and less restrictive methods that would accomplish the same purposes must be unavailable (for example, educational measures or the application of existing laws).

6 The potential for significant harm from incompetent or unethical practitioners must exist and must be extremely well documented.

7 Practitioner incompetence must be shown to be the source of harm.

8 The purpose of licensing laws must be the prevention of harm.

9   Adequate enforcement mechanisms for disciplining those who violate the law must exist.

10 Adequate financial resources must be committed to ensure proper administration and enforcement of the licensing laws (Hogan, 1979a: Vol. 1, 365–8).

Applying the preconditions for licensing to psychotherapy, counselling and psychology

How do psychotherapy, counselling, psychology and associated activities measure up in the face of these preconditions? These occupations certainly have a significant degree of public impact but fail to fulfil any of the other preconditions. They are neither mature nor clearly differentiated from each other or from other occupations (Mowbray, 1995: 92–9; Howard, 1996: 30–5).[2] Whilst a degree of risk is involved in their practice, this risk is neither very large, nor unequivocally attributable to practitioner actions. Nor can this risk be readily influenced by those factors which a licensing system can address (Mowbray, 1995: 100–14). It can, however, be ameliorated by other means (Mowbray, 1995: 203–12).

Entry requirements (preconditions [4] *and* [8])   The requirements being established for entry to the so-called 'voluntary' registers intended as precursors for statutory registers are those which would be appropriate to the establishment of a postgraduate profession. The training standards espoused require or favour graduate entry, substantial academic content and extended duration (three or four, going on five, years). Training courses are increasingly run under the auspices of academic institutions, and the pursuit of the status of a postgraduate profession for psychotherapy in the UK is occurring at both national and European levels.[3]

Psychotherapy does 'work' (Smith et al., 1980); however, surveys of outcome research in psychotherapy reveal that the factors being given such prominence as part of the drive towards a professional status are of minor relevance to competence as a practitioner (Russell, 1981/1993; Mowbray, 1995). The theoretical knowledge and technical considerations that psychotherapy trainees will usually be required to spend much of their time learning and addressing, including the acquisition of a specialized professional language, account for only 15 per cent of the variation in psychotherapy outcome.[4]

The practitioner's contribution to outcome has mainly to do with the ability to relate to a range of people on a deep level, including those who have difficulty with relating itself. This depends upon personal qualities such as empathy, genuineness, integrity, autonomy and respectfulness, as well as idiosyncratic factors (Mowbray, 1995: 118–19, 132–5). These cannot be acquired from a study of theory and technique. Nor are they likely to be found in greatest profusion amongst university graduates.

Appropriate training for practitioners would emphasize the maximum emergence of those personal qualities which are known to be crucial (Mowbray, 1995). Not surprisingly, however, in view of the irrelevance of much of what passes for psychotherapy training, a growing body of literature shows *at best* only a very modest relationship between professional training and therapeutic effectiveness, whilst academic qualifications correlate with effectiveness hardly at all (see Russell, 1981/1993; Dawes, 1994; Mowbray, 1995, 115–19; Bohart and Tallman, 1996: 12–16; Roth and Fonagy, 1996: 346, 355; House, 1997a; Miller et al., 1997). Thus, in the occupations in question, the 'unqualified' are those who lack the appropriate personal qualities – however many hours of training they may have undergone and however many certificates they may have acquired.

In view of the negative side-effects discussed above, the legal establishment of occupational entry requirements of minor relevance to the fundamentals of competent practice would be harmful to the public interest rather than protective of clients, as usually claimed.

The risks of psychotherapy (preconditions [6], [7] and [8])   The prevalent preoccupation with the dangers posed by psychotherapists is a natural counterpart to the common erroneous amplification of the practitioner's potency to effect change in the client.

Congruent with their statutory aspirations, registration protagonists are inclined to foster an image of the practitioner's activities as the primary agent of change in the client, and hence, by the same token, the main source of potential danger for the client, who is usually also characterized as 'too vulnerable to choose' (Mowbray, 1997a). This scenario does not, however, accurately reflect the available empirical evidence:

> [M]uch of the writing and thinking about psychotherapy places the therapist at the centre stage of the drama known as *therapy*. Rarely is the client cast in the role of the chief agent of change. Nevertheless the research literature makes clear that *the client is actually the single most potent contributor to outcome in psychotherapy.* (Miller et al., 1997: 25, original emphases).[5]

The client is also the best judge of who is a competent practitioner for him or her: 'There is absolutely no evidence that emotional stress necessarily implies incompetence or an inability to judge what is helping or hurting in an attempt to alleviate that distress' (Dawes, 1994: 125).

The dangers of psychotherapy are, in Hogan's words, 'not of such epidemic proportions that the arm of the law should intervene to curb the problem' (1979a: Vol. 1, 370). As a former Chair of the United Kingdom Council for Psychotherapy ruefully admitted: 'It has been proved difficult to amass evidence that the public has a great need of protection from psychotherapists' (Tantam, 1996: 100).

Moreover, there is a notable lack of evidence that the risks are lower with licensed as opposed to unlicensed practice (Mowbray, 1995: 106–14;

Howard, 1996: 22, 28, 47). Indeed, there is a significant danger that the elevated status accompanying professionalization would actually increase rather than reduce client vulnerability by encouraging the false assumption that safety had already been assured: 'Official recognition based on unconfirmed criteria *begets* vulnerability' (Mowbray, 1997a: 43, original emphasis).

Psychotherapists or counsellors are not experts whose efficacy derives from the application of an elaborate and specialist body of knowledge to a particular case. Nor do they act as 'agents' who do things 'for' their clients. Nor are they appropriately equated with professionals such as doctors, whose duties include actions performed on behalf of the state. Nor are they capable of functioning as expert witnesses who can make reliable diagnostic predictions about individuals appearing in court – statistical formulae do better (Dawes, 1994: 75–105). These occupations are not appropriate candidates for professionalization – statutory or otherwise – and claims that people would be protected from exploitation or incompetence thereby have little validity.

Viable alternatives to statutory registration [precondition 5]   The situation regarding the regulation of psychotherapy and counselling in the UK does not in general require any specific remedial legislative interventions. However, various enhancements are possible: educational initiatives to make the public more aware of the relevant criteria for selecting a practitioner; the application of existing laws; the encouragement of clear practitioner–client contracting; practitioner 'self and peer assessment'; and the implementation of full-disclosure provisions as part of general legislative improvements in the area of consumer law. 'Non-credentialled registration' is not necessary overall, but is an option for serious consideration in medical settings where a model of psychotherapeutic 'treatment' for mental disorders holds sway (Mowbray, 1995: 203–12).

Jenkins (1997: 77–114, 296), amongst others, has argued that general laws are inadequate as a means for addressing negligent practice because of both the costs of litigation and the difficulty in proving, as required by tort law, that a breach in the practitioner's duty of care actually caused damage to the client. However, this latter concern is mostly indicative of the inherent difficulty of establishing causality in this type of activity.

Difficulties in achieving justice through the general legal system on the grounds of cost point to a need for reform of access to the legal system and for the promotion of general systems of mediation and conciliation, rather than the development of further specialist law. The UK government's sponsorship of a 'no win, no fee' system for civil proceedings (White and Dyer, 1997) may go some way to addressing the issue of the cost of 'going to law' – given a reasonable case.

However, in view of the predominant role of the client in the determination of psychotherapy outcome, and the importance of relationship in that endeavour, contract is a more pertinent area of law than tort. By contrast, the drive for the professionalization of psychotherapy and counselling can be seen as an effort to establish status rather than contract as the legal basis for these occupations.

Stone and Matthews (1996: 191, 292–6) argue that a contractual model of regulation is the most appropriate form for the related field of complementary medicine, rather than status-oriented mimicry of the medical profession, since the relationship between practitioner and client in most forms of complementary medicine is the antithesis of the legal relationship assumed by professional negligence cases on the basis of an allopathic medical model. In the latter cases, for example, contributory negligence on the part of the patient finds no place, whereas, from the point of view of complementary medicine, 'It is certainly arguable, at least, that a patient's responsibility to take an active part in his or her own health management should find expression in the law' (1996: 294).

De facto registration

In the UK, the principle role of statutory registration in this area to date has been that of a threat evoking fears of exclusions on the part of practitioners and training organizations. Misinformation about the inevitability or likelihood of statutory registration, as well as the supposed benefits, has served as an effective recruiting officer for the would-be professional bodies. Their dominance of practitioner training and, increasingly, of eligibility for employment or fee reimbursement means that *de facto* registration through oligopolistic control of the market by these 'proto-registers' is a prospect to reckon with (Mowbray, 1995: 146–7). Since their criteria for entry are geared to future hopes for licensing and are typically inappropriate to the fundamentals of competence, these so-called 'voluntary' registers can have a negative impact on the field of practice approaching that which would apply if their statutory endorsement had already been achieved.

Conclusion

In view of the weight of argument and evidence against it, the starting point, the 'ground zero', for any discussion of the appropriateness of registration as a system of regulation for the fields of psychotherapy, counselling and psychology should be the exact opposite of the usual assumptions referred to earlier. *Statutory registration should be assumed detrimental unless proven to be both necessary and beneficial.* There is thus a clear ethical obligation upon the protagonists of professional registration to logically and empirically justify their position.

In the case of registered charities such as the United Kingdom Council for Psychotherapy, and the British Psychological Society and the British

Association for Counselling, this obligation is not just ethical but legal as well:

> A charity must not base any attempt to influence public opinion or to put pressure on the government . . . to legislate or adopt a particular policy on data which it knows (or ought to know) is inaccurate or on a distorted selection of data in support of a preconceived position. (Charity Commissioners for England and Wales, 1997: 13)

These organizations cannot therefore simply ignore the 'case against' while lobbying for a change in the law. They are obliged to refrain from such political activity unless they can present a balance of evidence that statutory registration would actually protect the public as they claim.

Notes

1. At the time of publication of *The Case Against Psychotherapy Registration*, the notion that there was a 'case against' was distinctly novel in 'therapy' circles in the UK. In addition to that book, a considerable body of literature which addresses the issue is now readily available. Dawes (1994), Parker et al. (1995), Saks (1995), Howard (1996), Stone and Matthews (1996), Brown and Mowbray (1997), House and Totton (1997), and Jenkins (1997) all contain pertinent material. Hogan's (1979a) inspiring and exhaustive study is unfortunately out of print.

2. In particular, there are major differences in the intentions of work which is practised on the basis of a medical or behaviourist model as opposed to a personal growth model. These differing goals are not, however, reflected in consistency as to the titles adopted, which leads to much confusion and misunderstanding (Mowbray, 1995: 172–97).

3. The European Association for Psychotherapy, with close links to the United Kingdom Council for Psychotherapy, is promoting a European Certificate of Psychotherapy requiring a seven-year training (Deurzen and Tantam, 1997).

4. Forty years of research reveal that the factors which account for variance of outcome in psychotherapy are, in descending order of importance: extra-therapeutic factors, that is, the client's pre-existing resources and concurrent life events (40 per cent); therapy relationship factors (30 per cent); expectancy, hope and placebo factors (15 per cent); theoretical model and technique factors (15 per cent) (Bohart and Tallman, 1996: 17; Miller et al., 1997: 24–31). Even if the validity of psychotherapy outcome studies is doubted, the fact remains that there is a dearth of empirical evidence *in favour* of the accreditation criteria being promoted. As Dawes says: 'there is no *positive* evidence supporting the efficacy of professional psychology. There are anecdotes, there is plausibility, there are common beliefs, yes – but there is no good evidence' (1994: 58, emphasis in original).

5. See note 4. The notable Georg Groddeck came to a similar conclusion many years ago (House, 1997b).

References

Alberding, B., Lauver, P. and Patnoe, J. (1993) 'Counselor awareness of the consequences of certification and licensure', *Journal of Counseling and Development*, 72 (September/October): 33–8.

Bohart, A.C. and Tallman, K. (1996) 'The active client: therapy as self-help', *Journal of Humanistic Psychology*, 36 (3): 7–30.

Brown, J. and Mowbray, R. (1997) *The Case Continues: Responses, Subsequent Developments and Further Support for 'The Case Against Psychotherapy Registration'*. London: Trans Marginal Press.

Charity Commissioners for England and Wales (1997) *Political Activities and Campaigning by Charities. CC9*. London: Charity Commission.

Dawes, R.M. (1994) *House of Cards: Psychology and Psychotherapy Built on Myth*. New York: Free Press.

Deurzen, E. van and Tantam, D. (1997) 'Developing a European Certificate of Psychotherapy', *International Journal of Psychotherapy*, 2 (1): 93–7.

Foster, J.G. (1971) *Enquiry into the Practice and Effects of Scientology*. House of Commons Report 52, London: HMSO.

Hogan, D.B. (1979a) *The Regulation of Psychotherapists*. 4 vols. Cambridge, MA: Ballinger.

Hogan, D.B. (1979b) 'A position statement on licensing counsellors and psychotherapists', *American Psychological Association Division of Community Psychology Newsletter*, 12 (3): 9–12.

House, R. (1997a) 'Training: a guarantee of competence?', in R. House and N. Totton (eds), *Implausible Professions: Arguments for Pluralism and Autonomy in Psychotherapy and Counselling*. Ross-on-Wye: PCCS Books.

House, R. (1997b) 'Therapy in new paradigm perspective: the phenomenon of Georg Groddeck', in R. House and N. Totton (eds), *Implausible Professions: Arguments for Pluralism and Autonomy in Psychotherapy and Counselling*. Ross-on-Wye: PCCS Books.

House, R. and Totton, N. (eds) (1997) *Implausible Professions: Arguments for Pluralism and Autonomy in Psychotherapy and Counselling*. Ross-on-Wye: PCCS Books.

Howard, A. (1996) *Challenges to Counselling and Psychotherapy*. London: Macmillan.

Jenkins, P. (1997) *Counselling, Psychotherapy and the Law*. London: Sage.

Miller, S.D., Duncan, B.L. and Hubble, M.A. (1997) *Escape from Babel: Toward a Unifying Language for Psychotherapy Practice*. New York: Norton.

Mowbray, R. (1995) *The Case Against Psychotherapy Registration: A Conservation Issue for the Human Potential Movement*. London: Trans Marginal Press.

Mowbray, R. (1997a) 'Too vulnerable to choose?' in R. House and N. Totton (eds) *Impossible Professions: Arguments for Pluralism and Autonomy in Psychotherapy and Counselling* Ross-on-Wye: PCCS Books.

Mowbray, R. (1997b) 'A case to answer', in R. House and N. Totton (eds), *Implausible Psychotherapy and Counselling* Ross-on-Wye: PCCS Books.

Parker, I., Georgaca, E., Harper, D., McLaughlin, T. and Stowell-Smith, M. (1995) *Deconstructing Psychopathology*. London: Sage.

Pfeffer, J. (1974) 'Administrative regulation and licensing: social problem or solution?', *Social Problems*, 21: 468–79.

Roth, A. and Fonagy, P. (1996) *What Works for Whom? A Critical Review of Psychotherapy Research*. New York: Guilford.

Russell, R. (1981) *Report on Effective Psychotherapy: Legislative Testimony*. Lake Placid, NY: Hilgarth Press (with 1993 update).

Saks, M. (1995) *Professions and the Public Interest: Medical Power, Altruism and Alternative Medicine*. London: Routledge.

Sieghart, P. (1978) *Statutory Registration of Psychotherapists: The Report of a Profession's Joint Working Party*. London: Tavistock.

Smith, M.L., Glass, G.V. and Miller, T.I. (1980) *The Benefits of Psychotherapy*. Baltimore, MD: Johns Hopkins University Press.

Stone, J. and Matthews, J. (1996) *Complementary Medicine and the Law*. Oxford: Oxford University Press.

Tantam, D. (1996) 'The structure and formation of national umbrella organisations in psychotherapy', *International Journal of Psychotherapy* 1 (1): 95–101.

Trebilcock, M.J. (1982) 'Regulating service quality in professional markets', in D.N. Dewees (ed.), *The Regulation of Quality: Products, Services, Workplaces, and the Environment*. Toronto: Butterworths.

Trebilcock, M.J. and Shaul, J. (1982) 'Regulating the quality of psychotherapeutic services', in D.N. Dewees (ed.), *The Regulation of Quality: Products, Services, Workplaces, and the Environment* Toronto: Butterworths.

White, M. and Dyer, C. (1997) 'Lawyers face fee shake-up', *Guardian*, 18 October.

23   Registration benefits and is necessary to the public and the profession

Digby Tantam

It seems best to me to start with some trends and speculations. Psychotherapy and counselling are becoming common activities. The public is
becoming increasingly interested in them, and increasingly concerned about
them. It is likely that there will continue to be a growing demand for them
and that it will be met by a growth in private practice even if, as seems
likely to happen in the UK and the US, a cap is put on what managed
health care schemes will pay. Furthermore, it can be expected that the
dominant scientific paradigm will continue to shift from genetics and other
information sciences, which have been the successors of the physical
sciences, to the human sciences. What will people's concerns be in this new
era? Probably less about amassing the latest technology, which will anyway
become increasingly cheap and therefore freely available. Less too about
mobility or communication, as the burdensome aspects of these media
become more apparent. Instead it seems probable that people will be
concerned with the quality of their lives and with the close relationships
that account for most of the variance in that quality.

Such a future will present new dangers as well as new opportunities.
There will be excesses, pollution and overexploitation, but of the social
environment, not the physical. There will be a tendency to lose one's
perspective, and to become as acquisitive about relationships as people
have about technology. Experts on the subjects will be influential, and
there will be the temptation for psychotherapists and counsellors to lose
perspective on their own limitations and ignorance, as doctors have in the
past, and as social workers have more recently.

We should be planning now for these eventualities, and although this
chapter will apply to the situation that currently prevails, the arguments in
it will become much more pressing if the future that I visualize comes to
pass.

What is a profession?

Tawney (1986) defined a profession as (a) a trade (b) which is organized for the performance of duties, (c) is self-regulating, and (d) has rules designed to enforce standards (e) for the better protection of its members and (f) for the better service of the public. There seems little doubt that psychotherapy is a trade, and that it is organized for the performance of its duties – the recognition of supervisors, and the almost universal acceptance of the need for training, are examples of that. Most psychotherapists would consider themselves in a service trade, I think, and would accept some rules for the conduct of their duties: for example, abstaining from sexual relations with their patients, or from financially exploiting them. Most psychotherapists would also accept that the regulation should be self-imposed, and not the consequence of oversight by others.

Tawney's criteria that remain to be considered are: that there are rules designed to enforce standards, and that one goal of these rules should be to protect the members of the profession.

Do we need rules?

I doubt that any psychotherapists would want to advocate a rule-less practice, but some might want to argue – do, in fact, argue – that they should have each their own rules, and not be bound by some general structure of rules that applies to every psychotherapist. It is hard to imagine a profession which does not have some constitutive rules that govern the behaviour of every professional, for example not to exploit their relationship with their clients, and always to act in their client's interest. Particular professional practices also raise especial risks. Lawyers might be tempted to pass judgement on their clients, and not to mount the best defence of those whom they consider reprehensible. Doctors are often in a position to damage the bodies of those in their charge, and thus the principle of doing the least harm is an important one in their regulations. Psychotherapists and counsellors have emotional influence over their clients which increases the risk of exploitation, and this needs to be addressed in their ethical codes.

Of course rules of this kind are not like the instructions to assemble something. They normally work because they are internalized and only get consulted when a problem arises. Professionals conduct themselves properly because they think like professionals, and not because they regularly consult their own ethical codes. But then many people who sing tunes that they know do not consult the music, may indeed never have read the music. Despite this the music has a necessary relation to the correct performance of the song.

Should there be rules about training standards or just about ethical practice?

It seems hard to imagine a psychotherapist who does not subscribe to any ethical code since all human relations are embedded in an ethical framework. It is the specification of the code, and the agency responsible for enforcing it, which are controversial. I take the specification of the code – what should be included and what excluded, and whether all the rules apply to every type of psychotherapy – to be another controversy, and not relevant to the present issue of whether or not there should be an ethical code, of whatever kind, imposed by a professional body.

There may be less consensus that there should be any training standard, whether or not it is imposed. I would suppose that few people would argue that everyone is equally competent to provide psychotherapy, but there is a tenable position that competence comes about through innate ability or from lived experience, or both. Alternatively, it might be argued that a professional training such as in medicine or in psychology provides all the skills that are required to be a competent psychotherapist. Support for this argument comes from the often cited findings of literature reviews which conclude that there is little effect of training on outcome (Beutler et al., 1994), although one definitive review concludes that training has never been investigated independently of other confounding factors such as expertise, or age, and the 'inquiry into the differential effects of training as it relates to outcome' remains to be done (Lambert and Bergin, 1994: 172).

It is counter-intuitive to suppose that training has no effect on competence, and it would be premature to assume that it does. It could certainly be argued that it might be more appropriate to measure competence directly than to measure training, with its uncertain link to competence. But there does not seem at the moment to be a successful objective measure of competence. The considerable expenditure of time and money by the Lead Body for Advice, Guidance, Counselling and Psychotherapy on this project has yet to produce an assessment method which would be acceptable by the profession (although it may in the future). Assessing competence by measuring the outcome of a series of patients seen by an individual would not be ethical unless there was some assurance before starting the assessment that the practitioner had some baseline competence. It could be argued that it is up to the patient to assess the competence of the practitioner that he or she sees and to withdraw his or her custom from a seemingly incompetent practitioner. But this places an unreasonably heavy burden on the consumer in the case of a service with hidden dangers which are not easily assessed.

I conclude that, inadequate as it is, training standards are the best measure of competence that we have. There is clearly an urgent need to evaluate them against outcome and to dispense with those standards that are the product of prejudice or tradition rather than necessity. But at the moment we do not know which would be dispensed with, and which retained.

Perhaps this situation is less bad than might appear. Involvement in a training is not simply about the acquisition of competence. It is also about the acquisition of knowledge, which enables new competencies to be developed when required, and about the development of values and attitudes. The latter are the basis for ethical practice. Consider the following case example. A practitioner, not trained as a psychotherapist, saw a young woman about her headaches and picked up that she was socially isolated. He attributed her headaches, perhaps rightly, to the frustrations of this situation, and particularly the sexual frustrations which he sought to put right through 'helping her become more aware of her body', a practice which he described as psychotherapy, but which involved a great deal of discussion about sexuality and, as time went on, intimate touching and overt sexual activity. The client was exceptionally naïve and raised no objection to this, believing that it was, as presented, psychotherapy. I think it likely that a formal training in psychotherapy would have instilled in this practitioner much clearer understanding about the risks of developing sexual feelings during psychotherapeutic work, and given some ideas about the methods, like supervision, which can be used to prevent enacting the desires of the practitioner.

It is sometimes argued that the frequency of sexual activity between patients and registered medical or psychological practitioners, which studies suggest is significant, is evidence against the protective value of training or ethical standards. These studies do indicate that the risk of exploitation is high, but without comparable information from unregistered practitioners with the same level of access to patients, it cannot be concluded that regulation is ineffective – only that it should be more effective.

Is it right for professionals to look to their own interests?

Registration of the members of a profession brings a barrier into being between those on the register and those not on it. Publication of a register, and any promotion of that publication, is designed to encourage the public to use the services of registrants and, indirectly, to reduce the amount of psychotherapy provided by non-registered practitioners. There is clearly a self-serving element here which is the source of at least some of the hostility to the registration process (it may be said, to any registration process). It is sometimes implied that, because it is self-serving, it is somehow illegitimate or suspect. I want to consider this further.

The case for the defence of self-service is that there is considerable expenditure of time, some expenditure of money and some loss of freedom in becoming involved in a profession, and that it is unrealistic to expect those costs to be offset by altruism. There has to be a reward. The reward for the officers of professions may be sufficiently provided by the power and influence that their work brings them, but the reward for ordinary registrants has to come from the public, through increased referrals or better income. And, taking the long view, this reward is going to be greater if it is not obtained by coercing or misleading the public but is instead given willingly as a proper recompense for the benefit that the public receives.

The same defence could be made of any or all professions, but to do so would lead to a social model which presumes that the public and the professions have the best of all possible relations. Clearly we should not assume this to be the case. Professions may be in conflict with the public – Polish anaesthetists are on strike as I write this, for example – and the public may be in conflict with professionals, through litigation, public demonstrations or government action. Ultimately, the public has the power to control professions through its refusal to pay for them. The profession of 'pardoner' disappeared when the public stopped buying papal indulgences.

Although individuals may be dependent on particular psychotherapists, the public at large is not dependent on psychotherapy in the way it is dependent on medicine, law or the Church. However I do envisage a time when the public will become dependent on psychotherapists and coun-sellors – when, for example, counselling is not just offered to the victims of crime as it is now, but is believed to be essential if victims are to avoid the psychological sequelae of crime. We should anticipate this increase in our power to impose ourselves on the public, and provide adequate safeguards to ensure that psychotherapists do not abuse it.

In particular we should be aware that professionals can try to put themselves beyond accountability to the public by mystifying their practice and by exploiting the fact that the public may be dependent on their professional activity.

In a debate on the professions in the upper house of the British Houses of Parliament (the House of Lords) in 1991, criteria about the conduct of *professionals* were proposed which are relevant to the self-discipline which professionals should exercise to prevent them abusing their power or authority. Professionals should, their lordships argued:

(a) allow fair and open competition between themselves;
(b) give the public information about their experience, competence, capacity to do the work, and fees payable;
(c) whether in practice or in employment, be independent in thought or outlook, willing to speak their minds without fear or favour, and not be in the control or dominance of any person or organization.

An additional safeguard, not mentioned in the debate, is the inclusion of lay members in the governing boards of the professions, where they can encourage professionals to look at themselves more sceptically than is sometimes the case, and in disciplinary bodies where they can ensure that the interests of the public and not of the professionals are served.

How can registration best be achieved?

Even if there is acceptance that practitioners should conform to ethical, and possibly training, standards, some practitioners may still wish to argue against this conformity being achieved by registration. After all, there are many ethical precepts that influence how a parent brings up a child, but the notion of registration of people suitable to be parents is anathema. Why are psychotherapists different? An argument of this sort might expand on the means by which society ensures that children are protected from unethical or incompetent parents. It might emphasize the relative rarity of children being removed from their parents because of the parents' conduct if this can be taken as an indication of the success of parents' voluntary regulation of their own ethical standards and parental competency.

Are psychotherapists' clients like children, or is this analogy misleading? This depends on the extent to which an ordinary person can be expected to be aware of, and be able to guard against, deviations from good practice. Before considering this, it is worth reminding ourselves of other trade activities which have developed accreditation procedures: they include fitters of gas appliances, travel agents and financial advisors. These trades consider that members of the public either cannot be expected to know what good practice is, or to be in a disadvantaged position that inhibits the practice being challenged. I think that both of these handicaps apply to members of the public dealing with psychotherapists, particularly if emotional distress or personal catastrophe already burdens them. Even if some members of the public – say, other psychotherapists – are able to weigh up a practitioner for themselves, regulation needs to be assessed against the most vulnerable user. This may be someone who has become dependent on a practitioner, or who has been given misleading information, or simply is desperate for relief.

Let us suppose then that an analogy of patient and child is applicable. Can we assume that psychotherapists will be like parents? I think not. Many people before becoming parents have amassed considerable experience of being in a parental role, and also of being parented themselves. Through experience, conversation, films, books, and other means, they will have become familiar with many of the ethical dilemmas of parenthood, and the socially accepted rules that apply to them. This cannot be said of psychotherapy: novel ethical dilemmas regularly arise and, as I have already argued, competence does not 'come naturally'.

Some opponents of registration have extended the parental to a family model, proposing that psychotherapists are like young parents of a first baby: reliant on regular advice from grandparents and other experienced parents about how to solve problems, and exposed to constant ethical scrutiny from the same sources. However, such a model assumes that experienced psychotherapists are like grandparents, that is, that they have acquired their knowledge of parenting, and of monitoring other parents, 'naturally'. The same arguments for needing external criteria of competence and ethical practice for psychotherapists, and not relying on what is acquired 'naturally', apply *a fortiori* to any psychotherapists who have the responsibility of monitoring the practice of neophytes.

If external criteria are needed which practitioners should meet before they can be recommended to the public, who should develop and implement these?

It is one of the hallmarks of the professions that they are self-regulating. The simple reason for this is the presumption that their activities are too complex to be effectively scrutinized by non-professionals. It might be argued by a few psychotherapists that this is not true of psychotherapy – that it could be, for example, regulated by a commission of civil servants, or doctors, or psychologists. But I doubt that many would wish to argue this. It is conceivable that a person might argue that the rules should be developed by the profession but that the register should be held by some other body, but I shall assume that the body that registers is the body that regulates, and vice versa.

If it is accepted that regulation should be by the profession, it is almost inevitable that this requires a professional association to do the job. There already exists a professional association for all generally accepted psycho-therapy organizations in the UK – the United Kingdom Council for Psychotherapy. The method of regulation adopted by the Council conforms to the pattern for all professional bodies outlined in the debate in the House of Lords referred to earlier:

(a) a governing body, set against the selfish interests of any particular section of the profession;
(b) adequate standards of education on entry to training, of training on entry to the profession, and of continued professional development;
(c) ethical rules and professional standards for the protection of the public, and not for the private advantage of members;
(d) expulsion from membership;
(e) statutory recognition of the governing body.

The fact that these are also the methods adopted by other professions is some evidence that they have been proven to be effective.

Is a profession of psychotherapy a good thing, whether or not registration protects the public?

There is a close relationship between the development of a profession and the registration of its practitioners. This essay has mainly concerned the justification for registration, but it is worth noting that there may be benefits in bringing a profession into being which themselves provide some justification for registration. Not least amongst these is the responsibility for leadership to the public which a professional association has. We may not yet have experienced sufficient authority as psychotherapists to take this responsibility seriously. But there is no doubt in my mind that the public will expect guidance in the future over the issues of quality of life, of relationship ethics, and of life goals which people individually bring to psychotherapists.

A final caveat

The acceptance of the principle of registration should not impede debate on its practice. Registers do rightly have an impact on practice, and some practitioners may be disadvantaged as a result. In some cases this will be an unfair disadvantage. Having a register means devising a registration procedure that is just. There are many practical difficulties in achieving this. There should be no complacency about the procedures for registering practitioners, and an awareness of the need to strive to do it better. But the fact that the reality has faults does not, in my view, mean that the principle is flawed.

Acknowledgement

I am very grateful for the suggestions of Emmy van Deurzen on how this chapter could be improved.

References

Beutler, D., Machado, P. and Neufeldt, S. (1994) 'Therapist variables', in A.E. Bergin and S.L. Garfield (eds), *Handbook of Psychotherapy and Behavior Change.* 4th edn. New York: John Wiley.
Lambert, M.J. and Bergin, A.E. (1994) 'The effectiveness of psychotherapy', in A.E. Bergin and S.L. Garfield (eds), *Handbook of Psychotherapy and Behavior Change*, 4th edn. New York: John Wiley.
Tawney, R.H. (1986) *The Acquisitive Society*. London: Peter Smith.

24   Psychotherapy and counselling are indistinguishable

Brian Thorne

Not boredom but anger

I am aware that I have been putting off writing this piece for some months. As I consider myself a well-disciplined person who does not on the whole procrastinate, my behaviour intrigues me. I had concluded that boredom with the subject was the probable explanation. Five years ago I was rash enough to accept an invitation from the British Association for Counselling (BAC) to deliver the keynote address at their Annual Conference on the subject 'Psychotherapy and counselling: the quest for differences' (Thorne, 1992). Since delivering that paper and its subsequent publication I have been plagued with appreciative and hostile letters and have been frequently asked to reiterate my views so that I can be further lauded or reviled. The original paper states clearly, with what I consider to be powerful supportive arguments, that there is no essential difference between the activities currently labelled 'counselling' and 'psychotherapy', and that to suggest that there is is the result of any one or a permutation of the following: muddled thinking; a refusal to accept research evidence; a failure to listen to clients' experiences; a lust for status; needless competitiveness; power mongering; a desire for financial gain; or some other unworthy motive prompted by professional protectionism. Over five years later I have not changed my views – if anything they have hardened – but I believed that I had simply become wearied by the whole debate to the point of being bored out of my mind.

I now realize that, as if often the case, my apparent boredom has been masking a mounting anger, and that the counselling–psychotherapy debate is merely symptomatic of a much wider malaise within the ranks of the counsellors and psychotherapists. Briefly and bluntly put, I believe that those of us who practise as therapists are caught up in a complex tangle of forces which threaten our very integrity and which, if they are not negotiated with ethical clear-sightedness, will simply turn us into compliant collaborators with the sickness which brings many of our clients to our doors. The tangle of forces to which I refer has resulted in the creation of a culture where the business ethic (so-called) has permeated into almost every area of human activity and where human beings are conceptualized as commodities, customers or complainants. Counselling and psychotherapy, on the other hand, are supposedly directed towards the relief of mental suffering, the promotion of personal development, the honouring of individual uniqueness and the enhancement of human relationships. The contrast is stark, and it is not surprising that the potential for muddle, contamination, hypocrisy and moral equivocation is enormous. It is my contention that there is much evidence of the presence of all these factors in the current debate about the supposed differences between psychotherapy and counselling.

Problems, goals and 'suitable' clients

In my 1992 paper I did my best to demolish some well-rehearsed arguments which are still sometimes trotted out to differentiate between the two activities. Problems and goals are the two favourite areas for deploying such arguments. It is suggested, for example, that counselling is concerned with problems which are reality-oriented, environmental, situational, specific and conscious, whereas psychotherapy is reserved for problems which are intrapersonal, general, personality disturbances, embedded and unconscious. Such a differentiation runs contrary to the experience of countless psychotherapists and counsellors, and a moment's thought exposes the futility of attempting to categorize problems according to their cognitive or affective content or in terms of 'depth' or duration. The focus on goals is equally non-productive, especially when it is suggested that counsellors are really only concerned with the relief of immediate mental pain whereas psychotherapists are primarily interested in the total life experience of their clients (Einzig, 1989). In this context it is worth noting that in recent years writers from the person-centred tradition, which is characteristically committed to the 'no difference' stance, have made significant attempts to demonstrate the applicability of their approach to 'in-depth' work and to the relief of deeply embedded psychological disturbance (Thorne, 1991; Lambers, 1994; van Werde, 1994; Prouty, 1995; Mearns, 1996). Recently I was also struck by an article by Michael Jacobs, the well-known psychodynamic practitioner, in which he substantially reverses his earlier thinking about which clients are suitable for counselling and which for psychotherapy (Jacobs, 1988, 1996). Jacobs readily acknowledges that in previous publications he had made 'errors of judgement' about this matter, and, speaking of counsellors whom he currently supervises, he writes: 'This highly responsible group of counsellors, whose training is good but usually by no means as lengthy or as deep as that of most psychotherapists, is working with clients whom I myself have listed in some of my publications as "not suitable for counselling, but suitable for psychotherapy"' (1996: 3).

Jacobs, with refreshing frankness, goes on to explain possible reasons for his previous 'errors of judgement'. One such explanation (his fourth) for the lack of clarity over the suitability of clients for counselling or psychotherapy is that there is a developing recognition that 'there are no clear distinctions between counselling and psychotherapy. The terms are interchangeable' (1996: 5). Although Jacobs does not entirely accept this explanation, he readily admits that he now has reservations about the degree of difference. What for me, however, is most remarkable (and wholly to be welcomed) is the fact that a leading psychodynamic theorist and clinician can give expression to his doubts and confusions on this matter at all. This seems to me a 'breaking of ranks' with enormous implications. It stands in stark contrast, for example, to the expressed opinion of Alan Naylor-Smith, who, in 1994, in the pages of the BAC journal *Counselling*, published a riposte to my 1992 paper. The article is courteous in tone and respectful of counsellors and counselling. Naylor-Smith also acknowledges that for client-centred practitioners and for cognitive therapists too the two words may be used interchangeably, but he also insists that this 'leads to confusion'. He then goes on to claim that in the psychodynamic tradition the words 'express a difference that is real and useful' (Naylor-Smith, 1994: 284). Unlike Jacobs, Naylor-Smith has no doubt where he stands. He postulates the 'continuum' theory according to which counselling and psychotherapy overlap for much of the way before we reach the area on the continuum where psychotherapy has the field to itself. Naylor-Smith describes this area authoritatively and succinctly: 'With more frequent sessions, more focus on the unconscious, on dreams and phantasy, and on the transference and countertransference; and with the allowance of greater dependence and of regression, the work is now, in my view, clearly psychotherapy' (1994: 285). This statement, in *my* view, gives the game away. Psychotherapy, according to this definition, requires more frequent sessions (presumably more than once a week), depends on an acceptance of notions of the unconscious, transference and counter-transference and sees dependence or regression as likely behaviours. Once more we are plunged into issues about 'depth', severity of disturbance and, by implication, training.

Training issues

Jacobs notes that the training of counsellors is 'usually' neither as lengthy nor as deep as that of psychotherapists, but the very use of the word 'usually' indicates that he is well aware that this is not invariably the case. It is now acknowledged that there are many examples of training programmes leading to qualifications in counselling or psychotherapy which in terms both of length and of rigour are not distinguishable. In any case, the usefulness of debates about the importance of the length of training is powerfully called into question by repeated research findings that neither the length nor the therapeutic orientation of a given training seems to have much bearing on the practitioner's effectiveness or on the client's perception of the helpfulness of what is being offered (Russell, 1981/1993;

Hattie et al., 1984; Howe, 1993). This somewhat embarrassing state of affairs is particularly irksome for those like Naylor-Smith who, having defined psychotherapy in terms of concepts of the unconscious and the transference, must argue for the necessity of lengthy and frequent personal therapy. He writes:

> It is surely a good rule that we should not work with clients on a more frequent basis to that we have experienced in our own therapy. The necessary qualifications for intensive work includes the ability to work in the transference; to analyse the counter-transference; and to be competent to work with dependence and regression. (Naylor-Smith, 1994: 286)

This scarcely holds water in the light of research findings and begs the question anyway of what constitutes 'intensive work'. Many a person-centred counsellor would claim with justification that he or she is daily involved in 'intensive work' but does not wish to be encumbered with such concepts as the unconscious or the transference – which is not to deny the reality of phenomena which psychodynamic practitioners choose to categorize in this way.

It was Ivan Ellingham who drew attention to the fact that arguments such as Naylor-Smith's for establishing the case that counselling and psychotherapy are marked by different activities *depend entirely* on the Freudian concepts of the unconscious and transference. In words which caused some offence at the time, Ellingham pulled no punches. 'Dispense with the concepts of the unconscious and transference and not only does the psychodynamic case for a difference between counselling and psychotherapy become shaky but the entire structure of psychodynamic thought begins to wobble' (Ellingham, 1995: 289). It is perhaps scarcely surprising that Ellingham's hard-hitting article caused some consternation, especially as its central thesis is that counselling and psychotherapy are still in what Thomas Kuhn (1970) has called a pre-paradigmatic state and that the person-centred framework of thought rather than the psychodynamic is more likely in the long run to provide an adequate base on which to ground a paradigm for the whole field. Should this occur, then the belief that counselling and psychotherapy are indivisible and indistinguishable activities will become paradigmatic, that is to say, a logical corollary of the generally accepted, precise and comprehensive explanatory scheme of the whole field.

The Trojan horse

Michael Jacobs, it would seem, is showing all the signs of becoming the Trojan horse in the psychodynamic camp. In a remarkable paragraph towards the end of the article already quoted he throws a spanner in the works of those for whom the continuing differentiation between counselling and psychotherapy is crucial to their livelihood and to the maintenance of their professional status. Windy Dryden (1996), the arch-deflator of pseudo-experts, has written that the difference between a counsellor and a psycho-therapist is about £8,000 a year. Jacobs, more gently – almost meditatively – concludes his reflections on his previous errors of judgement with this quietly revolutionary statement:

> There is, however, a fifth explanation, which may ultimately point the way to a clearer sense of who might be suitable for counselling and who for psychotherapy and *which entails dropping these particular labels altogether!* The only plausible reason I can find for the ability of some counsellors to work with clients whom I had previously ruled out as unsuitable is that their level of expertise is the same as that of psychotherapists. Their training may be shorter, and their personal therapy less intense but their experience with clients and good ongoing super-vision has given them the same skills and intuitive capacities *as paid (or more highly paid) psychotherapists.* Who sees whom depends more upon the particular therapist and counsellor than upon the professional label they use to advertise their function. (Jacobs 1996: 5–6, my emphasis)

A sinister iceberg

The lid is finally off as Jacobs, the psychodynamic practitioner, acknowl-edges that the labels of counsellor and psychotherapist could, and perhaps should, be dispensed with altogether. They serve only to obscure that what matters is the capability of the practitioner to form a working alliance with the client and to offer a relationship which is experienced as psycho-logically nurturing and productive. What is more, Jacobs' reference to paid or highly paid psychotherapists underlines the bitter humour of Dryden's cryptic judgement. Counselling and psychotherapy have become con-taminated – perhaps inevitably – by the culture of which they are part. They too are rapidly becoming big business where no holds are barred in the rush to corner the market. Guy Gladstone (1997) has written per-suasively and irreverently about the corruption of the training market and has exposed the closed-shop mentality which ensures that the training institutes flourish, that large sums of money are invested in personal analyses and accredited trainings so that high fees can subsequently be legitimized. And yet we know that lengthy trainings, high fees and prestigious titles have little or no bearing on the efficacy or otherwise of the therapy which is offered (cf. Russell, 1981/1993). A counsellor working unpaid and with only a comparatively short training is just as likely – some research studies suggest *more* likely – to offer effective help as an expen-sively trained psychotherapist with hours of personal therapy to his or her credit and years of theoretical study and supervised practice. It seems that there must be something crazy going on here until we face the unpalatable truth that the business ethic is all-pervasive and that what counts is persuading the customers to part with their money. In such a marketplace it is not politic to affirm that counselling and psychotherapy are indistinguishable let alone to acknowledge that what counts in the eyes of clients is not a practitioner's technical skills or theoretical orientation but his or her attitude and personality combined with the ability to offer the core conditions of acceptance, empathy and genuineness and to form a 'therapeutic alliance' (Howe, 1993). It serves the interests and the pockets of the psychotherapeutic élite to suppress or dismiss such unwelcome findings and to perpetuate the myth that counselling and psychotherapy are different activities. And that is why I am angry and not bored and why this particular debate exposes but the tip of a sinister iceberg.

From counsellor to psychotherapist

The existence of this iceberg was powerfully underlined for me recently when I met a person who had changed identities. With a knowing and somewhat patronizing smile, she assured me that she *knew* there was a difference between counselling and psychotherapy because once she had been a counsellor and now she was a psychotherapist. She could therefore speak with authority on the matter. I asked her how she perceived her behaviour as a psychotherapist to be different from her previous behaviour as a counsellor. The question seemed to bewilder her. She supposed that to the objective observer her behaviour had probably changed little. Behaviour was not the issue, it seemed, but rather the increase in her knowledge both of psychological theory and of her unconscious self. Unlike her training as a counsellor, her training as a psychotherapist had involved, *inter alia*, intensive personal therapy over a year, the close supervision of her work with three clients, and attendances at many theoretical seminars which had proved intellectually very challenging. As a result she felt altogether more confident and believed she was equipped to work in more depth with those seeking her help. What was more, she was now a registered psychotherapist and clients regarded her with more respect than they would have done if she had remained as a counsellor, even if she had achieved accreditation with the BAC. I could not help wondering as she spoke how much her training as a psychotherapist had cost her, and was pretty sure it would have run into many thousands of pounds – this on top of what she had already paid out for her training as a counsellor. It would be difficult for anyone in such a position to embrace the role of psychotherapist without the conviction that he or she was now doing qualitatively different and superior work. After all, the financial investment had been considerable and there was the undoubted sense of being more expert. Sadly, however, nothing in this practitioner's story proves that the activity of psychotherapy differs in any significant way from that of counselling. When challenged she acknowledged that she believed that she now did rather more effectively what she had done somewhat inadequately as a counsellor. Improvement in performance however, does not indicate a changed activity: it simply means that the person concerned – in her judgement anyway – is operating at a higher level. This particular woman had chosen to follow a training in psychotherapy; she might equally well have undertaken intensive personal development work through participation in encounter groups, engaged in the advanced academic study of personality theory and assiduously taped most of her therapeutic sessions for subsequent analysis. Or she might simply have acquired more courage and knowledge and gained more confidence through experience. Would she then have decided to call herself a psychotherapist? Perhaps, but the overriding reason, I would suggest, would be nothing to do with any essential change in the nature of her activity but everything to do with status, remuneration and power in the marketplace. It might even be to do with self-worth. As a counsellor she may not have felt too good about herself, but as a psychotherapist she had more esteem in her own eyes. Again, however, shifts in a practitioner's self-concept say little or nothing about the nature of the work in which he or she is involved.

Better things to do

My anger is now diminishing to be replaced by a deep melancholy. I suppose I long for counsellors and psychotherapists to be rather more glorious human beings than we self-evidently are. We do not need an Oliver James (1997) to tell us that the developed world is in the grips of an epidemic of aggression, depression, paranoia, obsessions, panics, addictions, compulsions and fragmented relationships. We know this all too well from our daily experiences in our various consulting rooms. We know too that there appears to be real malevolence abroad in certain quarters of the media which manifests itself in repeated attacks on therapeutic practitioners as if they were the cause of the world's ills instead of its potential healers. At such a time and in such a climate we urgently need a united therapeutic fellowship dedicated to helping people find meaning in their suffering and committed to the restoration of the human spirit. To be arguing about whether counselling and psychotherapy are the same or different activities is to fiddle while Rome burns. What is more, the realization that such arguments often have their source in competitiveness, status seeking and the love of money shows such fruitless debate to be not only irrelevant but also immoral. We have much to do to put our house in order.

References

Dryden, W. (1996) 'A rose by any other name: a personal view on the differences among professional titles', *Self and Society*, 24 (5): 15–17.

Einzig, H. (1989) *Counselling and Psychotherapy: Is it for Me?* Rugby: British Association for Counselling.

Ellingham, I. (1995) 'Quest for a paradigm: person-centred counselling/ psychotherapy versus psychodynamic counselling and psychotherapy', *Counselling*, 6 (4): 288–90.

Gladstone, G. (1997) 'The making of a therapist and the corruption of the training market' in R. House and N. Totton (eds), *Implausible Professions: Arguments for Pluralism and Autonomy in Psychotherapy and Counselling*. Ross-on-Wye: PCCS Books.

Hattie, J.A., Sharpley, C.F. and Rogers, H.F. (1984) 'Comparative effectiveness of professional and paraprofessional helpers', *Psychological Bulletin*, 95: 534–41.

Howe, D. (1993) *On Being a Client: Understanding the Process of Counselling and Psychotherapy*. London: Sage.

Jacobs, M. (1988) *Psychodynamic Counselling in Action*. London: Sage.

Jacobs, M. (1996) 'Suitable clients for counselling and psychotherapy', *Self and Society*, 24 (5): 3–7.

James, O. (1997) *Britain on the Couch: Treating a Low Serotonin Society*. London: Century.

Kuhn, T. (1970) *The Structure of Scientific Revolutions*. 2nd edn. Chicago: University of Chicago Press.

Lambers, E. (1994) 'Borderline personality disorder, psychosis, personality disorder', in D. Mearns, *Developing Person-Centred Counselling*. London: Sage.

Mearns, D. (1996) 'Working at relational depth with clients in person-centred therapy', *Counselling*, 7 (4): 307–11.

Naylor-Smith, A. (1994) 'Counselling and psychotherapy: is there a difference?', *Counselling*, 5 (4): 284–6.

Prouty, G.F. (1995) *Theoretical Evolutions in Person-Centered/Experiential Therapy*. Westport, CT: Praeger.

Russell, R. (1981) *Report on Effective Psychotherapy: Legislative Testimony*. Lake Placid, NY: Hilgarth Press (with 1993 update).

Thorne, B.J. (1991) *Person-Centred Counselling: Therapeutic and Spiritual Dimensions*, London: Whurr Publishers.

Thorne, B.J. (1992) 'Psychotherapy and counselling: the quest for differences', *Counselling*, 3 (4): 242–8.

van Werde, D. (1994) 'Dealing with the possibility of psychotic content in a seemingly congruent communication', in D. Mearns, *Developing Person-Centred Counselling*. London: Sage.

25   There are real differences between psychotherapy and counselling

Jan Harvie-Clark

There is a great deal of argument and some evidence to 'prove' that there is not any difference between counselling and psychotherapy; that 'talking treatment' is described in one setting as psychotherapy, in another as counselling, in yet another as counselling psychology (James and Palmer, 1996); that in each setting a trained, competent, experienced practitioner (or someone training to be such) is sitting with someone who has come for help in alleviating the distress which is probably acute, help in finding understanding and solace, help to ease a distressed state of mind. There have been many pieces of research which have shown that the training or the orientation, the nomenclature or the setting are not the factors which matter to those who seek help. Rather it is the quality of the experience, the sincerity of the helper; in the terminology with which I am familiar, it is 'the nature of the therapeutic experience' which is vital to the subjective experience of being helped.

I shall argue that there is a very great difference between counselling and psychotherapy. But I must at the earliest stage declare my own limitations. I only 'know' (in the sense that I am going to talk about knowing later in this chapter) about psychodynamic counselling and about psychoanalytic psychotherapy. It is in these disciplines that I am trained and that I practise. I have come from being a social worker back in the 1960s, when preventative case work was the prevailing culture: I started my own psychoanalysis at the same time as I started training as a psychodynamic counsellor in the early 1980s; and I trained as a psychoanalytic psychotherapist thereafter. After working in various hospital settings I now work privately. I have continuously maintained my connection with the counselling centre, as a counsellor, in long-term and brief work and assessment, and more recently as a teacher and supervisor.

Over the last 10 years my practice has changed. I am no longer a counsellor, I am a psychoanalytic psychotherapist. The sort of therapy I practise has changed – because my understanding of myself and my role in the therapeutic relationship has changed; therefore I can listen differently, and hear differently. This is not an article of faith, although it may seem so to those who have no idea of what I am describing; nor is it crazy, though once again I may sound so to some people. In many ways, visibly, I am doing the same things as I was when I was a counsellor. I am sitting with one person, in the same room, at the same time each week, for 50 minutes, and we are talking to each other. True, 10 years ago I was in a hospital working with patients, or in the counselling centre working with clients; they each came once a week, they sat in a chair, some came for a prescribed limited length of time, twelve weeks, six months, one or two years. There was no financial interchange between us, although counselling clients were asked for a weekly contribution to the centre. Nowadays patients visit me in my consulting room, often but by no means always three or more times a week; we agree on a sessional fee, they usually lie on the couch, they stay in therapy for an indefinite period. But the essential, fundamental ingredient, the confidential relationship between my client/patient and myself, is still central to what I am doing, and, as I say, is visibly unchanged. This is what patients/clients so often say, that what is important to them in their subjective experience of being helped, what they most appreciate, is the quality of the relationship in the room at the moment of meeting. Most recipients will claim to have benefited, no matter what training their helper has undertaken, and maybe no matter for how long their treatment lasted; although the effectiveness of different types of therapy, and therapist, is by no means proven (Brown and Pedder, 1991; Roth and Fonagy, 1996). Certainly the perceived benefit will not depend on how much they have paid, although actually I believe that some payment relative to income, with all the symbolic meaning, is an important ingredient of the therapy, an important part of the unequal relationship between the two people in the room.

One way that I can appreciate how my own expectations of my work have changed is in reading my earlier reports, or remembering work with a particular client. I expected to work through the particular crisis which had brought the client to counselling. I would have understood the crisis in terms of the psychodynamics of that unique geneogram, and the present situation of my client's life; I would have thought about the biological and sociological factors, the ethnic origin and cultural past and present (Jacobs, 1986). However, whether I was hoping to work for six weeks or two years with this client, I would not have been able to stay alongside my client to encourage and support the psychic changes which I now know to be possible. Change, I thought, meant visible, actual change to my client's life; psychic change I now know to be something different.

I have come to expect more of my patients, in every sense, in the 18 years that I have been working in this field. More fundamentally, though, I have come to expect a great deal more of myself. I am now talking about the 'depth' argument, so despised by the very many critics of psychoanalysis. I am sure everyone reading this is familiar with the arguments: there is no scientific proof that going deeper is better or more effective; Sigmund Freud was not a scientist, not a genius, not important, merely a man of his time in bourgeois Vienna at the turn of the century. There are and always have been critics; often the most virulent and damaging are those who are more knowledgeable about Freud's life and work, who may have had some personal psychoanalytic help and so do know what they are criticizing (Jacoby, 1983; Masson, 1989). As in any other field of human endeavour, there is a place for vicious reprisals, for revenge thinly disguised as objective criticism, for hatred and for envious attacks (the very stuff of the analytic process can be misused so easily). Other critics are suspicious of a theory of the invisible, untestable unconscious; they do not understand the need to know about their own or another's unconscious processes; they dismiss theories of the mind, the Oedipus complex, the importance of infantile experiences and sexuality, as ridiculous, unprovable and so irrelevant (Dryden and Feltham, 1992). For many, 'depth' seems a murky darkness.

People came to see me when I was a counsellor, as now when I am a psychotherapist, because they believed or hoped that I, or someone like me, could help them. I too hope that I can be of help. I do not think that I can cure, or heal; but I may be able to help, to help alleviate suffering, ease distress, bring understanding and therefore tolerance of what previously seemed intolerable, beyond the possibility of thinking about; and through understanding and greater tolerance, help in the process of change. It is in this last phrase that I believe there arises a distinction between psychodynamic counselling and psychoanalytic psychotherapy. As a counsellor, and for the counsellors whom I supervise now, my aim is to alleviate mental suffering, ease distress by bringing tolerance and understanding to what had seemed incomprehensible, crazy, uncontainable. I do think that 'being listened to', 'being heard', is what it is all about. The opportunity, the space and time to talk and think about oneself is invaluable: so often feared as being selfish, greedy, immoral; so often found to be an opportunity to explore and roam around territory which has always been felt to be dangerous, prohibited, terrifying, on one's own. It is a fearful expedition to undertake, into territory hitherto unexplored for various excellent reasons. No wonder too that a time limit and so limits on the boundaries of the exploration are entirely acceptable – for both parties on the expedition. And so psychodynamic counsellors will aim to discover why the past is presented with its strangely unique colouring, why it is hurting in its particularly painful way.

The metaphor of an expedition, voyage or journey seems a useful way of trying to explain the differences, as I understand them, between counselling and psychoanalytic psychotherapy. In the UK few people set out on any such expedition without being in distress; few people venture forth solely in search of great self-knowledge, as is the case in other places where psychoanalysis is considered more acceptable in medical, social and even political circles. Nevertheless, the recent explosion of interest in talking treatments in the UK has led to a huge increase in various trainings and also to a demand for the services. Particularly when in distress, people do want to be heard, with respect, with dignity, with humanity; perhaps more so in an age of increasing reliance on machines for communication. So this previous one-to-one business is booming. What makes the difference, which I am arguing is critical to what this help is called, is how far that hearing and that help go in understanding, intervening, exploring the causes and symptoms of the distress; and, furthermore, what psychic changes emerge in the changed internal landscape, which enable future choices to be different, which relieve the repetitive behaviour of the past so that different solutions can be found; in other words, what depth, what distance, that expedition goes, how much of a journey can be afforded.

Being with a person in distress, wherever he or she is at that particular stage in his or her life, is what this sort of help is about. Being non-judgemental, and supportive is valued and is extremely valuable. It is often not easy, even for the most experienced and well trained, for it can be extremely disturbing to hear and be with a very disturbed or distraught person. It is hard to stay with a curious but non-directive listening stance, being aware of one's own feelings, and thoughts, longing to give advice or criticism, and longing to make things better. Staying with someone to allow the person to find his or her own way through is very far from easy, and in trying to do this one needs to find one's own ongoing support and care to enable oneself to continue to be there for another person. This seems to be the essence of counselling; but only part of the stuff of psychotherapy (Brown and Pedder, 1991: 87–8).

If you want genuinely and sincerely to help a fellow human being, I am sure that you can and will, with or without training. However, a thoughtful, well-structured training based on respect for humanity will help and contain such a wish to help, and make it more possible to structure and sustain such helpfulness; and should provide you with colleagues whom you respect. I think their respect for you and your work is one of the most important safeguards you have that you are doing good work. Personal therapy will make it more likely that you distinguish what is yours from that which belongs to the other; the more good personal therapy you have, the more likely you are to know and understand more of yourself, and, under pressure from your client/patient, maintain your neutral stance. There is no way of objectively testing this most controversial and fundamental point, yet it is the vital underpinning of good therapy. This paradox, the untestable essence, is part of our human, paradoxical nature, is the keystone of all controversies in our field. There is no proof, no definitive. Yet it makes sense to me that the further you can 'afford' to travel yourself, in both distance and time, the more likely you are to be able to stay alongside a fellow-traveller. The affording is not just a financial affording and investment; more vitally, it is an emotional affording and investment: first in yourself, and only subsequently in another. If you value your own inner world, your psyche, your unconscious, if you have a respect for your own exploration, understanding and tolerance of your suffering and mental life as well as physical life, your mind as well your body, you will transmit that respect to another.

I think that it is only by having been there oneself, and accompanied by another, and by being able to access that 'being there', that one can be there, wherever that is, with someone else. The sense of such a journey, of such a long, arduous, painful journey into one's own unconscious, is not part of everyone's need or wish for themselves. It is not, of course, that I have to have suffered the same trauma as another, since even if I were to be in the same accident, I will have experienced it in my own unique way; but I do have to have suffered, and to know what that suffering, confusion, pain, helplessness, rage, and so on, feels like. Suffering is part of the human condition – we do not need professional help to know this; but how much one wants to know about that condition and its results is not part of everyone's essential kit for living. But if I know that what any human being has felt like doing, and maybe has done, I too can feel and even *in extremis* might possibly do that too; I am no different in my feelings from anyone else. I do also have to know that I often don't know and can't make sense of my own or someone else's feelings, but that I can wait and stay with not knowing until and for as long as it takes for things to become a bit clearer; because they will, eventually. This is the journey that I am on, and some of the places I have been to. So I now know for myself, and because I keep on travelling, I continue to find and lose and rediscover this for myself.

I have now changed to the personal pronoun because this is a personal statement. I imagine that my colleagues would agree with all this, but what is important in this field is that we can talk as authentically and sincerely as we possibly can to ourselves, to our patients and clients, and amongst ourselves. A historical overview, a trawl through the literature, a research into effectiveness and outcomes, is interesting, vital if that is what is sought. But 'hard facts' are not available for this particular controversy, and, it seems to me, have to be scrutinized and may not be worth so much in this highly subjective world of mental health, of differences and distinctions. There is a great deal of fascination in this world around us, a vast array of fields of inquiry, a plethora of paths through life; so why should I or anyone else be fascinated by this dark underworld of the unconscious? Why should anyone set out on such an uncharted and extraordinary (expensive, time-consuming) mission to explore such a lonely region? Why should one be concerned with one's dreams, the oddities of one's body and mind workings, one's patterns of relationships, family history: one's internal world? Maybe, as indeed I did, one might start out on such a quest because all other avenues have been exhausted, because nothing and no-one else on offer seems to help or have real meaning. Maybe, once started, one might find one wants to continue; maybe one might find this is both endlessly fascinating and absolutely invaluable. Maybe it will help to make some sort of sense where there seemed to be no sense before; maybe such intimate understanding of oneself can be used to lead to an understanding of others, and so one's loneliness and sense of isolation decreases, one's life and relationships become immeasurably enriched: maybe . . .

Then maybe you will find, or have found, as I have done, that there is an enormous difference between what you were doing when you were sitting and listening and what you are now doing; that because you yourself have eventually been well-enough attended to, you can and wish to attend to others; that you wish to accompany another on a journey, to try to share with another the sense of being accompanied that has meant so much to you. At its best and most desirable, it is surely such a motivation which instigates good parenting, and being a good counsellor or therapist is very similar. Just as there is no recipe for good parenting, nor is there a recipe for a good therapist (Winnicott, 1947/1975); in fact, as Winnicott so aptly puts the dilemma, there is every reason to hate one's baby/patient. The current bitter arguments over accrediting bodies embodies the controversy: what is good enough? BAC? UKCP? BCP? But for me the fundamental key is a good enough personal therapy, good enough to sustain both professional and personal life, good enough to enable someone to know when and how to overhaul his or her tools of self-examination and understanding throughout his or her life. At present the only method we have of trying to ensure this is through the regulations of accrediting bodies, imperfectly human and divisive though these are.

I hope that this makes some sense, and that readers can understand how much can go wrong, what space there is for imperfection, as in any human endeavour, as with parenting or journeying. So that the outcome of this investment in any, even the most intensive, therapy is uncertain, cannot be foreseen by either party to the relationship, cannot be guaranteed. I am not advocating any one method of therapy as being better than any other. However, the sort of help I received has gradually changed my perceptions of myself; and therefore my perception of others. But primarily of myself: as I come to comprehend how my mind works, the feelings which influence my behaviour have changed; as my sense of the immediate differences between myself and any other human being have diminished, so has my understanding and 'connectedness' with another human being grown. Ethnic, age, cultural, gender, class, differences of course exist, so do social, religious, political, differences. But as I have become more aware of my own personal sense of separateness, individuality and uniqueness, I can allow for another's 'otherness', and yet attempt to connect with the other. In the realms of unconscious processes it seems that age, gender, race, matter little: love, hate, joy, pain, danger, security, fear, all early primitive feelings, are with us from the cradle to the grave, and transcend biological and sociological differences. My own instincts and feelings, the top and bottom of them – why and how they arise in the way that they do – how my thoughts and actions are influenced by my feelings; what the landscape of my mind is like; how and why it shifts and is shaken; what has gone into the formation of my internal world and how my perception of the external world is coloured by my internal one; what are the objects of my internal world – and why, always why, the internal and external world appear to me as they do – this is my own personal realm, and these are the basic tools of my trade. I started to gather these tools, because I needed them at a time of great personal distress (although they were always lying around, waiting to be used, to borrow from Winnicott [1971]); I was extremely fortunate to be directed to a trusty companion, my helper, who stayed with me until it seemed as if I could continue my journey, albeit uncertainly sometimes, alone, to continue with my companion no longer in the external world, but tucked away internally to be found and used whenever required.

I am not healed, or cured. I still feel miserable, depressed, lonely, anxious, unbearably excited, crazy, ill, and sometimes intolerably so. But now, after a while which I can bear more easily because I know it will pass, I can think my way through, to work out why this particular catastrophe has hit me in the particular way it has. I can find perspectives which comfort me, and which enable me to search for and find appropriate help and comfort elsewhere. What a relief it is to make sense of what a moment ago seemed like a bottomless pit of senselessness, isolation, desolation. And so, starting from this premise, I offer to help others, to listen, to reach out, to offer a prompt, an intervention, a way of thinking beyond where someone has been able to reach on his or her own. Maybe we can think together, maybe my patients can continue until once again they get to a sticky point; and maybe, if I am alongside, I can offer another prompt, unlock another thought, allow a further degree of feeling . . . I use my own, constantly overhauled, tools to help them find that they too have such tools lying around in their minds, and they too can use them to think for themselves, and find their own understanding and choices in their own lives.

It seems that, first, being heard, as a fellow human being, is what we are all attempting in this talking treatment business. Whether the human being is big or little, male or female, black or white, we all need to have our experiences heard, validated, accepted, shared, and this in itself is thera-peutic, and is the very stuff of all talking treatments. But then, to be permitted and even encouraged to explore those experiences, gently, slowly, to go over them as often and from every angle until the sting is taken out of them; to think then about why they happened, how they happened, to face our own part in the happening, is to understand; to wonder about the effect of those experiences, to see how we engineered a repetition over and over again, to see how and why we have reacted against them. We humans have such complex ways of trying to encompass our early experiences in our adult lives, and often lose sight of the ordering of our later experience on the pattern of the early ones; of our defence mechanisms, defence against pain and guilt, repression, denial, fixation, reversal and more (Freud, 1936). The unfolding recognition of our unconscious, as played out and understood in the transference and countertransference in the consulting room, is exciting, and is inevitably painful. Perhaps if it were more manageable it would not need to be unconscious. Our increasing recognition enlarges our equipment to deal with life and its exigencies; it enables a whole new, previously immobilized and fossilized, part of ourselves to be ready for use; and so it enriches our lives and those around us. It is a great privilege to be allowed to join another on his or her journey, however far we are permitted to accompany.

I argue that the further we can go, the further we leave psychodynamic counselling behind, and the closer we get to psychoanalytic psychotherapy.

References

Brown, D. and Pedder, J. (1991) *Introduction to Psychotherapy*. 2nd edn. London: Routledge.

Dryden, W. and Feltham, C. (eds) (1992) *Psychotherapy and Its Discontents*. Buckingham: Open University Press.

Freud, A. (1936) *The Ego and the Mechanisms of Defence*. London: Hogarth Press and the Institute of Psycho-Analysis.

Jacobs, M. (1986) *The Presenting Past*. Milton Keynes and Philadelphia: Open University Press.

Jacoby, R. (1983) *The Repression of Psychoanalysis*. Chicago and London: University of Chicago Press.

James, I. and Palmer, S. (eds) (1996) *Professional Therapeutic Titles: Myths and Realities*. British Psychological Society Division of Counselling Psychology, Occasional Papers, Vol. 2. Leicester: BPS.

Masson, J.M. (1989) *Against Therapy: Emotional Tyranny and the Myth of Psychological Healing*. London: Collins.

Roth, A. and Fonagy, P. (1996) *What Works for Whom? A Critical Review of Psychotherapy Research*. New York: Guilford.

Winnicott, D.W. (1947/1975) 'Hate in the counter-transference', in *Through Paediatrics to Psychoanalysis*. London: Hogarth Press.

Winnicott, D.W. (1971) *Playing and Reality*. Harmondsworth: Penguin.

PART IV

SOCIAL ISSUES

---

26   Stress discourse and individualization

Tim Newton

This chapter is concerned with why stress has become a widespread phenomenon in Western society. It aims to explore the way in which stress discourse is constructed and how this is reflected in stress management practice. It draws on material I have presented in an earlier book in which a more detailed account is given (Newton et al., 1995).

The chapter will consider attempts by stress researchers to legitimize the subject of stress as an area of academic study; examine the image of the 'stressed subject' and of 'stress management'; and explore possible explanations as to the 'popularity' of stress. In so doing the aim is to challenge much of the conventional thinking about stress.

Legitimizing stress

According to both popular and academic media, the legitimacy of stress as a subject of study has largely been scientifically established. Yet when we come to examine this legitimacy, work on stress appears closer to scientism rather than something resembling conventional senses of 'science'. In the first place, the definition of stress is highly ambiguous. As Soderberg (1967) observed some time ago, stress represents a remarkably imprecise concept, a comment which has lost little of its currency. In the second place, the interest in stress gains much of its validity through its supposed relationship with psychological well-being and ill-health. In crude terms, the relationship appears as:

Source of stress, or 'stressor' $\longrightarrow$ psychological strain $\longrightarrow$ mental/physical ill-health and disease

Stress researchers may note that there are possible 'moderators' of this relationship such as individual differences (for example, tendency towards the 'Type A' behaviour pattern; Newton and Keenan, 1990), but the above nevertheless captures much of the implicit assumption. Yet when we examine this relationship more closely we find that its causal assumptions lack any clear support. First, the relationship between 'sources' of stress (job or domestic 'stressors') and both psychological strain and mental ill-health has been difficult to reliably establish, in part because of a general lack of precision in the 'operationalization' of these concepts (Kasl, 1983; Newton, 1989). In a similar fashion, we still lack any clear indication that stress is related to physical ill-health. The supposition that stress leads to physical ill-health is of course supported by popular experience, such as that of having a headache or a backache in 'moments of stress'. Yet the existence of such temporary psychosomatic experiences does not mean that 'stress' has any permanent impact on the immune system or that it necessarily 'leads to' longer term physical ill-health. Equally, while many of us may find our lives 'very demanding', this does not mean that such demands will seriously affect our physical (or mental) health. For it remains the case that we still lack any reliable evidence of a stress–ill-health relationship. Briner and Reynolds have recently summarized the very heavy layer of doubt which surrounds this central assumption of stress research:

> [T]he evidence for the relationship between general stress and health is not particularly strong: Lazarus & Folkman (1984, p. 205) describe the link between stress and illness as '. . . still only a premise, albeit widely assumed'; . . . Pollock (1988, p. 391) states that the link is 'unclear and unproven': Schroeder & Costa (1984, p. 853) write that '. . . the link . . . has been exaggerated'; and Cohen and Manuck (1995) observe that '. . . convincing evidence that stress contributes to the pathophysiology of human disease is sparse, and, even where evidence exists, relatively small proportions of variance are explained'. (Briner and Reynolds, 1998: 14)

There is little sign of change to this pattern. Stress researchers continue to acknowledge the lack of support for the stress–health relationship. For instance, one of the most recently published reviews admits that 'at the moment, there are only hints and guesses' as to the way in which stress may affect the immune system or lead to physical ill-health (Evans et al., 1997: 306). The phrase 'at the moment' is significant. It reflects stress researchers' continued optimism even though they lack 'evidence'. That is to say, in spite of the inability of five decades of research to establish a link between stress and illness, stress researchers still clearly want to believe in it. To do otherwise would be to severely question the rationale of their project.

Even though we lack evidence supporting a stress–health relationship, stress researchers continue to promote the image that stress is a dire 'cost' to industry and society. Cooper and Cartwright (1994) typify such promotion with regard to 'occupational stress'. They assert that 'the costs of occupational stress to business and industry in monetary terms have been increasingly well documented' (1994: 65). Illustrative of such 'documentation' is their observation that 'the Confederation of British Industry (Sigman, 1992) calculate that in the UK, 360 million working days are lost annually *through sickness*, at a *cost* to organizations of £8 billion' (1994: 65, my emphasis). The trick of such melodrama lies in the phrase 'through sickness', whereby stress once again receives its legitimacy through the myth of its supposed relationship to ill-health – for which, as we have seen, there is little clear evidence. Yet, though the putative 'costs' of stress are not even estimates, but often wildly exaggerated 'guesstimates' (Newton, 1992), they serve to further demonize stress and enhance its legitimacy as a subject of 'scientific' study.

Why stress?

Given that academic legitimation to stress appears open to serious doubt, the question remains as to why stress is such a popular subject (in a Foucauldian sense, well and truly 'spread over the surface of things'). There are few other areas of medical or social science discourse which are 'spoken' by academic and lay publics alike, where both groups appear to actively theorize about the subject. In consequence, if only from the perspective of an interest in discourse, it is fascinating to conjecture as to why so many people 'believe' in stress.

The conventional answer to this last question is that we believe because we have 'in reality' become more stressed throughout the twentieth century. But there is a notable problem with this argument since there is no way of knowing if we have all become more stressed. For example, imagine that you could compare the experience of people working in 1898 with those working in 1998 (admittedly something of a fictitious example). Those working in 1898 would probably not report job stress, those at work in 1998 well might. Does that mean that work in 1898 was not stressful? Clearly the ability to 'express' stress depends on the ability to learn the language of stress and the parameters of the stress discourse. Since the largely social science formulation of this language was hardly articulated in 1898, it is unlikely that anyone should report it. Following a similar line of argument, Pollock has argued that stress is 'not something naturally occurring' but instead represents 'a product of social and behavioural science research' (1988: 390). Her argument in effect is that we have all become stressed not so much because life 'really' is more stressful, but because social science has had a 'spectacular success' in persuading us that stress is a 'scientific' 'objective' fact. But are we so gullibly open to discourse? Do we simply follow the 'regimes' of social science? The problem with Pollock's argument is that it doesn't explain why the stress discourse has been so much more successful in its 'colonization' than other social science 'discursivities'. Post-World War II social and medical science has presented us with a host of novel subjects, but few can match the colonizing power of stress.

At the same time, we need to question why we have adopted a particular account of what it means to be stressed. As will be argued below, current explanations of stress present a very narrow view of the stressed subject as someone who is apolitical, individualized, decontextualized, and so on. This implies that even if for the sake of argument we accept that something which we now call 'stress' has 'really' increased in the twentieth century, this does not explain why we have adopted a particular kind of explanation of stress. In other words, the question of interest is not just that of why we believe in the reality of stress, but why we believe in current representations of stress (Newton, 1996).

In what follows, three possible explanations of the popularity of current stress representations will be considered, namely its mystery, its individualizing tactic, and its relevance to late modernity. These themes are, however, by no means exhaustive, and a number of other possibilities are considered in Newton et al. (1995). At the same time, the latter text considers stress discourse from a number of theoretical perspectives such as that of labour process theory, and the work of Foucault and Elias.

The power of 'mystery'

If we apply a rough Foucauldian metaphor, it can be argued that stress discourse was relevant to the discursive 'space' created by the inability of medical discourse to adequately explain the major health plagues of the West, such as coronary heart disease (CHD) and cancer. As Pollock's (1988) anthropological work illustrates, stress has become a common device for explaining the inexplicable in health. This ability of the stress discourse to fill the discursive space left inadequately explained by medical accounts in part derives from the mystery of stress, and by the tantalizing difficulty of 'forcing its secret' (cf. Foucault, 1981: 35). Researchers have continually emphasized how stress cannot be observed in the way that a body cell can. Stress is only knowable indirectly through the subjective eyes of the stressed, using error-prone analyses of their 'psychological space' (Newton, 1995a). It is true that some psychophysiological assessment can be made through neuro-endocrinal activity, but such measures are both subject to error, and are still only indicators of a stress experience which can only be truly known subjectively. In consequence, stress has the power of being never totally knowable, whilst being always potentially everywhere. It is always possible that someone is highly stressed since they may be 'denying it', 'covering it up'. So, for example, if someone dies from a heart attack, there is always the possibility to reconstruct their illness with stress at its base ('they never looked stressed, but then that was their problem, they never let it out'). As with any account founded on subjectivity, its unknowingness (to the 'outside observer') makes it highly appropriate for filing discursive spaces left by the unknown (such as CHD, cancer). By providing scientific 'dressing' to legitimize this problematic unknown, researchers have participated in the development of a discourse with a very wide application. It may not have the pervasiveness of some of Foucault's great unknowns (for example, sexuality), but it does have a mystery which enables a particular kind of discursive strength.

Stress, counselling and individualization

Stress discourse fosters an ideal of the individual as one who defines her psychological and physical well-being in terms of her ability to cope well with stress. Stress management practices can be seen to aid this process through the promotion of individuals who have successfully learned to cope with the stresses and strains of their lives, who might be said to be more 'stress-fit'. At the same time, the stress discourse tells us how the person who is not 'stress-fit' and cannot cope is likely to suffer mental and physical ill-health (such as the 'coronary-prone' tendencies associated with the 'Type A' behaviour pattern). Being stress-fit therefore has the considerable advantage of avoiding such ill-health.

The implications of such messages can be further illustrated through considering their application in the workplace. In the work context, the assessment of whether someone is 'stress-fit' is generally based on ability to cope with the demands of his or her job environment (Newton, 1992, 1995a). In consequence, the 'stress-fit' employee is someone who can do his or her job well, who in traditional terms might resemble 'a good little worker'. Practices such as employee assistance programmes or stress management training aid in the 'maintenance' of such employees by providing the 'oil' which keeps the human machine functioning efficiently, ensuring it doesn't break down 'mentally'. Through an introduction to 'stress concepts', the employee is taught to be wary of getting stressed ('stress leads to heart attacks'), whilst also being shown how stress is chiefly a function of the individual, and outmoded patterns of behaviour, such as that engendered by 'fight or flight' reactions, instincts suitable to the cave-dweller but not to modern business environments (Newton, 1995a). The message is that a stressful work environment is not necessarily 'bad', but that the 'primitive' psychosocial nature of human beings hasn't caught up with the modern technological world we have built. Thus the reason we get frustrated and feel like expressing our grievances is not because our work environment is overly stressful but because our own 'in-built technology' is inappropriate, suited to the 'Stone Age' but not the complex modern world.

Help is at hand, however, in the form of employee assistance programmes (EAPs) or stress management training which provide the basis to overcome these in-built handicaps so common to everyone, so that rather than getting stressed by the nature of the work organization in which we find ourselves, we are brought 'up-to-date'. A 'new-improved' human being can supplant her 'out-moded' 'Stone Age' patterns of behaviour with appropriate stress management skills so that what were once seen as job stressors can become the 'exciting challenges' of the modern business world (Newton, 1995b). A central problem with this argument, however, is that it relies on a dubious image of a socially simple 'Stone Age' society where stressors only arise from the occasional meeting with a dangerous animal. In such a society there appear to be few social stressors, and one can only assume that people either did not talk to each other (for example, they just grunted), or that they lived in peaceful harmony because somehow or another life was socially extremely simple. Yet anthropological research indicates that pre-industrial societies were just as complex in their social nature as industrial societies (Sahlins, 1972; Pollock, 1988; Newton, 1995a). In consequence, it appears specious to suggest that modern industrial/post-industrial life is necessarily more complex or that our socio-psychological patterns are suddenly outmoded.

Implicit in this language of stress and its management is an individualization of everyday life. In addition, if we adopt perspectives such as that of labour process theory, stress rhetoric can also be seen as highly convenient to employee control. For since the stress-fit worker is also the productive worker, the stress discourse conveniently conjoins individual *and* 'organizational' health. For instance, by 'helping' their employees to learn stress management skills, organizations promote workforces who are committed to being effective stress 'copers'. Since coping with stress is also evidenced by an ability to cope with the job, we have a seemingly happy union of the interests of the individual and the organization. Yet from a labour process perspective, the employee within stress discourse begins to look rather like a Marxist caricature; an individual who is keenly concerned to remain 'stress-fit', a good 'coper' who can, whatever the pressures, deliver the last drop of her labour to her employer.

In order to explore the individualization and the control implications of stress discourse, it is helpful to return to the forerunner of EAPs, namely the interwar counselling activities at the Hawthorne works of the Western Electric Company, Chicago (Levinson, 1956; Murphy, 1988). What is striking about the Hawthorne experience is the way in which work difficulties which might elsewhere have been treated as legitimate employee grievances were re-presented as being a reflection of 'latent' problems within *the individual*. The focus in the Hawthorne counselling programme was on analysing the individual and what they might 'reveal' about themselves, not the particularities of the work that they did. This is in spite of the fact that the problems which employees experienced at Hawthorne did appear to be directly related to their job and their work experience. For instance, the five main categories of 'employee concern' reported in Hawthorne counselling sessions were: keeping and losing a job; unsatisfactory work relations; felt injustices; unsatisfactory relations with authority; and job development – issues which do appear to be the stuff of traditional grievance complaints. Yet rather than accepting such grievances at face value, the Hawthorne counsellors adopted the psychoanalytic distinction between the manifest problem and the latent or underlying issue. According to Dickson, the head of the Hawthorne counselling programme: '[F]requently the complaint as stated was not the real source of the individual's trouble. Consequently, action based upon the manifest content of the complaint did not assure us that the difficulty would be eliminated' (1945: 344).

Thus problems such as felt injustices or unsatisfactory relations with authority were not accepted as legitimate grievances. Rather they were treated as the 'presenting problem' and analysed for what they revealed about the individual, and the 'latent' difficulties she experienced. The counselling interview would allow the employee to explore their underlying feelings, and the possible problems with the ideas and fantasies which they may have (incorrectly) built up:

> [T]he interview . . . stimulates the employee to re-examine the ideas, beliefs and fantasies which have been built up in his mind. Frequently this process brings about a modification of the interpretations the individual makes of his experiences. It is not unusual, for example, for an employee to start out making extreme accusations of unfairness against a particular individual and at the end of the interview to remark, 'Well, I guess he's got his problems and it's not so bad after all'. (Dickson, 1945: 347)

In this way the individual worker could be 'helped' to realize that what she at first might have felt to be a legitimate complaint relating to 'extreme unfairness' was really 'not so bad after all'. At the same time, they became aware of how problems which they had originally associated with their work *context* were often just a reflection of their *individual* 'ideas, beliefs and fantasies' (see above quotation). In this way, the individualization of work experience went hand in hand with its decontextualization, aided and abetted by the deployment of the psychoanalytic distinction between the manifest and the latent. In consequence, issues which might hitherto have been seen as common and *collective* in nature were effectively re-presented as the concern and responsibility of the individual employee (Storey and Bacon, 1993). As Wilensky and Wilensky noted in one of the few early pieces of critical commentary on Hawthorne, by letting out frustrations and 'irrational demands', the Hawthorne counselling guarded against any threat of militancy, and helped to guard against 'grievances that might otherwise find expression in other channels' (1951: 276). Or as Lasch later put it, this kind of 'personnel management treats the grievance as a kind of sickness, curable by means of therapeutic intervention' (1977: 184).

Elsewhere I have argued that such individualizing imperatives remain common within contemporary stress discourse and practice, and that they still contain considerable scope for employee direction and control (Newton,

1995a, 1995c). Nevertheless, stress discourse continued to be presented in a scientistic garb, seemingly apolitical, impartial and objective. It apparently does not represent the voice of management or shareholders, but rather that of an objective science benevolently applied to enhance the welfare of all employees.

Finally it is worth noting that the individualization of the stress discourse can be seen to operate in tandem with the privatization of emotion which it encourages. For instance, in the workplace employees are generally expected to maintain emotional control, especially when operating 'frontstage' (Goffman, 1971), relegating any emotional difficulties to 'backstage' or 'offstage' arenas (Hochschild, 1983; Wouters, 1989). Stress management practices are also very largely the province of 'offstage' arenas, enacted either through 'confidential' arenas at work (such as in counselling), or through special 'supportive' training environments (for example, learning 'progressive muscle relaxation') or through private self-help (for example, practising meditation in private). Rather than challenging such tacit emotional codes in the workplace, the stress discourse promotes them by effectively arguing that the 'relief' of work pressure should not be done in public, and that distressful emotions should generally be contained (if not hermetically sealed), aided by the private use of relaxation, meditation, counselling, and so on. But so long as stress remains a private matter, it is more likely to remain depoliticized, because it is seen as something that individuals are meant to deal with by themselves. After all, if employees did openly express their feelings of anger, distress, upset or frustration in the workplace, they might be more likely to notice the commonality amongst their feelings, and even to express *collective* grievances in relation to them.

Processes of individualization entail complex shifts in social relations (for example, Elias, 1991; Storey and Bacon, 1993). Yet if we restrict our attention to stress discourse, it is difficult to deny that it embodies a powerful individualizing rhetoric in its ability to represent social issues in individualistic terms.

Late modernity?

One obvious explanation of the 'rise of stress' is that it provides a 'catch-all' for a range of subjective experience relating to 'late modernity' (Giddens, 1991). For instance, people are bombarded with different ways of seeing our world, the physical, the statistical, the literary, the biological, the psychological, and these discourses relate to a diverse range of practices carried out through media, schools, hospitals, workplaces, and so on (Gergen, 1991). The technological products of these discourses, whether hard technology such as micro-chips, or human technology such as psychotherapy, appear to develop on an ever-accelerating curve. It is partly because of the multiplicity of such discursive developments that our modern world seems far less certain than that of the village serf (though, as noted above, not necessarily more socially complex). And ironically, because of this very uncertainty, we appear more in need of the help of modern discourse, so that we know how to lead our lives. For example, to avoid being duped by 'green' advertising, we must delve further and further into the environmental discourse so that we can discover the right and true way to be 'green'. To take another example, sex can never be taken for granted since psychological and demographic discourse tells us that relationships are increasingly unstable, whilst also revealing how important sex is to 'committed relationships'. A plethora of statistics tell us about how fast our world is changing, and reveal its inherent unpredictability. To cope we need to be not just 'sex-fit', but 'diet-fit', 'green-fit', 'global-fit', and so on.

Within this kind of analysis, the stress discourse, like other discourses of fitness, appears important because of the uncertainty of modern life, an uncertainty itself promoted by the array of discourse, and the continually competing 'priests' of authority and expertise. Stress appears almost as a necessary kind of 'comfort' discourse, a tranquillizer to cope with the diversity of competing messages about the truth of this world, and the dreadful uncertainty of our times. The stress discourse reassures us by explaining how it is 'normal' to feel stressed in these conditions, and it provides strategies to help us to cope with them by being vigilant and stress-fit. The scientific 'dressing' of stress discourse aids its ability to reassure us of our normality and of our ability to cope. The world may appear to be falling apart, but all we need to do is to 'relax' and develop our coping skills. Put crudely, 'Superman' becomes 'Stress-fit Man', and just as with 'Superman', a complex world context can be conveniently reduced to a range of individualistic palliatives.

Conclusion

We all experience certain types of distressing emotion such as worry, anxiety, frustration and anger. These are emotions which people probably experienced long before the development of stress discourse. What the stress discourse can be seen to do is to 'capture them' through re-presenting their significance to social and medical scientists, and to lay people. Within the discourse, emotions are portrayed as potentially dangerous, since if they are continually aroused, they may set up psychophysiological maladaption (for example, 'heightened' adrenalin, noradrenalin levels) which then results in serious illness, such as that of heart disease and cancer. To this extent, stress discourse can be seen to further pre-existing problematizations of emotion such as those associated with courtly and early industrial society, or within psychoanalytic discourse (Newton, 1995b). This problematization of emotions, as well as patterns of 'ineffective' coping behaviour, calls out for the 'solutions' of stress management practice.

One aim of this chapter has been to question the current scientistic legitimation of the stress discourse and the supposed link between stress and mental and physical ill-health. But my principal concern has been to question the way in which stress is represented, its individualization, decontextualization, apoliticism, and so on. Explaining why this representation of stress has arisen remains difficult. In the foregoing, the ambiguity of stress, its individualizing rhetoric and issues of modernity have been emphasized. In order to be succinct, other emphases have been neglected, such as the relationship of stress discourses to broader global patterns of individualization (Baumeister, 1986; Elias, 1991; Beck, 1992), or to other discourses of 'change' (Newton, 1995b). I hope the reader has, however, gained a sense of how both stress discourse and stress management are currently rather narrowly written and deployed. I do not wish to necessarily decry the value of all counselling and psychotherapy, or the host of stress management practices currently available. Rather my concern has been to query the current legitimation and representation of stress discourse and to question whether stress management practices necessarily benefit the 'total' welfare of those upon whom they are practised.

References

Baumeister, R.F. (1986) *Identity, Cultural Change and the Struggle for Self*. New York: Oxford University Press.

Beck, U. (1992) *Risk Society: Towards a New Modernity*. London: Sage.

Briner, R. and Reynolds, S. (1999) 'The costs, benefits, and limitations of organizational level stress interventions', *Journal of Organizational Behaviour*, in press.

Cohen, S. and Manuck, S.B. (1995) 'Stress, reactivity and disease', *Psychosomatic Medicine*, 57: 423–6.

Cooper, C.L. and Cartwright, S. (1994) 'Stress-management interventions in the workplace: stress counselling and stress audits', *British Journal of Guidance and Counselling*, 22 (1): 65–73.

Dickson, W.J. (1945) 'The Hawthorne plan of personnel counselling', *Journal of Orthopsychiatry*, 15: 343–7.

Elias, N. (1991) *The Society of Individuals*. Oxford: Blackwell.

Evans, P., Clow, A. and Hucklebridge, F. (1997) 'Stress and the immune system', *The Psychologist*, 10 (7): 303–7.

Foucault, M. (1981) *The History of Sexuality, Vol. 1*. Harmondsworth: Penguin.

Gergen, K.J. (1991) *The Saturated Self: Dilemmas of Identity in Contemporary Life*. New York: Basic Books.

Giddens, A. (1991) *Modernity and Self-identity*. Cambridge: Polity Press.

Goffman, E. (1971) *The Presentation of Self in Everyday Life*. London: Pelican.

Hochschild, A.R. (1983) *The Managed Heart*. Berkeley: University of California Press.

Kasl, S.V. (1983) 'Pursuing the link between stressful life experiences and disease: a time for reappraisal', in C.L. Cooper (ed.), *Stress Research: Issues for the Eighties*. Chichester: Wiley.

Lasch, C. (1977) *Haven in a Heartless World: The Family Besieged*. New York: Basic Books.

Lazarus, R.S. and Folkman, S. (1984) *Stress, Appraisal and Coping*. New York: Springer.

Levinson, H. (1956) 'Employee counselling in industry: observations on three programs', *Bulletin of the Menninger Clinic*, 20: 76–84.

Murphy, L.R. (1988) 'Workplace interventions for stress reduction and prevention', in C.L. Cooper and R. Payne (eds), *Causes, Coping and Consequences of Stress at Work*. Chichester: Wiley.

Newton, T. (1989) 'Occupational stress and coping with stress: a critique', *Human Relations*, 42 (5): 441–61.

Newton, T. (1992) 'Stress management in the caring services', in C. Duncan, *The Evolution of Public Management Concepts and Techniques for the 1990s*. London: Macmillan.

Newton, T. (1995a) 'Knowing stress: from eugenics to work reform', in T. Newton, J. Handy and S. Fineman (eds), *'Managing' Stress: Emotion and Power at Work*. London: Sage.

Newton, T. (1995b) 'Rethinking stress and emotion: labour process theory, Foucault and Elias', in T. Newton, J. Handy and S. Fineman (eds), *'Managing' Stress: Emotion and Power at Work*. London: Sage.

Newton, T. (1996) 'Postmodernism and action', *Organization*, 3 (1): 7–29.

Newton, T. (1995c) 'Becoming "stress-fit"', in T. Newton, J. Handy and S. Fineman (eds), *'Managing' Stress: Emotion and Power at Work*. London: Sage.

Newton, T. and Keenan, A. (1990) 'The moderating effect of Type A Behaviour pattern and locus of control upon the relationship between change in job demands and change in psychological strain', *Human Relations*, 32 (12): 1229–55.

Newton, T., Handy, J. and Fineman, S. (eds) (1995) *'Managing' Stress: Emotion and Power at Work*. London: Sage.

Pollock, K. (1988) 'On the nature of social stress: production of a modern mythology', *Social Science and Medicine*, 26: 381–92.

Sahlins, M.D. (1972) *Stone Age Economics*. Chicago: Aldine-Atherton.

Schroeder, D.H. and Costa, P.T. (1984) 'Influence of life event stress on physical illness: substantive effects or methodological flaws?' *Journal of Personality and Social Psychology*, 46: 853–63.

Sigman, A. (1992) 'The state of corporate health care', *Personnel Management*, February: 24–31.

Soderberg, U. (1967) 'Neurophysiological aspects of stress', in L. Levi (ed.), *Emotional Stress*. Basle: Karger.

Storey, J. and Bacon, N. (1993) 'Individualism and collectivism: into the 1990s', *The International Journal of Human Resource Management*, 4 (3): 665–84.

Wilensky, J.L. and Wilensky, H.L. (1951) 'Personnel counseling: the Hawthorne case', *American Journal of Sociology*, 17: 265–80.

Wouters, C. (1989) 'The sociology of emotions and flight attendants: Hochschild's *Managed Heart*', *Theory, Culture & Society*, 6: 95–123.

27   Employee assistance programmes and stress counselling: at a crossroads?

John Berridge

In recent times, it has almost become requisite behaviour for employees to state that they are 'stressed', if not 'stressed out'. The incorporation of the word 'stress' into the organizational vernacular is found almost universally in most advanced post-industrialising countries. Indeed, often the word is used untranslated from English (the French use 'le stress' for example), illustrating the near ubiquity of the perception of stress, if not a unanimity over the concept.

Individual stress is experienced by employees across the spectrum of blue-collar jobs (Kornhauser, 1965; Shostak, 1980; Briner and Hockey, 1988) to white- or gold-collar occupations (Kahn and Cooper, 1990), from entry-level positions to top executive posts and board-level directors (Cooper and Sutherland, 1991). Research into stress in employment has been conducted for and by a variety of interested persons as diverse as mental health professionals, management consultants, health and safety officials, human resource management specialists, production engineers, environmental consultants and industrial chaplains.

More recently, attention has turned towards *organizational stress* as a potential corporate cause of economic under-performance, lack of innovation (Burke, 1988) or adaptative capacity, or loss of key staff members (Jick, 1985). The stressed organization is seen as more than the sum of its stressed individual components. It may also be the product of the multiple interactions of those individual stressed components, who in their turn are acting in a stressed corporate environment which can include:

(a) an inappropriate mission, philosophy or goals;
(b) unsuitable or outmoded structures, communications or control processes;
(c) lack of attention to job design and demands;
(d) ineffectual or ill-adapted managerial criteria and supervisory styles.

In times of rapid organizational change, organizational stress may be produced from outside the organization, including:

(a) competitors' aggressive tactics;
(b) governmental over-regulation;
(c) corporate reorganization and relocation;
(d) mergers, take-overs and business closures.

All these phenomena are occurring with increasing frequency, intensity and incidence in a world of employment where change and uncertainty are the only sure elements of the future.

The interaction of such individual and organizational stress with stress from non-work causes (personal, familial, social and other causes) composes a complex set of pressures even for the resilient, coping and well-adjusted individual. With the continuing increase in the salience of work as a referent of economic and social standing, individual employees often experience needs for knowledge, skill and (when necessary) support in handling stress. In such a context, workplace employee counselling plays a role in assisting the individual, and also in the performance of the organization – whether for profit or public good (Megranahan, 1994).

This chapter will evaluate the employee counselling and assistance role, with a particular focus on stress in organizations. First, stress will be defined and its conceptual validity examined, and employment sources of stress and its symptoms will be described. Second, stress interventions in organizations will be critically categorized, and the forms of current employee counselling practice will be developed. Third, an analytical evaluation will be made of certain key issues in employee and organizational counselling, examining its espoused philosophies and enacted practices. Finally, brief assessment will be offered of the likely future patterns of employment counselling for individuals and organizations.

Towards defining stress

The existence and validity of the notion of stress is widely accepted in popular thinking, and increasingly so in the professional corpus of knowledge of psychology and physical medicine (Schabracq et al., 1996). It is far more problematic, however, to achieve any consensus of the definition of the slippery concept of stress.

In the domain of mental and physical health, the word 'stress' has been in usage in English since 1843 (*OSED*, 1978) in the sense of 'a strain upon a body organ or mental power', derived from the old French *estresse*, meaning narrowness or oppression. The writings of Selye (1956) served greatly to legitimize and define stress in terms of its *physiological* aspects of alarm (high arousal, followed by preparation for fight or flight), resistance (arousal drops, combat or coping occurs) and exhaustion (arousal largely disappears, inaction sets in and physical deterioration may occur). At the same time, stress has an *emotional-subjective* element, usually of a negative nature.

Selye (1975) further elaborates stress in its three forms of stress (a neutral concept in terms of mental and physical well-being), distress (with negative implications) and eu-stress (with positive connotations, even allowing for Selye's incorrect etymology of combining a Greek prefix with a Latin-based noun). His work provided the impetus for a veritable research industry into the mental and physical strains caused by a multi-plicity of stress sources across a wide range of occupations and types of work.

Building on this basis, we can define stress as

> a condition experienced at the level of the individual of interlinked physiological responses and reactions combined with negative emotional-subjective states, occurring in situations where individuals perceive frustrations and threats to their significant and important goals and concerns, which they feel they will be incapable of combating or coping with.

Nevertheless, an understanding of stress is characterized by a high degree of subjectivity. It might be argued that stress is in the mind of the individual, and its objective and physical evidence is capable of different interpretations of causality. For instance, in an industrial relations context, stress experience depends on the differing perspectives of labour and management, although all actors in the system recognize the existence of stress (Neale et al., 1982; Bluen and Barling, 1986). An extreme (if defi-nitional) viewpoint in this approach is the assertion that stress does not in itself exist at all, but is at best an inchoate and ill-defined catch-all term for a miscellaneous range of physical symptoms which may or may not have a common origin or explicable interconnections. This fundamentalist view receives little professional or popular support, however, and will not be pursued further in this chapter, however controversial the case may be.

Stress and its symptoms

In any social context, an individual will be subject to desired and undesired stresses. All the more so in the employment context, where expectations are multiple, often formalized, often deliberately demanding, often non-negotiable, and perhaps even unwelcomed and feared. Pressures are gener-ated by performance-oriented organisations, by the individualization of work, by new technologies, by organizational change, and by increasing emphases on service, quality and customer relationship maintenance or enhancement (Lazarus, 1991). In all too many cases, employees find that new goals are set for them, but the social and interpersonal facilitation and support required in order to achieve the goals are not provided to the same level. Employees are left to work out largely for themselves how to cope, achieve and excel in their enlarged and more challenging tasks.

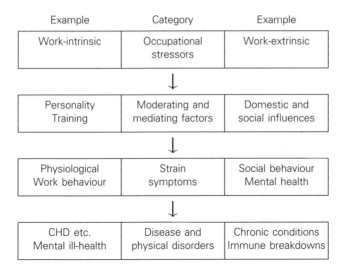

FIGURE 27.1 *Stressor–strain categorization of occupational stress (adapted from Fletcher, 1988)*

Individual employees vary in their perception of stress at work, quantitatively and qualitatively, and in terms of its origins. This may be illustrated in the stressor–strain model of occupational stress, which is represented in greatly simplified form in Figure 27.1. An alternative representation of similar elements is the NIOSH model of job stress/health relationships, which posits job stressors, influenced by individual and non-work factors and buffered by support mechanisms, which produce outcomes of acute reactions and physical illnesses (Hurrell and Murphy, 1992).

Interventions with stress at work

When an employing organization agrees to intervene in order to try to eliminate a source of stress at work, or to reduce or mitigate its effects, it is implicitly making several admissions. First, it is recognizing the cogency of employees' perception that stress exists in the workplace, and that they feel they are adversely affected by it (Dewe et al., 1993). Second, the employing organization is taking the first step towards an acknowledgement of its responsibility for causing stress, as a result of the work process – rather than attributing it to individuals' shortcomings, or to factors external to the organization. Third, it is accepting that the employer must bear the financial cost (in part or in full, whether legally or informally) for past detriment and present troubles experienced by employees. Fourth, the employing organization is beginning to realize that it must move forward from blaming or compensating to a more proactive role in creating the positively healthy work organization – as far as that is possible (Berridge and Cooper, 1994). In this framework of response categorization, three levels of stress intervention and prevention can be identified (Berridge et al., 1997).

Primary interventions aim to tackle stress issues by eliminating stress at its origin, where and when it shows itself. Initially many primary interventions remove a risk or danger (or the threat of it) or reduce its incidence. These steps could include noise reduction, disease or injury prevention, reduction of workloads, improved working hours and shift patterns. When these negative aspects have been tackled, attention often turns then to more positive primary interventions which can remove stressors, such as mechanical assistance to reduce the burden of physical effort, incorporation of information technology to assist decision making, ergonomically informed changes in working methods such as job redesign and improvements in layout of work stations or operations, or modified production systems. In most instances, there are few (if any) counselling elements in these objective organizational interventions.

Secondary stress interventions can be introduced at individual or collective levels. Both types depend on information, education and training to encourage people to know about the symptoms of stress in the work context, to recognize stress symptoms and behaviour personally, in colleagues or subordinates, and to develop or refine coping skills and personal hardiness in the face of stressors. At the individual level, the forms of secondary prevention can include awareness raising on conflict handling and avoidance (with colleagues or the public), relaxation techniques, time management techniques, assertiveness training, teamworking and leadership skills, and lifestyle advice. Collectively, the secondary interventions comprise measures such as the introduction of personal stress evaluation into medical screening programmes, employee fitness programmes, including both on- and off-site exercise and sport facilities, corporate dietary, smoking and drug-abuse control programmes, and well woman/ man programmes. Within such collective initiatives, there frequently is an element of individual advice and counselling, but provided by the expert in the specialist knowledge or technique. This intervention is more informational than therapeutic, and usually assumes that the employee is a relatively rational-functional individual.

It is at the *tertiary level of stress intervention* and prevention that counselling provisions become prominent. These interventions comprise counselling for individual troubled employees who have suffered from stress as a result of the absence or inadequacy of primary interventions, and who have not acquired coping skills and behaviours from secondary-level interventions. Tertiary interventions are essentially rehabilitative, aiming at restoring the client-employee to full adjustment, capability and competence in coping with stress, whatever its origin. This is provided through counselling, whether in-house or supplied externally to the organization, and without distinction as to the referral method, therapeutic philosophy or practice model adopted. The focus of this chapter is the employee counselling and employee assistance programmes (EAPs). They are a particular development of employee counselling, related to stressed employees, and designed to deal directly and quickly with 'troubled' employees in the context of the organizations.

Employee counselling and EAPs

A sympathetic definition of an employee assistance programme is 'a confidential and professional service provided as an employee benefit which complements and extends in-company resources in the constructive and supportive management of people impacted by concerns in their personal and work lives' (Megranahan, 1995). The difference between the EAP and traditional employee counselling is its compatibility and integration (by design) with the corporate goals and culture of the employing organization. The EAP provider accepts to work within the organization's structure, processes, leadership and motivation methods in a professional non-judgemental manner, and to professional standards (Reddy, 1993).

Most British EAPs are 'broad brush', tackling a range of issues from informational (for example, debt counselling) to psychosocial (for example, relationships) to psychoanalytical (for example, severe substance abuse). An effective diagnostic procedure, referral mechanisms and both micro- and macro-linkages with specialist and community resources are essential to cope with employee-clients whom the counsellors do not feel they are able to help themselves.

The majority of clients approaching British EAPs are self-referrals, but managerial persuasion or authority may occur in some cases, especially in cases of a disciplinary nature. In many instances, EAPs are preceded and paralleled by education and training initiatives on the programme itself, its benefits, its confidentiality, and on health promotion or stress reduction techniques. Managers and trade union officials are often targeted as the potential facilitators and 'champions' of the EAP (Davis and Gibson, 1994).

EAPs hence represent a more developed and organizationally integrated effort spanning tertiary interventions and aspects of secondary or primary interventions. Although focused on and partly integrated with the employing organization, they deliver professional standards of service to clients, yet at the employer's expenses. In these ways, they differ from the more dissociated employee counselling, which lacks the linkages with the organization, and which is individualized at the tertiary level of intervention (Summerfield and Van Oudtshoorn, 1995). The therapeutic approaches of the two variants are arguably similar, and their inward and onward referral methods resemble each other. The two types of counselling are not necessarily a progression towards EAPs, but they will be treated together for the following discussion of selected controversial aspects.

Problematic areas in employee counselling

The activity of employee counselling and assistance stands at a crossroads of various disciplines and different interest groups. In disciplinary terms, it is not exclusively the preserve of the psychologist, since the contextual and originating rationale of employment introduces elements of organizational analysis, human resource management and industrial relations. The interest groups involved within the organization are the line managers of the 'troubled' employees, the top management concerned with the culture and economic viability, and the trade unions or professional associations who defend their members' rights. Nor should the individual's own legitimate interests be overlooked.

The contentions and controversies surrounding employee counselling therefore embrace not only professional concerns in psychotherapy; they also have to be drawn more widely, and in particular they include management of the employing organization, and (at the risk of reification) the behaviour of the organization itself. This chapter therefore is written with a perspective which de-emphasizes professional concerns within their own terms of references to some extent. Instead it places them within the wider organizational frame of reference, and introduces economic, social, political and legal considerations of professional practice.

Eight main problematic scenarios are discussed, but the author is well aware that this choice of topics is necessarily limiting. As a consequence, numerous central topics of professional practice have only been touched upon peripherally – notably confidentiality, practice models and evaluation, confrontation, ongoing therapy following referral, counsellor selection, programme audit and the role for statutory support and protection in employee counselling.

Employers' disinterest in employee counselling

For a counselling professional, employee counselling is a problematic area of practice because of doubts over the employer's motives in establishing and funding a counselling programme. If the counsellor is an associate with an EAP contractor-provider, the question becomes even more acute, since the motives of her or his employing company also enter into the decision to work in this sector. What is the overall scenario within which the counsellor works, and is it delineated explicitly or formally? How does that scenario equate with the therapeutic framework within which a counselling professional should expect to offer an expert service and develop a professional career (Bond, 1993)? Has the counsellor been equipped with the necessary skills to work effectively within an economic organization (Dryden and Feltham, 1994)?

An employer's motives for instituting employee counselling are wide-ranging in nature, and may include the following (Berridge et al., 1997):

(a) a disinterested concern for employees' welfare, based on humanist principles;
(b) a recognition of the increasingly stressful nature of work in organizations;
(c) a willingness to accept the social responsibility of paying to rehabilitate troubled employees, out of profits or surpluses (the organizational equivalent of 'the polluter pays');
(d) a desire to create a positive image as a caring employer, in order to maintain internal morale or to attract a better quality of recruit to a sympathetic employment culture;
(e) a need to reduce costs by cutting absenteeism, preventing early retirals, lowering insurance premiums for accidents, avoiding training and retraining costs, not incurring overtime or agency staff costs for cover, and so on;
(f) a wish to improve quality of product or service by having fewer and less stressed employees providing more commitment;
(g) a plan to avoid legal costs and awards to employees bringing stress or injury suits against the organization;
(h) an intention to cope more effectively with disruptions in work patterns caused by change such as relocation, delayering, restructuring, down- or rightsizing, redundancy, take-over or merger (Straussner, 1988).
(i) a tactic to supplement disciplinary procedures by incorporating counselling and subsequent behavioural conformism as a condition, element or stage in the disciplinary sequence: an employee who is unwilling to participate, to complete a course of counselling and to abide by agreed outcomes in that course, or who subsequently reoffends is thus more susceptible to lawful dismissal, and the employer's defence is thereby strengthened.

The problem for the employee counselling professional lies in the sequences of motives described above – where should the employer's motivation be placed in this continuum from altruism to unrequited self-interest? In effect, most employers have a mixture of many of these motives (Schmidenberg et al., 1992). But how does the counselling professional evaluate which orientation she or he is supporting or opposing, albeit implicitly? The in-house counsellor probably has a clear view of the employing organization, and can decide whether to remain in post, according to the balance of organizational motives for providing employee counselling. The associate of an EAP contractor-provider does not have such detailed organizational knowledge, and is probably dealing by telephone with a range of employing organizations whose philosophies are not known at all. How to decide one's professional values, other than on universalistic professional principles – which then disregard the employee-client's organizational context?

Organizational economics and values

The juxtaposition of professional counselling and economic organizations may well not be happy. Employee counselling is predicated upon work-originated and related 'troubles'; it is paid for by the employer, and is designed to return the individual back into the organization, functioning productively. Employing organizations are economically and financially maximizing entities – whether in the private or not-for-profit sectors. Their psychosocial and philosophical dimensions are often conspicuously absent in practice, even if ritually alluded to in chief executives' public discourse or in annual reports. It may hence appear counterproductive if not cynical for counselling services to rehabilitate corporate warriors and cannon-fodder alike, in order to return them to the corporate conflict.

The professional education, training and socialization processes of counsellors encourage idealism, and individual client focus and altruistic service – all of which are antithetical to corporate commercialism, competitiveness and aggression. It is scarcely surprising, therefore, that many counsellors see employee organizations as inherently destructive to the healthily functioning individual (Bakalinsky, 1980). Also in reverse, corporate managers sense this oppositional stance of counsellors, and find their analyses and suggestions to clients impractical if not unhelpful – particularly so since the employer is paying for counselling (Schmidenberg et al., 1992).

The problem arises most acutely with external provision of counselling through public-service agencies and with EAP contractors, whose large number of associates may include those with a wide range of professional training and orientations. Where counsellors have no employment experience in a non-professional capacity, or hold views about organizations being destructive to individuals, then the dichotomy between the programme objectives and the orientations of the counsellor becomes acute. Clients may feel that counselling is proceeding in irrelevant or impractical directions; company executives may feel that counselling is dysfunctional to company policy or even subversive.

In-house and externally provided employee counselling

The choice to be made by an employer between an in-house or external counselling service causes much debate among counselling professionals.

The choice of an in-house counselling service appeals to the employer. It is capable of being integrated to the mission and culture of the organization. From time to time it can be fine-tuned to the internal economic, political and control systems of the enterprise through periodic modifications of services to clients, referral methods, and so on. The counsellors (as employees themselves) will understand the organization *realpolitik* as well as the minutiae of a client's work context (Straussner, 1988). But counselling professionals will have concerns over the confidentiality of the service, their own independence of action in the light of the activities of other functions (for example, human resource management) and the professional integrity of an employer-defined and -funded programme – whatever assurances are given (Reddy, 1997).

The externally sourced counselling or employee assistance programme has grown greatly in Britain since the mid-1980s, not only supplanting some existing in-house services, but expanding into sectors of employment where welfare had withered away, or where counselling had never existed in connection with employment. For an employer, externally contracted employee counselling or EAP provisions offered service delivery advantages such as independence, perceived confidentiality and a creative, original approach (Carroll, 1997). It also gave advantages of cheapness of unit costs, flexibility of service provision, low capital costs and known revenue costs over the contract period, continual cost and quality benchmarking through contract renewal, cheaper access to a wider range of counselling specialisms and service delivery modes, and conformity to the economic fashion of outsourcing.

For most British employers, the case was irrefutable, especially when reinforced and reiterated by the able marketing and sales staff of the leading employee counselling and employee assistance programmes. What were the implications for counselling professionals? The increased employment opportunities for psychologists were no doubt welcomed, but they also brought disadvantages. These included counselling firms being overly concerned with volumetric growth, increase in market share, reduction of unit costs, enhanced return on capital employed, and satisfying client firms' needs. While counselling and EAP providers were originally run mainly by entrepreneurial professional psychologists, the concern was not too prominent. With the increasing acquisition of counselling firms by large players in the personal and financial services sectors, professional standards of quality may be under threat. The aspects threatened by non-professional control are referral methods and triage procedures, sound recruitment methods for counsellors with sufficient verification of professional suitability, reasonable case loads, clear identification of clients' needs, limitations on sessions to be supplied at the counsellor's discretion, onwards micro- and macro-linkages with community and specialist services, and professional supervision and development. Only a few counselling contractor-providers are sources of concern for all such practices, however, and many remain eminently scrupulous in their methods.

Yet the counselling industry is still economically immature, and during the process of market rationalization, intense competition exists. This places pressure on professional practices in the counselling contractor-provider industry. While statutory requirements do not exist, and while the professional-industrial association (EAPA or Employee Assistance

Professionals Association) and the qualifying association (BAC or British Association for Counselling) are dissociated, the commonality of interest and standards normally associated with a therapeutic profession does not prevail. It is in the interests of the employee counselling profession to resolve this issue.

Counsellors' training and practice bases

Employee counsellors need a particular blend of knowledge, skills and experience. They deal with a special section of clients:

(a) employees with work-related problems on presentation;
(b) employers who provide the funding;
(c) employees expecting quick results within an organizationally compatible framework (Megranahan, 1994).

They practise in a field which is traditionally the preserve of lay counsellors (almoners, welfare officers, personnel specialists) or well-intending but totally untrained persons (colleagues, supervisors, shop stewards). The origins of employee counselling are sentiments of moral superiority ('do-gooding' in Britain, 'social secretaries' in the US) or in Alcoholics Anonymous (especially in the US) using group persuasion methods. It is hence unsurprising that recent British research (Highley and Cooper, 1995) reveals that 22 per cent of counsellors involved in work-related practice are not professionally qualified: half of these have a counselling skills certificate but half have no formal qualifications, relying on experience, received wisdom and personal empathy with clients.

British employee counselling practice centres on short term therapy (Malan and Osimo, 1992) (typically three to eight funded sessions) to assist the client in working through a 'trouble'. The assumption is that the client is moderately functioning, and counsellors argue that interventions (often derived from Rogerian theories or from rational emotive behaviour therapy) will suffice to return the individual to relatively normal functioning. The concern persists whether such methods will fully meet clients' needs, and whether onward referral mechanisms will operate adequately within the funding arrangements of the employer or of the state or community.

Assessing the effectiveness of employee counselling

The evaluation of the outcomes of employee counselling of necessity must be a key activity of any employee counselling activity but one that is multiply problematic (Balgopal and Patchner, 1988). The two main sets of professional outcomes are those for the client and those for the counsellor. Most counselling services will carry out these activities as a matter of professional quality assurance, and will supply aggregated statistics to the funding employing organization. There is far less evaluation of the continuing effect of an employing counselling provision on the organization (Orlans, 1991). Frequently no organizational evaluation occurs beyond a scrutiny of the statistics supplied by an external provider-contractor. The potential exists for more fundamental cultural change, but in practice few organizations make this evaluation, which is surely necessary for the continuation of any counselling service.

Numerous US-based studies of employee counselling programmes show impressive cost savings per dollar expended: for instance, one study states savings of US$4.23 for every dollar spent on counselling programmes (Intindola, 1991). The economic bases of such savings may be open to criticism in the methods of calculation, as well as the rationale for inclusion/exclusion of benefits and costs (Holosko, 1988). A major British study (Highley and Cooper, 1995) takes a more qualitative approach, as well as including certain key quantitative indicators. A very brief and undifferentiated view of employee counselling that can be made from its data is as follows:

1 Absenteeism is considerably reduced – but at the expense of presenteeism?
2 Employees' awareness of stress and stressors is much greater – does this mean they are more susceptible?
3 Coping behaviour of employees is enhanced in their opinion – but of course awareness is heightened.
4 Employees' general satisfaction with their work is not substantially affected, and neither is their relationship with the employing organization.
5 Those employees who have not had contact with the professional counselling services do not experience sizeable modification of their stress-related behaviour or expectations.

As a consequence, many of the claimed intangible benefits of employee counselling remain asserted and anecdotally debated rather than empirically demonstrated. These advantages potentially could include the following:

(a) changes in company cultures, affecting all staff members, not just those using counselling;
(b) development of a more responsive, mutually responsible and open atmosphere in an organization, which starts to develop self-learning characteristics;
(c) a greater orientation towards relationships of all sorts in the organization, including customers or users, colleagues, different functional or product groups, and vertically within a hierarchy.

An economic as well as a social calculus is evident in these objectives for employee counselling, and the potential pay-off could be immense in terms of corporate prestige and revenues. The counselling professional could well have misgivings over the smallness of his or her fee, the restricted micro-benefits which are provided to the employee, and the size of the corporate financial gain.

Employee counselling in the enterprise society

Many employers currently are taking a more holistic approach to adopting employee counselling and to developing it to meet the contingent problems which they face. In the 1980s in Britain, many early programmes were of the 'bandaid' type – imposed by a concerned organization on troubled employees to treat the immediate symptoms with little concern for the underlying causes. Where these causes lay within the organization, a fundamental cultural change was often required. This would entail a move away from engineering and Taylorian logic concerning the structure of jobs and work processes, away from economistic and Freidmanesque rationales for judging success, and away from authoritarian forms of social control within the employment relationship.

Thus employee counselling represented a tertiary-level intervention, treating employee clients as the inevitable victims of organizational Darwinism in an enterprise culture promoted by Thatcherism. Managers often even opposed employee counselling as being soft on employees, and implicitly condoning indiscipline if not organizational deviancy in a hard-driving, individualistic, commercial environment.

Counselling professionals in Britain were reluctant to move outside the one-to-one client relationship in order to tackle the organizational stressors, valuing their professional independence. They seldom wished to become enmeshed in the business consultancy sector of organizational development (OD), having neither the experience, training nor inclination to do so. In the US the employee counselling profession had developed earlier, and by the 1990s was a more mature occupational sector, in terms of specialized experience, qualifications and length of service. Counsellors hence developed the wish to tackle the origins of stress in organizations, and such expertise was built into Master's degree in Social Work pro-grammes (Cunningham, 1994). Therefore employee assistance has mutated much more widely than in Britain, into organizational assistance pro-grammes (OAPs). This variant combines OD and individual counselling, at the same high standards of professionalism, but with the independence of viewpoint not easily achieved by the business consultant in the OD field.

The counselling profession in Britain may also be facing this choice of expansion of practice, or risk being marginalized within the power struc-ture of their corporate funding clients by other new experts (Berridge, 1996). These could include the organizational analysts (using sociological models), the human resources specialists (using socio-economic tools) or the cultural-change consultants (using politico-anthropological notions). It remains to be seen how appropriate is 'downstream' counselling in dealing with the 'upstream' issues of the types mentioned (Walton, 1997).

The ownership of employee counselling

The professional ownership of an employee counselling service or EAP is often contested within an organization. The service is a crossroads of interests in many respects, having elements of personal service to individuals as clients, as well as control of performance and behaviour by the organization. There are also implications less clearly in terms of statutory duty, legal protection and commercial prudence. Hence claims of ownership may be advanced by the functional specialisms of occupational health, welfare or human resource management. Alternatively, an in-house counselling service or EAP may assert its own distinctiveness and independence, reporting only to the chief executive, or to a board-level committee. An external provider of counselling or EAP will have more operational independence, but the reporting issue will still arise annually on evaluation of the service, and even more acutely at the renewal of contract every few years. The locus and level of professional counselling expertise may well determine the ownership. In an organization where lay counselling is still used, in some cases the welfare function may still be in charge. With sophisticated human resource management in an enterprise, that function may wish to use externally contracted counselling as part of its array of managerialist techniques. Ownership by occupational health sends signals of independent confidentiality to employees, but the traditional emphasis of the function has been preventative physical health (for medical officers) and skills-level counselling for support staff. Given such confusion of claims to ownership, it is not surprising that many organizations opt for mixed models of control for counselling services. This compromise sometimes also reflects the fact that EAPs are often first suggested by or sold to chief executives with an intention of assisting with organizational change, including the overall culture. Hence they do not want to see them fall into a particular organizational fiefdom.

But all this confusion over organizational ownership diminishes the status of counselling, inhibits professional expertise and may lead to conflicts over the funding and purpose of the service. In such circumstances, professionally qualified counsellors may not be attracted to work in such contested terrain. Alternatively, they may find that inappropriate controls or accountabilities are imposed on practice, and they may not wish to remain in this sector of professional activity.

Funding for employee counselling

The growth of employee counselling services and EAPs in Britain since the mid-1980s has been dramatic. By 1996 some 1.3 million employees (5–6 per cent of the working population) were covered by EAPs (Berridge et al., 1997). In the US estimates of EAP coverage regularly revealed that 75–80 per cent of the Fortune Top 500 corporations have EAPs (Luthans and Waldersee, 1989), and some 25 per cent of all employees are so covered (Feldman,1991), particularly in the large corporations, where it is a significant employee benefit. Questions may therefore be asked justifiably: 'Where and how far is employee counselling going?'

One area of concern is whether the Department of Health and the Department of Trade and Industry via the Health and Safety Commission are seeking to transfer some or all of the cost for mental health issues of employed persons from the state to the employer. It is clear that some employees have some problems whose origin is in the employment process. Equally, the nature of some problems is in social or interpersonal activities unconnected with work. Does the employment or workplace counsellor wish to become a proxy functionary of the state or the employer through his/her professional practice?

A second major worry is whether employee counselling is becoming cost-driven, to the detriment of the client. Ownership patterns among the major counselling providers are moving towards control by leading financial services sector firms (insurance, business consultancy) as the financial resources escalate in order to operate and market an employee counselling or assistance service. The locus of managerial control is also moving away from the professionally qualified counsellors who founded the services. Instead marketing and financial specialists are assuming operating control as the founding fathers tire of commercial competition and opt to move sideways or out.

A third disquieting factor which is entering into employee counselling is managed care (Hahn and Kleinke, 1991). As a rationing and decision-making mechanism in more wide-ranging health provision, it is prevalent in insurance-funded health care (Cunningham, 1994). If both counselling providers and managements adopt an increasingly economistic-utilitarian approach to employee counselling, will this be at the cost of altruistic and universalistic perspectives?

Conclusion

Two decades ago, employee counselling in Britain would have been considered moribund, if not outmoded. The EAP has revitalized employee counselling in numbers of clients, in the range of issues treated, in its social acceptance, and not least in its professional standing and robustness of practice in short-term therapy. Yet if it is to remain functional to clients and also to the providers of finance, it has challenges to resolve. Within the counselling profession, these will centre around recruitment and training of counsellors, and especially around ensurance of the highest standards. In its environments, the challenges relate to defining its sphere of competence, and its distinctiveness in the eyes of organizational clients, while retaining its independent contribution to the resolution of their problems. Such are the continual dilemmas of any profession. Can the counselling profession solve them not just competently, but creatively? Employee counselling and assistance faces a multiple crossroads, professionally and organizationally, with few if any signposts which it can rely upon.

References

Bakalinsky, R. (1980) 'People vs profits: social work in industry', *Social Work*, 25: 471–3.

Balgopal, P.R. and Patchner, M.A. (1988) 'Evaluating employee assistance programs: obstacles, issues and strategies', *Employee Assistance Quarterly*, 3 (3–4): 95–105.

Berridge, J. (1996) 'New roles for employee assistance programmes in the 1990s: occupational social work is back and different', *Personnel Review*, 25 (1): 59–64.

Berridge, J. and Cooper, C.L. (1994) 'The employee assistance programme: its role in organizational coping and excellence', *Personnel Review*, 23 (7): 4–20.

Berridge, J., Cooper, C.L. and Highley-Marchington, C. (1997) *Employee Assistance Programmes and Workplace Counselling*. Chichester: John Wiley.

Bluen, S.D. and Barling, J. (1986) 'Psychological stressors associated with industrial relations', in C.L. Cooper and R. Payne (eds), *Causes, Coping and Consequences of Stress at Work*. Chichester: John Wiley.

Bond, T. (1993) *Standards and Ethics for Counselling in Action*. London: Sage.

Briner, R. and Hockey, R.J. (1988) 'Operator stress and computer-based work', in C.L. Cooper and R. Payne (eds), *Causes, Coping and Consequences of Stress at Work*. Chichester: John Wiley.

Burke, R.J. (1988) 'Sources of managerial and professional stress in large organizations', in C.L. Cooper and R. Payne (eds), *Causes, Coping and Consequences of Stress at Work*. Chichester: John Wiley.

Carroll, M. (1997) 'Counselling in organizations: an overview', in M. Carroll and M. Walton (eds), *Handbook of Counselling in Organizations*. London: Sage.

Cooper, C.L. and Sutherland, V. (1991) 'The stress of the executive life style', *Employee Relations*, 13 (4): 3–7.

Cunningham, G. (1994) *Effective Employee Assistance Programs*. Thousand Oaks, CA: Sage.

Davis, A. and Gibson, L. (1994) 'Designing employee welfare provision', in J. Berridge and C.L. Cooper (eds), 'The employee assistance programme: its role in organizational coping and excellence', *Personnel Review*, 23 (7): 33–45.

Dewe, P., Cox, T. and Ferguson, E. (1993) 'Individual strategies for coping with stress at work', *Work and Stress*, 7 (1): 5–15.

Dryden, W. and Feltham, C. (1994) *Developing Counsellor Training*. London: Sage.

Feldman, S. (1991) 'Today's EAPs make the grade', *Personnel*, 65: 3–40.

Fletcher, B. (1988) 'The epidemiology of occupational stress', in C.L. Cooper and R. Payne (eds), *Causes, Coping and Consequences of Stress at Work*. Chichester: John Wiley.

Hahn, S. and Kleinke, J.D. (1991) 'Managed wealth for the 1990s: integrating managed care and employee assistance', *Compensation and Benefits Management* (manuscript).

Highley, J.C. and Cooper, C.L. (1995) 'An assessment of employee assistance and workplace counselling programmes in British organisations'. *Report for the Health and Safety Executive*, unpublished.

Holosko, M.J. (1988) 'Perspectives for employee assistance program evaluations: a case for a more thoughtful evaluation planning', *Employee Assistance Quarterly*, 3 (3 & 4): 59–68.

Hurrell, J.J. and Murphy, L.R. (1992) 'Psychological job stress', in W.N. Rom (ed.), *Environmental and Occupational Medicine*. 2nd edn. Boston, MA: Little Brown & Co.

Intindola, B. (1991) 'EAPs still foreign to many small businesses', *National Underwriter*, 95: 21.

Jick, T.D. (1985) 'As the axe falls: budget cuts and the experience of stress in organisations', in T.D. Beehr and R.S. Bhagat (eds), *Human Stress and Cognition in Organisations*. New York: John Wiley.

Kahn, H. and Cooper, C.L. (1990) 'Mental health, job satisfaction, alcohol intake, and occupational stress among dealers in financial markets', *Stress Medicine*, 6: 285–95.

Kornhauser, A. (1965) *Mental Health of the Industrial Worker*. New York: John Wiley.

Lazarus, R.S. (1991) 'Psychological stress in the workplace', in P.L. Perrewe (ed.), 'Handbook in job stress' [Special Issue], *Journal of Social Behaviour and Personality*, 6 (7): 1–13.

Luthans, F. and Waldersee, R. (1989) 'What do we really know about EAPs?', *Human Resource Management*, 28: 385–401.

Malan, D. and Osimo, F. (1992) *Psychodynamics, Training and Outcomes in Brief Psychotherapy*. London: Butterworth-Heinemann.

Megranahan, M. (1994) 'Counselling in the workplace', in W. Dryden, D. Charles-Edwards and R. Woolfe (eds), *Handbook of Counselling in Britain*. London: Routledge.

Megranahan, M. (1995) 'Employee counselling'. Unpublished presentation to postgraduate course in organisational psychology, Manchester School of Management, UMIST, 29 November.

Neale, M.S., Singer, J., Schwartz, G.E. and Swartz, J. (1982) 'Conflicting perspectives on stress reductions in occupational settings'. Report to NIOSH on PO No. 82-1058, NIOSH, Cincinnati OH.

Orlans, V. (1991) 'Evaluating the benefits of employee assistance programmes', *Employee Counselling Today*, 3 (4): 27–31.

OSED (Oxford Shorter English Dictionary) (1978). Oxford: Oxford University Press.

Reddy, M. (1993) *EAPs and Counselling Provision in UK Organisations*, 1993. Milton Keynes: ICAS.

Reddy, M. (1997) 'External counselling provision for organisations', in M. Carroll and M. Walton (eds), *Handbook of Counselling in Organisations*. London: Sage.

Schabracq, M.J., Winnubst, J.A.M. and Cooper, C.L. (1996) *Handbook of Work and Health Psychology*. Chichester: John Wiley and Sons.

Schmidenberg, O., Blaze-Temple, D. and Cordery, J. (1992) 'Supervisors and EAPs: a clash between the real and the ideal', *EAP International*, 1 (1): 4–8.

Selye, H. (1956) *The Stress of Life*. New York: McGraw-Hill.

Selye, H. (1975) 'Confusion and controversy in the stress field', *Journal of Human Stress*, 1: 37–44.

Shostak, A.B. (1980) *Blue-Collar Stress*. Reading, MA: Addison-Wesley.

Straussner, S.L.A. (1988) 'Comparison of in-house and contracted-out employee assistance programs', *Social Work*, 33: 53–5.

Summerfield, J. and Van Oudtshoorn, L. (1995) *Counselling in the Workplace*. London: Institute of Personnel and Development.

Walton, M. (1997) 'Counselling as a form of organizational change', in M. Carroll and M. Walton (eds), *Handbook of Counselling in Organizations*. London: Sage.

28   Psychotherapy and counselling as unproven, overblown and unconvincing

Alex Howard

The growth of counselling has been explosive in the past ten years. Rising demand exceeds the ever-growing supply in relation to:

(a) clients and health sector counsellors;
(b) counselling students and counselling courses;
(c) counsellors and budgets to employ them.

Clients want to be counselled and counsellors want clients and employment. They routinely follow police, fire and ambulance personnel to deal with trauma of whatever kind. The practice of counselling has moved ahead, beyond and out of sight of sensible definitions, discipline and demarcation of boundaries, varieties of therapy, aims, values, theories and practices.

The case for support of one kind or another from third party outsiders is unassailable. We cannot manage every problem and crisis from within our own immediate family or social group. Most societies have provided, and do and will provide 'outside' assistance in a wide variety of institutional and informal contexts, no doubt with highly variable results.

We all like to receive systematic time and attention, and doctors often prefer to hand over patients to someone else when there is no particular physical ailment. Currently this plethora of (hopefully) healing human activity is called 'counselling' or 'psychotherapy'. Counselling is the flavour of our time. Who am I, then, to suggest that we should all slow down, take stock, look again, think carefully, do some arithmetic, find some evidence worthy of the name?

Certainly counselling has its critics, and it is easy to become overly shrill, either in support of counselling, or against it. Instead, we might pay more attention to the facts and to (what is much more commonly the case) our absence of worthwhile evidence. We shall find that, at present, it is much easier to ask questions about counselling than to find answers.[1]

Of course, if people want to spend their own money on their chosen counsellor, they are free to do so. There might be better ways of using their time. They might get lucky or unlucky in their choice of healer and there is a great deal of chance at work here. They might be happy with the result, with or without good reason. They will almost certainly appreciate having someone to listen, especially if no-one else in their daily lives is willing or able to do so.

I am confident that counselling is sometimes helpful, sometimes harmful, sometimes neither. Generally clients may appreciate the time and attention in any event. It may sometimes be harmful even when the client is highly satisfied. As an extreme illustration of the dangers of relying entirely on client satisfaction, in 1997 adherents of the Heaven's Gate cult in the USA, following their leader, committed mass suicide, happy in the expectation that they would thereby meet up with an alien spacecraft hovering behind comet Hale-Bopp. Counsellors are unlikely to be so dangerous or clients so misguided. But let's remember the following:

1   Most healing remedies offered before this century appear to have had no active ingredients whatsoever (see, for example, Kennedy, 1983).
2   Most patients were none the less happy with their chosen healer, even though their remedies were either dangerous or impotent. For example, thousands of sick people were literally bled white because doctors thought this would help. Patients were duly grateful, and often got better despite these efforts.
3   Any expert has to believe in his or her expertise and dress and act accordingly. Until all too recently, they have often had no other real skill. Yet customers and would-be professionals have generally been unwilling or unable to confront the monumental incompetence, ignorance and impotence in the history of 'healing'.[2]
4   Many chronic, intractable problems and ailments remain, to this day, chronic and intractable.

If we tried to prohibit goods and services on the grounds that, however much in demand, they were of no real use to customers, we might find ourselves attempting to disallow a significant proportion of the buying and selling within contemporary economies. The key question, then, is should the taxpayer be funding this new service because it is so good that the poorer than average within society need their fair share?

My answer, given the present stage of development in counselling/psychotherapy,[3] is an emphatic 'no', for the following reasons:

1   The counselling industry has reached (much) too far beyond its current ability to define, develop and assess its theories, practices and purposes.
2   If it is an effective treatment rather than a cultural fashion, it is not enough to show that it often produces a 'feel-good' experience among its clients.

3 If it is to be funded as a public service, then it must deliver more than the alternative remedies and expenditure options: for example, friendship, material-support, other social or economic initiatives.
4 I fear that it is a symptom of, more than a solution to, social fragmentation.

Would-be professionals tend to profess their expertise long before they can actually provide it or prove it.[4] As taxpayers, we ought not to be happy to fund promises, however well presented. We deserve evidence and we need to know, beyond platitudes, clichés and vague generalizations, just what it is that is being provided.

'The overall aim of counselling is to provide the opportunity for the client to work towards living in a more satisfying and resourceful way.' So says the British Association for Counselling. So would every other service provider. No-one is actively seeking for people to be less satisfied and resourceful. Hence this definition is far too broad and vague to be of general use. This might not matter if everyone in practice meant the same thing when they referred to counselling. In fact there is a cacophony of voices and schools with complementary, contrary and contradictory views about the nature of counselling. The word has become a substitute for thought rather than an aid to it.

Perhaps there should be a moratorium on its use? Anyone tempted to use it would be required to be more specific about what s/he thought s/he was describing. We would then more easily be able to analyse and make some sense of this vast and variable undertaking. This would help us to prise away components that deserved to be supported. We might then seek to scrap other activity that produces no worthwhile results and/or does not deserve the investment of private, let alone public, funds.

Holmes and Lindley argue that 'psychotherapy should be much more widely available; indeed it should be regarded as no less essential than other forms of health care, or education' (1989: 17). They agree that supporting evidence of the value of psychotherapy is important and claim that they have it. They cite research showing that clients of psychotherapy tend to do better than those in control groups. 'Control subjects here means patients who are offered brief non-specific "chats" or unfocussed discussion groups' (1989: 33). Should we be impressed? I think not.

A real control would surely require that clients in an experiment do not know if they are getting 'real' counselling or not. They must not be allowed to know who is the 'real' expert since the very belief that an expert is helping us lifts our hope and our morale very substantially indeed. Trials of drugs are carried out in 'double blind' conditions. What this means is that neither the person delivering the treatment nor the individual receiving it knows if the pill on offer contains the powerful ingredient being tested, or chalk and flavouring.

People who are offered a 'non-specific chat' know at once that they are receiving the verbal equivalent of chalk and flavouring. Their hopes and responsiveness are adjusted accordingly. Control pills have got to look like pills, taste like pills and even, if they are really to be plausible, deliver a few physical side-effects. Similarly, control therapy has got to look and feel like the real thing to discerning clients if placebo effects are to be discounted. We will then have an experiment where the clients, at least, are genuinely blind. There is, of course, no way of keeping the practitioner in the dark unless you take people through a long, fake, training programme built on folk wisdom and common sense. This would not be fair on the trainees, but might be more worthwhile than some of the wilder and more exotic therapy training offered in this highly variegated industry.[5]

It is not surprising, exciting or significant to discover that almost anyone can be more helpful than the control alternative of a 'non-specific chat'. If therapists are to justify a claim to professional status, they will surely have to defeat stiffer competition than can be delivered via such a feeble control trial.

So let's suggest a more real and realistic test condition. Offer, say, 10 sessions of counselling. Ensure that each counsellor looks and sounds reasonably intelligible, intelligent, accessible. Have one group of trained counsellors deliver a 'real' service according to their professional training. Set up another group of untrained lay persons, with similar levels and ranges of intelligence, life experience and personality. Let the clients take their problems to one or other group, without knowing if they are meeting a professional or an amateur listener. Who might get the best results and by how large a margin?

In such a contest it becomes anything but clear that counselling professionals can reliably out-perform serious amateurs.[6] It becomes difficult to say what 'success' ought to consist in. It becomes clear that professionals don't necessarily do what they were trained to do but that this doesn't seem to matter since the nature of the counsellor training doesn't make much difference to the outcome.

Holmes and Lindley acknowledge that 'there is no one major type of psychotherapy that is consistently more effective than others; Luborksy's "Dodo-bird" verdict (from *Alice in Wonderland*) "everyone has won and all shall have prizes" has yet to be refuted' (1989: 37). They also acknowledge that 'therapists, as opposed to therapies, differ significantly in their effectiveness' (1989: 37). Moreover, personal qualities seem to be more crucial than the nature of the training received: 'Accurate empathy, non-possessive warmth, and honesty are essential attributes' (1989: 37). Do we need a new, or old, profession to remind us that empathy, warmth and honesty go a long way? Does this really justify research money? We surely do not need to prove that these qualities are more desirable, desired and helpful than being misunderstood, or treated coldly, or lied to, manipulated and deceived. What we do need is to show which professionals, using which therapeutic approaches, can achieve significantly more than amateurs do. Carol Sherrard (1991), for example, reviewed 41 studies comparing the effectiveness of professional with non-professional helpers.

Twenty-eight of these revealed no difference in outcome, 12 showed the non-professionals to be more effective, and only one study concluded that the professional group was more effective. In the teeth of this thoroughly disappointing evidence, Sherrard concluded that Masters-level training in counselling should be restricted to psychology graduates only!

Let us imagine a lobby of counsellors meeting a health, or education, minister or manager. There will be a series of predictable, essential questions that will need answering. I presume that the counsellors with their core values would, unlike other mortals, answer questions honestly and tell the truth, the whole truth and nothing but the truth with no dressing or spin of any kind.

Minister: What is counselling actually?

Counsellors: We're working on an answer to that. The word is used, abused and over-used in a wide variety of ways.

Minister: Is it the same as counselling psychology or psychotherapy?

Counsellors: These distinctions are essentially spurious. Counselling psychologists want to be paid more than counsellors but there is no evidence that their degree in psychology helps them to produce better results.

Minister: You want counselling to be made available on demand to all who need it? How much will that cost?

Counsellors: It will be expensive but we have made no costing.

Minister: How much demand will there be? How do you define 'need'?

Counsellors: The demand is likely to be more or less limitless. Everyone likes to receive time and attention and everyone seems to be too busy to provide it. We have not yet defined 'need'. Currently those who use it most and are most rewarding for counsellors are people who are young, attractive, verbal, intelligent and successful.

Minister: What kinds of counselling are best?

Counsellors: They mostly seem to be as good as each other. Psychoanalysis has the highest cost, status and training requirements and appears to perform least well. They are all generally better than nothing but we haven't shown them to be better than cheaper, amateur efforts with folk wisdom and common sense.

Minister: When you say 'better' or worse, what do you actually mean? For example, after couple counselling will a couple be more likely to stay together or separate? Who will decide what is best?

Counsellors: It is difficult. It depends. Clients may not know what is best; but counsellors might not be in a better position to judge, and often do not like, or believe in, making judgements.

Minister: What skills and theories are used?

Counsellors: They vary enormously. Counsellors will often do quite different things. Some very actively challenge client ideas and attitudes, some try to be completely non-judgemental. Human qualities seem to matter most, like warmth, empathy, genuineness.

Minister: So virtue matters more than skill. Can you actually train people to be virtuous?

Counsellors: Perhaps not. Priests and philosophers have spoken out against lies, aloofness and coldness for millennia. People do not always listen, and, when they do, they may not actually change their ways in practice.

Minister: Do counsellors practise cooperation, warmth and understanding more than others do?

Counsellors: We have no evidence, except that there are huge battles for power, status and a secure income going on at present among counsellors and trainers.

Minister: After training, can you ensure that trainees will deliver to the required standards?

Counsellors: Well, we have not managed to define the standard. There are huge variations between individual counsellors both before and after training. Often they do not do in practice what they claim to be doing and what they have been trained to do.

Minister: Are clients happy with the result?

Counsellors: Generally they very much like to receive time, and attention, from anyone who looks and sounds like an expert. They do not like to be abused, as happens rather often.

Minister: Does training make this happen less often?

Counsellors: The abuse seems to be worst among the most highly trained.[7]

Minister: How much training do they need?

Counsellors: We have a minimum of hours of theory, practice and supervision that trainees must complete before they can be accredited.

Minister: What particular theories and practices are best?

Counsellors: We do not know. Professional, 'umbrella', organizations have tried to avoid this question by concentrating on the necessary hours rather than the required content. This is the only way to avoid arguments between the competing theoreticians and practitioners. We don't want the public to lose confidence in us by seeing how divided we are about theories and skills.

Minister: So, for example, will astrology be accredited? There are 40,000 astrological counsellors in France. There has to be a free movement of labour within the European Union. Will astrologers be eligible for professional status if they have completed enough hours of supervised, accredited astrological theory and practice? What about the I Ching? Scientology? There are scores, hundreds, of different theories and practices. Who will you admit and exclude? How? Why?

Counsellors: These are difficult questions.

Minister: Have you got any answers? I need some answers if I am to act. Is there a core curriculum?

Counsellors: No, not yet, not at all.

Minister: Who are the 'big names' in counselling?

Counsellors: Fashions come and go. Freud was a huge authority for years. Freudians had the most training, the highest pay and status and, within the USA, the largest inclusion within the medical establishment. But much of what Freud said now looks very questionable. Different counsellors follow different gurus whose fortunes can rise and fall again very rapidly.

Minister: Can we assume that those currently in fashion will stay in vogue for long?

Counsellors: No, definitely not. Carl Rogers is still a big name, but his ideas have received a great deal of fundamental criticism recently. He has been accused of naïveté, innocence and is thought, by some, to be highly superficial.

Minister: When did counselling begin?

Counsellors: Some say in the 1950s, others the 1960s, some say with Freud, some think serious progress only really began at the University of Iowa in the 1980s.[8]

Minister: Surely you know that serious attempts to find, and cultivate, meaning, purpose, self-discipline, compassion and consolation were made before then? Have you no sense, or knowledge, of your own vast and rich cultural history? Can you demonstrate more progress and insight than earlier sages and artists? The liberal-humanist tradition began with the ancient Greeks. It has a long, chequered and sophisticated history. Are you aware of any of that? The Stoics predate Albert Ellis by 2,000 years. Epicurean exploration of humanist principles is equally ancient, and arguably more sophisticated than contemporary individualism.

Counsellors: We do not include much history or philosophy in our training, beyond the last generation or two, if at all.

Minister: Surely people have always employed many kinds of personal, social, cultural, spiritual and physical strategies to stay sane, survive, find meaning and direction? A wider availability of professional counselling might give people an excuse to take even less responsibility for helping themselves and each other. Our communities are decayed enough as it is. You just focus on individuals and bits of contemporary psychology. Is this not a rather narrow and shallow agenda?

Counsellors: Perhaps it is.

Minister: Yet you want me to write a blank cheque and provide you with a legally enforced licence so that you can all be employed within a middle-class lifestyle. Is this not rather hasty and premature? Perhaps you should come back later when you have got clearer answers to some of these important questions.

Counsellors: We will go away and think again. When shall we return?

Minister: Well, given how much you still have to do, I think another thousand years would be about right!

Maybe a hundred will be enough? Contemporary science has allowed huge advances to be made on earlier medical understanding. 'Social science' (so-called) is not doing so well in relation to earlier humanist efforts. The best novelists and artists still have far more subtle and sophisticated insights into human nature, its circumstances and dilemmas than our contemporary psychologists and counsellors, however chartered and accredited they try to be. Perhaps this will change. But change is not yet evident.

Certainly we all need, and like, care, attention, compassion, comfort. I do not need research evidence to tell me that these can be profoundly helpful and healing. The demand for such a 'virtue-package' is bottomless. The state budget is not. Perhaps we should try to listen to, comfort and help each other and ourselves as best we can, without waiting for a fee or a certificate? Perhaps our efforts to turn all these obvious virtues into saleable commodities and would-be professions, far from providing a solution to our current social and spiritual sickness, is just a part of our problem, our malaise, and our desperate efforts to find secure, paid employment?

Holmes and Lindley provide one, particularly negative, client view of one counsellor that is worth sharing:

> You middle-class bastard, you don't give a damn about me, sitting there with your well-paid job, your nice wife and kids, and comfortable home in the suburbs. What do the likes of you know about the way I live – in a damp room with no money, noisy neighbours, no job, walking the streets in the freezing cold? You're just doing your job, waiting to go home. You don't care about me one bit. (1989: 82)

This is strong stuff. I am sure that clients are generally more satisfied, and counsellors more sensitive. But, as a nation, we are short of cash for so many good causes, not least poor housing, low pay and unemployment and community decay. If we were to spend more humane amounts of time, energy and cash on these problems, how much would be left to deliver counselling services, even after the counsellors had answers to the questions raised above by your sceptical Minister of State?

Holmes and Lindley do not address this question, suggesting only that the money would have been better spent on counselling than on Trident submarines. Thus far, I might agree with them.[9] But no further, not now, yet. Not, I suspect, for quite some long time to come.

Notes

1. In my last book, *Challenges to Counselling and Psychotherapy* (Howard, 1996), the questions about therapy greatly outnumbered the available answers. In my newest, *Philosophy in Counselling and Psychotherapy* (Howard, 1999), I am attempting to redress this imbalance by summarizing what I think have been the most useful contributions from liberal-humanist philosophy from ancient Greece to the present.

2. How much of today's 'expertise' will be rejected, in one or two centuries from now, just as totally as we dismiss the claims of medieval magicians? It may not be a question that contemporary experts are keen to ask.

3. In this chapter I use the terms 'counselling' and 'psychotherapy' almost interchangeably since I am unconvinced that a worthwhile distinction can be made between them.

4. Perhaps that is why they are called 'professionals'? They *profess* to skill and insight more often, and more reliably, than they *provide* it.

5. It is worth remembering that the clients of all manner of fringe healers and cult leaders generally claim that: (a) they are happy with the service and (b) it has made them 'better'. If anything, there may be an *inverse* law: the more eccentric, crazy and charismatic the guru, the more enthusiastic and convinced are the disciples!

6. 'One hundred and fifty four comparisons from 39 studies indicated that clients who seek help from paraprofessionals are more likely to achieve resolution of their problems than those who consult professionals' (Hattie et al., 1984: 534–41). 'In general, there was no difference between the outcome of patients treated by trained and untrained persons' (Berman and Norton, 1985: 451–61). Both are cited in Bergin and Garfield (1994: 171).

7. As summarised by Michael Pokorny, Chair of the Registration Board for the United Kingdom Council for Psychotherapy at a British Association for Counselling conference workshop (1992).

8. See, for example, Duck (1988).

9. Though not even this is obvious. Nuclear weapons are cheaper than conventional alternatives. Without them World War III might well have begun during the 1950s or 1960s.

References

Bergin, A.E. and Garfield, S.L. (eds) (1994) *Handbook of Psychotherapy and Behavior Change*. 4th edn. New York: John Wiley.

Berman, J.S. and Norton, N.C. (1985) 'Does professional training make a therapist more effective?', *Psychological Bulletin*, 97: 451–61.

Duck, S. (1988) *Relating to Others*. Milton Keynes: Open University Press.

Hattie, J.A., Sharpley, C.F. and Rogers, H.F. (1984) 'Comparative effectiveness of professional and paraprofessional helpers', *Psychological Bulletin*, 95: 534–41.

Holmes, J. and Lindley, R. (1989) *The Values of Psychotherapy*. Oxford: Oxford University Press.

Howard, A. (1996) *Challenges to Counselling and Psychotherapy*. London: Macmillan.

Howard, A. (1999) *Philosophy in Counselling and Psychotherapy*. London: Macmillan.

Kennedy, I. (1983) *The Unmasking of Medicine*. London: Paladin.

Sherrard, C. (1991) 'The rise in demand for counselling'. Unpublished paper (Leeds University) presented to the British Psychological Society, Lincoln.

29 Psychotherapy as essential health care

Jeremy Holmes

Controversy is inherent in the nature of psychotherapy. Almost every advance, whether theoretical or empirical, has been met with backlash and repudiation. There are several reasons why this might be so. One is that psychotherapy inevitably contains moral as well as scientific assumptions about what constitutes a good life – for example that it is preferable to become aware of one's painful feelings rather than to suppress them – and morality is inherently contestable (Singer, 1979). Others argue that psychotherapy is a covert ideology, a modern opiate that diverts people from the real material causes of their unhappiness (Epstein, 1995), and that much of what psychotherapists believe is based not on science, but on professional self-interest (coinciding with that of the dominant class), and needs to be rebutted as part of a political struggle for liberation. Third, the Freudian view, commonly put forward by therapists themselves, is that opposition to psychotherapy is based on unconscious *resistance*. They argue that people are reluctant to concede how little the conscious mind is able to control our emotions and actions, and that there is a tendency to resist any theory which emphasizes the power of the unconscious.

Finally, even if psychotherapy *is* a valid and effective way of helping overcome psychological distress, there are genuine scientific debates about what kinds of therapy are most useful for what kinds of disorder, how training is best carried out, how professional standards should be maintained, and so on (Holmes and Lindley, 1998).

This chapter starts with a discussion of the evidence for and against the efficacy of psychotherapy. I go on to consider the move to establish psychotherapy as a profession, and finally explore what it might mean to have a 'right' to psychological help, and whether this is different in kind from help for physical illness.

By 'psychotherapy' and 'counselling' I mean the attempt to bring about psychological or emotional change by the systematic use of the relationship between therapist and patient/client. I make no clear distinction between counselling and psychotherapy, which I see as mainly a difference of quantity (counselling being briefer and less intense) rather than quality.

Does psychotherapy work?

A century of scientific medicine has seen the rise of 'evidence-based' treatment as the dominant ideology guiding practice and health investment for the twenty-first century. The gold standard is the randomized controlled trial, and with finite resources, publicly funded health care seeks increasingly only to support treatments of proven efficacy. The culture in which the psychoanalytic pioneers established modern psychotherapy was very different.

Psychotherapy has always relied on authority, anecdote, narrative and historical method to establish its theories and methods. To say that psychotherapy works because a particular patient got better after a course of it, or because Rogers or Klein or Winnicott said it does, carries a certain kind of conviction, but one very different to the stringent requirements of evidence-based medicine. Quacks and charlatans have always justified their nostrums on the basis of individual case histories or appeals to higher powers.

Psychotherapy is today subject to the same rigours which would be expected of any drug or technique purporting to ameliorate physical pain or unhappiness. Although this 'drug metaphor' (Shapiro, 1995) has its limitations, it has, over half a century, stimulated invaluable psychotherapy research. Much of this stems from Eysenck's (1952) claim that psychotherapy produced no better results than those which occur spontaneously in the course of a neurotic illness. He purported to show that about two-thirds of a group of patients treated with psychotherapy got better over a two-year period, but a similar proportion of untreated controls also improved in the same period. Therefore, he argued, psychotherapy is no more effective than 'real life' in helping people solve their difficulties.

Eysenck based his paper on other people's research, and reanalysis of the data (McNeilly and Howard, 1991) has established just how biased his interpretations were ('science' can be used to justify as well as dispel prejudice). It seems that in fact the treated patients improved much faster than the untreated group – eight weeks into therapy 50 per cent were already better as compared with 2 per cent of controls. Even though by the end of two years the untreated group had more or less caught up, there were undoubted benefits to therapy.

Following Eysenck, determined efforts were made to subject psychotherapy to controlled trials. A statistically new method of investigation was created, 'meta-analysis', which amalgamates the results of many different trials and compares the average improvement of the treated patients with that of controls (a methodology which has passed into general use within medicine). This produces an 'effect size', a number which quantifies the impact of any given treatment. The well-known meta-analytic study of Smith et al. (1980) concluded that there were 'consistent, positive and large effects of verbal psychotherapy compared with placebo treatment'. The average effect size for psychotherapy is around one standard deviation, which means that the average psychotherapy patient is, after treatment, significantly better off than 85 per cent of control subjects.

By the 1980s the efficacy of psychotherapy was firmly established, but many unanswered questions remained, stimulating a new era of psychotherapy research, which continues today. One consistent negative finding has been the apparent lack of differential effects of different types of therapy. The 'narcissism of minor differences' (Freud's phrase) means that people passionately espouse their own particular variety of therapy, whether it be Jungian or Kleinian analysis, cognitive therapy or structural family therapy, yet psychotherapy research has, on the whole, not been able to show that any one treatment is more successful overall than any other (Luborsky et al., 1986).

This 'Dodo-bird verdict' – namely that 'everyone has won and all shall have prizes' – seems to contradict the clinical impression that matching patient and problem to therapist and therapeutic model is in reality very important. As clinicians we are constantly trying to find the 'right' therapist who has the right personality and technique to help the patient. Psychotherapy assessment and brokerage of this sort is seen as vital, especially in publicly funded therapy, where resources are limited and need to be used as efficiently as possible.

A major research problem flows from the fact that what we call 'psychotherapy' is a multifaceted mixture of different components which include the therapist's personality, basic technique and capacity to engage with the patient, as well as any specific therapeutic models he or she may happen to use. It is necessary to standardize ('manualize') and where possible isolate the active ingredients in any particular psychotherapy package before we can be confident about 'what works for whom' (Roth and Fonagy, 1996), and yet such procedures seem inimical to the holistic nature of therapy.

Despite the difficulties of this sort of research, a number of salient findings stand out. First, there is a 'dose-effect' in psychotherapy (Orlinsky et al., 1994) – in general, the longer the treatment, the greater the benefit. However the dose-response curve is a negative logarithmic one, so that there are diminishing returns as therapy progresses. By session 27 three-quarters of the total gain has been achieved. It is important to note, however, that these are summed findings from many different kinds of study, often involving only moderately neurotic university students, and with an emphasis on behavioural treatments whose outcomes are easier to quantify.

Second, there are demonstrable links between severity of disturbance in the patient, and the length of treatment needed to bring about change. For example, Shapiro (1995) and his colleagues, comparing a 16-session and an 8-session treatment for mild–moderate depression, have shown that where symptoms were mild the outcome was roughly the same with either length, but the more disturbed patients needed longer therapy if they were to recover. Level of patient disturbance has, third, also been shown to interact with the type of therapy and outcome. Horowitz et al. (1984) compared outcome following abnormal grief reactions with two different types of therapy, supportive and expressive. Patients using more 'primitive' defences, such as splitting and projection, did better with supportive therapy, while the more mature patients fared best with the expressive approach.

Another consistent, although hard-won finding has been the demonstration of a relationship between therapist skill and experience and outcome. With only moderately disturbed patients inexperienced therapists seem to do as well as their mentors, but with more disturbed patients experience counts, especially in engaging difficult patients in therapy and reducing drop-out (Rounsaville et al., 1988).

There is a growing literature looking at the effects of particular types of psychotherapy in specific psychiatric conditions. For example, both cognitive-behavioural therapy and interpersonal therapy are effective in depression (Elkin et al., 1989), and are probably as effective as anti-depressant drugs in all but the most severe cases. Furthermore, continuing intermittent therapy sessions appears to delay relapse even after the symptoms of depression have lifted (Kupfer et al., 1992). Family therapy and cognitive-behavioural therapy have an important part to play in the treatment of psychotic illnesses such as schizophrenia, in preventing relapse and reducing the intensity of delusions (Garety et al., 1994). Conversely, classical psychoanalysis is probably ineffective, and may even induce relapse (Goldstein, 1991). Specific therapy programmes for eating disorders are also effective, especially in bulimia (Hartmann et al., 1992).

The research evidence from primary care is somewhat contradictory. Some studies have failed to show any benefit of counselling compared with 'routine care' as normally provided by the patient's general practitioner (Friedli et al., 1997); others have shown reductions in psychotropic drug prescribing, frequency of surgery attendance and improved symptomatology. On the whole, patients prefer 'talking' to 'prescribing' (Friedli et al., 1997), although the evidence is that for depression the combination of drugs and therapy together is more effective than either alone (Blackburn et al., 1981). The balance of evidence suggests that focused, problem-solving approaches are more likely to produce benefit than unstructured psychological interventions (Tylee, 1997).

This brief survey of the research evidence takes us some way towards answering some of the questions posed at the start of the chapter. We can confidently assert that wholesale dismissal of psychotherapy (Masson, 1990; Webster, 1996) is nowadays untenable, and can only be based on prejudice rather than facts. There is overwhelming evidence that, under the right conditions, with well-selected patients and properly trained therapists, using techniques appropriate to the presenting problem, therapy can produce both immediate symptom relief and valuable long-term benefits such as improved social adjustment and prevention of relapse.

There are, however, many areas in which psychotherapy and counselling remain open to serious challenge. First, the evidence supporting structured, goal-oriented, time-limited therapies is much stronger than that for longer-

term analytic therapy. This is not to say that psychoanalysis is not beneficial: there is weak evidence suggesting that it is (Bateman and Holmes
1995), and the methodological problems inherent in evaluating it are much
greater than for less complex forms of treatment. But a major research
challenge exists here.

Second, the fact that a proportion of the benefit of therapy seems to be
based on 'non-specific' factors suggests, as implied in the opening controversial statement, that 'lesser' forms of counselling such as befriending,
self-help groups, bibliotherapy (that is, self-improvement based on written
material), and measures to reduce social stress are also likely to help people
feel better and more able to tackle their problems. Some proponents of
these methods even claim that they are superior to formal psychotherapy in
that they empower people rather than foster dependence, although there is
no hard evidence to support this view.

Third, one of the stubborn facts of psychotherapy research is the finding
that 'client factors' are consistently better predictors of outcome than are
factors relating to the therapy/ist – in other words, very ill patients do not
do particularly well with any sort of therapy, and motivation is a crucial
determinant of outcome.

All this suggests that *selection* for psychotherapy is vital. Therapy is
certainly not a panacea that should be available for all psychological ills.
Those most likely to benefit are a middling range of patients with moderately severe illnesses, who nevertheless manage to cope to some extent with
their lives, and who are also well motivated for change. Some of those who
are very ill can improve with therapy (usually as part of a package of
treatment which includes other input such as psychotropic drugs and
milieu therapy); they require skilful engagement if they are to benefit at all,
and some will not. People whose problems are relatively minor will probably improve whatever therapy is applied and may do as well with 'peer
support' as formal therapy.

Given the problematic nature of uncritically applied therapy, it might
seem that the recent moves towards the professionalization of psychotherapy are to be welcomed. However, as we shall see, that too is not without
its worrying aspect.

Psychotherapy as a profession

With some notable exceptions, the psychotherapeutic pioneers were all
members of established professions such as medicine, psychiatry, psychology or social work. Their ethical codes and working practices derived
from their parent disciplines. Contemporary psychotherapy looks very
different. Today many people train as counsellors or therapists with relatively little background in the helping professions. Psychotherapy is
emerging as a discipline in its own right, with its own set of ethical pitfalls
and training requirements. Although predominantly still based in the

private sector, counsellors and therapists are increasingly working in public settings such as general practice, mental health units and industry. Public funding rightly demands public standards of practice and probity.

The United Kingdom Council for Psychotherapy (UKCP) is an umbrella organization set up to regulate the training, standards of practice and ethical behaviour of its member psychotherapy organizations. It is partly modelled on the regulatory body for medicine, the General Medical Council, and its long-term aim is statutory legislation which would sanction psychotherapy practitioners in the same way that doctors are licensed. The aims of the UKCP are laudable, and already it is undoubtedly doing a good job in protecting the public from unscrupulous or exploitative practitioners.

But professionalization has its drawbacks. A profession is necessarily self-serving, and the existence of the UKCP is no guarantee that, for example, vulnerable members of the public will not be encouraged to undertake lengthy and often costly courses of treatment without definite benefit. Although the UKCP is respectful of research, its structure and functioning if firmly rooted in the idea of *modalities* of treatment – analytic, integrative, systemic, and so on – rather than in generic therapies geared to particular disorders. Also, as with any young organization, there are mutual hostilities between different branches, each of which claims to hold the most valid form of treatment. This has led to the formation of a rival body, the British Confederation of Psychotherapists (BCP), comprising therapies based around intense psychoanalytic training.

The government is rightly suspicious of a would-be profession which is unable to collaborate effectively, and the chances of regulatory legislation are currently not high. What regulation there is in the profession is generally self-regulation. The College of Psychiatrists and the British Psychological Society each have registers of their members who have had special training in psychotherapy, and they are of course subject to the strictures of their parent disciplines, which in the case of psychiatrists is statutory by virtue of the fact that psychiatrists are medical doctors. The British Association for Counselling similarly attempts to ensure that accredited counsellors have had reputable and reasonably extensive training.

In conclusion, people seeking treatment from a UKCP- or BCP-registered practitioner can perhaps be assured that their therapist will have had a reputable training within its own terms, and that he or she is subject to an ethical code with built-in sanctions, but could still not be certain that the therapy they were offered was 'evidence-based' or necessarily the most appropriate for their particular problem.

A 'right of citizens to mental health support'?

The question of rights is complex and contentious (Dworkin, 1977). Two basic rights are usually discussed: the right to well-being, and the right to freedom. Jeremy Bentham famously described the French Revolutionary claim that there were natural and unrevisable (that is, unalterable) rights as 'nonsense upon stilts' (Honderich, 1995). Rights have to be seen in a social and historical context. The rights of individuals have to be weighed against the needs of the community as a whole. Rights are closely related to equity. Thus the principle of the National Health Service is that all citizens should have equal access to the best possible health care irrespective of income or geography.

The question of the right to psychotherapy is problematic for two reasons, according to which of the two basic rights is being considered. The first, concerning the right to well-being, is pragmatic and quasi-political. The principle of equity in the NHS means that, given limited resources, there is competition between different branches of medicine for which should take priority. If people have a right to health and well-being, then there is clearly a hierarchy from physical survival through absence of handicap to psychological health and happiness. Faced with a choice between an investment which would save life and one which would merely improve well-being, most people would give precedence to the life-saving measure.

This has meant that in the struggle for resources in the NHS, psychiatric care, and psychotherapy in particular, has tended to be pushed to the back of the queue. If, as some have argued, the only aim of therapy were the enhancement of autonomy (Szasz, 1969) and freedom, this might be acceptable. But, as the research mentioned above suggests, psychotherapy can itself save life, for example by helping a suicidally depressed patient to feel better. Similarly therapy can help alleviate the effects of disability, for instance in working with the delusions of patients suffering from schizophrenia.

Thus it can be argued that if people have a right to health, then they have a right to psychotherapy in so far as psychotherapy can promote health, both physical and mental. This is the strong case for the right to psychotherapy (Holmes and Lindley, 1998).

But psychotherapy also aims to promote people's well-being – their ability to flourish and to lead a more satisfying life. Clearly the distinction between this right and the right to health is not absolute – ill-health is in itself a powerful impediment to flourishing. Nevertheless, these two aspects of therapy can be separated. Many people seek psychotherapy who are not ill in any meaningful sense. They are troubled, unhappy, stuck, miserable, unable to move forward or to form satisfying intimate relationships – but not sick. Help with these problems is legitimate, and it is inequitable that those who are able to pay can get psychotherapeutic assistance, while those who are poor can't.

But, unlike in the case of illness, psychotherapy is certainly not the *only* way to achieve such goals – joining an evening class, taking up a new interest or sport, learning to dance or play a musical instrument, even joining a dating agency may equally help. So may improvements in material conditions such as housing, reducing noise and providing places for children to play safely and creatively.

Here we can only argue that people have a right to a *range* of opportunities to help enhance their freedom, of which psychotherapy is an important component. Therapists argue that the changes *they* can bring about are more profound than the necessarily superficial impact of the alternatives mentioned, and that, for example, someone with recurrent relationship difficulties is likely merely to repeat them via a dating agency, unless he or she has first undergone the maturational process of psychotherapy. So there is a case here – albeit weaker than the right to well-being – also for the right to psychotherapy as part, possibly one of the most significant parts, of a pluralistic range of freedom-enhancing opportunities.

Conclusion

In conclusion, the increase in psychotherapy within society is to be welcomed. Therapy provides a unique opportunity to overcome certain forms of psychological and physical ill-health, and, alongside other means, can also increase people's sense of freedom and well-being. Public recognition of the values of psychotherapy has been slow in coming. This volume is a good example for much-needed debate. Work needs to be done to reinforce psychotherapy's research base; to sift the helpful from the less useful aspects of therapy; and to strengthen the assessment and brokerage needed if the right kind of therapy is to be offered to prospective clients. The professionalization of therapy still has a long way to go before it can legitimately claim to put the needs of patients first. Humility, balance, and constructive scepticism are needed – the very values which therapy might itself hope to instil.

References

Bateman, A. and Holmes, J. (1995) *Introduction to Psychoanalysis: Contemporary Theory and Practice*. London: Routledge.

Blackburn, I., Bishop, S. and Glen, A. (1981) 'The efficacy of cognitive therapy in depression: a treatment using cognitive therapy and pharmacotherapy, each alone and in combination', *British Journal of Psychiatry*, 139: 181–9.

Dworkin, R. (1977) *Taking Rights Seriously*. Cambridge: Cambridge University Press.

Elkin, I., Shea, M.T., Watkins, J.T., Imber, S.D., Sotsky, S.M., Collins, J.F., Glass, D.R., Pilkonis, P.A., Leber, W.R., Docherty, J.P., Fiester, S.J. and Parloff, M.B. (1989) 'National Institute of Mental Health Treatment of Depression Collaborative Program: general effectiveness of treatments', *Archives of General Psychiatry*, 46: 971–82.

Epstein, W.M. (1995) *The Illusion of Psychotherapy*. New Brunswick, NJ: Transaction Publishers.

Eysenck, H. (1952) 'The effects of psychotherapy: an evaluation', *Journal of Consulting Psychology*, 16: 319–24.

Friedli, K., King, M., Lloyd, M. and Horder, J. (1997) 'Randomised controlled assessment of non-directive psychotherapy versus routine general-practitioner care', *Lancet*, 350: 1662–5.

Garety, P., Kuipers, L. and Fowler, D. (1994) 'Cognitive behavioural therapy for drug-resistant psychosis', *British Journal of Psychiatry*, 67: 259–71.

Goldstein, M. (1991) 'Psychosocial (nonpharmacological) treatments for schizophrenia', *Review of Psychiatry*, 10: 439–78.

Hartmann, A., Herzog, T. and Drinkman, A. (1992) 'Psychotherapy of bulimia nervosa: what is effective? A meta-analysis', *Journal of Psychosomatic Research*, 2: 159–67.

Holmes, J. and Lindley, R. (1998) *The Values of Psychotherapy*. 2nd edn. London: Karnac.

Honderich, T. (ed.) (1995) *The Oxford Companion to Philosophy*. Oxford: Oxford University Press.

Horowitz, M., Marmar, J. and Weiss, D. (1984) 'Brief psychotherapy of bereavement reactions: the relationship of process to outcome', *Archives of General Psychiatry*, 41: 438–48.

Kupfer, D., Frank, E. and Perel, J. (1992) 'Five year outcome for maintenance therapies in recurrent depression', *Archives of General Psychiatry*, 49: 769–73.

Luborsky, L., Crits-Christoph, P. and McLellan, R. (1986) 'Do therapists vary much in their success? Findings from four outcome studies', *American Journal of Orthopsychiatry*, 51: 501–12.

Masson, J.M. (1990) *Against Therapy: Emotional Tyranny and the Myth of Psychological Healing*. London: Fontana.

McNeilly, C. and Howard, K. (1991) 'The effects of psychotherapy: a re-evaluation based on dosage', *Psychotherapy Research*, 1: 74–8.

Orlinsky, D., Grawe, K. and Parks, B. (1994) 'Process and outcome in psychotherapy', in A.E. Bergin and S.L. Garfield (eds), *Handbook of Psychotherapy and Behavior Change*. 4th edn. Chichester: John Wiley.

Roth, A. and Fonagy, P. (1996) *What Works for Whom? A Critical Review of Psychotherapy Research*. New York: Guilford.

Rounsaville, B., O'Malley, S., Foley, S. and Weissman, M. (1988) 'Role of manual guided training in the conduct and efficacy of interpersonal therapy for depression', *Journal of Consulting and Clinical Psychology*, 56: 681–8.

Shapiro, D. (1995) 'Finding out how psychotherapies help people change', *Psychotherapy Research*, 5: 1–21.

Singer, P. (1979) *Practical Ethics*. Cambridge: Cambridge University Press.

Smith, M., Glass, G. and Miller, T. (1980) *The Benefits of Psychotherapy*. Baltimore, MD: Johns Hopkins University Press.

Szasz, T. (1969) *The Ethics of Psychoanalysis*. New York: Dell.

Tylee, A. (1997) 'Counselling in primary care', *Lancet*, 350: 1643.

Webster, R. (1996) *Why Freud was Wrong*. London: Fontana.

Mind at the end of its tether

Fay Weldon

Once there was religion, then there was science, then there was Marxism: now we have therapy, which, in its wider political and social context outside the consulting room, I shall call Therapism. Our belief structures rise and fall with the centuries. We feel safe serving, whether it's God, knowledge, patterns of history – obsessions which overlap but seldom coincide – but now turn inwards to serve the inner self. I give Therapism perhaps another fifty years before our brave new caring society collapses under the weight of its own by-product, an excess of empathy – as shatteringly and suddenly, no doubt, as did the Berlin Wall, leaving the human race to find itself some new wheeze in its quest for purpose. What next, once self-understanding fails to bring about heaven on earth? We'll think of something. The human race is ingenious in its search for explanations and solutions.

In the meantime, Therapism offers a new idea of what people are, one which denies God, denies morality and is value-free; Therapism replaces the old doctrine of original sin, that notion that we were born flawed but must struggle for improvement, with the idea that we were all born perfect, bright, happy and good, and if we are not, why then someone or something – harsh circumstances, faulty parenting or personal trauma – is to blame. Freud's concept of the superego, the controlling conscience which accompanies the id on all its errant voyaging, seems now an unnecessary concession to the old religious ways: even this has drifted from our thinking. Jung wins, okay!

It is a cheerful enough doctrine, this Therapism, but it is also a dangerous one, if in believing that the original bliss of being can be regained by kindness and talk, we also believe that society can be left to get on with itself. It can't.

In the world of extreme Therapism the physiological is denied, and genetic determinism ignored: the psyche is all. To suggest that the human condition is incurable, that discontent is endemic to the species, that not feeling properly loved is inevitable – inasmuch as it takes two to make a third, and we all know two's company and three's none, so how can any of us be truly satisfied as parent or child? – is the equivalent in Therapism to the Pelagian heresy. To suggest that Nature did not create us to be happy, but simply to survive long enough to procreate, that discontent is endemic to the species, is pretty much the Manichean heresy under a new name, and the response the same. Burn the wrong-thinkers alive!

Otherwise Therapism is a kindly and hopeful doctrine, espoused by the nicest and most intelligent of people, and on that very account the harder to refute. See the extremes of Therapism in, say, the happy idea that the fat aren't greedy or genetically doomed; no, eating disorders are caused by abusive fathers. See it in the idea that – as in Erewhon – criminals are mentally sick (and conversely, as in AIDS, that the sick are criminals); that depression is a curable disorder not a natural response to circumstances; that schizophrenia is caused by schizophrenogenic mothers – always the mothers, God bless 'em. That, solipsistically, we do better to fit ourselves to the world than the world to ourselves. In the refusal to acknowledge that the paedophile and the rapist are merely dwellers at the extreme end of the bell curve of sexual inclination, and in the insistence that they are 'curable' by talk: let the world be what we'd like it to be, not what it is. Hit on the head? Burgled? That wasn't *real* – that was trauma in the head. The police run a victim's support group – that being a cheaper and simpler solution than employing more policemen, let alone changing the society which produces the crime. The NSPCC now asks for money not to rescue, feed or save children at home or abroad, but to 'counsel' them.

Therapism suits governments, is cheaper than change, and stops people rioting in the streets. The energy of thought is turned inwards, not outwards; too many are too busy coming to terms with their true selves to have time left over for judgemental thoughts about society. In Texas today, those who can convince a counsellor they are in touch with their inner child are allowed to carry concealed weapons. Make of that what you can. The reversal is complete. The inner child, the tumultuous id, becomes the saving grace; it's the controlling superego becomes the murderer.

Therapism demands an emotional correctness from us – we must prefer peace to war, tranquillity to stress, express our anger, share our woes, love our children (though not necessarily our parents) and sacrifice our own contentment to theirs, ban guns, refrain from smoking, give voice to our low opinion of men (if we are women), refrain from giving voice to our low opinion of women (if we are men) and agree with one another that we were all born perfect, bright, happy and free and, what is more, equal. We produce our own inner Prozac: how we smile and drift, while enemies hammer at the gate.

Therapism murmurs in our ear that certain research should not be done in case it reports things we do not want to know: that, say, the reason men get more first class degrees than women is not that examiners are biased against women, but that when it comes to intelligence the bell curve of distribution flattens for men, so there are more very bright (*and* con-comitantly more very stupid – no, forbidden word: more less mentally-able) men around than there are women, and that these men on the outskirts of normality tend to end up in Oxford taking degrees and getting Firsts. Don't even think about it. Easier just to conclude women are victims and discriminated against. I see today research coming out of Sweden to suggest that those of us who go to the opera and enjoy cultural pursuits live longer than those who don't. Research acknowledges, but only as an afterthought, that income may have something to do with it. It is not fashionable to say, simply 'the rich live longer'; though it is observably true. One of the truisms of the New Age, the New Therapism, is that money doesn't make you happy or healthy: 'love' does.

In the age of Therapism it is assumed that we have reached the pinnacle of wisdom, and that there is nothing more to be learned, just some things to be unlearned, and that if facts are unpalatable it is better to disregard them. In this climate it is difficult for social and educational policies to be effective since they are based on wishful thinking rather than on what actually goes on. The government must test seven year olds and rate schools as if all seven year olds were equal in intelligence: the fall-back position being that, yes, true, some children may be socially disadvantaged and so don't do as well as others – background will be blamed, or uneducated parents, or bad teachers; but the fact that children are born within a wide range of intelligence will be ignored. The word 'intelligence' must be used cautiously: there is something here that smacks of unfairness; of things inherited rather than merited, of a problem that cannot be cured. In the age of Therapism-out-of-Marxism all of us are equal – in the age of Therapism-out-of-Science all folk are curable. In the age of Therapism-out-of-Religion love is all you need.

Psychoanalysts are the new popes: psychotherapists the new priests and counsellors, the lay workers of this dangerous religion of Therapism. I exempt psychiatrists and psychologists since they belong to a different genus: they have come down to us through the medical line, their aim is to heal the body; they see the mind as a physiological entity called 'the brain'. Snip that synapse, change that dose! In the eighteenth century the College of Physicians and the College of Lawyers argued over which of them should claim the mad as their particular areas of concern. In those days insanity presented itself as a legal problem as much as a medical one, to do with an incapacity to make or honour contracts, rather than as a falling-away from a physical, albeit mental, norm. (Some people are just like that.) But the doctors won the argument, and since doctors 'cure', they have been trying to 'cure' the mad ever since. And though with modern medicines symptoms can be subdued, behaviour moderated and distress relieved, 'cure' remains elusive. Some people just go on not knowing how to behave. If they were dangerous we kept them locked away and as happy as we could, according to the standards of the time: now we try to 'cure' them, make them live as we do, and they are wretched and fill the prisons.

A cure by means of talk also remains elusive; unprovable. That is not to say that the conversations are not profoundly interesting: they are, to all concerned. This is not to say that an inspiring body of work has not been built up in relation to the way the human mind works. Of course it has.

Our lives are illuminated and enriched by the ideas of Freud, Jung, Klein, Adler, Eric Berne, among others. Of course. Of course. Some patients report 'cure', though I suspect them of being the ones who end up in love with their therapist. A positive transference, in other words. Some patients report failure, but tend to be the ones who enjoy victim status and have no intention of relinquishing it. Far too many brave and lonely women living desperate lives come up to me and say 'but it was my therapist gave me the courage to leave my husband'. And others – well, after two hours on a British Airways counselling course to cure fear of flying, most reported greatly increased fear, not less. Make of that what you will.

Anyone can set up in their own front room as a psychotherapist – and the length and structure of their training probably has very little to do with the degree of their insight or their ability to influence others or cheer them up. I am not going to posit here the desirability of registration, let alone declarations of ethics as a solution to the anyone-can-join problem. Anyone can set up a register: anyone can pull down some terminology from the sky and assemble a collection of pious ethical statements. While sanctions remain unenforceable, while the occupation of healing others by talk remains *not* a chartered profession, such as the psychiatrists and psychologists enjoy, letters after the name and noble talk and earnest dedication mean nothing.

Rather see the practising psychotherapist as narrator, and 'good' or 'bad' as writers are seen to be. Many, I suspect, are indeed thwarted novelists. The patient comes into the room and delivers a halting, unprofessional, emotional, inexact narrative of their life to date. Boldly and professionally the psychotherapist rewrites this narrative, giving it a proper beginning and middle, sharpening the plot points, interpreting the tale according to professional training or his or her own obsessions, whichever is most powerful, and directs the story towards a desired end. Change the therapist and you change the narrative. But perhaps any will do. The therapist validates the client's right to be the central character in the drama; absolves the client from guilt, denying 'ought', gratifying 'want'. (Satisfying, at least temporarily, to the client, though probably not to spouse, family, friends or colleagues, those who constituted the 'family' pre-therapy.) The psychotherapist undertakes to draw the narrative to the right conclusion in due course, at so many pounds the chapter. 'It will take us six months to work through this' or 'This will be two years' hard work on both our parts.' A living novel to be written of so many words, long or short, as dictated by the decision of the publisher! If the psychotherapist is writing in a certain genre, sexual abuse by the father always makes for a dramatic, satisfying and lucrative resolution. But the genre is rather less acceptable than it was.

In the heyday of religion we had a Father God, whose good work was being spoiled by witches: now we have Mother Nature as the benign creator whose work is being spoiled by abusive fathers. Well, men's turn, I suppose. Confession was the mainstay of the Catholic Church; it seems to be in our natures to need to confide in others the sins which bother us; we want to be granted absolution, and pay a price (once Hail Marys said, now money handed over), and forget them. Finite, like a one-off TV drama. Begin again. And why not? Therapy is our contemporary version of confession: the non-stop soap opera of the soul. Except that in the New Confession it's not what you did to others but what they did to you that must be so mulled over. The therapist offers absolution in the same way as did the medieval pardoner. Mind you, the pardoner was at the sleazy end of the clerical profession. Licensed by a corrupt Pope, he was entitled to offer you time off purgatory; your sin could be purged by a money payment. 'What, left your children? Oh dear! Well, cheer up. That's normally five years in purgatory before you can go off to heaven, but give me a couple of guineas now and God will let you off with three years. I have his assurance of that.' The modern equivalent is 'What, left your children? Oh dear! fifteen hundred pounds – say fifty sessions at £30 a go – and I'm in a position to relieve you of guilt and sorrow.' If happiness and peace of mind is on offer, we pay up, as then. So little changes. We all need someone to talk to.

Only now (thanks partly, I suspect, to Therapism, and our growing worship of 'aloneness' and 'independence', and our growing disinclination to put up with one another, and our habit of blaming others for our own discontent) 28 per cent of us live in single-person households. We are worse off than we were in the old days: there is often no-one to talk to; no friends, no priest to hear confession, and a doctor who can give us only seven grudging minutes of his or her time. So we take ourselves off to the therapist, the Pardoner, and pay, humiliatingly, to be listened to and shrived. No longer a miserable sinner, just someone seeking the validation of his or her own conduct, searching for the authenticity of his or her emotion, in the name of which all things will be forgiven. Even leaving the children, in the search for the hidden self.

There was a time, of course there was, when I saw psychoanalysis, psychotherapy, as the way forward for humanity. A group therapy on every street corner! That was in the fifties, sixties. Psychotherapy was then indeed a subversive force for change, working away on the edges of a stubborn, reactionary, militaristic, punitive, patriarchal society. It was everything that was progressive, radical; therapy stood for change, understanding, for personal and social advance. But it just isn't like that any more. Psychotherapy, like feminism, has been absorbed into the mainstream, has become a tool of the establishment, part of the establishment. This of course is the fate of all revolutionary movements. Revolution works away hidden for years, then seizes power, becomes that power, is in itself the new reactionary force, and has to be resisted. The wheel turns; the truth, as Ibsen remarks in *An Enemy of the People*, in the end becomes the lie.

I had a moment of insight in relation to psychotherapy: a revelation, an anti-conversion experience. Let me share it with you. You know the archetypal haunted house? The castle of the demon lover? Where the witch lives? On top of the hill, mean and craggy against a windswept skyline? Every now and then the attic windows open, and flocks of black bats, like demons, shrieking, stream out across a stormy sky to do all manner of ill. You see it in *The Wizard of Oz*, you see it in *The Addams Family*: it's in our fairy tales, it's in our psyche. The archetype. Thank you, Jung. I acknowledge the debt.

Well, there I was, a couple of years back, in this perfectly pleasant house upon a hill in North London: headquarters of a very respectable association of Jungian psychotherapists, addressing a gathering of their literary society. They wanted to know – or said they did – what was 'the function of the archetype' in my novels. 'You tell me,' I said, 'What do I know?' – and this they agreed to do. Now this very large house, I observed, was a hive of industry, full of busy, soft-voiced people brimming over with good intent, and every room had some kind of training course or other going on inside it, with an official certificate at the end of it – courses either for individual psychotherapists or for probation officers, stress counsellors, policemen, magistrates and the like – here indeed was a seminary of Therapism, a hot-house for the creation of the new priests and priestesses. Money was changing hands like no-one's business – these courses are not cheap – and every now and then the front door opened and a stream of the therapeutically certified poured out into the world to spread their talking cure abroad – and suddenly where once I would have seen soft-voiced angels of mercy, now I saw demons. I saw a business, not a healing profession.

After the talk we all went out to a Chinese meal, and there, when the guard of my hosts was down, I listened while clients were freely named, individual cases were discussed – 'So and so must leave her husband; he's a horror.' 'Yes, I know him: he's a frightful bully – after the same job as me, actually' – and all manner of confidences were revealed: all at the level of simple, smug and cynical gossip. Not even the rules of the old confessional applied. And someone turned to me as I protested against this unpicking of family life, and said, 'Oh, we don't talk about "loneliness", we talk about "aloneness".' That was when the angels, for me, turned to demons, the doves to vampire bats. I saw a hapless population put its trust where no trust should or could be. I saw language taking over from experience, and distorting it. I saw a dangerous doctrine spreading: I saw Therapism in the making.

Yet why should therapists be better than the rest of us? Any more than priests have proved to be? We are all so gullible, and love to trust. *Nostra culpa.*

By all means let the intelligent help the not-so-bright, let the informed pass on their knowledge to the uninformed, the competent guide the incompetent, the middle class help the underclass out of the black pit of incomprehension. *'If you hit your wife, of course she'll give you a hard time.' 'What, doesn't she like it? No? Oh, I hadn't thought of that. I'll stop hitting her.'* Of course those who know should help those who don't, and always have, and of course it will 'work'. Call it 'cognitive therapy' if you like, because in the age of Therapism even the word 'guidance' is suspect, and the idea that someone might know more than anyone else, other than by 'training' which is open to anyone on equal terms, isn't quite on.

Look at it like this. At the turn of the century when Freud and Jung acted as midwives at the birth of psychoanalysis, their baby was born into a room of Stygian black. We knew nothing, nothing, about ourselves. To help us we had the merest glimmer of light, produced over past centuries by poets, playwrights, novelists; just enough to help the baby into being. But the glimmer grew into a brilliance, and thereby changed the world, as much as ever did Jesus, Darwin, Marx. But now it's so bright it could blind you.

I heard a story ten years ago: in 1938 eight psychoanalysts fled Hitler's Germany and set sail for Australia and safety. The ship was diverted to New York, the psychoanalysts were obliged to disembark there, and that's why New York is what it is, and Sydney what it is. One subtle and alive with self-knowing, the other energetic but blind. That story is outdated now: Sydney catches up with New York. The arcane knowledge which was once the preserve of psychoanalysts is arcane no longer. It is everywhere. Insights and opinions pile on top of one another, battling for space. A soupçon of *Women Who Love Too Much*, a dollop of *I'm Okay, You're Okay*, a shot of *The Cinderella Complex*, of Freud's *Interpretation of Dreams*, of the 15 volumes of the *Complete Works of Jung*, and the brew's just fine. (An owl flew in my window and left its droppings as it flew on every single Jung volume – what are we to make of that?) Find the new knowledge in every magazine, on the Oprah Winfrey show, in the pop-therapist, on the radio show, the agony aunt; in the rows upon rows of self-help books on the bookshop shelves. But on the whole it is still the bright leading the not-so-bright, the cheerful cheering up the sad, the ingenious leading the plodders, in the new world order Freud and Jung created (and don't forget Adler): which in time, I fear, will collapse under the weight of its unthought of and unpredicted by-product, that is to say, an excess of empathy combined with a belief that language and reality are the same thing. Talk doesn't pay the rent. Understanding is no substitute for benefits. Fine words, as we have always known, butter no parsnips.

31 Counselling and psychotherapy as enabling and empowering

Sheelagh Strawbridge

My brief is to defend psychotherapy and counselling as 'empowering and enabling activities and more often than not as positively assisting clients to become more autonomous'. In my view there are too many variables for it to be possible to know whether these activities are *more often than not* empowering and enabling, but I do think some light can be thrown upon *what it is* in effective counselling and psychotherapy that is empowering and enabling. In order to do this it will be necessary to explore the nature of counselling and psychotherapy and empowerment and the ways in which they can be linked.

Counselling and psychotherapy

Debates about the similarities and differences between counselling and psychotherapy are seemingly endless. However, I do not believe that, from the point of view of practice, a useful distinction can be made (see, for example, O'Brien, 1996). Whether or not we call ourselves psychotherapists, counsellors or counselling psychologists depends largely on the professional body through which we have gained accreditation and does not imply, for example, long- or short-term work or a particular therapeutic model. Like many people working in the field of counselling and psychotherapy, I have built up a portfolio of training and experience over a number of years. With the development of more formal routes to accreditation, my decision to pursue that of the British Psychological Society (BPS) and become a 'Chartered Counselling Psychologist' was more to do with being a psychology graduate and having a sense of a 'professional home' in the BPS than my specifically therapeutic training and experience. Some colleagues chose the British Association for Counselling and United Kingdom Council for Psychotherapy routes, whilst others have remained independent of professional bodies, some taking a principled stand against formal accreditation.

Debates about difference highlight issues about power and status rather than approaches to practice. In this context, Windy Dryden's (1996) comment that the difference between counselling and psychotherapy is about £8,000 per year is a telling one which emphasizes the political aspects of the process of professionalization, associated with power in relation to both clients and other professions. A particular aspect of this process relevant to the current controversy is the higher status of practices termed 'psychotherapy' over those termed 'counselling', and the sometimes uneasy association of the former with the medical profession. The lower status of practices termed 'counselling' has something to do with their non-medical and even popular and self-help associations.

A working definition

Definitions of counselling and psychotherapy are always from particular perspectives, usually of practitioners, employers or opponents. Recent National Health Service reviews define psychotherapy from an employer's position. They broadly distinguish it from pharmacological methods and include 'all approaches to helping individuals (alone, in couples, families and groups) of all ages which work directly with behaviour, thoughts and feelings through talking and therapeutic relationships and experience' (Daimon, 1997: 11). The reviews usefully note the confusing effects of professional rivalry in debates over definitions but discuss psychotherapy solely in relation to distress defined in terms of 'mental health', which, from the point of view of this chapter, is problematic.

A broad-based practitioner view offered by Holmes and Lindley is quite similar and will serve as a working definition. They define psychotherapy as 'the systematic use of a relationship between therapist and patient [client] – as opposed to pharmacological or social methods – to produce changes in cognition, feelings and behaviour' (1991: 3–8), and they contend that the basic elements of all forms of therapy are the use of structure, space and relationship. Structure is given by the contractual conditions such as regular meeting times in a secure environment. Space is thus provided for exploration in relationship with the therapist and it is essentially upon the quality of this relationship that the therapy[1] depends.

Empowerment

The concept of 'empowerment' is a tricky one. It is a buzz-word widely used in the 'helping' professions and has a moral flavour. However, what can easily be forgotten in this context is its political force in clearly locating therapy in a discourse of power. It highlights the positive dimensions of power and suggests that a capacity of the therapeutic relationship is to enhance a client's power. However, used in this context and when, as in the posing of this controversy, it is linked with 'enabling', the essentially social nature of power can be glossed over and the wider political meaning of 'empowerment' lost: 'It can act as a "social aerosol" covering up the disturbing smell of conflict and conceptual division' (Ward and Mullender, 1993: 147). As empowerment makes the stronger claim, I shall focus on this term.

Using the concept of empowerment in the context of therapy recognizes the source of many problems, experienced by individual people, as lying in their 'powerlessness'. Moreover, there is an at least implicit acknowledgement that individual powerlessness is often linked with social oppression. Empowerment implies recognizing and, where possible, challenging oppressive aspects of existing power relationships. This in turn implies knowing something about how power relations are produced and reproduced and the nature of their effects. If it can be argued that therapy is empowering, it must be possible to conceptualize clients' difficulties and distress in terms of powerlessness and to demonstrate how therapeutic practice works with this. It will only be possible, within the scope of this chapter, to sketch an answer. I first wish to acknowledge that therapy can disempower.

Part of the problem?

The sociopolitical discourse of power accessed by the concept of empowerment contrasts sharply with a competing medical health/illness discourse. In the context of professionalization, and the relatively automatic acceptance of the NHS as the main source of state-funded therapy, medical discourse often predominates. Whilst not wishing to deny the appropriateness of medical discourse to some forms of psychological disturbance, I would argue that the widening circle of its application is connected to the competition for professional power and is disempowering to service users. Briefly, medical discourse disempowers when it reduces to individual pathology forms of personal distress linked to social and political structures and relationships.

There is a long and well-documented history of the role of psychology and psychiatry in the development of a variety of 'scientific' versions of racism (for example, Littlewood and Lipsedge, 1989; Fernando, 1991, 1993). Feminist work, over many years, has drawn attention to the political nature of the personal, and recent books (Showalter, 1987; Miles, 1988; Ussher, 1991) have traced the misogynies of psychology, psychiatry and various therapies. All locate many of the problems which women face, and which result in common psychiatric diagnoses, firmly in the socio-political arena. We might also note work in the area of disability (Oliver, 1990; Finkelstein, 1993) which argues that people with disabilities are disempowered by the medical model of health care professionals which locates disability within the individual's personal impairments. Relating disablement to the powerlessness of people with impairments living in environments designed by people with 'able' bodies raises awareness of its political dimensions.

Given this dismal history, it is important to acknowledge that therapy has been and can be part of the problem, and how in the current climate of professionalization practitioners are drawn more and more into adopting the higher-status medical model. Nick Totton (1997) has described a worrying tendency to enlarge the scope of this model through shifting the emphasis from 'mental illness', claimed to affect about 10 per cent of the population, to lack of 'mental health', identified as the chronic low-grade unhappiness that many people tolerate in their jobs and relationships. Such imperialistic extensions might well merit Fay Weldon's (1997; and this volume) charge of 'Therapism' and Raj Persaud's (1996) criticism of defining people as sick and encouraging dependency. Totton also draws attention to the way in which working in medical contexts and the struggle for funding reinforce the medical model. He warns that the American experience of therapists being required to use *DSM* (*Diagnostic and Statistical Manual of Mental Disorders*) diagnostic categories in order to obtain reimbursement from medical insurers is quite logical: 'If the Health Service is paying then the client must be presumed to be sick' (1997: 7).

I do not intend to devalue the work of medicine or the health services, only to draw attention to the inappropriate extension of the medical model and to suggest that this is encouraged by the push towards profession-alization in therapy. A vast literature in the sociology of professions demonstrates the thrust to power involved, and the often acrimonious debates around accreditation, registration and the use of professional titles serve to demonstrate this in the case of therapy. One way of increasing power is by association with more powerful allies, and the medicalization of therapy can be seen as an example of this. More generally, it is worth reminding ourselves of telling arguments against 'disabling professions' (Illich et al., 1987), and Roger Gomm points out that 'to empower some-one else implies something which is granted by someone more powerful to someone less powerful: a gift of power, made from a position of power' (1993: 137). So there is a paradox in any profession claiming to empower its clients as this implies giving its own power away.

Not all of the attacks on therapy are about professionalization and medicalization, but some of the more telling ones do say as much about professional power and its abuse as about the therapeutic process itself; indeed the two are often closely linked, as in Jeffrey Masson's (1990) arguments. It is also the case that disempowerment is internal to some forms of practice which impose interpretations that fail to respect clients' perspectives, by for example insisting on the pathology of a gay man's 'homosexuality'. Others openly advocate what David Winter (1997) has described as 'the heroic approach to resistance'. Such practices can be seen as constituting a form of religious or psychological correctness. Given all this, it may seem that the case for the opposition has been conceded. This is not so, although I do believe that there are some telling criticisms which must be addressed. Having acknowledged these, I want to argue that the distress experienced by many clients can be conceptualized in terms of powerlessness. Moreover, powerlessness is a source of real suffering which has psychological and sometimes physical effects. It is inappropriate to reduce these to internal 'health' problems, and therapy is empowering when it recognizes and works with clients' struggles with powerlessness.

Power and identity

Therapists are concerned one way or another with the personal relationships and identities of clients. Therefore an understanding of how power relationships affect identities will help us to conceptualize therapeutic work in terms of a discourse of power. Structuralist and post-structuralist theories are useful in seeing the 'subject' (preferred to the term 'self') as being produced socially in relationships through systems of meaning within language and culture. Many have drawn on Louis Althusser's (1969/1971) work on ideology in showing how power relationships are reproduced through the construction of the personal identities of 'subjects'. Althusser uses the metaphor of an 'authorless theatre', and ideology is conceptualized as a system of symbolic representations which works by constructing individuals as subjects and calling us out to play our parts. It is as if a mirror is held up to us in which we recognize ourselves. This mirror of society is rather like the mirror in the fairy tale which tells us who is the fairest of us all, and as we recognize ourselves as male, female, Christian, Islamic, English, black, white, and so on, we locate ourselves in positions in society and take on appropriate attitudes, beliefs and feelings. Inasmuch as our social positions are structured by relationships of inequality, discrimination and oppression, these will be experienced as integral to our identities and have a 'natural' feel. For example, it is difficult for women and men in our society not to experience gender inequalities as somehow natural.

Many people who have eventually recognized themselves as 'oppressed' have described their experience of being invisible except as a negative image. Ralph Ellison (1951/1976), for example, shows black Americans rendered invisible by being represented only through white eyes, lacking a positive identity of their own. Toni Morrison takes this further and shows how, in white American literature, a negative presence of African-Americans becomes 'the vehicle by which the [white] American self knows itself as not enslaved, but free; not repulsive, but desirable; not helpless, but licensed and powerful . . .' (1993: 52). She describes the way in which white literature constructs the African-American as a 'serviceable other' whose existence serves the needs, interests and desires of the dominant group. Similar observations can be made about the construction of 'woman' in relation to 'man', 'disabled' in relation to 'able-bodied', 'homosexual' in relation to 'heterosexual', and so on. Each person who inhabits an identity defined by a dominant group as inferior or abnormal serves the interests of that group by providing them with a construction of what they are not.

This process can be compared to how colonized people learn the language and history of the colonizer. Frantz Fanon writes powerfully about his personal experience of colonization:

> Every colonized people . . . finds itself face to face with the language of the civilizing nation; that is, with the culture of the mother country. . . .
>
> The black schoolboy in the Antilles, who in his lessons is forever talking about 'our ancestors, the Gauls', identifies himself with the explorer, the bringer of civilization, the white man who carries truth to savages – an all-white truth. There is an identification – that is, the young Negro subjectively adopts a white man's attitude. (1952/1970: 14, 104)

This conveys well a sense of being taken over from the inside. All successful processes of colonization involve the imposition of language and culture, and Paulo Freire (1972) has described in some detail how in learning the language of the dominating culture, oppressed people lose their own voice and are imprisoned in a 'culture of silence'. The process of liberation and de-colonization involves a struggle by oppressed people to find a voice in a language of their own. It is a struggle for identity not defined in terms of 'otherness'. Feminists have written much about women's struggle to find a voice and an identity when the only words available are those of masculine language. So oppression works in the very heart of personal identity, and this accounts for the difficulties that oppressed groups have in overcoming their internalized homophobia, racism, sexism or some other form of self-hatred. 'Glad to be Gay' and 'Black is Beautiful' are, first of all, self-affirming messages.

Therapy as empowerment

We can find links with the above themes in much writing about therapy, and there is an increasing emphasis on the way selves are created socially in relationships even when power is not emphasized as a central dimension. Significantly, Carl Rogers conceptualizes the source of clients' distress in terms of the 'conditions of worth' attached to their identities during development (Kirschenbaum and Henderson, 1990: 236–57). More directly, Showalter (1987) has linked both the 'hysterical' symptoms of women in the nineteenth century and the 'war neurosis/male hysteria' of World War I with powerlessness and loss of a sense of control, and recent stress research clearly identifies 'locus of control' as an important factor (Palmer, 1997). David Smail (1987, 1993) has made explicit connections between social conditions and psychological distress and Oliver James (1997) links advanced capitalism, which promotes dissatisfaction, a sense of failure and low status, with reduced levels of serotonin, the brain chemical boosted by antidepressants such as Prozac. Certainly the devalued identities, loss, stress, abuse and trauma which are the daily business of practice are experienced by clients in terms of lack of self-worth, or more directly in terms of loss of power or control.

So if at least a substantial proportion of the distress encountered by therapists can be conceptualized within a discourse of power, how can therapy empower clients? In the working definition of therapy as providing 'structure, space and relationship', emphasis is placed on the quality of the relationship. This is justified by the evidence. The recent meta-analysis of research, commissioned by the NHS, provides substantial evidence of benefit from psychological 'treatment' across the field of 'mental health' but little to support particular methods and approaches (Roth and Fonagy, 1996). The NHS Executive Report concludes, on the basis of this evidence, 'that a substantial proportion of the variability in therapeutic outcomes is unexplained by differences between therapeutic procedures or differences between client groups', and that the 'most significant process variable contributing to outcome is the therapeutic alliance' (Parry and Richardson, 1996: 52–3). This research reinforces David Howe's (1993) study of clients' experiences. Howe also argues that within the 'core conditions' or 'therapeutic alliance' it is the talking that helps. Talking, he says, 'activates the language field in which the self was formed' (1993: 4), and he argues that therapeutic frameworks themselves constitute a set of non-specific factors in that they help clients to make their personal experience meaningful.

If powerlessness can be understood, at least in part, as losing one's voice, being individually silenced or being in some way imprisoned in a 'culture of silence', we can see how therapy empowers when clients are helped to find a voice and that voice is validated in an accepting relationship. Myra Grierson, for example, contrasts her experiences of treatment for depression:

> I was given drug therapy and Electro-Convulsive Therapy . . . nothing was explained. I do not remember telling my story or being listened to by anyone. What I do remember was a feeling of being judged to be weak and without value either to myself or others.
> [In contrast, the] way I experienced change in counselling seems important. All the things I discovered came at my pace and from my frame of reference. As each new shift was internalised I could sense a pattern developing. Feeling myself moving towards some unknown insight meant that I began to experience great faith in my ability to take power over my life and change my ways of relating. The most important fact was that it came from *within me* and I was free to choose how and when I used my change (1990: 8, 39, original emphasis)

Unlike novelists, who tell their own stories, therapists facilitate the telling of others' stories – stories which have not been thought worth telling or have been actively silenced. As Erving Polster (1987) tells us, 'every person's life is worth a novel'. However, this is a difficult and painful process and good therapy is as risky as good literature. At first, we are likely to feel worse not better when we confront and own pain we have previously denied. Fay Weldon's recommendations and warnings about literature apply equally to therapy: 'It takes courage, to comprehend not just what we are but why we are', and she admits to stopping reading for some time after *Jude the Obscure* for fear of encountering, for example, 'the Giant Despair' (1995: 10, 17).

The significance of storytelling in therapy is increasingly emphasized (for example, White, 1995; Dwivedi, 1997; Gersie, 1997; McLeod, 1997). In the present context it is worth stressing that recognizing the myriad of possible stories, facilitating a client's telling of his or her own story and respecting his or her capacity to find personal meaning is likely to be more empowering than insisting on one particular 'therapeutic story' embedded, say, in a core theoretical model. Indeed, insisting on one can be oppressive (Feltham, 1997). It is also worth reflecting, in a word-saturated therapy world, on the contribution of the more creative and expressive approaches which show us other ways than words of telling and facilitating stores (for example, Jennings and Minde, 1993; Gersie, 1996). Moreover, stories link us to others, and storytelling is a social activity with wider significance, as shown in Ken Plummer's (1995) study of sexual stories, which connects therapeutic storytelling with sociopolitical processes. He is interested in the nature of stories, their forms and content; the social process of producing and consuming stories; the social role of stories, including the ways in which they contribute to maintaining and changing identities and social relationships; and in the social and historical conditions that enable particular stories to be told and received. 'The power to tell a story, or indeed not to tell a story, under conditions of one's own choosing, is part of the political process' (Plummer, 1995: 26).

Plummer chooses one genre of story for his study,'the personal experience narrative'. He considers three forms of this genre: 'breaking the silence' stories, about rape or abuse; lesbian and gay 'coming out' stories; and 'recovery' stories about therapeutic transformations. These are all stories of the twentieth century, stories 'whose time has come'. They are stories of sexual suffering, silence and secrecy, the need for action, transcendence, redemption and transformation. Plummer asks, what is it that allows a story to be told at a particular point in history and in a particular cultural place? Rape stories, for instance, could rarely be told and hardly ever heard and believed just a quarter of a century ago. Today, at least some stories are told and heard, they are politically more feasible and, as they are told, some lives are empowered. Moreover, the telling and hearing contribute to the creation of more spaces for women to come together and talk and for their collective voices to contribute to the transformation of police and court practices.

Stories are produced and consumed in social worlds; they require 'interpretative communities' in which they make sense, and in being told and received they contribute to producing, reproducing and changing identities, social relationships and communities. An effective therapeutic relationship provides the conditions under which clients' stories can be first told, heard, validated, reworked and perhaps rehearsed for a wider community. In my view, it is this that makes therapy enabling and empowering, and it is this that connects therapy to the wider sociopolitical sphere.

Note

1. Hereinafter 'therapy' is used as shorthand for counselling and psychotherapy.

References

Althusser, L. (1969/1971) 'Ideology and ideological state apparatuses', in *Lenin and Philosophy and Other Essays*. London: New Left Books.

Daimon, S. (1997) *The Commissioning and Funding of Training in Psychotherapies for the NHS in England: An Independent Preliminary Report*. Commissioned by the NHS Executive.

Dryden, W. (1996) 'A rose by any other name: a personal view on the differences among professional titles', in I. James and S. Palmer (eds), *Professional Therapeutic Titles: Myths and Realities*. British Psychological Society Division of Counselling Psychology, Occasional Papers, Vol. 2. Leicester: BPS.

Dwivedi, K.N. (ed.) (1997) *The Therapeutic Use of Stories*. London: Routledge.

Ellison, R. (1952/1976) *Invisible Man*. Harmondsworth: Penguin.

Fanon, F. (1952/1970) *Black Skins White Masks*. London: Paladin.

Feltham, C. (1997) 'Challenging the core theoretical model', *Counselling*, 8 (2): 121–5. (Reproduced in R. House and N. Totton (eds), *Implausible Professions: Arguments for Pluralism in Psychotherapy and Counselling*. Ross-on-Wye: PCCS Books, 1997.)

Fernando, S. (1991) *Mental Health, Race and Culture*. Houndmills: Macmillan.

Fernando, S. (1993) 'Psychiatry and racism', *Changes*, 11 (1): 46–58.

Finkelstein, V. (1993) 'From curing or caring to defining disabled people', in J. Walmsley, J. Reynolds, P. Shakespeare and R. Woolfe (eds), *Health, Welfare and Practice: Reflecting on Roles and Relationships*. London: Sage/Open University.

Freire, P. (1972) *Cultural Action for Freedom*. Harmondsworth: Penguin.

Gersie, A. (ed.) (1996) *Dramatic Approaches to Brief Therapy*. London: Jessica Kingsley.

Gersie, A. (1997) *Reflections on Therapeutic Story Making*. London: Jessica Kingsley.

Gomm, R. (1993) 'Issues of power in health and welfare', in J. Walmsley, J. Reynolds, P. Shakespeare and R. Woolfe (eds), *Health, Welfare and Practice: Reflecting on Roles and Relationships*. London: Sage/Open University.

Grierson, M. (1990) 'A client's experience of success', in D. Mearns and W. Dryden (eds) *Experiences of Counselling in Action*. London: Sage.

Holmes, J. and Lindley, R. (1991) *The Values of Psychotherapy*. Oxford: Oxford University Press.

Howe, D. (1993) *On Being a Client: Understanding the Process of Counselling and Psychotherapy*. London: Sage.

Illich, I., Zola, I.K., McKnight, J., Caplan, J. and Shaiken, H. (1987) *Disabling Professions*. London: Marion Boyars.

James, O. (1997) *Britain on the Couch: Treating a Low Serotonin Society*. London: Century.

Jennings, S. and Minde, A. (1993) *Art Therapy and Dramatherapy: Masks of the Soul*. London: Jessica Kingsley.

Kirschenbaum, H. and Henderson, V.L. (eds) (1990) *The Carl Rogers Reader*. London: Constable.

Littlewood, R. and Lipsedge, M. (1989) *Aliens and Alienists: Ethnic Minorities and Psychiatry*. London: Unwin Hyman.

McLeod, J. (1997) *Narrative and Psychotherapy*. London: Sage.

Masson, J.M. (1990) *Against Therapy: Emotional Tyranny and the Myth of Psychological Healing*. London: Fontana.

Miles, A. (1988) *Women and Mental Illness: The Social Context of Female Neurosis*. Brighton: Wheatsheaf.

Morrison, T. (1993) *Playing in the Dark: Whiteness and the Literary Imagination*, London: Pan.

O'Brien, M. (1996) 'Counselling psychology: identity vs identity diffusion', in I. James and S. Palmer (eds), *Professional Therapeutic Titles: Myths and Realities*. British Psychological Society Division of Counselling Psychology, Occasional Papers, Vol. 2. Leicester: BPS.

Oliver, M. (1990) *The Politics of Disablement*. Houndmills: Macmillan.

Palmer, S. (1997) 'Stress management programmes: from theory and research to development', *Counselling Psychology Review*, 12 (2): 90–104.

Parry, G. and Richardson, A. (1996) *NHS Psychotherapy Services in England: Review of Strategic Policy*. London: NHS Executive.

Persaud, R. (1996) 'The wisest counsel?', *Counselling*, 7 (3): 199–201.

Plummer, K. (1995) *Telling Sexual Stories: Power, Change and Social Worlds*. London: Routledge.

Polster, E. (1987) *Every Person's Life is Worth a Novel*. London: Norton.

Roth, A. and Fonagy, P. (1996) *What Works for Whom? A Critical Review of Psychotherapy Research*. New York: Guilford.

Showalter, E. (1987) *The Female Malady: Women, Madness and English Culture, 1830–1980*. London: Virago.

Smail, D. (1987) *Taking Care: An Alternative to Therapy*. London: Dent.

Smail, D. (1993) *The Origins of Unhappiness: A New Understanding of Personal Distress*. London: HarperCollins.

Totton, N. (1997) 'Inputs and outcomes: the medical model and professionalisation', *Self and Society*, 25 (4): 3–8.

Ussher, J. (1991) *Women's Madness: Misogyny or Mental Illness?* Hemel Hempstead: Harvester Wheatsheaf.

Ward, D. and Mullender, A. (1993) 'Empowerment and oppression: an indissoluble pairing for contemporary social work', in J. Walmsley, J. Reynolds, P. Shakespeare and R. Woolfe (eds), *Health, Welfare and Practice: Reflecting on Roles and Relationships*. London: Sage/Open University.

Weldon, F. (1995) *Letters to Alice: On First Reading Jane Austen*. London: Sceptre.

Weldon, F. (1997) 'Mind at the end of its tether', *Guardian*, 11 January. (This volume, ch. 30.)

White, M. (1995) *Re-authoring Lives: Interviews and Essays*. Adelaide: Dulwich Centre Publications.

Winter, D. (1997) 'Everybody has still won but what about the booby prizes?', *Psychotherapy Section Newsletter*, 21 (June). Leicester: British Psychological Society.

Index

Kihlstrom, J., 45
Kingsley, Charles, 159
Kline, P., 68, 70, 81
Kluft, R., 56–7
Kohut, H., 203
Kopelman, M., 56
Kopta, S.M., 79
Kornreich, M., 144
Krell, R., 60
Kuhn, T., 228
Kulish, N., 146

labour process theory, 246
Lacan, J., 189
Lacanians, 110
Laing, R.D., 34, 105, 121
Lake, F., 26, 34, 38, 40, 41
Lambert, M.J., 65–6, 82, 166, 167–8, 174–5
Langs, R.J., 137–9
language
  and deception, 134
  and memory, 30
  and social relations, 98–9
  and the unconscious, 17–18, 19–20
Larsen, D.J., 200
Lasch, C., 247
late modernity, 248–9
Laub, D., 59
Lead Body for Advice, Guidance,
    Counselling and Psychotherapy, 219
learning from experience, 158–60
Leavitt, F., 58
Leboyer, F., 26
Lees, Susan, 57
Leventhal, H., 28, 29
Lindley, R., 271, 272, 276, 295
Lipsey, M.W., 78–9, 80
Lipsitt, P.L., 39
lithium carbonate, 115, 117, 120
Little, M., 135
Luborsky, L., 76, 96, 144–5, 146–7, 149, 165,
    272
Luria, A.R., 30
lysergic acid (LSD), 26

Macaskill, A., 148, 149, 150, 151
Macaskill, N.D., 148, 149, 150, 151
McCarthy, B., 54
McDevitt, J., 150, 151
MacFarlane, A., 39
Macmillan, M., 68
McNair, D., 145, 147
McNally, J., 180
Mahrer, A.R., 195
Masson, J.M., 12, 125, 175, 177, 160, 165,
    297
Matthews, J., 213
Mearns, D., 176

medical model, 297
Meltzoff, A.N., 40
Meltzoff, J., 144
memory
  around birth, 26–8, 35, 36
  childhood, 30–1
  contemporary theories, 29
  dual memory system, 27, 29
  effects of depression, 26, 55
  muscular and cellular, 37
  see also false memories; recovered
      memories; repressed memories
mental health construct, 75–6
meta-analytic studies, 66–7, 78–9, 81, 165,
    166, 175, 180, 279–80, 300
microcounselling approach, 180
Miller, A., 27, 31, 38
mind
  inherent consciousness, 7
  Freudian model, 19
  social creation, 98
Mirvish, A., 20
Modell, A., 58
Mollon, P., 59, 60
mood, effects on memory, 26
mood (bipolar affective) disorder, 115, 117,
    120
Morris, S., 57
Morrison, T., 298
Mott, F., 34
mourning, 18

narrative therapies, 105, 108
narratives and stories, 20, 137, 187, 200, 290,
    300–2
National Health Service (NHS), 284, 295,
    296, 300
National Vocational Qualification (NVQ),
    198
Naylor-Smith, A., 227, 228
negligence, 212–13
neonatal research, 28, 38–40
Neufeldt, S.A., 169
neuroscience, 29, 58
neurosis, 16, 17, 23n, 25, 26, 27, 36, 41, 110
neutrality, 126
Newton, T., 244
Nietzel, N.T., 166
Norcross, J.C., 148, 186–8, 189

object permanence, 30
obsessional symptoms, 119
obsessive compulsive disorders, 78, 94, 116,
    117, 119–20
Oedipus theory, 12, 19, 34
Oliver, J.E., 55, 60
organizational assistance programmes
    (OAPs), 264

outcome studies
  brief history, 74–5
  contemporary summaries, 65–7
  criticisms answered, 80–1
  effectiveness, 77, 79–80, 95–6, 160, 165,
    271–2, 279–82
  effects of personal therapy, 144–7, 151–2
  effects of supervision, 168–9
  effects of training, 165–8, 174–5, 210–11,
    219, 229, 272–3, 276n
  efficacy, 76–7, 77–9
  employee counselling, 262–3
  factors affecting, 214n
  further directions, 82
  primal therapy, 25, 32n
  relationship factors, 88, 89–90, 96–7, 300
  scientific nature, 75–6
  scientific transgression, 67–9

Papousek, H., 40
parent–child relationship
  compared to therapist–client relationship,
    98–102, 129, 159, 222, 238
  Freudian theory, 18–19
  as metaphor for training, 203
Parker, I., 121
past-life experiences, 25
patients *see* clients/patients
Paul, G.L., 100
Peebles, M.J., 148
Perlesz, A.J., 167
Perls, F., 200
Persaud, R., 297
person-centred approach, 176, 184, 199, 203,
  226, 228
personal therapy, 228, 236–8
  defended, 155–63, 176, 228, 236–8
  questioned, 142–54
Pfeffer, J., 208
phantom pain, 29
phobia, 120
physical contact, 127–8
Pilgrim, D., 191
placebo effects, 66, 67, 80–1
Plummer, K., 301
Pollock, K., 243–4
Polster, E., 300
post-traumatic stress disorder (PTSD), 41,
  58
presence, 187, 188–9
presenting problem, histories of, 105–6
primal integration, 32n, 34
primal therapy, 25–33
primary therapy, 27
Prioleau, L., 67
process studies, 147–9, 177
Prochaska, J.O., 186–8, 189
Proctor, B., 198–9

profession
  criteria for establishment, 209–10
  definition, 218
  and power, 295, 297
  psychotherapy as a, 210–13, 223–4, 282–3
  and self-interest, 220–1
psy-complex, 106–7, 110
psychiatry, 26, 34, 108, 119–20
  deconstructing the power of, 106–7
  diagnosis, 105, 109, 110, 113–14, 118
  as hard truth, 110–11
psychoanalysis, 8, 16, 17–18, 125, 157–8,
  273, 289, 293
  boundaries in, 125, 127, 137–8
  dependence on interpretation, 9, 12
  effectiveness, 68, 74, 281, 282
  importance of communication, 19, 20
  potential for harm, 13–14
  training analysis, 142, 143, 155–62, 171n
psychoanalytic therapy, 27, 76, 183, 196, 247,
  283
  distinguished from psychodynamic
    counselling, 233–40
  see also evolutionary psychoanalytic
    perspective
psychodynamic approaches, 142–3, 157, 178,
  196, 198, 199, 203, 227, 228
psychological-mindedness, 110
psychopathology
  diagnosis as, 109–11
  as reality, 113–23
psychosis, 108, 110
psychosocial theories, 97–102
psychotherapy
  distinguished from counselling, 176, 233–40
  indistinguishable from counselling, 164–5,
    225–32, 276n, 278, 294–5
Pulos, S.M., 157

race and racism, 105, 110, 196, 238, 296 *see
  also* black identity
randomized clinical trials (RCTs), 76–7
Rank, Otto, 27, 34, 35
rapid eye movement (REM) sleep, 9
rational emotive behaviour therapy (REBT),
  90–1, 92–3
Read, J., 53, 54
rebirthing, 25, 32n
recovered memories, 44–5, 49, 56–60, 68
recovered memory therapy (RMT), 44, 46,
  50–1
registration (licensing), 283, 290
  as necessary, 217–24
  as unnecessary, 206–16
relationship therapy, 91
relationship-based theories, 97–102
repressed memories, 25, 43, 44, 47–8
repressed memory syndrome, 45–6